DARK
PARADISE

David T. Courtwright

DARK
PARADISE

Opiate Addiction in
America before 1940

Harvard University Press
Cambridge, Massachusetts
and
London, England
1982

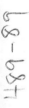

Library of Congress Cataloging in Publication Data

Courtwright, David T., 1952–
  Dark paradise.

  Bibliography: p.
  Includes index.
  1. Opium habit — History. 2. Opium — Therapeutic use — History.
3. Morphine habit. 4. Heroin habit. 5. Narcotic addicts — History.
6. Opium trade — Law and legislation — United States — History. I. Title.
[DNLM: 1. Narcotic dependence — History — United States. WM 286
C866d]
HV5816.C648   362.2'93'0973   81–6958
ISBN 0–674–19261–3   AACR2

Weave a circle round him thrice,
And close your eyes with holy dread,
For he on honey-dew hath fed,
And drunk the milk of Paradise.

— Samuel Taylor Coleridge,
  "Kubla Khan"

Acknowledgments

I am deeply indebted to Harold M. Hyman, Allen J. Matusow, William C. Martin, Albert Van Helden, Martin J. Wiener, Richard J. Smith, David W. Martin, Terry and Carol Parssinen, Gerald N. Grob, Barbara Rosenkrantz, Michael Gross, William I. Bennett, Susan Wallace, and Vivian B. Wheeler for their advice, criticism, and support at various stages in the evolution of this book. Generous financial assistance was provided by Rice University, the Institute for the Medical Humanities of the University of Texas Medical Branch at Galveston, the University of Texas School of Public Health, and the National Endownment for the Humanities. I particularly want to thank Chester R. Burns and Reuel A. Stallones for making possible extended periods of uninterrupted research and writing.

Librarians Inci Bowman, Manfred Waserman, Ferne Hyman, Charles Gibson, Dick Perrine, and Barbara Kyle patiently answered all manner of questions; with equal patience Ann-Marie Vermillion, Kathryn Hunt, William Pinkston, Jesse Amos, Susan Pridmore, Kay Flowers, Anne Krum, and Phyllis Burger filled a multitude of requests for numerous interlibrary loans. My access to important Treasury Department documents was facilitated by Russ Aruslan, Darrell Skaggs, and Linda Vettori of the Drug Enforcement Administration. Sylvia Ross, Gay Robertson, Betty Hall, Carolyn Mallery, Barbara Fredieu, Carol Roark, and Harriet Baggish provided clerical assistance; John C. Hubbard supplied the graphics. Special thanks are due my wife, Shelby Miller, and my good friend Patricia Toomey for long hours spent helping me to read over the manuscript.

Contents

A Note on Terminology and Spelling

The term *opiate addiction* has been used in many different senses by many different authors. When I refer to opiate addiction, I mean to describe a condition characterized by both physical and psychological dependence. Physical dependence is the state in which discontinuance of an opiate will bring on a train of withdrawal symptoms: tearing, sweating, cramps, diarrhea, and so forth. Psychological dependence can be described as intermittent craving for the drug, even after detoxification. Persons physically, but not psychologically, dependent are not addicts by this definition. A physically dependent infant, for example, does not crave an opiate, because it does not understand the connection between pleasure and the presence of the drug or pain and the absence of the drug. Addiction thus has a cognitive element, a point to be developed in Chapter 2.

In the United States the word *addiction* was not commonly employed, at least with respect to opiates, until the twentieth century. Owing perhaps to Thomas De Quincey's influence, persons who manifested the symptoms of opiate addiction were often called *opium eaters* or *morphine eaters* during the nineteenth century. *Opium habit* and *morphine habit* were other popular phrases. Among medical specialists a series of *isms* gained currency after 1870: *opiokapnism, opiophagism, morphinism,* and finally *heroinism.* For consistency and simplicity I shall use the term *addiction* throughout this study, except in direct quotations.

The spelling of the names of the various opiates prescribed during the nineteenth and early twentieth centuries was idiosyncratic. Among the variants of morphine, for example, were *morphinum, morphia, morphium,* and *morphin.* I employ the modern spelling throughout, again unless quoting directly.

Introduction

Within the span of a century the pattern of opiate addiction in the United States has undergone a transformation so profound that it has altered the very ways in which we think and feel about the problem of addiction. During the nineteenth century the typical opiate addict was a middle-aged white woman of the middle or upper class. Mary Tyrone in Eugene O'Neill's autobiographical play, *Long Day's Journey into Night,* exemplified the characteristics of this generation of addicts: female, outwardly respectable, long-suffering — and thoroughly addicted to morphine. But from roughly 1895 to 1935 the Mary Tyrones of this country were supplanted by a new and radically different sort of user. Lower-class urban males, down-and-outs like Frankie Machine, the hustling, poker-dealing junkie of Nelson Algren's *Man With the Golden Arm,* became increasingly conspicuous and were identified in the public mind with the problem of opiate addiction. Gone was the stereotype of the addicted matron; in its place stood that of the street criminal. What brought about such a dramatic change?

For liberal critics of American narcotic policy (including Charles E. Terry, Alfred R. Lindesmith, Rufus King, Morris Ploscowe, Edwin M. Schur, William Butler Eldridge, Edward M. Brecher, Norman H. Clark, and others) the answer was relatively simple. With varying degrees of emphasis, these authorities stressed that the transformation had resulted from an abrupt and ill-considered change in the legal status of the addict. During the nineteenth century, the argument runs, opiate addiction, although socially stigmatized, was perfectly legal. Then, beginning in 1909, with the enactment of the Smoking Opium Exclusion Act, a series of laws was passed that made legal access to opiates increasingly difficult. The key statute was the Harrison Narcotic Act, passed late in 1914. Not a prohibition statute per se, the Harrison Act merely required physicians, pharmacists, and certain other persons who dealt in narcotics to register with the U.S. Department of the Treasury, pay a nominal tax, and keep records of the narcotic drugs they dispensed. However, the law contained a number of ambiguities, the most important of which involved a provision that physicians in the course of their professional practice might prescribe narcotics to their patients. The question arose whether a physician who prescribed opiates merely to support an addict's habit — to "maintain" it — was acting within the bounds of the law. The Treasury Department, with the sometime compliance of the federal courts, answered in the negative. Physicians suspected of maintaining addicts were prosecuted or harassed; by 1921 most of the ad hoc municipal clinics established to supply and in some instances treat addicts had been closed.

As the legitimate narcotic supply dried up, addicts were forced to turn to the burgeoning black market; since black-market prices were exorbitant, they were also forced into petty crime to raise the large amounts of cash they needed. The "hustling" behavior associated with addicts thus was a concomitant of the antimaintenance policy that evolved after 1914; the transformation of the American addict into a street criminal was held to be an unnecessary tragedy.

This interpretation of history, it should be added, has been of considerable use politically, serving as the rationale for methadone and other forms of maintenance that found favor during the 1960s and 1970s. Since the prohibition-minded policy had proved counterproductive, it seemed logical to switch back to a cheap and legal supply of drugs.

While I believe there are important elements of truth in this view, and while (to state my biases openly and at the outset) I am generally in favor of some form of legal supply, I nevertheless remain unconvinced that the antimaintenance interpretation of the Harrison Act was primarily responsible for the transformation of the American addict. The key events occurred not from 1914 to 1924, but from 1895 to 1914, and involved not the legal, but the medical, profession. Greatly simplified, my argument is that opiate addiction increased throughout the nineteenth century, peaked in the 1890s, and thereafter began a sustained decline. The major reason for the rise, as well as the fall, in the rate of opiate addiction was the prevailing medical practice of the day. Prior to 1900 most addiction resulted from the activity of physicians; it was, to use a shorthand term, iatrogenic. Doctors liberally dispensed opium and morphine to their patients, many of whom were female and many of whom subsequently became addicted. There was also in the nineteenth century a pattern of nonmedical addiction, mainly opium smoking among Chinese and members of the white underworld. Later, in the early twentieth century, heroin and morphine supplanted smoking opium and became the underworld drugs of choice. At the same time the number of iatrogenic opium and morphine addicts was diminishing, as a wider range of effective therapies, improved sanitation, and improved medical education became available.

The net result was that opiate addiction, while declining relative to population, began to assume a new form: it ceased to be concentrated in upper-class and middle-class white females and began to appear more frequently in lower-class urban males, often neophyte members of the underworld. By 1914 the trend was unmistakable. This is not to deny that the emerging anti-maintenance policy accelerated the trend toward criminalization, but rather to affirm that the transformation was well under way before the basic narcotic statutes were enacted.

This analysis of the transformation of the American opiate addict population is useful, not only as a corrective to the widely accepted liberal interpretation, but for understanding a series of important theoretical and attitudinal changes that took place within the medical profession. During the 1920s and 1930s a growing number of physicians and public health professionals came to view addiction as a manifestation of psychopathy or some other form of twisted personality, to support mandatory institutionalization of addicts, and to refuse to supply addicts (especially the nonmedical type) with opiates. The average doctor came to think of the average addict as somehow beyond the pale, an unstable and compulsive personality better left to the management of the police or other authorities. This hardening of attitudes resulted at least in part from the fact that physicians were exposed to an increasingly lower-class type of addict; witnessing the transformation first hand, they did not much like what they saw. In previous decades, however, when addicts were drawn primarily from the middle and upper classes and often were addicted through medical practice, attitudes of both doctors and laity were generally more tolerant. Willis P. Butler, a crusty, nonagenarian physician who in 1919 established a morphine maintenance and treatment program in Shreveport, Louisiana, likes to illustrate this point with an anecdote. One day a prominent citizen walked up to him and denounced his addicted patients as "hopheads" who ought to be run into the river. Irritated, Butler took the visitor aside and confided that the man's own 75-year-old mother, an asthma sufferer who had been addicted for more than 20 years, was a regular patient at the clinic. Once he overcame his surprise and shock, the erstwhile critic became one of the program's staunchest supporters.[1] The moral of this story is one of the central themes of this book: what we think about addiction very much depends on who is addicted.

The lesson, in fact, can be generalized. Pronounced changes in the pattern of a disease entail corresponding changes in attitudes — or, as Susan Sontag would put it, the creation of a new set of illness metaphors. Tuberculosis, for example, seemed romantic, even chic, when it afflicted such great artists as Shelley, Keats, and Chopin;[2] today, when it is largely confined to crowded urban slums, tuberculosis is decidedly unglamorous. Nicotine addiction furnishes another, somewhat more speculative illustration. It may well be that today's growing intolerance of smoking is related to the fact that proportionately more members of the middle and professional classes are kicking the habit, leaving a residue of poorer and less future-oriented smokers.

It would be wise at this point to introduce a note of caution, to anticipate a possible misinterpretation. A number of colleagues who have considered my thesis have ventured that it might be used to explain American narcotic prohibition, that the whole edifice of laws, rulings, and court decisions upon which the anti-maintenance approach was predicated was itself a reaction to the relative increase in nonmedical addiction. Society saw more and more of a less and less desirable type of user and therefore sanctioned a variety of measures aimed at control and incarceration. While there is some merit in this hypothesis, it must be carefully qualified. Its greatest defect is its tidiness. As David F. Musto, Arnold H. Taylor, and others have shown, the sequence of events that led up to the passage and interpretation of American narcotic laws was extremely complex. There were diplomatic motives, pressures from special-interest lobbies, constitutional problems, and the ulterior political motives of disingenuous individuals, notably Dr. Hamilton Wright. It would be wrong, therefore, to describe American narcotic policy simply as a function of the changing addict population. Yet there is a sense in which the transformation can be viewed as a necessary condition for the emerging hard-line approach: it would certainly have been more difficult to deny drugs and mete out sentences if, in the 1920s and 1930s, the addict population still had been largely composed of ailing ladies and crippled war veterans. To state the matter another way, this study is not meant to contradict previous accounts that emphasize the diplomatic and legal dimensions of American narcotic policy; rather, it is meant to show that changes in that policy paralleled and were entirely consistent with the independent and underlying transformation of the addict population.

Analyzing the changing characteristics of American opiate ad-

4

dicts has generated a number of other insights that may prove valuable to (or at least provoke controversy among) historians, sociologists, psychologists, ethnographers, criminologists, lawyers, physicians, and others interested in the phenomenon of addiction. First and foremost, the problem of opiate addiction, though mutable, has thus far been intractable. None of the countless regimens of treatment, drug free or otherwise, has resulted in permanent abstinence for more than a minority of addicts.[3] Moreover, no narcotic policy, either promaintenance or antimaintenance, has come close to eradicating addiction. Instead, the number of addicts has been largely determined by exogenous factors: the introduction and popularization of new alkaloids and new techniques of administration; war and its aftermath; or fundamental demographic changes, such as the aging of an unusually large cohort of late-nineteenth-century medical addicts or, in more recent times, the presence of large numbers of susceptible adolescents as a result of the postwar baby boom. The most that can be expected of any legislation is that it will minimize the problem. Given the present state of medical science and the dynamics of the addictive process, there seems little chance of complete success.

I do not mean to imply, however, that one law is as good as another; legislation still needs to be evaluated carefully from the standpoint of the addicts' health and behavior. As liberal critics have insisted, there is an inverse relation between the availability of legal drugs and the amount of crime committed by users; moreover, there is a close connection between the law and the types of opiates consumed and the methods used to administer them. The "mainlining" (intravenous injection) of adulterated heroin, often using shared "works" (needle and syringe) — a practice that has had the most catastrophic impact on the lives and well-being of nonmedical addicts — was one particularly unfortunate response to the changing legal status of opiates.

Another fundamental feature of American narcotic laws is that they were passed, interpreted, and defended on the basis of misleading, even fraudulent, information. In attempting to assess the extent of addiction at different points in time, I have necessarily considered a variety of official estimates. These figures consistently were shaded either upward or downward, depending on whether government officials were attempting to obtain more stringent regulations or defending the stringent regulations already in place. The ethic that intelligent narcotic policy should be predicated on accurate data was almost totally lacking prior to 1940; no student of this period should assume, without the most careful corroboration, that government estimates reflected the true number of addicts.

Attempts to reconstruct the pattern of opiate addiction over an extended period of time also yield some insight into its etiology. Over and over again the epidemiologic data affirm a simple truth: those groups who, for whatever reason, have had the greatest exposure to opiates have had the highest rates of opiate addiction. This is as true of doctors and their patients in the nineteenth century as it is of delinquents and slum dwellers in our own day. There is little need to posit elaborate personality theories, as a number of psychologists and psychiatrists have done[4] — although, simultaneously, one can appreciate how such theories are themselves a manifestation of the relative increase in apparently deviant users. "Addiction," summarized William S. Burroughs, "is an illness of exposure. By and large those who have access to junk become addicts . . . There is no pre-addict personality any more than there is a pre-malarial personality, all the hogwash of psychiatry to the contrary."[5] Although one might not wish to state the case so bluntly, there is relatively little in the historical record to contradict Burroughs' essential insight.

A final theme to emerge from this study is that addict subcultures date back at least as far as the mid-nineteenth century. American social scientists, who tend to focus on recent and quantifiable data, have generally assumed that addict subcultures did not exist prior to 1914 and were formed as a result of national legislation.[6] This was not the case. There were separate, sometimes overlapping subcultures of Chinese and white opium smokers in the nineteenth century; subcultures in the sense that each of these groups had its own terminology, procedures, loyalties, and common standards of appropriate behavior. It is interesting in this context to note that many of the terms still in use today (*yen, dope fiend, hophead*) derive from these prototypical nonmedical addict subcultures.

I should add a word about the scope, method, and organization of this study. I have chosen 1940 as a terminal date for two principal reasons: first, the essential transformation of the addict population was complete by then, and second, World War II marks a watershed in the history of opiate addiction in this country. The war disrupted smuggling routes, and the ensuing panic forced many users into periods of involuntary abstinence. There was, of course, a postwar revival, especially among urban minorities; but that story is so complicated, and so shrouded in controversy, that I have thought it best to set it aside for a separate study.

The fact that I have chosen to focus primarily on the opiates, and secondarily on cocaine, also requires comment. It is true that other drugs, notably chloral hydrate and cannabis, were used before 1940; and while I in no way intend to dismiss such substances as unimportant or unworthy of serious study, the fact remains that contemporaries, when they talked about drug addiction, by and large meant addiction to opiates. Addiction to chloral hydrate (a foul-tasting and foul-smelling hypnotic) does not seem to have been widespread, and cannabis does not produce physical dependence. Neither does cocaine, but it has an important place in this narrative, for there were close links between underworld cocaine sniffing and early, nonmedical heroin use.

The method of this study is best described as eclectic. I have relied throughout on the traditional approach of the historian, the close reading and interpretation of printed and manuscript sources (catalogued here in an extensive bibliography). Beyond the traditional sources, I have sought to impart rigor to the analysis by basing generalizations, where possible, on statistical data. The statistical techniques employed range from simple, descriptive measures (such as graphs and averages) to more complex and analytical techniques (correlations and multiple regressions). Although some historical studies relegate their data, like familial skeletons, to the darkness of footnotes, appendixes, or even separate volumes, I have chosen to bring most of my statistical material into the light of the text, to facilitate the reader's consideration of key evidence. The problem with this approach is that it risks reducing human experience to mere numbers and charts. To counteract this tendency, I have also incorporated interview material, from both oral and written sources. Individual narratives have the advantage of enabling us to see the situation through the addicts' eyes, as well as through those of the legal, political, and medical elites who sought to control and cure them. While the nature of the surviving sources makes perfect balance impossible, I have tried throughout to present the points of view of both addicts and nonaddicts, to make this book an act of historical empathy as well as an exercise in historical epidemiology.

Each of the chapters is a step in a larger argument. Since a key part of my case hinges on the timing of the overall decline in opiate addiction, the entire first chapter is given over to the question of extent; in it I attempt to show that addiction began to decrease around the turn of the century, well before the passage of restrictive legislation. Chapters 2 to 4 explore the reasons for the decline, and the ways in which different addict groups were affected. For the sake of simplified analysis, opiate addicts are divided into three major classifications: those who used opium or morphine, those who used smoking opium, and those who used heroin. Finally, in Chapter 5, my analysis of the rise and fall of medical opium and morphine addiction is combined with the separate discussions of smoking opium and heroin to explain why opiate addiction underwent such a marked change, and to provide a basis for discussing some of the consequences of that transformation.

The Extent of Opiate Addiction

1 Reconstructing the pattern of opiate addiction in the United States is difficult, not only because addicts tended to conceal their condition, but because much of the historical evidence has been exaggerated and distorted. Fortunately, there are four categories of statistical evidence upon which objective estimates can be based: surveys of physicians and pharmacists, records of maintenance programs, military medical examinations, and opiate import statistics. Although each type of data has its limitations (which will be analyzed in detail), it is nevertheless possible to reach certain general conclusions: the rate of opiate addiction in America increased throughout the nineteenth century, from not more than 0.72 addict per thousand persons prior to 1842 to a maximum of 4.59 per thousand in the 1890s; thereafter the rate began a sustained decline. In round figures there were never more than 313,000 opiate addicts in America prior to 1914.

The above conclusions run contrary to the findings of several important government reports issued between 1910 and 1919. These documents indicate that as late as 1910 the rate of addiction was still increasing and that by 1919 there were 1,000,000 or more drug addicts in the United States. This discrepancy can be resolved, however, by revealing the sources of error and bias in the government reports, and by showing how in some cases their authors manipulated or even fabricated data in order to sway public opinion and achieve political ends.

Surveys

Surveys of physicians and pharmacists, the first and most problematic type of evidence, vary in format. Some investigators confined themselves to asking whether or not addiction was increasing in the respondent's locale.[1] Responses to this sort of question are of little use in reconstructing a rate and are not considered here. The first systematic survey which attempted to pinpoint the number of addicts was that of Orville Marshall in 1877.[2] Marshall asked 200 physicians scattered throughout the state of Michigan how many opium and morphine eaters resided in their locales; his respondents reported a total of 1,313 addicts. The 1874 population of the 96 cities, villages, and townships for which replies were received was 225,663, yielding a rate of 5.82 addicts per thousand persons. Because of the "supposed impossibility of getting reliable information of the number [of addicts] in the larger cities," no questionnaires were sent to physicians in Detroit, Grand Rapids, or East Saginaw. The effect of this bias was probably not too great, however, as opium and morphine addicts were fairly well distributed with respect to urban and rural areas.[3]

In contrast to Marshall, later investigators tended to direct their inquiries to pharmacists rather than physicians. In 1880 Charles W. Earle inquired at 50 drug stores scattered throughout Chicago and discovered 235 addict-customers, or 4.70 per store.[4] In 1885 Justin M. Hull sent 1,500 questionnaires to Iowa druggists. He received only 123 replies, mostly from small towns; 235 opiate addicts were reported, an average of 1.91 per store.[5] Finally, in 1902 a special committee of the American Pharmaceutical Association sent questionnaires to pharmacists in New York, Brooklyn, Philadelphia, Baltimore, and several unnamed towns in Pennsylvania and New Jersey. In this instance 4.00 was the average number of addicts reported.[6]

Conversion of these per-store averages into a rate requires the ratio of drug stores to population. If, for example, one knows that there are 5 addicts per store and one store for every 2,000 persons, one can infer that there are 2.50 addicts per thousand persons (exclusive of opium smokers, who procured their drug elsewhere). While the exact ratio is not known, it appears that there was approximately one drug store for every 1,850 to 2,250 Americans during the late nineteenth and early twentieth centuries.[7] Table 1 lists the range of addiction rates that this ratio yields.

How much of the disparity among the three surveys was genuine, and how much was caused by different methods, is hard to determine. It is probably not coincidental that Earle's Chicago study, which produced the highest rate, was also the most thorough; the Iowa and American Pharmaceutical Association surveys were both characterized by a low percentage of questionnaires returned. Because it was considered professionally *déclassé* to cater to addicts, one suspects that those with the greatest number of addict-customers were the least likely to reply, or that those who replied may have revised their totals downward. In either case the result was underreporting. Yet, paradoxically, some overreporting is also apt to have occurred, for several druggists in the same city may have reported the same customer. It is possible, but unlikely, that the overreporting and underreporting factors exactly canceled each other. The imprecision of the drugstore-to-population ratio compounds these problems and further diminishes the value of the survey data.

Maintenance Programs

The records of the maintenance programs are somewhat more reliable. On March 3, 1919, the Supreme Court held, in *Webb et al.* v. *United States,* that a physician might not provide opiates for the sole purpose of maintaining an addict.[8] Several municipalities

Table 1 Selected surveys of pharmacists, 1880 to 1902.

Year	Place	Average number of addicts per store[a]	Addicts per thousand persons[b]
1880	Chicago	4.70	2.09 to 2.54
1885	Iowa towns	1.91	0.85 to 1.03
1902	Eastern cities and towns	4.00[c]	1.78 to 2.16

a. Assuming one pharmacist-respondent per store.
b. Assuming one drugstore for every 1,850 to 2,250 persons.
c. All drug habits. Survey conducted by the American Pharmaceutical Association.

responded by establishing narcotic dispensaries to furnish addicts with an alternative source of legal supply. Some intended to distribute opiates only until treatment facilities became available; others were geared to long-term maintenance. These hastily organized "clinics," as they were dubbed, might have become the nucleus of a national maintenance program, had it not been for the adamant opposition of the Narcotic Division of the Prohibition Unit of the Bureau of Internal Revenue, then under the direction of Levi Nutt. By 1921 the division had succeeded in closing nearly all of the clinics.[9]

In the cities that established clinics, it is unlikely that every addict made use of the facility. Many wealthy and socially prominent addicts, for whom anonymity was more important than cheap drugs, undoubtedly sought to secure their supplies elsewhere.[10] But for the majority of addicts in the lower and middle classes, the clinic was an attractive alternative to the escalating price of black-market drugs.[11] Addicts from surrounding communities might also be drawn in by the prospect of a licit supply, thereby increasing the total number of patients.

In 1924 two U.S. Public Health Service officials, Lawrence Kolb and Andrew Grover DuMez, using Bureau of Internal Revenue reports, tabulated the number of addicts attending clinics in 34 cities in 12 states.[12] Their findings are displayed in Table 2. "In compiling the . . . figures from the reports," they remarked, "the highest number of addicts recorded at any one time or in a certain year are given . . . No reduction whatever was made in the total for transients, although the reports show that many of the clinics treated addicts from distant as well as near-by places."[13] The average rate for the 34 cities was 0.99 per thousand. Applying this figure to the country as a whole, there would have been 104,933 addicts in 1920. Of the individual cities listed, one in particular stands out: Shreveport's rate of 9.55 addicts per thousand was more than nine times as great as the average for all 34 cities. Kolb and DuMez attributed this to the relative longevity of Willis Butler's clinic, which was not closed until 1923. As clinics in Houston, New Orleans, and other southern cities were shut down, addicts made their way to Shreveport, where morphine could still be purchased for 6 cents a grain. Butler, who was aware of the problem of transients, later went back through his records, dividing residents from nonresidents. He found that, of 542 cases treated during 1920, 211 had resided in Caddo Parish (where Shreveport is located) a year prior to registration at the clinic, yielding a resident rate of approximately 4.81 addicts per thousand.[14]

Table 2 Number of addicts attending clinics in 34 cities.

Location	Population	Reported addicts	Addicts per thousand
California			
Los Angeles	576,673	481[a]	0.83
San Diego	74,683	179	2.40
Connecticut			
Bridgeport	143,555	79	0.55
Hartford	138,036	105	0.76
Meriden	29,867	2	0.07
New Haven	162,537	80	0.49
Norwalk	27,743	19	0.68
Waterbury	91,715	86	0.93
Georgia			
Atlanta	200,616	515	2.57
Augusta	52,584	42	0.80
Macon	52,995	52	0.98
Kentucky			
Paducah	24,735	35	1.41
Louisiana			
New Orleans	387,219	250	0.65
Shreveport	43,874	419[b]	9.55
New York			
Albany	113,344	120	1.06
Binghamton	66,800	32	0.48
Buffalo	506,775	250	0.49
Corning	15,820	22	1.39
Elmira	45,393	10	0.22
Hornell	15,025	16	1.06
Middletown	18,420	30	1.63
Oneonta	11,582	37	3.19
Port Jervis	10,171	17	1.67
Rochester	295,750	160	0.54
Saratoga Springs	13,181	12	0.91
Syracuse	171,717	92	0.54
Utica	94,156	25	0.27
North Carolina			
Durham	21,719	36	1.66
Ohio			
Youngstown	132,358	65	0.49
Rhode Island			
Providence	237,595	175	0.74
Tennessee			
Knoxville	77,818	184	2.36
Memphis	162,351	325[c]	2.00

Table 2 continued

Location	Popu-lation	Reported addicts	Addicts per thousand
Texas			
Houston	138,276	122	0.88
West Virginia			
Clarksburg	27,869	49	1.76

SOURCE: Lawrence Kolb and A. G. DuMez, "The Prevalence and Trend of Drug Addiction in the United States and Factors Influencing It," *Public Health Reports,* 39 (1924), 1182.
  a. Terry and Pellens, 37, gives a total of 564 for the Los Angeles clinic.
  b. Resident addicts numbered about 211, yielding a resident rate of 4.81 per thousand.
  c. "Drug Addicts in the South," 147, gives a total of 456 for the Memphis clinic.

In addition to the clinics listed in Table 2, several other maintenance programs produced statistics of interest. In August 1912 Jacksonville, Florida, passed an ordinance drafted by the city health officer, Charles Edward Terry, requiring that the health department be sent duplicate copies of prescriptions for medicines containing more than 3 grains of morphine or its equivalent. The law also stipulated that the health officer might, upon acquiring "satisfactory evidence of habitual abuse," offer free prescriptions to the addict, to be filled by a local druggist. The system thus was designed to supply, as well as keep track of, addicts. In the Jacksonville Board of Health's *Annual Report* for 1913, Terry recorded that 541 persons out of a population of 67,209 were addicted to opiates, a rate of 8.05 per thousand.[15] These were the basic figures to which he would refer in all of his subsequent writings. His findings did not go unchallenged, however; Kolb and DuMez attacked them on the ground that they included many transients, drawn in by Jacksonville's liberal narcotic policy.[16] While Terry later admitted that his total included some nonresidents, he asserted that their presence was balanced out by resident addicts who surreptitiously obtained their supplies. His defense was somewhat undermined, however, by the fact that the *Annual Report* for 1912 showed, after more than four months of operation, a total of only 383 opiate addicts, a rate of approximately 5.70 per thousand.[17] It is remotely possible that a massive epidemic of opiate addiction overtook Jacksonville during 1913, but a simpler explanation would be that outsiders were attracted by free drugs.

Another likely reason for Jacksonville's relatively high rate was its location deep in the South, a region that suffered a disproportionate amount of opium and morphine addiction.

In 1913, a year after the Jacksonville program was formulated, Tennessee passed a law forbidding the refilling of narcotic prescriptions unless the holder of the prescription had previously registered with the state as an addict. After a year of operation, State Food and Drugs Commissioner Lucius P. Brown reported a total of 2,370 registrants. At that time, Brown estimated, Tennessee had 2.30 percent of the national population, representing a rate of 1.04 addicts per thousand. He seriously doubted, however, that all or even a majority of addicts had registered; his best guess was that there were "in the neighborhood of 5,000 addicts in Tennessee."[18] The problem of underreporting also confronted the Pennsylvania Bureau of Drug Control, another state agency charged with keeping track of drug addicts. By 1920 there were 3,104 registrants; by 1922 there were 9,000, or 1.03 per thousand. Again, officials thought this represented slightly less than half the total.[19]

Finally, there was the New York City clinic, unique because of its size and problems. During its brief existence from April 10, 1919, to January 16 of the following year, 7,464 addicts were registered, a surprisingly low rate of 1.33 per thousand. There is good reason to suspect that the true rate was higher. For the New York City clinic practiced gradual reduction, that is, an attempt was made to wean the addict from his drug, whether he liked it or not. This factor, plus the brusque manner in which the clinic was run, undoubtedly led many to seek other sources of supply.[20]

Military Medical Examinations

One of the by-products of American mobilization for World War I was a wealth of data for public health researchers. Recruits were weighed, measured, tested, and checked for a variety of conditions, including drug addiction. Of the 3,764,101 men who appeared before their local draft boards, 3,284 were rejected for addiction—many for addiction to heroin. This represents a rate of only 0.87 per thousand.[21] Because of the difficulty of obtaining drugs in the army (at least in 1917), it is unlikely that many addict-recruits escaped detection.[22] On the other hand, some addicts never came under examination, since conviction of a felony was grounds for disqualification; and by 1917, addicts were more likely than the general population to have committed a serious crime. Another drawback is that the rate is based on males in the 21-to-30 age bracket, rather than on a cross-section of the country as a whole.

Import Statistics

Two premises underlie the use of opiate import statistics to estimate the extent of addiction: first, the amount (or value) of opium imported per capita is an indicator of whether addiction was increasing or decreasing; and second, if the daily dose required to sustain an addict is known, it is possible to compute the maxium number of addicts a given level of imports would have supported. Both of these assumptions are possible because, owing to a shortage of cheap labor, the opium poppy was not grown commercially in the United States.[23] The amount imported theoretically represents the total supply.

There is, however, a problem. To the extent that opiates were smuggled into the country, customs figures understate the amount actually available. In general, smuggling is liable to occur either when the government taxes a "good" (such as diamonds) or proscribes a "bad" (like pornography). The American opiate market has been characterized by both patterns of illicit traffic. Over the years 1842 to 1914 duties on the three categories of opiate imports—crude or medicinal opium, opium prepared for smoking, and morphine or its salts—fluctuated, but were generally high. Table 3 summarizes these imposts. By avoiding the duty and then selling the drugs at market value, smugglers could realize substantial profits.[24]

A 1909 case illustrates the profits to be earned from such illicit traffic. Stewards aboard the North German Lloyd liner *Kronprinzessin Cecilie* routinely smuggled large quantities of codeine and opium into New York. They had the cooperation of the liner's watchmen and a corrupt customs inspector. Their American connection was a Dr. George Van Der Schulenberg, who in the guise of a wholesale druggist sold the drugs to pharmaceutical firms. Schulenberg's suicide on December 29, 1908, abruptly terminated this arrangement. His replacement, Alfred E. Willembricher, sold the codeine to wholesale candy makers, who used it in the manufacture of cough drops. Willembricher proved less discreet than his predecessor, however, and in February 1909 customs agents exposed the ring. Subsequent investigation revealed that

Table 3 Imposts on crude opium, smoking opium, and morphine or its salts, August 30, 1842 to June 30, 1914.

Date	Crude opium	Smoking opium	Morphine or its salts
August 30, 1842 to July 30, 1846	$0.75/lb	Not mentioned	Not mentioned
to March 3, 1857	20% ad valorem	Not mentioned	Not mentioned
to March 21, 1861	15% ad valorem	Not mentioned	Not mentioned
to July 14, 1862	$1.00/lb	Not mentioned	$1.00/oz
to June 30, 1864	$2.00/lb	80% ad valorem	$2.00/oz
to July 14, 1870	$2.50/lb	100% ad valorem	$2.50/oz
to March 3, 1883	$1.00/lb	$6.00/lb	$1.00/oz
to October 1, 1890	$1.00/lb	$10.00/lb	$1.00/oz
to July 24, 1897	Duty free	$12.00/lb	$0.50/oz
to April 1, 1909	$1.00/lb	$6.00/lb	$1.00/oz
to August 5, 1909	$1.00/lb	Banned	$1.00/oz
to October 3, 1913	$1.50/lb	Banned	$1.50/oz
to June 30, 1914	$3.00/lb	Banned	$3.00/oz

SOURCE: *Tariff Acts Passed by the Congress of the United States from 1789 to 1909,* House Document no. 671, 61st Cong., 2nd sess. (1909); and U.S. Department of the Treasury, Customs Division, *The Tariff Act of October 3, 1913, on Imports into the United States* (Washington, D.C.: G.P.O., 1913).

the stewards had purchased the codeine for 440 marks per kilo — roughly a dollar an ounce. The duty avoided was also a dollar an ounce. "The drug sells here for $5.00 an ounce after duty is paid," commented the *New York Times,* "which gives some idea of the profit made by the gang in its smuggling career."[25]

The traffic in smoking opium was equally lucrative. Since this type of opium was associated with Chinese, as well as gamblers, prostitutes, and other undesirables, Congress sought to discourage its use by means of a stiff impost.[26] Duties ranged as high as $12 a pound, equivalent to 182 percent ad valorem. The result was smuggling on a massive scale, much of it organized by the

Chinese tongs.[27] U.S. Opium Commissioner Hamilton Wright stated that customs returns for the decade 1890 to 1899 represented only 60 percent of the total smoking opium that actually entered the country.[28] Wright, who was prone to exaggerate opiate consumption, may actually have underestimated the problem. Another investigator, Frederick J. Masters, observed that "during the years of heavy duties the regular traffic fell off more than half, although it is well known that during these years the local market was glutted. There is no doubt that heavy duties encourage a vast smuggling trade, amounting in the opinion of ex-Collector Phelps, to double the regular importations."[29] The situation became so serious that in 1888 the secretary of the treasury, Charles S. Fairchild, urged Congress to prohibit all importation of smoking opium. He argued that an outright ban would be more effective than the existing near-prohibitive tariff. "If, however," he added, "Congress is not disposed to prohibit or restrict the importation of opium for smoking, and desires to obtain revenue therefrom, the tax should be materially reduced so that the inducement to smuggling and attendant difficulties and expense of administering the law may be lessened."[30] Congress was not so disposed; two years later the impost on smoking opium was raised by two dollars a pound.

Crude opium was also smuggled into the country, except during those years when it was duty free.[31] Wagons loaded with up to 800 pounds of the drug rumbled across the Canadian border. Another scheme involved shipments of cattle from Hong Kong. The horns of the cattle were removed, fitted with an inner thread, filled with crude opium, then screwed back into place. This system was exposed when an agent noticed that one cow's horn was askew, but not before "tremendous quantities of the drug had been smuggled in."[32] Another case in New York involved four smugglers selling local druggists pound packages of opium and phenacetine (an antipyretic); drugs worth $5,000 were confiscated when the ring was broken.[33] Such seizures were not consigned to the furnace, as they are today, but instead were auctioned off to legitimate dealers.[34] Thus virtually all smuggled drugs, intercepted or not, eventually found their way to the consumer.

The ingenuity of the opiate smugglers knew no bounds. One supercargo reportedly packed $500 worth of opium into the false bottom of a snake cage. Upon landing in San Francisco, he sold both snake and opium for a tidy profit.[35] Another technique involved shipping smoking opium to Victoria or Nanaimo, British Columbia, then slipping it across the border concealed in hollowed-out planks of lumber.[36] "Recently completed facilities for transcontinental transportation," complained Secretary Fairchild, "have enabled opium smugglers to extend their illicit traffic to our Northern border."[37]

Smuggling, it should be added, was not the only illicit source of smoking opium. Hundreds of Chinese immigrants set up scores of illegal "opium kitchens" to convert crude opium into smoking opium,[38] in defiance of an 1890 law which stipulated that smoking opium could be manufactured only by native Americans who paid an excise of $10 a pound.[39] Although police raided scores of these makeshift labs, others escaped detection, a situation that reminded one reporter of "whisky distillers . . . in the wilds of Kentucky and Tennessee."[40]

The consequence of all this clandestine activity is that import statistics do not necessarily reflect domestic demand, particularly during periods of high duty. This should be kept in mind when examining the import statistics themselves, which, because of changes in reporting procedures, fall into three separate periods: fiscal 1827 to 1842, fiscal 1843 to 1861, and fiscal 1866 to 1914. No statistics are available prior to 1827, and customs returns after 1914 are problematic, because of the substantial increase in illicit traffic engendered by the Harrison Act. The figures for the Civil War years must also be deleted; they represent only the returns of northern customhouses and therefore are abnormally low.[41]

Treasury Department records for fiscal 1827 to 1842 list the annual dollar value of opium imports and exports, charted in Figure 1. These sums were based on a somewhat unusual definition of foreign trade. Most of the so-called imports never reached the U.S. shore; rather, they represented cargoes of crude Turkish opium picked up by enterprising American merchants in European or Near Eastern ports for shipment to China.[42] The Treasury Department chose to regard such consignments first as imports, then, when landed in the Orient, as exports. Thus both totals were artificially high. Of interest, however, is the average net difference between imports and exports. Turkish opium not exported, it is reasonable to assume, was either lost at sea or consumed at home. Let us suppose, for the sake of establishing a maxium level of domestic consumption, that all of the consignments not landed in foreign ports were landed safely in America. The average dollar value of imports minus exports for these 16 years was $75,448.56. To express this as a quantity, some approximation of value per pound is needed. For fiscal years 1843 to 1853 the average value per pound of imported opium was $2.77,

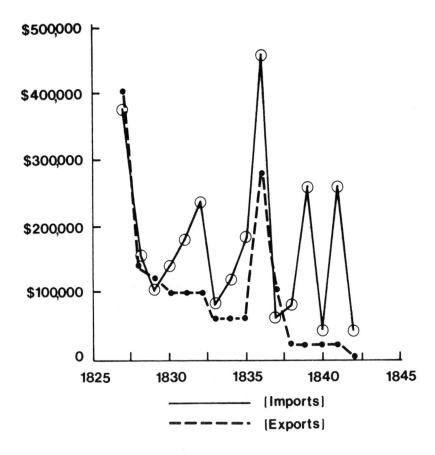

Figure 1 Value of opium imports and exports, fiscal years 1827 to 1842. Source: J.B. Biddle, "Value of Opium Imported and Exported from 1827 to 1845," *American Journal of Pharmacy,* 13 (1847), 18.

which yields an average consumption of 27,238 pounds per annum. This amount is of particular interest in that prior to August 30, 1842, there was no duty on opium. No duty means no smuggling;[43] thus one can be reasonably sure that the estimated 27,238 pounds does not understate the maximum average annual consumption for fiscal 1827 to 1842.

Beginning in 1843, customs returns specified the actual number of pounds entered for consumption, rather than aggregate value. Figure 2 plots pounds imported per capita over time. The graph reveals a sharp upward trend; imports rose from 1 pound or less per thousand persons in 1843 to 1845 to 4 or 5 pounds per thousand persons in the mid-1850s. The rate of addiction, however,

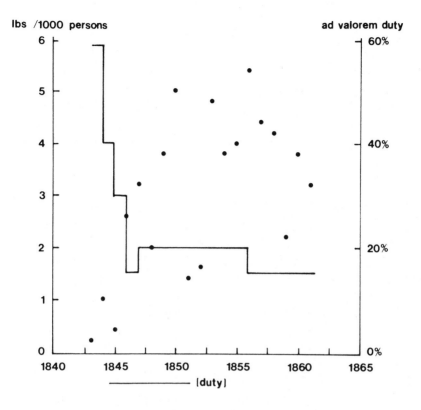

Figure 2 Pounds of opium imported per capita, fiscal years 1843 to 1861. Sources: "Estimated Population of the United States: 1790 to 1957," Bureau of the Census, *Historical Statistics of the United States: Colonial Times to 1957* (Washington, D.C.: G.P.O., 1960), 7; "Importations into the United States of various forms of opium . . . ," *Conference Internationale de l'Opium, Actes et Documents,* 2 (The Hague: Imprimerie Nationale, 1912), 36. Ad valorem duties are as given in Table 3. (For consistency the duties for fiscal years 1843 to 1846 have been expressed in ad valorem form.)

did not necessarily quintuple during this period, since imports were lowest when duties (expressed in Figure 2 as a solid line) were highest. The correlation between pounds imported per capita and duty is -0.59. This suggests smuggling activity in proportion to the duty, which in turn suggests that the official returns understated the amount actually consumed, especially during fiscal 1843 to 1845. A second point is that smoking opium began to be imported in significant quantities in the mid-1850s, when the first wave of Chinese immigrants arrived in California.[44] (Prior to July 14, 1862, crude and smoking opium were reported together.) Per capita opium importation rates for fiscal years 1854 to 1861 necessarily reflected this sudden, exogenous increase in demand.[45]

The third and final group of import statistics stretches from the end of the Civil War to the eve of the Harrison Narcotic Act. During this period customs returns were divided into three categories: pounds of crude or medicinal opium, pounds of smoking opium, and ounces of morphine or its salts. Because most of the crude opium was eventually converted to morphine, it is simpler to combine the first and third categories into one group, hereafter referred to as *medicinal opiates*. This is accomplished by expressing pounds of crude opium as equivalent ounces of morphine sulfate, then adding the ounces of morphine or its salts imported directly.[46]

Figure 3 plots the per capita importation of medicinal opiates, expressed as ounces of morphine sulfate, over time. It appears that imports peaked in the mid-1890s, but these years were also characterized by low or nonexistent duties on medicinal opiates, which would have discouraged smuggling and inflated customhouse returns. The correlation between per capita imports and duty (-0.62) is negative, as would be expected. It is significant that the import rate for fiscal 1897 was inordinately high, and for 1898 inordinately low. This is attributable to a large speculative importation during fiscal 1897, in anticipation of the reimposition of a $1 per pound tariff, with a corresponding slackening of imports the following year—a further demonstration of the sensitivity of the market to duties.

Legitimate imports of smoking opium, plotted in Figure 4, behaved in much the same way. Once again the correlation between per capita imports and duty (-0.41) is negative.[47] There is comparable evidence of speculative importation, notably in fiscal 1883, when a record 298,153 pounds were imported in anticipation of a $4 per pound increase in the tariff. As with medicinal opiates, the recorded level of smoking-opium imports was a function of tariff policy, as well as of domestic demand.

Given the impact of smuggling on import statistics, the interpretation of customs returns must be guided by two principles. First, in assessing whether or not the use of a particular opiate was increasing, we can compare directly only those periods with equal duties. For example, in analyzing smoking-opium returns, it is legitimate to compare fiscal 1871 to 1883, when the tariff was $6 a pound, to fiscal 1898 to 1909, when the duty was also $6 a pound, but not to fiscal 1891 to 1897, when the duty was $12 a pound. The reason, of course, is that the incentive to smuggle during

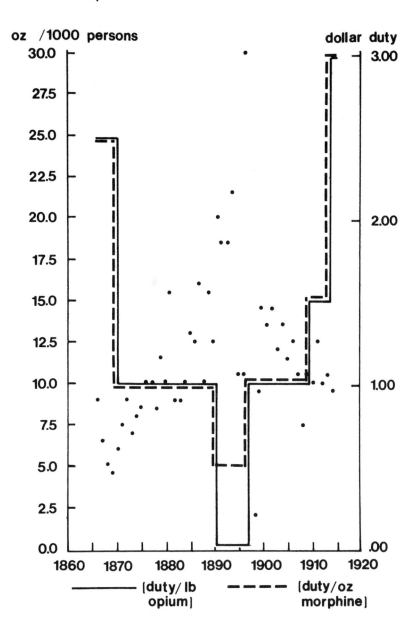

Figure 3 Imports of medicinal opiates, in equivalent ounces of morphine sulfate, fiscal years 1866 to 1914. Sources: Same as Figure 2, except for imports during fiscal 1906 to 1914, which were taken from the Department of Commerce and Labor's annual *Foreign Commerce and Navigation of the United States.* The totals for these years include opium alkaloids and derivatives other than morphine, mentioned separately from (but taxed at the same rate as) morphine or its salts after 1906.

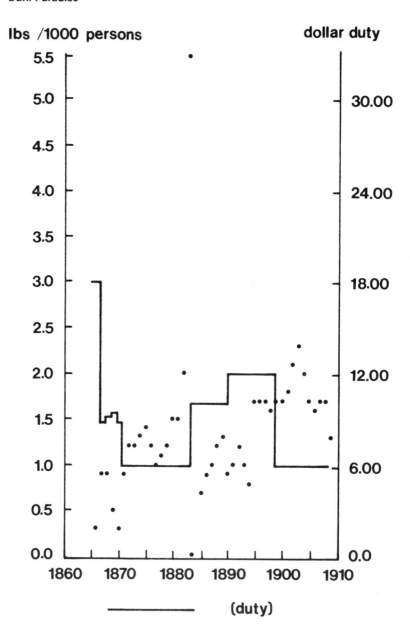

lbs /1000 persons   **dollar duty**

Figure 4 Imports of smoking opium, fiscal years 1866 to 1909. Sources: Same as Figure 2.

1891 to 1897 was double that of 1871 to 1883. The second principle is that estimates of the maximum number of addicts that imports could have supplied should be based on years when there was little or no duty. Smuggling causes underreporting; but smuggling will not occur unless there is a duty, or an outright proscription.

Duties on medicinal opiates were the same, $1 a pound, for two extended periods, fiscal 1871 to 1890 and fiscal 1898 to 1909. Observations for these years are enclosed within polygons in Figure 5. During the first period imports doubled, from roughly 7.50 to 15.00 ounces of morphine sulfate per thousand persons. But during the latter period imports per capita declined almost as precipitously.[48] An analysis of smoking-opium returns (Figure 6) reveals much the same pattern. In fiscal 1871 to 1883 the trend was sharply upward, but in fiscal 1898 to 1909, years characterized by the same $6 per pound impost, per capita imports began tapering off. Taken together, Figures 5 and 6 indicate that the rate of opiate addiction was declining well before the passage of national narcotic legislation.

In addition to the comparison of periods of like duty, it is useful to analyze years when there was no duty — and hence no smuggling. During fiscal years 1827 to 1842 there was no charge on any form of opium, and during fiscal 1891 to 1897 no charge on crude opium and only a nominal charge on morphine or its salts. During both periods the amount imported represented the total supply. Based on a review of several thousand cases, the minimum average daily dose required to sustain the nineteenth-century opiate addict was the equivalent of 6 grains of morphine sulfate.[49] The 27,238 pounds (average per annum) imported during 1827 to 1842 thus could have supported a maximum of 10,875 addicts, or 0.72 addict per thousand persons.[50] By way of comparison, the annual average equivalent of 1,109,822 ounces of morphine sulfate imported during duty-free fiscal years 1891 to 1896 could have supported (exclusive of opium smokers) 221,559 addicts, or about 3.25 addicts per thousand.[51] Because up to 35 percent of these medicinal imports were either wasted or went to nonaddicts;[52] because an undetermined amount of the drug was re-exported in the form of narcotic patent medicines;[53] and because, as mentioned earlier, some crude opium was secretly converted to smoking opium; it can be said with certainty that there were no more than 222,000 persons addicted to medicinal opiates at this time.

Of course, this does not represent the maximum for all opiate

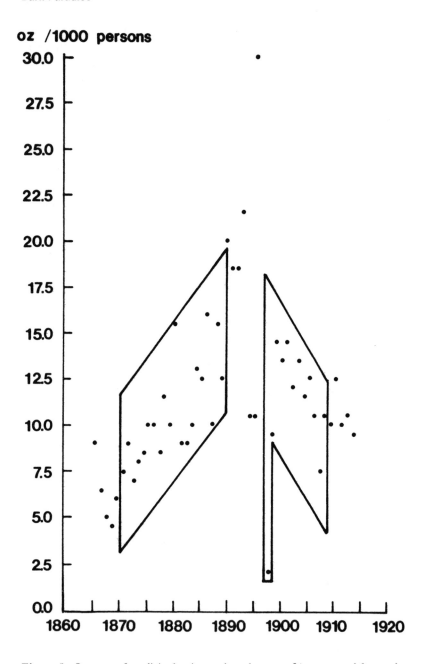

oz /1000 persons

Figure 5 Imports of medicinal opiates when duty was $1 per pound for crude opium and $1 per ounce for morphine. Sources: Same as Figure 3.

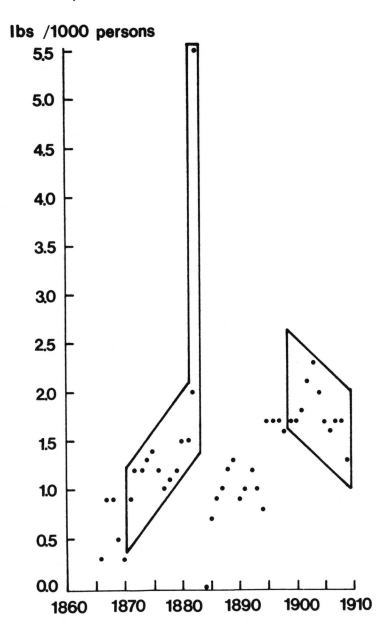

Figure 6 Imports of smoking opium when duty was $6 per pound. Sources: Same as Figure 2.

addicts, since it does not include opium smokers. Because of the high duty, arriving at the maximum number of opium smokers for fiscal 1891 to 1896 is problematic, but a rough estimate can be made. The most liberal estimate made by a knowledgeable authority of the amount of smoking opium smuggled into the country when duty was high (that of Collector Phelps) was "double the regular importations." Regular importations for fiscal 1891 to 1896 averaged 76,348 pounds; one can therefore assume that the true total was closer to 229,044 pounds (76,348 × 3). Several contemporary studies indicated that the average amount of opium required to sustain a smoker for one year was no less than 2.5 pounds,[54] a dose that yields a maximum of 91,618 opium smokers at this time. Combining these totals (221,559 + 91,618) gives a maximum of 313,177 persons addicted to all types of opiates during fiscal 1891 to 1896, for a rate of 4.59 addicts per thousand.[55]

To recapitulate, it is possible to use import statistics to establish the maximum number of opiate addicts at specific times. Prior to 1842 it is virtually certain that the national addiction rate was no more than 0.72 per thousand. But by the mid-1890s the maximum had more than sextupled to 4.59 per thousand. Thereafter the rate of opiate addiction, as reflected in opiate imports per capita, began a sustained decline. Because per capita consumption fell faster than population grew,[56] it is safe to assume that there were never more than approximately 313,000 opiate addicts in America after 1900 and before 1914.

Official Estimates

The foregoing analysis clashes sharply with earlier official assessments of the problem, notably Hamilton Wright's *Report on the International Opium Commission* for the U.S. Senate (1910), Andrew DuMez's "Some Facts Concerning Drug Addiction" (1918), and the Treasury Department's *Traffic in Narcotic Drugs* (1919). The first report distorted the trend of opiate addiction, the second and third its prevalence; all three documents made a deep and lasting misimpression.

Hamilton Wright was appointed in 1908 to be one of three American delegates to the Shanghai Opium Commission. By training a physician and a scientist,[57] Wright was by instinct a politician and not above bending facts to achieve legislative ends. His 1910 *Report* is better understood as a carefully constructed brief than as a disinterested scientific document. Wright lobbied for domestic narcotic legislation as part of his larger strategy for controlling the international traffic. Essentially, he believed that in order to assume moral and diplomatic leadership on the world question, the United States must itself possess exemplary narcotic laws. Shortly after the Opium Commission convened on February 1, 1909, Congress passed, at the behest of the State Department, the Smoking Opium Exclusion Act.[58] Wright saw the ban on imported smoking opium as a step in the right direction, but he wanted more comprehensive legislation — and he wanted it before the projected Hague Opium Conference began. He drafted a series of bills, which were introduced by House Foreign Affairs Committee Chairman David Foster on April 30, 1910. Two were relatively noncontroversial measures designed to supplement the Smoking Opium Exclusion Act, but the third, generally known as the Foster Antinarcotic Bill, was clearly designed to circumscribe domestic narcotic traffic. Its elaborate provisions for registering dealers and recording all narcotic sales, backed by stiff fines for infractions, were vigorously opposed by the drug industry.[59]

Rather than compromise with the drug interests, Wright sought to secure passage of the Foster bill through scare tactics. His *Report* painted a lurid picture of the domestic drug problem; he especially stressed the danger to white women posed by black cocaine users — probably to secure the votes of negrophobic southern congressmen.[60] On the question of extent, however, he shifted to more subtle tactics. As has been shown, per capita consumption of both smoking and medicinal opium was declining during the years 1900 to 1910. Wright himself had been advised repeatedly by leading drug wholesalers of the downward trend.[61] Yet he attempted to circumvent this problem by presenting his data in such a way that consumption appeared to be increasing. By combining the recent, lower per capita import figures with those for years in which imports were relatively high, and by taking a 50-year span as his point of reference, he created the statistical illusion of a sustained increase in the per capita consumption of opiates. "Thus against the 351 per cent increase in our importations of all forms of opium *for the last five decades* we find a 133 per cent increase in our total population," he concluded. "These figures speak louder than words." So loudly, in fact, that they completely obscured the decline in per capita consumption of opiates that had taken place during the previous decade.[62]

Although the *Report* failed to achieve its immediate goal (the Foster bill died in committee), Wright's disingenuous statistics lived on. Within a short time his 351 to 133 ratio had resurfaced in a presidential message, a book-length public health bulletin, a manual of pharmacology, a *Journal of the American Medical Association* editorial, and a *New York Times* feature entitled "Uncle Sam Is the Worst Drug Fiend in the World."[63] When the Harrison Narcotic Act, essentially a watered-down version of the Foster bill, was being considered, the figures turned up again in a favorable House report.[64] Diplomatic historian Arnold H. Taylor was not far from the mark when he noted that, even though "Wright greatly exaggerated the extent of opium consumption," his figures were significant because "they provided the conceptual basis for remedial legislation regarding the problem in the first two decades of the twentieth century."[65]

Although Wright intimated that addiction was growing, he did not venture an exact estimate of the increase. Somewhat more explicit was Andrew DuMez's 1918 report. At the time DuMez prepared his document, he was working as a technical assistant for a special Treasury Department committee on narcotic drugs. He concluded that "an estimate of 750,000 drug addicts in the United States would appear to be conservative. The Bureau of Internal Revenue places the number at 1,500,000." DuMez explained that the committee had received replies to 52,693 of 136,745 questionnaires sent to physicians, and that these indicated a total of 270,662 addicts (drug unspecified). Extrapolating, there would have been approximately 694,000 addicts nationwide. DuMez took this figure to be too small, however, since he thought that addicts of the upper and lower strata tended to avoid physicians. Moreover, he was impressed by the testimony of a Lieutenant Deidlebaum, who appeared before the committee with a list of names and addresses of over 8,000 male, draft-age addicts in New York City alone. "[Deidlebaum] had obtained these names, personally, at Albany," wrote DuMez. "Unfortunately, he died a short time later, and we have never been able to obtain this data."[66]

DuMez was not able to obtain these names because they did not exist: the total number of draft-age addicts rejected nationwide was only 3,284. Worse, DuMez based his physician-survey estimate on grossly inaccurate figures. When the special committee published its final report, it stated that only 73,150 addicts were reported by respondents—not 270,662. The revised extrapolation indicated a total of 237,665 addicts.[67] And even that figure may have been too high. Shortly after the final report appeared, Byron U. Richards, secretary of the Rhode Island State Board of Health, wrote to Surgeon General Rupert Blue, objecting that the committee's estimate of nearly 1,000 addicts in his state was entirely out of line. Richards based his objection on the fact that a comprehensive, statewide registration program had turned up only 200 addicts.[68]

Inaccurate though they were, the statistics in "Some Facts Concerning Drug Addiction," like those in Wright's *Report,* had an important impact on policy. DuMez's preliminary estimates were quoted in the government briefs for two crucial Supreme Court cases, *Webb et al.* v. *United States* and *United States* v. *Doremus.* The former case dealt with the status of the physician-addict relationship, the latter with the constitutionality of the Harrison Act itself. Citing the special committee's work, the government stated that there were at least 750,000 addicts in the United States, and perhaps as many as 1,500,000. Playing on the theme that adverse social conditions justified the exercise of federal powers, the brief concluded, "Congress, no doubt, having facts somewhat similar to these before it, in its wisdom saw fit to adopt the method it did in this law for the imposition of the tax and the assurance of its payment."[69] Finding for the government, the court upheld the constitutionality of the law and, reversing an earlier promaintenance decision, held that a physician might not prescribe "for the purpose of providing the user with morphine sufficient to keep him comfortable by maintaining his customary use." The margin in both cases was one vote.[70]

The final report of the special committee, *Traffic in Narcotic Drugs,* also had significant impact. In addition to DuMez, the report's authors included Congressman Henry T. Rainey, representative from Illinois; Reid Hunt, professor of pharmacology at Harvard University; Barnett C. Keith, deputy commissioner of internal revenue; and Benjamin R. Rhees, a physician. The basic conclusion of the report, widely publicized, was that "the number of addicts in this country probably exceeds 1,000,000 at the present time." The basis for this estimate was not made clear. Certainly it was not supported by the (revised) physician survey, or by an additional survey of public health officers—but these findings were dismissed as "much too low." Instead, the report called attention to Terry's 1913 enumeration of 887 addicts (541 opiate, 346 cocaine) and a statement by the New York City health officer that there were 103,000 addicts in that city alone.[71] The Jacksonville rate, as we have seen, was singularly high, and once again the New York data turned out to be totally erroneous: only 7,464 addicts registered at the New York City narcotic clinic the following year.

"We accepted in good faith some data which now appears to have been incorrect," was Reid Hunt's understated summary of the affair.[72] DuMez implicitly repudiated his work with the committee when he argued, in a 1924 article coauthored by Kolb, that the amount of opiates legitimately imported could never have supported more than 246,000 addicts, let alone 1,000,000.[73] Kolb too was highly critical of the 1,000,000 estimate. In a 1932 letter to his son he dismissed it as "merely a statement . . . a belief that was not based on any facts and which was arrived at by ignoring all the facts which they, as well as others, discovered before the report was made." Only deference to the other committee members prevented Kolb and DuMez from discussing the matter in print.[74]

Rainey, however, was not so reticent. While serving as chairman of the committee, he was simultaneously sponsoring legislation, drafted by Keith, that was designed to strengthen the Harrison Act. On September 18, 1918, he delivered a major speech on the floor of the House in support of the proposed legislation. A man of impressive bulk (over 6 feet tall and weighing 275 pounds), Rainey was equally impressive as an orator. Referring to some of the more sensational testimony before the committee — the same testimony that had misled DuMez — he painted a grim picture of the domestic narcotic situation:

We find as a result of computations and estimates as far as we have gone with the investigation that there are in all probability in the United States . . . 1,500,000 drug addicts, every one of them needing treatment. There were 80,000 drug addicts in the first draft . . . Sixty per cent of the addicts in the city of Baltimore are of draft age. There are 200,000 addicts in the city of New York . . . We have names of 8,000 young men in New York City between the ages of 21 and 31 who are drug addicts.[75]

Rainey alluded twice to the scientific expertise of the committee, in an effort to impart credibility to his startling statistics. By emphasizing the prevalence of addiction among draft-age men, he appealed to the fears of a wartime Congress. He also hinted that the rate of addiction would worsen, owing to the prohibition of alcohol and the likelihood that war widows and veterans would resort to drugs to alleviate their grief and injuries. This combination of tactics ultimately proved successful, as most of the proposed amendments to the Harrison Act were adopted.[76] Rainey was not content to rest his case before Congress, however. Well before *Traffic in Narcotic Drugs* was released, he leaked the revised estimate of 1,000,000 drug addicts to the press.[77] His remarks on draft-age addicts were also widely circulated.[78] By the time the final report, dated June 1919, appeared in print, the American public was convinced that addiction was a problem of massive dimensions.

Not the least important of the readers of *Traffic in Narcotic Drugs* was Richmond P. Hobson. Described by one of his biographers as a man of "virtually unlimited moral indignation," Hobson was a Spanish-American War hero turned temperance lecturer and organizer. He proved quite adept in that role, but when Prohibition went into effect, he became a reformer without a cause—a victim, as it were, of his own success. Hobson soon realized the potential of the addiction issue, however, and in the early 1920s launched a new crusade designed to awaken the nation to the perils of narcotic drugs, particularly heroin. He resorted to the by-then-familiar tactic of sensationalism, depicting addicts as dangerous and deranged individuals, bent on criminal acts and determined to enslave all with whom they came in contact. Of particular concern here, he further claimed that there were 1,000,000 or more addicts in the United States and that their numbers were constantly increasing. Hobson based this allegation primarily on *Traffic in Narcotic Drugs,* which he quoted prominently in feature-length newspaper articles.[79] His use of this document proved a source of embarrassment to Treasury Department and Public Health Service officials, who by this time realized the extent of the report's inaccuracies. Although the shortcomings of *Traffic in Narcotic Drugs* were candidly discussed in a series of internal memorandums, it was difficult for the Treasury Department to denounce publicly the findings of its own blue-ribbon committee. Officials of the Public Health Service successfully halted some of Hobson's more grandiose schemes, such as government-sponsored distribution of 50,000,000 copies of his article, "The Peril of Narcotic Drugs—A Warning," but they could not prevent him from broadcasting and publishing his claims about the "army of addicts." Hobson continued agitating until his death in 1937, and his mix of questionable statistics and pseudoscience was instrumental in persuading Americans that addiction was both pervasive and malignant.[80]

During the decade 1910 to 1920, the crucial period for the formulation of American narcotic policy, public opinion concerning opiate addiction was profoundly influenced by inaccurate and even falsified data. Laws were passed and interpreted on the premise that addiction was a widespread and worsening social problem, rather than a limited and diminishing disease. The statistics that Wright, Rainey, Hobson, and others quoted are important, not as an index of epidemiologic reality, but as a clue to understanding why legislators and citizens reacted the way they did.

The larger goal of this study, however, is to explain the transformation of the American opiate addict. To that end it is necessary to attempt to reconstruct the true prevalence and trend of opiate addiction. Objective evidence indicates that, far from increasing during the early twentieth century, the rate of addiction declined steadily from 1900 to 1914, from a peak of perhaps 4.59 per thousand in the mid-1890s. Per capita opiate imports during these years, compared to earlier periods when duties were similar, dwindled; moreover, virtually all addiction rates derived from the records of maintenance programs were substantially lower than rates based on surveys taken in the 1870s and 1880s (such as Marshall's in Michigan or Earle's in Chicago). Even allowing for 100 percent underreporting, the clinic records indicate a maximum of 209,866 addicts in 1920, or 1.97 per thousand persons. Furthermore, if the rates based on addicts registered in the Tennessee (1913), Pennsylvania (1920–1922), and New York City (1919–1920) programs are doubled, as some officials suggested they should be to arrive at the true rate, it is still apparent that there were not more than approximately 2.06 to 2.66 addicts per thousand persons in these places. Add to this the fact that, in spite of their limitations, military medical examinations turned up only 3,284 drug addicts, and the case for an early-twentieth-century decline in opiate addiction becomes overwhelming. To understand why the overall rate of addiction dropped so sharply, after nearly a century of increase, we need to examine the background and characteristics of the various groups of opiate addicts and determine how they became addicted in the first place.

Addiction to Opium and Morphine

2 The term *opiate addiction,* as it has been used thus far, serves as a unifying concept. Like the word *alcoholism,* it is a way of speaking about diverse people who have in common their dependence on a certain drug. The aim of this and subsequent chapters, however, is to divide opiate addicts into smaller, more homogeneous classifications. The histories of these separate groups provide a basis for understanding the overall decline in addiction, as well as for explaining the transformation of the addict population.

Nineteenth-century and early-twentieth-century opiate addicts were distinguished by the form of opium they used. The background of a morphine addict, for example, was different from that of an opium smoker. Not only was the morphine addict a "better" person in the conventional social sense, but he (or more likely, she) typically began using the drug for medical, rather than euphoric or experimental, purposes. Recognizing the presence of such distinct patterns of addiction, each centering on the use of a particular drug or drugs, is the key to organizing opiate addicts into more meaningful categories.

The first pattern is addiction to opium and morphine. By opium and morphine I have something quite exact in mind. *Opium* means the dried milky juice of white poppy capsules, except when it has been prepared for smoking. (For clarity I always refer to opium in the latter form as *smoking opium.*) *Morphine* means the principal active alkaloid of opium, or any of its salts, such as morphine acetate, morphine hydrochloride, or morphine sulfate. It does not include diacetylmorphine or heroin, a semisynthetic derivative which, like smoking opium, is discussed in a separate chapter. When referring to opium and morphine addiction, I mean addiction to these substances either alone or as part of a medicinal preparation. Opium and morphine were commonly included in official preparations, such as Dover's powder or laudanum, as well as unofficial preparations, particularly patent medicines.[1] While some opium and morphine addicts took their drug as a pure powder or salt, others ingested it as a part of a polypharmaceutical concoction. Both are considered here.

While there were many sources of opium and morphine addiction, four were especially significant: administration by physicians, the Civil War, self-dosage, and nontherapeutic usage. Prior to an examination of each of these factors, it will be useful to consider the background and characteristics of the addicts themselves. Fortunately, there is sufficient information on their sex, age, race, national origin, geographic distribution, class, and occupation to fashion a detailed composite portrait.

Characteristics of Opium and Morphine Addicts

The outstanding feature of nineteenth-century opium and morphine addiction is that the majority of addicts were women. Orville Marshall's 1878 Michigan survey, Charles Earle's 1880 Chicago survey, and Justin Hull's 1885 Iowa survey indicated that 61.2, 71.9, and 63.4 percent of their respective samples were female.[2] Marshall further differentiated between opium addicts, of whom 56.3 percent were female, and morphine addicts, of whom 65.6 percent were female.[3] The location with the highest percentage of female addicts allegedly was Albany, where it was reported that "fully four-fifths of the opium-eaters are women."[4]

The disproportionate number of female opium and morphine addicts persisted in some places well into the twentieth century. In 1912 Charles Terry reported that 68.2 percent of Jacksonville's opium and morphine addicts were female; in spite of an influx of male transients, the figure at the end of 1913 was still 61.0 percent female.[5] Tennessee's 1913 registration and maintenance program revealed that 66.9 percent of morphine users, 75.0 percent of laudanum users, and 66.7 percent of gum opium users were female; in contrast, women comprised only 22.6 percent of the registered heroin users.[6] As late as 1919 a report from Memphis indicated that 57.0 percent of the morphine addicts in that city were female.[7]

Not every early-twentieth-century study disclosed a majority of female addicts, however. Of 34 morphine addicts studied by Dr. Harry H. Drysdale in Cleveland City Hospital in 1915, 23 — or 67.6 percent — were male.[8] Unpublished case summaries compiled by Lawrence Kolb in 1923 showed that 120 of 174 opium and morphine addicts were male, or 68.9 percent.[9] An even higher percentage was obtained from the records of the Shreveport clinic, which indicated that 76.4 percent of the patients were male.[10] Some of this disproportion may have resulted from the itinerant character of many of Willis Butler's patients;[11] nevertheless it appears that, at least in some places, by 1915 to 1923 men comprised the majority of morphine addicts.[12]

Most individuals who became addicted to opium and morphine did so between the ages of 25 and 45. "To no age is accorded an absolute exemption," wrote Alonzo Calkins in 1871, "but the medium period lies between the 30th and the 35th year." His view was shared by Charles Earle, who described it as "a vice of middle life."[13] Statistics from the Tennessee program confirm Earle's dating of addiction, if not his assessment of it as a vice. The average age at which addiction began was for males 37 years, 10 months; for females, 37 years, 6 months. For both sexes the average age at time of registration was 49 years.[14] Other studies published between 1871 and 1922 yield somewhat lower average ages, but generally support the characterization of opium and morphine addiction as a condition of middle life.[15]

With respect to race, whites were overrepresented among opium and morphine addicts, blacks underrepresented. In 1885 Dr. James D. Roberts of the Eastern North Carolina Insane Asylum, after making a number of inquiries, reported that he knew of "but three well authenticated cases of opium-eating in the negro."[16] In Jacksonville in 1912 and 1913 nearly three-quarters of the opium and morphine addicts were white, even though whites made up slightly less than half of that city's population.[17] Lucius Brown noted that only 10 percent of Tennessee's registered addicts were black, even though roughly a quarter of that state's population was black.[18] In Shreveport 91.5 and in Houston 95.5 of the clinic patients were white, remarkable statistics in view of the substantial black populations in these areas.[19] As late as

1923 only 7 of the 174 morphine addicts studied by Kolb were designated "colored."[20] The single exception to the pattern was Chicago, where Earle's 1880 study showed blacks to be over-represented among opium and morphine users.[21]

Most opium and morphine addicts were also native-born. In Chicago 73.2 percent of the addicts were listed as Americans, even though the native-born comprised only 59.3 percent of that city's population in 1880. Germans, Irish, English, and Scandinavians were all underrepresented among Chicago addicts; only the Scots were overrepresented.[22] An 1887 study of 12 morphine addicts in the Pennsylvania Hospital for the Insane showed all to be of American birth.[23] Finally, case summaries published in Drysdale's 1915 Cleveland study also indicated that the foreign-born were underrepresented among morphine addicts.[24] With the exception of Chinese opium smokers (to be discussed later), immigrants contributed relatively little to the incidence of opiate addiction in America.

In geographic terms, opium and morphine addicts were concentrated in the South. Table 2 shows the number of addicts attending narcotic clinics in 34 cities between 1919 and 1924. Most, though not all, of these addicts used opium or morphine. The 23 northern and western cities averaged 0.93 addict per thousand, while the 11 southern cities[25] averaged 1.53 addicts per thousand persons — a rate 64.5 percent higher. Maintenance programs in Jacksonville and Tennessee also produced addiction rates in excess of the northern and western average.

Further evidence for higher southern use is found in pharmacy records. A survey of the records of 34 Boston drug stores published in 1888 revealed that of 10,200 prescriptions sampled, 1,481 (14.5 percent) contained some type of opiate.[26] Unfortunately, there was no comparable study of prescriptions for a major southern city. I have, however, located and sampled the contents of two surviving New Orleans pharmacists' record books, dating from the late 1870s and 1880s. Fully 24.5 percent of these prescriptions contained opium or morphine, 10 percentage points more than the Boston average.[27] While a limited, two-city comparison does not prove that an entire region had a higher rate of addiction, it at least corroborates the differences indicated by clinic registration.

One important implication of the higher southern clinic and pharmacy figures is that southern whites ran the greatest risk of opium and morphine addiction of any regional racial group. Since southern blacks had a very low rate of addiction, and since blacks made up roughly a third of the postbellum southern population,[28] it follows that, to account for the low black rate, southern whites must have had a rate even higher than their regional average.

A second question bearing on the geographic distribution of opium and morphine addicts is whether they were situated in urban or rural areas. Contemporaries offered two competing theories. The first, advanced as early as 1869, held that addiction was concentrated in larger cities, where the demand for "stimulants" was proportionately greater.[29] This view, endorsed by several prominent specialists, was opposed by Thomas S. Blair, a physician and drug control officer who made a careful study of addiction in Pennsylvania. In 1919 he observed that although there was little addiction among active farmers, there was a good deal of addiction among

---

retired farmers, invalids on the farms, tenants, domestic farm help, and the much-harassed farmers' wives . . . Our reports . . . , while showing less free use of narcotics in rural communities than formerly, do very positively show a *per capita* consumption of opiates in the small towns and villages adjacent to the farms where the drugs are secured from physicians or on prescription, very far in excess of the *per capita* consumption in the large cities.[30]

Morphine use in Pennsylvania, Blair later reported, was concentrated as follows: towns with populations ranging from 1,000 to 30,000 had the highest per capita consumption, followed by cities of 30,000 to 100,000, and finally by Philadelphia and Pittsburgh, which had the lowest per capita consumption of all.[31]

Unfortunately, data drawn from surveys and maintenance programs outside Pennsylvania provide no clear-cut resolution of the controversy. In his Michigan survey, Marshall tabulated the number of opium and morphine addicts per town, together with the town's population.[32] Although the survey canvassed no large cities, it did include 96 locations ranging in population from 315 to 10,235. The statistical relation between rate of addiction and town size is exceedingly weak, however, with virtually zero correlation between the two variables. An analysis of the clinic data in Table 2 yields somewhat similar results; adjusting for regional differences, there is a negative relation between the rate of addiction and city size, but it is not pronounced (see Appendix). Opium and morphine addicts, in short, seem to have been well distributed with respect to urban and rural areas.

"While all classes of people are to be found in the ranks of morphine addiction," wrote addiction specialist Charles B. Pearson in 1918, "the better class of the native American stock seem to be the most susceptible."[33] Pearson's remark summarizes a half-century of medical testimony; there was a consensus that opium and morphine addicts were concentrated in the upper and middle classes.[34] Evidence of a statistical nature is scant, but what there is generally supports Pearson's view. In 1889 Dr. Benjamin H. Hartwell asked Massachusetts pharmacists and physicians which classes of people in their communities used opium or its preparations. The 446 pharmacists answered as follows: 22 percent, all classes; 22 percent, middle classes; 7 percent, upper classes; 7 percent, lower classes; 11 percent, "do not know of any who use opium"; and 31 percent, "do not know" or some other answer. The answers of the 166 physicians were 30 percent, all classes; 22 percent, upper; 12 percent, upper and middle; 8 percent, middle; 6 percent, lower; 14 percent, "nervous women"; and 8 percent, "do not know."[35] While Hartwell was counting questionnaires, Virgil G. Eaton was thumbing through the prescription records of 34 Boston drug stores. He observed that a drug store with a distinctly upper-class clientele had more prescriptions containing opium or morphine (16.3 percent) than stores patronized by "poorer people" or "poor Italian laborers" (12.0 and 10.7 percent, respectively).[36] Evidently American laborers and factory operatives did not take to opium and morphine with the enthusiasm of their English counterparts.[37]

In addition to strictly statistical evidence, contemporary accounts abound with allusions to addicts of refinement and position; their plight served to drive home the point that addiction was, as Charles B. Towns put it, "no respecter of persons."[38] Discreet references tantalize: Who were the several congressmen and senators whom Washington physician D. Percy Hickling supplied with opium, or the congressman-addict who resorted to opium to bolster his oratorical efforts? Who was Mrs. E. D. P., sister of a governor and U.S. senator, mentioned by pamphleteer Edward Sell as a former addict, or the brilliant and famous inventor cited by Clyde Langston Eddy?[39] In some cases we know the identities of famous addicts, principally because their medical histories (or those of their families) have been closely studied. Benjamin Franklin and John Randolph, for example, almost certainly became dependent upon opium in their declining days, while Harriet Beecher Stowe's daughter, Georgiana, became addicted to morphine following a sudden nervous prostration.[40] Letters and diaries occasionally provide clues about the use of these drugs in prominent families. Correspondence by Jefferson Davis' female relatives reveals how commonly opium preparations were resorted to for illness, as do the diaries of Confederate aristocrats Mary Boykin Chesnut and William Pitt Ballinger.[41] Henry S. Lane, a man of similar pharmaceutical practices if dissimilar political views, noted in his journal that he dosed himself with opium for the "cramp cholic" he suffered during the Mexican War.[42] Of course not all opium and morphine addicts were rich or distinguished—or even middle class; prostitutes and criminals used these drugs as well. Prior to 1900, however, opium and morphine addiction was primarily an upper-class and middle-class phenomenon.

The most common occupation among female addicts was that of housewife. The majority of nineteenth-century female addicts were married and therefore stayed at home. Unmarried female addicts were observed among domestics, teachers, actresses, and especially prostitutes.[43] Another type, mentioned as early as 1832, was the harried society lady, who downed opium or morphine to steady her nerve and enhance her wit.[44] Women associated with the medical profession—nurses and doctors' wives—also had an unusually high rate of addiction.[45]

Among male addicts the leading occupation was unquestionably that of physician; sources differ only on how large a percentage of the medical profession was addicted. The most widely quoted estimate was that of Thomas Davison Crothers. Based on a study of 3,244 physicians, he concluded that "from six to ten percent. [of the physicians] in this country are opium inebriates."[46] Thomas J. Happel thought the figure even higher. "I find," he wrote in 1900, "in a list of the names of one hundred and fourteen physicians . . . eighteen who became addicted to morphine—nearly 16 percent."[47] In 1913 Bittle C. Keister announced to a startled audience that fully 23 percent of the medical profession were victims of morphine addiction.[48] Asylum records, although they cannot be used to establish an exact percentage, on the whole support charges that physicians had a serious addiction problem.[49] Country doctors, with their especially arduous routine, were said to have made up a disproportionate share of physician-addicts.[50] However, no stratum of the profession was exempt; cases of physician-addicts as eminent as William S. Halsted, pioneering surgeon and professor at Johns Hopkins, have been documented.[51] Members of the allied health professions, notably dentists and pharmacists, also had a high rate of addiction.[52]

"Brain workers" and "professional men" were other occupational categories frequently cited in connection with opium and morphine addiction.[53] Data on white-collar addiction is sketchy, however. Businessmen, lawyers, clerks, clergymen, and the like are mentioned in surveys,[54] but in such a way that it is impossible to tell precisely how many of their number were addicted. Among male occupations with a low rate of addiction, sailors were prominently mentioned. Cut off for months or years at a time from a regular supply of opiates, it is unlikely that many of their number became addicted.[55] Active farmers and skilled and semiskilled workers were also cited as low-addiction groups, although the exact rates are not known.[56]

There is, by way of summing up, a character in Harper Lee's novel *To Kill a Mockingbird* named Mrs. Henry Lafayette Dubose. Mrs. Dubose is a propertied and cantankerous widow residing in a small Alabama town. She is also a morphine addict, having become addicted years ago as a consequence of a chronic, painful condition. Informed that she has only a short while to live, she struggles to quit taking the drug, for she is determined to "leave this world beholden to nothing and nobody."[57] Although fictitious, Mrs. Dubose personifies the American opium or morphine addict of the late nineteenth and early twentieth centuries. If all of the foregoing statistics were condensed into a single, modal type, it would closely resemble Mrs. Dubose: a native Southerner, possessed of servant and property, once married, now widowed and homebound, evidently addicted since late middle age. In all respects — her sex, age of addiction, race, nationality, region, class, and occupation (or lack thereof) — she is typical. Typical, too, is the origin of her condition: she was addicted by her physician.

Medical Administration

The administration of opium and morphine by physicians was the leading cause of addiction in the nineteenth century, and the principal reason opium and morphine addiction assumed the pattern just described. Estimates of the number of opium and morphine addicts who could trace their plight back to their doctor ranged from a simple majority to 99 percent.[58] The problem became particularly acute with the spread of hypodermic medication during the 1860s and 1870s, when morphine injection became a virtual panacea. In spite of repeated warnings, therapeutically engendered addiction remained a serious problem until the early twentieth century, when the American medical profession largely abandoned its liberal use of opium and morphine.

Before tracing in detail the course of iatrogenic addiction, I need to qualify one term, *physician.* When I speak of physicians causing or contributing to addiction, I refer to regular practitioners. Sectarian practitioners, thanks to their distinctive therapeutic regimens, seldom addicted anyone. Thomsonians denounced the use of opium; their successors, the eclectics, used it, but with circumspection; the homeopaths believed that opiates, as all drugs, should be administered only in minuscule amounts.[59] Hydropathy, osteopathy, chiropractic, and Christian Science all advocated drugless therapy.[60] Regular practitioners, on the other hand, freely used drugs, including opium and morphine, throughout the period.[61] It is on the regulars, therefore, that I intend to focus.

The therapeutic use of opium was passed down to the American physician as an ancient and honorable practice, sanctioned by the greatest medical authorities over many centuries.[62] The drug had been employed by figures no less illustrious than Galen (A.D. 130-201), Paracelsus (1493-1541), Franz de la Boë (1614-1675), Thomas Sydenham (1624-1689), Herman Boerhaave (1668-1738), and John Brown (1735-1788).[63] The basis for opium's lasting popularity is not its curative power, but rather its analgesic properties. No other naturally occurring drug can match it as an anodyne, a fact recognized by even the most skeptical contemporaries. When Oliver Wendell Holmes, Sr., made his famous remark, "I firmly believe that if the whole materia medica, *as now used,* could be sunk to the bottom of the sea, it would be all the better for mankind, — and all the worse for the fishes," he specifically exempted opium, a medicine "which the Creator himself seems to prescribe."[64]

The therapeutic use of opium was common in colonial America,[65] although one cannot even begin to estimate the total amount dispensed. During the eighteenth century the drug was given to dull pain, induce sleep, control insanity, alleviate cough, check diarrhea, and treat a wide range of communicable diseases, including malaria, smallpox, syphilis, and tuberculosis.[66] In 1785 an American physician, John Leigh, captured the Harveian Prize with his study, *An Experimental Inquiry into the Properties of Opium and Its Effects on Living Subjects.* Leigh's list of indications was typically long and comprehensive, and he ended it with the observation that opium also served "to afford much relief to the various spasmodic symptoms of dyspepsia, hysteria, hypochondriasis, asthma, & c & c."[67] The inclusion of psychosomatic disorders and the use of the double et cetera is revealing; it is almost as if he appended to his statement "and virtually any other distressing or painful mental or physical condition."

When available, opium was used by Continental Army physicians to treat sick and wounded soldiers during the Revolutionary War. British forces made use of the drug as well. The military demand, together with the disruption of trade, dried up the regular supply — a situation that alarmed civilian practitioners. "Opium is an article," wrote Dr. Thaddeus Betts in 1778, "which no physician ought ever to want; it is so extensively useful, and in cases so perilous and urgent, where no substitute will supply its defect, that physic . . . would be lame and deficient without it." Betts met the crisis by growing and harvesting his own poppies, a practice he strongly recommended to his colleagues.[68]

Some eighteenth-century American physicians had other cause to worry about sources of supply: they themselves were opium addicts. Dr. James Hurlbut (1717–1794), for example,

would not prescribe or even look at a patient in the last years of his life, till the full bottle of spirits was placed in his entire control, and daily replenished; it was his practice to take very frequently small potations, and at the same time swallow enormous quantities of opium. For many of his last years all the avails of his medical practice were expended in the purchase of this one drug; his spirits he obtained from his employers, which was a heavy tax, and he probably took as much opium as the most devoted Turk.[69]

Recorded cases are scarce, but there is at least one other, cited in 1803 by Benjamin Rush, of a German physician in Pennsylvania who became deranged through continuous use.[70] There are also a few sketchy case histories of laymen addicted during the eighteenth century, mostly for medical reasons.[71] On the whole, however, there is nothing to indicate that opium addiction was a widespread problem; at least there was no great outcry in the medical literature. In the letter mentioning the Pennsylvania physician, Rush remarked that he had been acquainted with but two other addicts during the previous ten years.[72]

Opium remained a popular therapeutic agent throughout the first half of the nineteenth century. When Alexander Hamilton lay dying, a bullet lodged in his shattered spine, it was for the laudanum bottle that his physician instinctively reached to alleviate his patient's suffering.[73] When Connecticut physician

Vine Utley was confronted with a double epidemic of pneumonia and typhus fever in 1812–1813, he resorted to the lancet and liberal doses of opium. "From the beginning," Utley explained, "I did not hesitate as to the most earnest and judicious principles to follow in the arduous task of combating the prevailing epidemic, for I had long ago adopted the American theory (ie 'to prescribe for the symptoms without being solicitous to give the disease a name.' "[74]

Lesser afflictions were treated with opium as well; Nathaniel Chapman, author of the first systematic treatise on pharmacology published in the United States (1817), judged it the most useful drug in the materia medica, "there being scarcely one morbid affection or disordered condition, in which, under certain circumstances, it is not exhibited, either alone, or in combination."[75] Opium's continued popularity was due in part to the Brownian cast of American medicine in the early nineteenth century. The influential Scottish physician John Brown held that diseases were of two types: *sthenic,* resulting from too much stimulus, and *asthenic,* resulting from too little. The latter could be cured by administering stimulants, notably opium and alcohol, to restore the body to its proper level of excitability.[76] Not every American physician held with Brown that opium was a stimulant; Valentine Seaman, for one, argued that opium acted as a sedative.[77] Whatever their opinion of opium's essential properties, most American physicians shared Brown's enthusiasm for the drug; by 1834 it was ranked as the single most widely prescribed item in the materia medica.[78]

Opium's principal alkaloid, morphine, was also employed after the method for its isolation was published in 1817.[79] Morphine crystals had definite advantages; they were pure and of consistent potency, qualities imported opium often lacked.[80] Nevertheless, morphine did not supplant opium as the therapeutic opiate of choice until the spread of hypodermic medication during the 1860s and 1870s. Not only did morphine cost more, but, as one student shrewdly observed, doctors "never . . . abandon an article whose virtues are known, and universally acknowledged, for one not yet proved, but just introduced."[81]

Although there was as yet no ground for criticizing professional overuse of morphine, a number of writers began commenting on the injudicious use of opium.[82] Prior to 1830 much of the literature on opium was concerned with overdose and its treatment, but after that date opium addiction was discussed more and more frequently.[83] In 1841, for example, a Mr. M'Gowan read a paper before the Temperance Society of the College of Physicians and Surgeons of the University of the State of New York, charging that there were 3,000 to 5,000 habitual opium users in New York City alone.[84] While the accuracy of M'Gowan's statistics may be questioned, the fears he voiced were genuine and seem to have been shared by a growing number of American physicians.

The newfound concern expressed between 1830 and 1860 suggests that something happened during those decades to increase the rate of addiction, or at least to make the problem more visible. One possible explanation involves a series of severe epidemics that struck the United States: cholera in 1832–1833, dysentery from 1847 to 1851, and cholera again between 1848 and 1854. Cholera and dysentery, diseases that afflicted thousands of persons, were routinely treated with opiates,[85] and it seems reasonable to suppose that some exhausted survivors continued the medication long enough to become addicted. Certainly this is consistent with the sharp increase in crude opium imports observed in the late 1840s (see Figure 2), when both cholera and dysentery were prevalent — although, as noted earlier, this increase was also partly due to changes in tariff policy. In any event opium addiction, whether from treatment of epidemic disease or some other factor, ceased to be regarded as a relative curiosity and by 1860 had assumed the status of a significant medical problem.

Problem became crisis during 1860 to 1880. Two events, the Civil War and the spread of hypodermic medication, triggered a massive increase in iatrogenic opium and especially morphine addiction. For simplicity I here consider only hypodermic medication, as practiced by civilian doctors upon civilian patients; the impact of the Civil War, a subject about which there is some controversy, will be discussed later.

Like any other new device, the hypodermic syringe (first brought to America in 1856) was greeted with skepticism.[86] But the writings of Antoine Ruppaner, Roberts Bartholow, and others, plus the firsthand experience of some physicians with it during the Civil War, helped persuade the profession of the value of the instrument.[87] Promoters also played upon professional insecurities, noting that practitioners of standing were quick to avail themselves of the advantages of the syringe and implying that those who did not were in danger of falling behind.[88] The percentage of American physicians who practiced hypodermic medication grew dramatically during the 1870s; by 1881 virtually every American physician possessed the instrument.[89]

The hypodermic syringe was developed for the purpose of injecting morphine, and this proved to be its most popular use during the nineteenth century.[90] Morphine injected hypodermically avoided the unpleasant gastric side effects of opiates administered orally;[91] it also produced stronger feelings of relief and euphoria, and it produced them much more quickly. New Orleans surgeon Charles Schuppert, called upon to treat a man wounded in a barroom fray, vividly described the strength and rapidity with which an injection of morphine worked. "I was immediately summoned," he noted in his casebook, "and on my arrival . . . found him in a deep stupor from the effects of liquor and bleeding profusely. I gave him an injection of morphine subcutaneously of ½ grain, this acted like a charm, as he came to in a minute from the stupor he was in and rested very easy."[92]

Although effective in the short run, such treatment enhanced the likelihood of addiction in several ways. The patient, instantly reinforced by the relief of pain and infused with a sense of well-being, would have remembered the wonderful effect of the drug administered in this way and would likely have requested the same treatment in the future, particularly if he suffered from a chronic disease and experienced recurring pain. The physician, for his part, was also reinforced by the injection. His patient responded quickly; pain disappeared and mood improved. Praise was effusive and patronage continued. More important still was the sense, which must have been precious for the frustrated nineteenth-century physician, that he could at last do something for the patient; for the first time in the entire history of medicine near-instantaneous, symptomatic relief for a wide range of diseases was possible. A syringe of morphine was, in a very real sense, a magic wand. Though it could cure little, it could relieve anything; doctors and patients alike were tempted to overuse.

I do not mean to imply, however, that all patients who received morphine injections subsequently became addicted. Why some succumbed and others did not is an interesting and potentially controversial question. Rather than postulate personality defects or endorphin deficiencies in those who became addicts, as some authors do, I propose that the circumstances of administration plus the nature of the patient's illness were the most important factors in determining who became addicted.[93] In order to become addicted to an opiate, one must first become physically dependent, that is, experience withdrawal symptoms if the drug is discontinued. In order to become physically dependent, one must consume the drug continuously over a period of time, perhaps 10 to 14 days.[94] Ideally, then, to avoid iatrogenic addiction, measures should be taken to ensure that opiates are administered as infrequently as possible.[95] Nineteenth-century physicians seldom achieved this ideal. If they did not by repeated administration addict the patient themselves, they often made addiction possible by leaving morphine and syringe with the patient or the patient's family, with instructions to use as needed for pain.[96] Nothing prevented the patient from increasing the frequency and amount of the dose on his own initiative. Another practice that heightened the risk of addiction was mentioning the name of the pleasing anodyne the patient was receiving. This information was dangerous for several reasons. First, if dependence resulted, addiction might still have been avoided if the patient was unaware that his withdrawal distress resulted from the absence of morphine and thought his discomfort a sequel to his illness; on the other hand, if the physician failed to disguise the medication, and the patient learned that he could alleviate withdrawal distress simply by continuing the morphine, addiction was bound to occur.[97] Another danger, particularly acute in the nineteenth century, when morphine and other opiates were freely available, was that the patient, if he knew what he was taking, could supplement the prescribed dose, or continue to consume the drug after the physician had ceased prescribing it.[98] These risks were compounded if the patient suffered from a chronic disease. For physical dependence will soon develop if, as soon as an injection wears off, symptoms recur and the patient's doctor or the patient himself immediately administers more of the drug.[99]

Case histories, clinical notes, and remarks in the medical literature support the view that although opium and morphine were ultimately given for practically everything, even for such unlikely disorders as masturbation, photophobia, nymphomania, and "violent hiccough,"[100] it was principally in those suffering from chronic ailments that use of these drugs led to addiction. Those afflicted with neuralgia seemed especially prone to addiction, as morphine was commonly employed to treat neuralgic attacks.[101] Another common recurring nervous disorder, headache, was also treated with opium and morphine.[102] Women suffering from "female complaints," particularly dysmenorrhea, were similarly dosed. "Uterine and ovarian complications," wrote one observer, "cause more ladies to fall into the habit, than all other diseases combined." As late as 1908 the State Hospital at Independence, Iowa, reported that most of the female addicts became addicted through palliation of dysmenorrhea.[103] Alcoholics seeking relief from hangover or delirium tremens often became addicted.[104] Patients suffering from chronic respiratory disorders (asthma, bronchitis, tuberculosis) or infectious diseases of long duration, especially chronic diarrhea, dysentery, malaria, or syphilis, were also likely candidates.[105] Other addicts had histories of rheumatism.[106] Postoperative syndromes, such as neuroma, took their toll.[107] Finally, it was often mentioned that insomnia, anxiety, and fatigue resulting from overwork could, if treated with opium or morphine, easily lead to addiction.[108]

The fact that the overwhelming majority of opium and morphine addicts suffered from one or more of these conditions goes far toward explaining why certain groups had an elevated incidence of addiction. The higher rate of women derives, in part, from the prevalence of dysmenorrhea and other gynecological disorders. The habit of middle-class and upper-class females' complaining of (or of being diagnosed by male doctors as suffering from) "diseases of a nervous character" could only have aggravated the problem.[109] The onset of opium and morphine addiction in middle age or later is also partially attributable to the nature of these disorders; it is unlikely that there were too many patients under the age of 25 suffering from arthritis, delirium tremens, chronic headache, bronchitis, and the like. The age factor may also help to explain the lower black addiction rate, as relatively fewer blacks lived long enough to develop the chronic diseases associated with aging.[110] Of even greater importance was the fact that, owing to poverty, discrimination, and a lack of physicians of their own race, many blacks were prevented from seeking professional medical care.[111] It is possible that the inaccessibility of doctors worsened the already high mortality rate of blacks, but at least it spared them the risk of iatrogenic opium and morphine addiction. Southern whites, on the other hand, did have access to drug-dispensing physicians and, of equal importance, were often afflicted with malarial and diarrheal diseases. The presence of these endemic diseases, together with the lingering trauma of the Civil War, ensured that Southerners would suffer a higher rate of addiction.[112]

There were, by contrast, fewer candidates for addiction among northern immigrants. Lack of funds for professional medical care undoubtedly played a role; the weeding out of the weak and the chronically ill by the Atlantic passage may have been an additional factor. As Oscar Handlin put it, "The crossing in all its phases was a harsh and brutal filter." Most of the immigrants who passed through the filter, moreover, were male, and men tended to have a lower rate of addiction, at least in the nineteenth century.[113] Similar circumstances may have protected native farmers and industrial workers. These groups too were predominantly male; they did not have a great deal of money to spend on doctors; and it was unlikely that many seriously or chronically ill persons were able to pursue such active callings. Finally, the widespread use of opium and morphine as tranquilizing and somniferous agents helps explain why so many physicians and other health professionals became addicted. Long and irregular hours, stiff competition, and constant pressure from impatient patients sorely tempted the physician to treat his headache or insomnia with opium or especially morphine, a drug that he knew to be quick, effective, and readily available.[114] As many as 12,000 physicians were addicted in this way, a professional pandemic that struck some as a kind of ironic justice.[115]

The creation of addicts through the hypodermic administration or self-administration of morphine for stress or chronic illness continued unabated until the late 1890s. This prolonged, excessive use of morphine was made all the more remarkable by the fact that, beginning in 1870 and continuing through the 1880s and 1890s, warnings about the possibility of iatrogenic morphine addiction appeared in numerous books, journal articles, and published speeches.[116] The physician was cautioned, often sharply, that the drug should be used sparingly, avoided in chronic cases, disguised if possible, never refilled without permission, and above all that the patient should never be left with a syringe and a supply of morphine with instructions for self-medication.[117] These animadversions were reinforced by a growing body of European addiction literature, in which English, French, and German doctors decried similar abuses in their own countries.[118] Why then, in spite of numerous warnings, did American physicians persist in creating addicts?

Critics of the profession charged that a major source of continued abuse was inadequate medical education. Not only was the graduate of a typical proprietary school ill-informed about the danger of repeated administration of opiates, but his general lack of diagnostic skills tempted him to fall back on blind, symptomatic treatment.[119] Ignorance combined with indolence was doubly dangerous. "When a doctor is called near a patient complaining of pains," wrote one experienced physician, "and he does not want to bother about making a diagnosis, or he wants to go fishing, he simply resorts to the ever-ready hypodermic of Morph. Sulp. ¼ grain." Another summed up: "Opium is often the lazy physician's remedy."[120] In a sense the indolent or incompetent practitioner was like the carrier of a communicable disease; though not necessarily himself an addict, he might succeed in transmitting addiction to patients with whom he came into contact. Thus the number of addicts in a given place hinged, in part, on the training and conscientiousness of the local practitioner, a fact that helps explain the apparently random distribution of addicts in the Michigan towns surveyed.[121]

In addition to laziness and incompetence, greed was cited as a reason for continued abuse. When a "physician is called for the first time to a well-to-do home," observed one group of skeptical pharmacists, he realizes that "a practice might be secured which would be valuable if he can only show his ability, and he does—there is not very much pain in the prick of a needle, and the result is so quick, so calming—wonderful man,—the patient begins to improve at once."[122] The upper-class background of many addicts is certainly consistent with the allegation that some doctors courted the wealthy client with a little morphine. Even worse, it was common practice for "quack cure joints" to offer 10 to 20 percent kickbacks for referring addicted patients.[123] The utterly unscrupulous practitioner could realize a handsome profit by addicting patients and then having them trek from one asylum to another—asylums with which he had an arrangement.

To the vast majority of physicians, of course, such practices were unthinkable. In fairness, too, it should be pointed out that there were formidable pressures acting on the individual physician to disregard the warnings and proceed as he had before. Simple distance, rather than laziness or incompetence, prompted many doctors to leave opium or morphine with the patient.[124] Before the automotive age it was practically impossible, especially in the countryside, for the physician to administer every dose himself, as the learned journals were admonishing. Moreover, doctors were often under tremendous pressure from patients and their families to continue the treatment indefinitely; it felt good, it relieved the pain. "Most impatiently did she await the injection," wrote one physician of a neuralgic female, "always exclaiming, as I entered—'Oh doctor, shoot me quick!' "[125] Complicating matters further was the doctor's knowledge that, if he did not "shoot quick," a competitor would, thereby gaining a patient.[126] Or the patient might simply persuade a druggist to refill the prescription without the physician's knowledge. Nineteenth-century pharmacists were notorious for their willingness to supply a user; opium and morphine were their bread and butter, and there is no steadier customer than an addict. "There are druggists in Houston, now," complained Dr. Newton J. Phenix in 1896, "making a living selling narcotics."[127] Confessed a New York apothecary, "If it were not for this stuff [morphine] and my soda-water I might as well shut up shop."[128] The efforts of even the most conscientious physicians to check repeated administration were thus undermined.

It was not until the years 1895 to 1910 that physicians managed to slow and then reverse altogether the growth of iatrogenic morphine addiction. Underlying this change was the growing acceptance of the germ theory of disease,[129] an event that had several important and interrelated consequences. Public health measures, reinforced and rationalized by the new bacteriology, reduced the incidence of gastrointestinal disorders, such as diarrhea and dysentery, for which opium and morphine had been freely given.[130] Vaccination, as against typhoid fever (1896), or chemotherapy, as against syphilis (1909), began to provide effective alternatives to opium and morphine for a few diseases. Moreover, the achievement of greater diagnostic precision, made possible by the discovery and classification of pathogenic microorganisms and by the development of new techniques, such as x-radiation, discouraged the unthinking palliation of disease; doctors who shot first and asked questions later were increasingly criticized for masking the symptoms of illnesses otherwise diagnosable and treatable.

In the event symptomatic relief was still indicated, a host of new and less dangerous anodynes became available. The introduction of milder analgesics, the salicyclates and aniline and pyrazolone derivatives, constitutes the second major reason for the decline of iatrogenic opium and morphine addiction. Although these antipyretics were originally introduced for the purpose of reducing fever, their pain-relieving qualities soon became apparent, and in 1889 James F. A. Adams published an important article in the *Boston Medical and Surgical Journal* urging their wholesale substitution for opiates.[131] A decade later Adams' proposal, which had already won a number of adherents,[132] received an important impetus with the accidental discovery of the analgesic properties of aspirin in 1899. The introduction of this common household drug, highly effective against head, muscle, and joint aches, undoubtedly saved thousands of persons from becoming addicted to opium or morphine.

Reinforcing the growth of narcotic conservatism brought about by bacteriological advances and the availability of safer analgesics were the stern injunctions against the liberal use of morphine issued by a new generation of medical educators. During the 1890s warnings previously confined to medical journals began percolating into medical curricula. Advice offered in one generation of textbooks was frequently contradicted in the next, as seen in the writings of two famous American gynecologists, William H. Byford and his son, Henry T. Byford. In his 1865 text, *The Practice of Medicine and Surgery Applied to the Diseases and Accidents Incident to Women,* the elder Byford counseled the use of opium in dysmenorrhea as a part of an "energetic palliative treatment," standard practice for the time.[133] However, in the 1898 *American Text-Book of Gynecology,* coauthored by the younger Byford, this course was condemned in the strongest possible terms: "He who is compelled to resort frequently to opium and stimulants in dysmenorrhea, must be considered devoid in diagnostic ability, and consequently ought not to be entrusted with the management of such cases."[134] Similar sentiments were expressed by neurologist William J. Herdman. "I have not failed in my attempt," he remarked in 1902, "to impress on the minds of my students how unwise is the indiscriminate use of these powerful drugs."[135] Other commentators directed their message to the practicing physician, emphasizing that the best doctors were the most sparing in their use of opiates. "In the last four or five years," boasted Professor Walter F. Boggess, "I have not written a prescription [of opiates] for the relief of pain."[136] On the legislative front physicians, joined by an increasing number of professionally minded pharmacists, pressed for laws restricting the availability of narcotics. From 1895 to 1915 most states and many municipalities passed laws limiting the sale of narcotics (usually defined as cocaine and the opiates) to those possessing a valid prescription.[137] Although these laws were unevenly and often inadequately enforced, their net effect could only have been to reduce the number of unauthorized refills.[138]

Fewer prescriptions for opium and morphine were being written in the first place. A 1908 sampling of 1,000 prescriptions from the files of a representative California druggist showed 18 containing opium, 11 morphine, and 7 codeine, plus 4 cocaine, altogether 3.6 percent with some form of opiate.[139] This represents a considerable drop from the 14.5 percent for Boston (1888) and the 24.5 percent for New Orleans (circa 1877-1889) cited earlier. Moreover, it was the younger and better-educated members of the profession who were primarily responsible for such decreases. In 1919 Thomas Blair published the results of a painstaking study of opiate prescription by Pennsylvania physicians. He found that 90 percent of all opiates were prescribed by one-third of all doctors. The conservative majority was composed largely of "modern practitioners, either young or keeping abreast of the times," skilled in diagnosis and case management, and thoroughly warned of the danger of iatrogenic addiction. The lax physicians, by contrast, were predominantly over 50 and had received their education when "the narcotics-menace was not stressed."[140] With time the conservative majority would grow even larger, as death and retirement thinned the ranks of the older practitioners.

By 1910 the reform movement within the medical profession was well on its way to eradicating iatrogenic addiction. Opium and morphine had fallen into such disfavor that some physicians began to worry that they might be withheld in even the most dire cases. "The present generation has been so thoroughly warned, both by teaching at college and by observation," wrote New Hampshire physician Oscar C. Young in 1902, "that now they are in many instances so very afraid to give it, even for the worst pain, that the patient suffers agonies worse than any hell for want of one-eighth of a grain of morphine."[141] Although a dwindling number of physicians continued — out of ignorance, expediency, or cupidity — to rely on the syringe, the overall effect of the profession's newfound narcotic conservatism was a reduction in the number of opium and morphine addicts; old addicts died off faster than new ones were created.[142] This was the principal reason that imports of medicinal opiates, the most sensitive barometer of iatrogenic addiction, declined in both per capita and absolute terms during the first decade of the twentieth century.[143]

Impact of the Civil War

The traditional explanation of the increase in opium and morphine addiction has focused not so much on the civilian practitioner as on his military counterpart. During the Civil War sick and wounded soldiers, liberally injected with morphine, frequently became addicted — as did many veterans who, in the course of treatment for war-related injuries, were also given opiates. Proponents of this view often refer to the fact that during the nineteenth century morphine addiction earned the sobriquet "the army disease."[144]

There are, however, several objections to this theory. In the first place, the majority of nineteenth-century opium and morphine addicts were women. If the Civil War was such an important factor, why should the Michigan (1878), Chicago (1880), and Iowa (1885) surveys have reported so many female addicts? In the second place, there is reason to doubt that hypodermic injection of morphine, the technique most likely to produce addiction, was common during the war. Hypodermic medication was still in its infancy; few American physicians had syringes in 1860; and it appears that the instrument was not issued in quantity by the medical department of either the North or the South.[145] Those army doctors who happened to have access to a syringe no doubt used it freely; they were, however, decidedly in the minority. For these and other reasons recent scholarship has downplayed the significance of the war; one writer, Mark A. Quinones, has gone as far as to label it a scapegoat on which the spread of addiction was subsequently blamed.[146]

The essential insight of the critics, that the explosive growth of addiction from 1865 to 1895 was more than an epidemic of the army disease, is undoubtedly correct. In making this point, however, one must take care not to overstate the argument; there is still a good deal of evidence that the war contributed to the spread of addiction, even if it was not the sole cause. Although morphine injection may have been relatively rare, oral administration of opium was not; massive quantities of the drug were consumed by both armies. Nearly 10,000,000 opium pills and over 2,841,000 ounces of other opium powders and tinctures were issued to Union forces alone. Soldiers recuperating from battlefield wounds were routinely dosed with opium, as were the victims of the common camp diseases — diarrhea, dysentery, and malaria. Circumstances of administration were casual. One Confederate physician, William H. Taylor, asked every patient he saw whether his bowels were open or shut. If the answer was open, Taylor handed him a plug of opium. Union Surgeon Major Nathan Mayer did his diagnosing from horseback. If he thought a soldier needed morphine, he would pour out an "exact quantity" and then let the soldier lick it from his hand.[147]

When, as often happened, soldiers' diseases and injuries developed into chronic conditions, the likelihood of addiction was enhanced. Even if a disabled soldier survived the war without becoming addicted, there was a good chance he would later meet up with a hypodermic-wielding physician. The anonymous Yankee author of *Opium Eating: An Autobiographical Sketch by an Habituate* suffered just such a misfortune.[148] As a consequence of deprivations suffered at Andersonville and other prisons, the young soldier developed constant headache and racking stomach pains. After he had been discharged, his doctor treated him with injections of morphine, to which he became addicted. His experience was repeated by J. M. Richards, an ex-army surgeon, who began taking morphine in 1867 to combat chronic diarrhea.[149] There were even cases of Methodist chaplains becoming addicted through the treatment of diarrhea.[150] Over 63,000 veterans were plagued with this lingering, debilitating disease; given what is known about the medical practice of the day, it seems likely that a substantial number of them eventually became addicted to opium or morphine.[151]

The significance of the Civil War, then, comes down to two points. During the fighting, large amounts of opium were issued in circumstances favorable to addiction; after the fighting, sick and wounded veterans greatly expanded the pool of candidates for iatrogenic addiction. The precise numbers and proportions involved are unknown, since addicted veterans went to great lengths to conceal their condition for fear of losing their pensions.[152] It is certain, however, that the war's greatest impact was felt from 1861 to 1900; after 1900 there were fewer and fewer surviving veterans, addicted or otherwise.[153] The timing is of interest, since the expected die-off of many aging veterans around the turn of the century coincides exactly with the decline in per capita imports of opium and morphine.

Self-Dosage

A third factor in the spread of addiction was self-dosage with medicines containing opium and morphine. In some instances this meant the outright purchase, on a friend's advice and without a doctor's prescription, of some official preparation of opium, such as paregoric.[154] Another common pattern involved the unwitting consumption of opium or morphine in the form of a patent or proprietary medicine purchased from a druggist, mountebank, or mail-order house.[155]

Patent medicines (the term is a misnomer, for most patent medicines carried no patent at all) were secret formulas marketed, usually with the most extravagant claims, by entrepreneurs seeking to capitalize on real or imagined ills.[156] Although these concoctions could contain virtually anything, opium and morphine, with their ability to alleviate a wide range of symptoms, were particularly attractive as ingredients. The career of "Scotch Oats Essence" is typical. One day the originator of this remedy, a young man with an eye on the main chance, asked his physician in an offhand manner how he would prepare a successful patent medicine. "Oh, well," replied the doctor, "make the basis whisky; put in some opiate; disguise the whole with a bitter tincture; get high-sounding testimonials or indorsements, and especially give it an attractive, 'taking' name. Then extensively advertise it from 'Dan to Beersheeba' and the thing is done." The young man, evidently impressed with the simplicity of the scheme, did precisely that. Scotch Oats Essence enjoyed a successful, if devastating, career as a nerve tonic, until someone analyzed the solution and announced that it contained morphine. "As a result the sales fell off, insolvency and financial ruin followed. Then the proprietor drank himself to death, mortified at his failure and public exposure."[157] Ruin following exposure was a fate common to many narcotic nostrums, a point to which I shall return.

The number of opium and morphine addicts who could trace their plight to self-medication is not known, but certainly they were in the minority. Statistical summaries of addicts seen by Charles Terry in Jacksonville (1912, 1913) and by Lawrence Kolb (1923) establish that prescription or administration by physicians, rather than self-medication, was the most important factor.[158] The social background of opium and morphine addicts underscores the importance of iatrogenic addiction. Patent medicines were used mainly by the poor,[159] yet the majority of addicts were from either the middle or the upper class, that is, they were people who could afford doctors.

One possible explanation for the observed class difference is that direct administration by a physician was more likely to lead to addiction than disguised consumption in the form of a patent medicine. This inference may seem counterintuitive; morphine by any other name is still morphine. The difference is that the farmer who nursed a bottle of Scotch Oats Essence was blissfully unaware of its habit-forming potential; if physical dependence occurred and withdrawal symptoms ensued, he still might have escaped addiction by attributing his sickness to something other than discontinuation of the medicine. If, on the other hand, he, like most doctors' patients, discovered that he had become dependent on morphine and that he could forestall withdrawal symptoms simply by consuming more of the drug, then he was almost sure to become addicted.[160] Hence the very secrecy that surrounded the nostrum served in some instances to prevent addiction to it.

There are other reasons why narcotic patent medicines did not spawn as many new addicts as physicians; these involve the purposes for which the products were advertised. First, there was a class of opiate-laced nostrums, known as soothing syrups, which were promoted as infant pacifiers. Bawling babies were regularly stupefied into silence by impatient mothers or nurses who resorted to these syrups, as well as to other opium preparations. "Paregoric by the bottle / Emptied down the baby's throttle," ran one old but true ballad.[161] Naturally, if the infant survived this regimen (and thousands did not), dependence might easily form. But, again, dependence was unlikely to develop into full-blown addiction, for the infant would not have comprehended the nature of its withdrawal distress, nor could it have done anything about it.[162]

The second special class of narcotic patent medicines was made up of the numerous habit cures. These nostrums, labeled "Opacura," "Denarco," and the like, were the most outrageous frauds; invariably they contained the drug from which they promised freedom. A person who set aside the syringe to take up the cure was simply maintaining his habit in a different and more expensive way. One man spent "over a thousand dollars endeavoring to get rid of the habit" before he discovered, after 11 years, that his bottled morphine cure contained largely morphine.[163] As reprehensible as these products were, they at least did not create new addicts; only persons already addicted would be tempted to buy them. So in the special cases of infants' soothing syrups and habit cures, narcotic patent medicines cannot be held responsible for the spread of opium and morphine addiction. It was instead those nostrums purporting to cure some specific, chronic disease (such as "Prof. Hoff's Consumption Cure," containing opium) that were likely to have contributed to the problem.

After 1906 the narcotic patent medicine situation was drastically altered by federal legislation. The provision of the Pure Food and Drug Act that packages and labels on medicines must state any narcotic content destroyed the market for habit cures and reduced the demand for other opium and morphine products. As one chemist put it, "The average sufferer . . . took alarm at the names of these familiar poisons on his medicine bottle, and feared to use the medicine."[164] Consequently opium and morphine were dropped from many proprietary formulas.[165] Other patent medicines retained their narcotic contents, but only at the risk of being shunned by the increasingly chary buyer. Thus unwitting addiction through patent medicines, a factor of limited importance before 1906, declined still further with the passage of the Pure Food and Drug Act.

Nontherapeutic Usage

The three factors examined thus far, administration by physicians, the Civil War, and self-dosage, have all been of a therapeutic nature: the addiction process commenced with the treatment or self-treatment of some injury or disease. Some addicts, however, began in an entirely different way. They turned to opium and morphine either as a stimulus to imagination, or as a substitute for alcohol, or even as a primitive form of birth control.

The use of opium as a stimulus to imagination was closely tied to the writings of Thomas De Quincey, whose popular *Confessions of an English Opium Eater* first appeared in serial form in 1821. Although the *Confessions* touched on many subjects, the passages contemporaries found most intriguing were those that dealt with De Quincey's fantastic opium dreams. As Alethea Hayter, a leading De Quincey scholar, has pointed out, these dreams were more a product of the author's own extraordinary imagination than the drug itself; nevertheless, it was easy for the reader to conclude that he too might journey through fantastic inner realms if only he downed a little opium.[166]

Translating De Quincey's influence into a precise number of opium and morphine addicts is, again, impossible. At best one can only attempt to assess the relative importance of the different sources of addiction. While the *Confessions* induced a few literati to dabble in opium, it is doubtful that its overall impact, especially in comparison with iatrogenic addiction, was great. Aside from the few spin-off confessions of writers who mimicked De Quincey,[167] it is extremely difficult to find documented cases of Americans whose addiction stemmed from a reading of the *Confessions*. It is true that nineteenth-century addiction literature contains a number of pointed references to De Quincey; but these remarks are better understood as pro forma warnings to the unwary than as actual evidence of the extent of his influence. It was almost a literary convention among addiction writers to denounce the famous English opium eater, even though the thrust of their argument was elsewhere.[168]

A more likely nontherapeutic route to addiction, at least in America, was the use of opium or morphine by women as a substitute for alcohol. Throughout the nineteenth century it was considered unseemly, by both males and temperance-minded females, for women to drink. Yet there was a powerful temptation, particularly for women of high social station, caught up in the social swirl, for women stranded in rural areas, thoroughly bored with their lot, and for seamens' wives, separated for long periods from their husbands, to resort to some euphoric agent.[169] Opium and morphine, which at least in the initial stages of their use produce euphoria, suited these purposes very well.[170]

Opiates also suited the purposes of frustrated women whose aspirations had been blocked by a male-dominated society. Remarked one anonymous lady of culture:

I am the last woman in the world to make excuses for my acts, but you don't know what morphine means to some of us, many of us, modern women without professions, without beliefs. Morphine makes life possible. It adds to truth a dream. What more does religion do? Perhaps I shock you. What I mean is that truth alone is both not enough and too much for us. Each of us must add to it his or her dream, believe me. I have added mine; I make my life possible by taking morphine. I have managed to prevent it from disfiguring my life, though I know other women who botched it horribly. I am really morphine mad, I suppose, but I have enough will left not to go beyond my daily allowance.[171]

Even allowing for a measure of self-justification, it seems reasonable to suppose that some embittered and disillusioned women drowned their sorrows with opiates. Alternately, repressed drives and suppressed ambitions may have manifested themselves in physical symptoms, which were in turn alleviated with opiates.

The soothing properties of opiates were not lost on another important female addict group, the prostitutes. Life in the "cribs," entertaining a succession of grunting, sweating males, must have been emotionally devastating; opiates offered an attractive, if temporary, escape. Moreover, the regular use of opiates conferred an important physiological benefit, the disruption or total cessation of menstruation.[172] An amenorrheal prostitute obviously did not have to contend with either the risk of pregnancy or enforced time off for her monthly period. (Some ladies of refinement, also anxious to conduct their affairs without risk of pregnancy, acquired this contraceptive practice from their sisters in the demi-monde.[173]) So it is not surprising that the prostitute-addict figured in several studies, especially those involving urban areas.[174] The particular opiate used, however, varied from time to time and from place to place. Between 1870 and 1910 smoking opium made considerable inroads on morphine as the drug of choice among prostitutes and their underworld companions. Then, between 1910 and 1920, there was a switch back to morphine or, in some places, to its new derivative, heroin.

Despite the undercurrent of nontherapeutic use, the predominant pattern of opium and morphine addiction was medical. As doctors put aside these drugs in favor of new and safer analgesics and superior therapeutic agents and techniques, and as narcotic patent medicines were subjected to adverse legislation, the likelihood of chronic disease or injury leading to addiction diminished sharply. After 1900, aging opium and morphine addicts, including veterans who had become addicted during or after the Civil War, died off faster than new addicts were created. As a result, the more disreputable types of users, notably opium smokers and heroin sniffers, came to constitute a progressively larger share of the total addict population. The transformation of the American opiate addict had begun.

Addiction to Smoking Opium

3 Unlike addiction to opium or morphine, addiction to smoking opium was almost never the consequence of medical treatment. As Hogarth distinguished between beer and gin, the American practitioner distinguished between medicinal and smoking opium; the former was beneficial and indispensable, the latter dangerous and unnecessary. There was controversy over opium and morphine, but the issue was not so much whether these drugs should be used as under what circumstances and with what precautions. Opium prepared for smoking, on the other hand, had no legitimate therapeutic purpose; it was a ruinous vice, practiced by the irresponsible and the wicked. In contrast to medical addicts, who had some extenuating disease or painful condition, opium smokers became addicted through the gratification of a "purely sensuous appetite." Reflecting the widespread opposition to the drug and displeasure with all who used it, the *Journal of the American Medical Association* called in 1892 for a ban on all imports of smoking opium.[1]

This attitude on the part of the medical profession, while it reveals much about the motives and characteristics of those who smoked opium, creates serious evidential problems. Because opium smoking was beyond the therapeutic pale, and because opium smokers (particularly Chinese smokers) were considered to be alien and offensive, relatively few serious and virtually no statistical studies of the problem were undertaken.[2] Nineteenth-century physicians who specialized in treating addiction concentrated on opium and morphine addicts, persons with whom they were in close contact and with whom their sympathies lay. Popular accounts of opium smoking yield some information, but they lack precision and are often marred by sensationalism. As a result, it is impossible to present a profile of opium smokers as detailed and accurate as that of opium and morphine addicts. It is possible, however, to sketch some of the prominent characteristics of opium smokers, and to suggest how sharply they differed from the majority of opium and morphine addicts.

Characteristics of Opium Smokers

Opium smokers fell into two distinct groups: the Chinese and the white. The typical Chinese opium smoker, as he would have appeared in about 1850 to 1880, was a young man of peasant stock. He had come to America as an indentured laborer, hoping to earn enough money to support his family, repay his creditors, save some money, and eventually return to his village. The determination to leave the family in China, plus the backbreaking nature of the work in the New World, precluded female immigrants; women comprised less than 10 percent of the Chinese population in America.[3] Many of the Chinese women who did come served as prostitutes,[4] and it seems reasonable to assume that some of them also smoked opium. There is at least one reference to this, in an 1886 story in the *San Francisco Chronicle*. "The Chinese women, . . . except those of the lower class, do not seem to be as addicted to the habit as are the men," a reporter noted.[5] "Lower class" in this context was almost certainly a euphemism for prostitutes. Even so, contemporary portrayals of opium dens, verbal as well as graphic, generally depicted the Chinese occupants as men.

Male opium smokers in China ranged in age between 20 and 55.[6] The majority of immigrants, however, were between 18 and 30, suggesting a lower average age among Chinese smokers in America.[7] There are only scattered references to elderly Chinese smokers in America before 1900.[8]

In the period from 1850 to 1870 opium smoking was strictly confined to the areas of Chinese settlement. This meant primarily California and the Far West, although sizable numbers of Chinese began working in the South and East after 1870.[9] The typical immigrant led a dual existence, dividing his time between a work camp, where he toiled as a gang laborer, and the Chinese quarter of a city or town, where he went on an occasional spree. This recreational quarter might be nothing more than a ramshackle store or laundry in a nearby mining town, or it might be San Francisco's Chinatown itself, with its gaudy array of vices; smoking opium was available in either place.[10] The Chinese had no counterpart to the lonely seaman's wife, comforting herself with a little laudanum; opium smoking was a social enterprise, carried on in a communal place.

After 1870 a new type of addict began to emerge, the white opium smoker. White smokers were drawn primarily, though not exclusively, from the underworld: prostitutes, gamblers, and petty criminals, their pimps, apprentices, and hangers-on.[11] Jansen Beemer Mattison, an otherwise sympathetic Brooklyn physician who specialized in the treatment of addiction, tersely dismissed them as "evil men and ill-famed women . . . [who], being undesirable patients, rarely come under regular care."[12] On the ratio of evil men to ill-famed women he did not elaborate. Still, it is clear that males predominated. Of 27 cases of addicted white smokers, dating from 1878 to 1915 and collected from a variety of published and unpublished sources, only 3 were listed as female.[13]

Concern was often expressed that opium smoking had spread or was about to spread to the upper classes, particularly to the "idle rich" and other wealthy neurotics who had nothing better to do than dabble in dangerous vices. The beautiful aristocrat enchanted by the pipe became a stock melodramatic character; a generation of would-be heroes toured the dens of Chinatown, hoping to "run across some females tricked out in the décolleté gowns and striped stockings affected by the 'ladies' who enlivened every issue of the old *Police Gazette.*"[14] While there were undoubtedly some upper-class opium smokers, it is unlikely that they ever comprised more than a small minority. In 1886 a Denver reporter was assigned to watch the local opium dens. He counted 145 persons coming and going, among them 27 women. Only 6 individuals of respectable occupation could be identified, the remainder being largely gamblers and prostitutes.[15]

Opium smokers tended to be young. Male addicts studied by Charles Earle in 1886 averaged 22 years, 6 months when they began smoking.[16] Former male opium smokers treated in Cleveland in 1915 started at an average age of 19 years, 9 months; World War I draftees rejected for opium smoking, at 18 years, 3 months.[17] The downward trend continued; cases examined by Lawrence Kolb in 1923 began at 17 years, 5 months; cases seen by R. B. Richardson in Philadelphia in 1927 at approximately 17 years, 7 months.[18] These averages are not based on large samples, but they give a consistent impression. Female smokers also were young; according to Allen S. Williams, a reporter who wrote a lengthy exposé of the dens in New York City, the "women who smoke are almost without exception under thirty years of age. A majority of those whom I have observed are under twenty-one years."[19] Several other observers remarked on the youth of the smokers, although they did not differentiate by sex.[20] The relatively early age of addiction differed noticeably from that of the opium or morphine user, who typically became addicted in mid-life.

Finally, the geographic distribution of white smokers closely paralleled that of the Chinese. The earliest smokers were situated in western cities and towns; it was there that white gamblers and prostitutes first learned to smoke opium. Later, as the Chinese fanned out into the South and East, the practice went with them. The presence of a few Chinese, in fact, was almost a prerequisite for opium smoking to take root in a given place.[21] As a rule, the Chinese controlled the supply and ran the dens. Peripatetic white smokers helped spread opium smoking to places like New York City, Boston, and Chicago, but it is doubtful that the practice would have flourished without the presence of Chinese communities in those cities.

Opium Smoking in China

The close association of the Chinese with opium smoking began well before the first wave of immigration to California. Opium was introduced into China by Arab traders around A.D. 700 and soon came to occupy an important place in the Chinese materia medica, much as it had in the West. Opium smoking, however, was not practiced until the seventeenth century. At first the drug was smoked in combination with tobacco, but sometime during the eighteenth century the tobacco was dropped and the opium smoked alone. It was not crude opium, but a refined product, of suitable strength, purity, and consistency for the pipe.[22] How, where, and precisely when the boiling, evaporating, and straining processes for refining opium were developed is not known.

During the late eighteenth and early nineteenth centuries

opium smoking was confined largely to the upper classes, especially to the idle young sons of wealthy families. But the practice soon spread to other classes, upward to the officers and belted gentry, and downward to the laborer and the tradesman, to the traveler, and "even to women, monks, nuns, and priests."[23] Opium smoking also made great inroads in the army, undermining efficiency and morale. Jonathan Spence, an authority on opium smoking during the Ch'ing period, has speculated that different groups had different motives for smoking: eunuchs, members of the imperial clan, and soldiers took to the pipe to overcome their ennui; the wealthy, to relax and put aside their worries; the merchants, to increase their business acumen; and the laborers and peasants, to escape for a while the drudgery of their lives.[24] Alcohol might have fulfilled these needs, as it did in the West; but the Chinese were rather moderate drinkers, so opium and tobacco emerged as the leading drugs.

Another important factor was the eagerness of the British, who began exporting opium from India in the late eighteenth century, to sell large quantities to the Chinese. The opium traffic, although prohibited by imperial edict, was seen by the British as a lucrative source of revenue and a means of redressing an unfavorable balance of trade; conversely, responsible Chinese officials came to view the traffic as a source of domestic corruption and a serious drain on the nation's specie. Chinese efforts to end the illegal traffic, culminating in Commissioner Lin Tse-hsü's seizure and destruction of over 20,000 chests of opium stored in hulks off Lintin Island, provoked the series of skirmishes known as the First Opium War (1839–1842). Western weaponry and tactics prevailed; the Chinese agreed to pay a stiff indemnity, cede Hong Kong, and open five ports—Canton, Amoy, Foochow, Ningpo, and Shanghai—to foreign trade. From the standpoint of the opium traffic, the opening of these cities can be likened to the raising of five flood gates; the drug poured into the country in ever-increasing quantities. Another blow fell in 1858, when the Treaty of Tientsin effectively legalized the opium traffic. Imports nearly doubled, from 40,000 chests in 1839 to 76,000 chests in 1865. The spread of addiction, with the constantly increasing demand it entailed, also stimulated the domestic industry; cultivation of the opium poppy in China was widespread by the 1870s.

Assessments of the overall rate of addiction vary enormously. Depending on the estimated supply, the estimated average daily dose, the date the calculation was made, the region studied, and the political sympathies of the authority, anywhere from 1 out of

166 to 9 out of 10 Chinese were said to be addicted to smoking opium.[25] In spite of the disparity of the estimates, one fact is clear: China maintained one of the highest rates of opiate addiction of any nation in the world throughout the nineteenth century. The immigrants who landed in California came from a society in which opium smoking was commonplace, the opium den an institution. Moreover, the overwhelming majority of immigrants came from the area around Canton, a region that had long been associated with the opium traffic, serving as the sole (though illegal) point of entry for the drug prior to 1842. Cantonese immigrants were especially likely to have knowledge of or actual experience with opium smoking.[26]

Opium Smoking in America

The Canton area, in addition to being a locus of the opium traffic, was in the mid-nineteenth century a region of profound turmoil. Political instability, widespread corruption, ethnic conflict, and population growth combined to put great pressure on the peasantry. Yet this pressure was matched by the peasant's determination to maintain his way of life; loyalty to family and clan were paramount. In the face of this conflict many Chinese resolved upon a course of temporary emigration. The idea was to work abroad, save as much as possible, and send money back to the family, with the ultimate goal of going back to China a wealthy and respected man. The embarking peasant's self-image was that of a sojourner, rather than a permanent emigrant, although relatively few who left managed to return to a life of ease.

The early sojourners found work in Southeast Asia, but with the discovery of gold in California in 1848, America's West Coast became the logical destination. The climate was amenable and cheap labor was badly needed to work the mines. The problem was how to finance the passage. Chinese merchants responded by devising a credit-ticket system, whereby the immigrant agreed to repay the cost of his passage, plus interest, through his labor in California. The debt repaid, the laborer could (at least in theory) accumulate enough money to sustain his family, buy a return ticket, and eventually retire to his homeland. But as long as he was in debt he was a virtual slave, forced to work where the merchant-creditor dictated and at the wages he stipulated. A network of "district companies," under the leadership of the merchants, evolved in California to ensure that the laborer upheld his end of the bargain.[27]

It was an oppressive system, and the indentured laborer, bound to toil in an alien land until his debt was cleared, was subject to tremendous psychological pressure. To prevent that pressure from bursting into open revolt, some sort of safety valve was required. A leading historian of Chinese immigration, Gunther Barth, has suggested that the emotional safety valve was found in the early Chinatowns, especially in the vices they offered. (*Chinatown*, as Barth uses the term, refers to the Chinese quarter of any city or town, from San Francisco to the meanest mining camp.) The most popular forms of recreation were gambling, prostitution, and opium smoking, often found together in single or adjoining establishments.[28] There the sojourner might lose his troubles in a game of fan-tan, in the company of a slave girl, or in the familiar fumes of smoking opium.[29]

In addition to serving as a safety valve, this triad of vices served as a subtle means of reinforcing the debt bondage system. Gambling, prostitution, and opium smoking were expensive pastimes, particularly for steady customers. Opium smoking was notorious in this regard, because of its addictive potential. The indentured laborer who became addicted to smoking opium was literally on the slippery slope; he could make no headway repaying his original debt and soon acquired new ones. By the early 1880s the cost of an addict's daily supply of the drug was fifty cents or more, though the maximum daily income a Chinese laborer could hope to earn was little more than a dollar.[30] Moreover, the time spent languishing in the den could not be used to earn income, a problem that worsened as the habit took deeper and deeper hold. The sense of despair the addict felt as the dream of returning to his homeland faded could only have increased his need for the soothing drug, creating a vicious circle of anxiety, opium smoking, more anxiety, and more opium smoking. Two groups benefited from the addicts' misery, the merchant-creditors and the secret criminal societies (tongs) that dominated the smoking opium traffic. The merchant-creditors retained control over the addicts' labor as long as their debts went unpaid, while the tongs fattened on the increasing consumption.

There were several variations on this basic safety-valve pattern. Some Chinese immigrants were undoubtedly addicted, or had at least experimented with smoking opium, before they set foot in California. The most important evidence for this, aside from the high rate of addiction in China itself, is the fact that searches of arriving immigrants often netted concealed smoking opium.[31] While the intercepted Chinese may have been doubling as couriers, as part of an organized smuggling operation, it is also possible that they were experienced users who had brought along a supply to tide them through the long sea voyage and the early uncertain weeks in the New World.[32]

It is also possible that some of the resident merchant-creditors were or became addicted to smoking opium, although there is conflicting testimony on this point. Cortlandt St. John, an experienced New York opium broker, wrote in 1908 that "the better or merchant class of Chinese rarely use it."[33] However, in 1870 William Speer, a missionary who instructed Chinese immigrants, complained that some of the brightest young merchants who entered his school fell victim to opium smoking, while San Francisco's health officer remarked that opium smoking was very general among the Chinese in that city, and not confined solely to the "loafing class."[34] The merchant-smoker's higher income at least would have permitted him to avoid (or forestall) the pauperism that beset the common Chinese addict.

Finally, there was a type of user who might be designated a social smoker. He was not addicted, smoking only on occasion. Such recreational use of opiates without addiction was not unprecedented, but more Chinese opium smokers managed it than whites, especially whites who injected morphine. Perhaps this was because many Chinese understood opium smoking as something especially appropriate to holidays.[35] Just as some American families imbibed wine only on sacred or festive occasions, these Chinese restricted their smoking to feast days, thereby minimizing the likelihood of physical dependence. They were also dealing with a somewhat milder drug; although opium prepared for smoking contained up to 9 percent morphine, when it was smoked only a fraction of the morphine was sublimated up the pipe.[36] Most of it remained in the ash, or yen-shee. Because less morphine was consumed, dependence took longer to develop—a full 15 days of regular smoking, according to one observer.[37] This helped the occasional smoker escape full-blown addiction to the drug.

Counting all types of users, what percentage of the Chinese immigrant community smoked opium? The estimates are even more variable than those for opium smoking in China. Benjamin S. Brooks, who testified in 1877 in favor of continued Chinese immigration, ventured that only 1 Chinese in 20 smoked the drug, and that only 1 in 100 was addicted to it. Brooks' figures were turned completely around, however, by San Francisco policeman George W. Duffield, who testified at a later hearing that "ninety-nine Chinamen out of one hundred smoke opium."[38] In 1886 the *San Francisco Chronicle* ventured that between 10,000 and 15,000 of the city's 30,000 Chinese were addicted to the use of smoking opium.[39] Hamilton Wright, who strongly supported a ban on imports of the drug, also stated that nearly half the Chinese in America smoked opium — 15 percent being heavy smokers, 20 percent light smokers, and 10 percent social smokers.[40] More cautious and disinterested authorities gave lower estimates. Frederick J. Masters, a Methodist missionary who made a fairly thorough study of the problem, thought 30 percent of San Francisco's Chinese population was addicted, though he noted that the Chinese consul, Colonel Frederick A. Bee, insisted that the rate was only half that.[41] Another missionary, Ira M. Condit, estimated that 30 to 40 percent of the Chinese smoked, 15 to 20 percent regularly.[42] Harry Hubbell Kane, one of the few nineteenth-century physicians to study opium smoking in any detail, wrote that "about twenty percent . . . smoke opium occasionally, and fifteen percent smoke it daily."[43] There is no objective way of choosing among these diverse estimates.[44] Those in the best position to know were the tong leaders, and they went to their graves — or back to China — without talking. Although the authorities differed over percentages, they were virtually unanimous on one point: that addiction to smoking opium afflicted a significant portion of the Chinese immigrant community.[45]

Opium Smoking by Whites

For 20 years, from roughly 1850 to 1870, opium smoking was confined to the Chinese. The principal reason the practice did not spread to whites during those years was the extreme isolation, physical and psychological, of the Chinese community. Since the typical immigrant saw himself as a sojourner, with no intention of settling, he had little incentive to abandon old ways and adapt to the new culture. Instead he banded together with his fellow sojourners, a tendency reinforced by the pooling of immigrants into labor gangs. The white community also contributed to this isolation. Ambivalence or outright hostility toward a strange race and their customs, coupled with a growing fear of cheap "coolie" labor, fueled a virulent anti-Chinese campaign, culminating in the 1882 Exclusion Act. Given their discordant goals and mutual distrust, Chinese and whites naturally avoided one another; they mingled, wrote political commentator James Bryce, "as little . . . as oil with water."[46]

There was, however, one element of the white community willing to mix with the Chinese: the underworld. Operating beyond the bounds of respectability, gamblers, prostitutes, and assorted other criminals would have had fewer scruples about associating with Orientals or experimenting with their vices. The identities of the original white smokers are uncertain, although there are at least two apocryphal stories. The first, and most commonly quoted, was reported by Kane:

The first white man who smoked opium in America is said to have been a sporting character, named Clendenyn. This was in California, in 1868. The second—induced to try it by the first—smoked in 1871. The practice spread rapidly and quietly among this class of gamblers and prostitutes.[47]

A second account appears in a testimonial published by Dr. Samuel B. Collins, proprietor of an addiction cure. The letter, signed "Wm. L. Kennedy," begins

Dear Sir:—I will probably reside in Kentucky this winter. You may use my name in your paper. I am known in all the large cities of the U.S. by most all OPIUM SMOKERS as I was one of the first who started use of the drug in the way of smoking it. That was in 1871, in the state of Nevada.[48]

It is just possible that William Kennedy was the second smoker alluded to by Kane, as the two accounts agree on the 1871 date.[49] It is also conceivable that there was no single chain of transmission, that the practice took hold in several different places at approximately the same time. In either instance opium smoking, once established, spread rapidly through the world of sporting characters in the 1870s.

The pipe's quick acceptance in the underworld poses some interesting questions. Why did so many gamblers, prostitutes, and other criminals take up smoking opium, in preference to some other opiate? The hypodermic injection of morphine was just becoming popular, and it was quicker, cheaper, and stronger. Moreover, prostitutes already had a history of opium and morphine use. Why should they not have continued as before?

The answer is twofold. In the first place, some gamblers and prostitutes continued to use opium and morphine, either because they happened not to be exposed to smoking opium or because they preferred the more traditional opiates.[50] One who was addicted to opium or morphine in 1865 and had developed considerable tolerance might find it difficult in 1875 to switch to the milder smoking opium. But for members of the underworld who were not yet addicted, smoking opium possessed certain charms that opium or morphine lacked. Above all, opium smoking was a social vice, a way of relaxing and indulging with friends. "The morphinist wishes to be alone to enjoy his drug," explained Thomas Crothers, but the opium smoker "wants company, is talkative, his mind turns in a philosophical direction, to monosyllabic comments on men and events. He goes to a 'joint,' or a room which persons of a similar desire frequent." Inhaling the vapors of burning opium he is "immediately at peace with every one."[51] Kane agreed with this assessment, declaring, "I have never seen a smoker who found pleasure in using the drug at home and alone, no matter how complete his outfit [pipe and paraphernalia], or how excellent his opium."[52]

In many respects it was the nature and complexity of opium smoking that ensured its status as a social, rather than a private, act. Smoking opium, unlike tobacco or marijuana, cannot be stuffed into an ordinary pipe and lit; a special pipe and method of preparation are required. The opium pipe typically consists of a 16-inch to 20-inch bamboo stem, with a ceramic bowl inserted about a third of the way down from the stoppered end. Also required is some sort of lamp (as a source of heat), a large needle (to manipulate the viscous drug), and a knife (to scrape the bowl). The smoker, reclining on a wooden platform, dips the needle into a container of prepared opium, usually purchased from the proprietor of the den. He then holds the globule of opium above the lamp's flame, where it swells and bubbles to several times its original size. Once it is properly "cooked" and distended, the opium is transferred to the pipe's bowl, where it is rolled into a small "pill." This pill is forced into the hole at the center of the bowl and heated, then the needle stuck through and withdrawn, leaving a ring of smoking opium around the hole connecting to the pipe stem. The pipe is tilted, the flame strikes the opium, and the smoker draws in the fumes. Then the whole process begins again, until the desired state is achieved.

Such a complex procedure must obviously be learned; it is not nearly so simple as downing a spoonful of Scotch Oats Essence or sticking a needle in one's arm. The neophyte who visited a den out of curiosity or at the urging of an associate was not unlike a student attending school; he was totally dependent on the experienced smokers for instruction. One he mastered the art, he might in turn assume the role of instructor and transmit the ritual to others.[53] All of this would have been impossible in isolation. Had smokers been as scattered and as secretive as morphine addicts, the practice would have died out in a single generation.

An opium den (or "dive" or "joint") was more than a school, however; it was also a meeting place, a sanctuary, and a vagabonds' inn. Members of the underworld could gather there in relative safety, to enjoy a smoke with their friends and associates. One addict has left us a memorable portrait of life in the New York City dens. "The people who frequent these places," he recounted, "are, with very few exceptions, thieves, sharpers and sporting men, and a few bad actors; the women, without exception, are immoral." In spite of the desperate character of the clientele, fights were practically unknown. Instead, the smokers passed the time between pipes by chatting, smoking tobacco, telling stories, cracking jokes, or even singing in low voices. They might venture out for a bite to eat and return for some sleep. Early in the morning the prostitutes who worked the nearby neighborhoods would begin drifting in, to have a smoke before retiring. Even those who did not smoke would sometimes stop by to visit their acquaintances. Within the den a rigid code of honor prevailed: smokers would not take advantage of other smokers, or tolerate those who did. "I have seen men and women come in the joints while under the influence of liquor," continued the New York addict, "lie down and go to sleep with jewelry exposed and money in their pockets, but no one would ever think of disturbing anything." "The joint," confirmed an experienced Denver smoker, "is considered a sacred sanctum, and to betray . . . any conversation between the fiends is considered an unpardonable offense, and a fiend who commits a second offense of this character is generally debarred from all the rights and privileges of the joint."[54]

Another advantage, from the underworld point of view, was that there was a den in every major city, and practically every western town. "It's a poor town now-a-days," remarked a white smoker in 1883, "that has not a Chinese laundry, and nearly every one of these has its lay-out [pipe plus accessories]. You once get the first ticket [letter of introduction written in Chinese] and you're booked straight through. I tell you it's a great system for the fiends who travel." Availability was an important consideration, since many smokers, especially gamblers and prostitutes, pursued itinerant professions.[55] Given all these advantages — comraderie, security, and availability — it is not surprising that the opium den became such a popular underworld institution during the 1870s.

More formally, the opium den had become the matrix of a deviant subculture, a tightly knit group of outsiders whose primary relations were restricted to themselves. "Another feature of the 'hop' fiend," explained the Denver smoker, "is his absolute aversion to the society of everybody, save and except the fiend or Chinaman . . . They are a society in themselves and care nothing for the outside world." Conventional laws meant little; they would cheerfully lie under oath to protect a den keeper from successful prosecution. Yet the same smokers would honor the implicit code of the den, even to the point of never challenging the tall tale of another smoker, however outrageous.[56] An individual's status was determined by his adherence to such group norms, and by his skill in performing the opium smoking ritual. Experienced smokers, for example, were set apart by their ability to inhale an entire pill of opium in a single breath, a talent referred to as the "long draw." Those who cooked the opium and prepared the pipe dextrously soon acquired reputations as skilled "chefs." In virtually all particulars — peer reinforcement, exclusive membership, common argot, and shared rules of appropriate behavior — opium smoking anticipated the pattern of the various twentieth-century drug subcultures.

Recruitment into the world of opium smoking followed a consistent pattern. The prospective smoker, often a young male, would be introduced to the practice by a friend. Curiosity and a desire to emulate would prompt him to smoke a few pipes. Although the first trial often resulted in nausea, the same motives would induce him to try again until he was able to overcome the nausea and enjoy the pleasurable sensations produced by the drug. If he kept at it long enough, he would become physically dependent; and once he recognized his dependence, a full-blown addict.

Opium smokers who recorded their experiences in letters or interviews often commented at length on their introduction to the drug. Here is the story of a white Californian who began smoking opium sometime before 1886:

I had become acquainted with a gambler, one of the most expert in the State, whether in front or behind the game. I noticed that he often left the table, when dealing, and after he returned, say in half an hour, his manner had undergone a change; he manipulated the cards with greater steadiness and ease. One day I asked him the plain question: "Why do you call on a substitute, and quit the table so often?"

"Opium, my boy," he said, in a feverish way. "I can do nothing without it. Steadies the nerves. Deprive me of my periodical pipe and I'm like a fiddle minus strings. Ever try a whiff?"

"No."

"Then you'd better take my advice and continue to let it alone."

But my curiosity was aroused, and after accompanying D—— to his favorite opium haunt several times, I resolved to realize the sensations derived from smoking, whatever they might be. I "hit" my first pipe, as the slang goes, about four o'clock one afternoon . . . [I smoked too much at first and, after drinking a cupful of water, I became terribly nauseated. D—— was summoned, and sat up with me until morning.] "Well, old fellow," said he, in a bantering tone, "how do you like it as far as you've gone?"

"It's a pretty rough introduction," I replied, "and I guess I'll go no further."

"That's right," said he; "you'd better stop right now, but I'll bet you a twenty you won't. Of course you smoked too much, and then drank water to make the matter worse. If thirsty after the pipe, all practised opium smokers drink only good strong tea."

"Well, I'm done with the stuff, anyhow."

"No, my boy," he said, quietly; "you'll tackle it again — you don't like to give up beat."

The gambler was soon proved correct. On the second try, the novice recalled, "I pulled away for about three minutes, consuming three pills, and this time I got a glimpse of what is called the opium devotee's paradise. With my body and limbs completely relaxed, I dropped into a state of delightful dreamy half sleep, languidly knowing all that was going on around me, but caring for nothing." However, "horrible mental images" intruded on his reverie, and these visions so frightened him that he stopped smoking completely.[57]

One of the most interesting aspects of this story is the attitude of the gambler. He warned his friend of the danger, yet he could not help urging him on, by piquing his curiosity ("Ever try a whiff?"), suggesting he would continue ("You'll tackle it again"), providing a motive for continuing ("You don't like to give up beat"), and cuing him on ways to avoid nausea ("You smoked too much"; "All practised opium smokers drink only good strong tea"). It is also apparent that the friend looked up to the gambler as a man of great skill, and as one worthy of emulation. Had disturbing visions not interrupted his pleasures, he probably would have continued smoking.

The next case was not so lucky. He ran away from home at age

16, ending up in Butte, Montana, and taking a job as a messenger boy, work which "consisted mostly of carrying trays of food and drinks from restaurants and saloons to the cribs where the sporting women worked." He soon discovered that most of the messenger boys doubled as pimps, and he resolved to acquire a prostitute too. When an opportunity presented itself, he struck up a conversation with a likely candidate. Learning that she was unattached and wanted him as "her man," he quickly agreed to become her pimp. The following morning

---

I was relieved from duty at the messenger office [and] I made a bee line straight for her crib . . . I was just a kid seventeen years old and I had never slept with a woman in my life and I was very bashful and hardly knew what to do . . . She said she liked me very much and she wasn't long in showing me what to do . . . We slept most of the day until late in the afternoon, and when I awoke she got up and got a tray out of the dresser drawer and brought it over and placed it on the bed. I had seen opium pipes two or three different times since I had been working on the messenger force, so I recognized the contents of the tray as an opium layout. She told me that she was a smoker and asked me if I had ever smoked any hop. I told her that I never had and she said that I ought to try it once, as she was sure that I would like it . . .[With her help] I smoked my first pill of opium [and] suddenly became very nauseated and had to leave the table to vomit . . . I slept two hours and when I awoke I felt all right . . . When I got ready to leave her crib to go to work that evening, she gave me thirty-two dollars and told me to be sure to come back when I finished work in the morning. I thought that it was a very easy way of getting money and she was young and very good looking, so it was not very hard for me to promise her that I would be back next morning . . . As soon as I was in bed she brought out the tray with the layout on it and placed it in the center of the bed and then she got into bed. She cooked a few pills and smoked them herself and than [sic] asked me if I wanted to smoke. It had made me so sick the night before that when she first started cooking the opium this morning it seemed to nauseate me again. So I declined . . . She smoked a few more pills and then put the tray away and got back into bed and we went to sleep. [When we awoke that afternoon] she got up and again got the tray and lit the lamp and got back into bed and started to cook her opium again. She cooked and smoked six or eight pills as I lay there watching her and then she offered me some. I told her that I was afraid to smoke again for fear that it would make me as sick as I was the night before. She told me that it wouldn't make me sick this time and she coaxed and coaxed, until I finally gave in and said that I would smoke a couple of pills with her just to be sociable. She cooked some more of the raw opium into pills and we both started to smoke again . . . Now, here is the first peculiar thing that I noticed from the

effects of smoking opium. We started carrying on our sexual intercourse, and where ordinarily it would have taken me only a few
minutes to finish it seemed as though after smoking the opium I
would never finish . . . When I finally finished she threw her arms
around me, laughing and seeming very happy. She told me that
she had more satisfaction out of our intercourse than she had from
anyone in her whole life, and she told me she loved me very much
and wanted me to promise never to leave her.

They lived together for six months, smoking daily. One day the
prostitute received word that her sister was very ill, so she left to
visit her, packing the layout with her. The young man thought
nothing of it until he began to experience withdrawal symptoms.
Another messenger recognized the problem and gave him three
pills of opium, washed down with coffee. He soon began to feel
better, and realized that his distress resulted from his not having
smoked that day, the first time in six months. He was an addict
for the rest of his life. Continuing his career as a pimp, he eventually beame involved in other crimes, including larceny, bur-
glary, drug peddling, and robbery. He also switched from smoking opium to morphine, then to heroin, which he injected in
quantities of about 16 grains a day.[58]

Although this story is unusual in that it did not involve a den, it
is a good illustration of the pressures and temptations operating
on a novice smoker. This young man was not inclined to smoke
again; but his lover coaxed and coaxed, and he realized that she
was in a position to withhold money and sexual favors. Once he
discovered that he could smoke without becoming ill and that the
drug enhanced intercourse, he no longer required her blan-
dishments to keep on smoking. Nor did the prostitute warn him of
the long-term effects of continuous smoking; either she was not
yet aware of them herself or, more likely, she dismissed addiction
as a small price to pay for a drug that kept her calm and dreamy,
and numb to the debaucheries of her besotted customers.[59] Not
yet disillusioned, she urged the pipe on a favored lover. This pattern was repeated elsewhere with other drugs, notably cocaine
and heroin, which were also popular with prostitutes. Prostitutes
contributed to the spread of opium smoking and other forms of
opiate addiction in another, indirect way: venereal disease, which
they often transmitted, was (at least in its initial stages) a powerful
incentive for anyone to continue inhaling an analgesic drug.

Not all white opium smokers began through prostitutes, however; nor were all smokers in or on the fringes of the underworld.
A number of actors and traveling salesmen, occupations for which

the ubiquity of the dens represented a great convenience, became addicted.[60] Of more concern to authorities was the alleged spread, after 1875, of opium smoking to upper-class whites, particularly white females. As mentioned earlier, there were public alarms that the idle rich of New York, San Francisco, and other cities were taking up the practice. A parallel concern was that respectable white women were being seduced in the dens. It was commonly reported that opium smoking aroused sexual desire, and that some shameless smokers persuaded "innocent girls to smoke in order to excite their passions and effect their ruin."[61] Fear of miscegenation made such a spectacle all the more shocking. "In the case of the white women who steadily cohabit with this [indolent] class of Chinese," lamented Frederic Poole, missionary in charge of the Chinese mission in Philadelphia, "it is found that they are invariably victims to this pernicious habit, the indulgence . . . in many cases having been the first inducement to settle down to a life of degradation."[62] San Francisco physician Winslow Anderson wrote, somewhat more graphically, of the "sickening sight of young white girls from sixteen to twenty years of age lying half-undressed on the floor or couches, smoking with their 'lovers.' Men and women, Chinese and white people, mix in Chinatown smoking houses."[63]

The Legal Response

Public outrage at this sort of behavior was soon translated into restrictive legislation. Municipal governments, especially those of cities with large Chinese populations, reacted first; San Francisco in 1875 and Virginia City in 1876 passed ordinances penalizing opium smoking. Enforcement of these ordinances was selective; dens patronized by whites were the most likely to be raided.[64] This had the effect of driving white smokers away from Chinatown into nearby lodgings, where they continued to smoke in small groups. Remarked San Francisco physician William S. Whitwell, "There are few second or third class lodging houses . . . where daily and nightly 'hitting the pipe' is not practiced by men and women, boys and young girls."[65] Wealthy smokers also set up private dens, albeit in more sumptuous surroundings, furnished with mattresses and jeweled pipes. The smoking opium itself was obtained from a network of Chinese dealers.[66] Although the route of supply was different, the new private dens mirrored the old public dens in at least one respect: they remained social centers, with several persons smoking together. Later, when enforcement abated (or in places where no antiopium smoking ordinance was enforced), some smokers would drift back to the Chinese dens, or to a den run by a Chinese but patronized chiefly by white customers. An incident, such as the death of a young female teacher in a Chinese den in Philadelphia, might trigger a crackdown, but in general enforcement was sporadic.[67] Moreover, as Kane pointed out, the fact that opium smoking was illegal led "many who would not otherwise have indulged to seek out the low dens and patronize them, while the regular smokers found additional pleasure in continuing that about which there was a spice of danger."[68] Municipal ordinances, in short, did not deter opium smoking.

State laws, although some carried stiff sanctions, also had relatively little effect. An 1881 California statute, for example, stipulated a fine of up to $500 and 6 months in jail for persons convincted of operating or patronizing a public den.[69] By 1915, 26 other states had passed antiopium smoking measures, most of which aimed at closing the public dens rather than forbidding the practice outright.[70] The outcome may be guessed: whenever there was a concerted effort to enforce these laws, white smokers moved their operations elsewhere. The net result was segregation, not cessation, although some observers felt the laws may have had a slight deterrent effect.[71]

In the end it was national legislation that had the greatest impact; congressional statutes, rather than municipal ordinances or state laws, eventually succeeded in making opium smoking sufficiently risky and expensive that many smokers were forced to switch to other opiates. The progress of national antiopium smoking legislation was slow and halting, but because of its ultimate impact, it is worth some study.

Efforts to check opium smoking began as early as 1880, when Congressman James F. Briggs of New Hampshire introduced a bill designed to increase the duty on imported smoking opium and tax its domestic manufacture.[72] In 1884 Congressman James H. Budd of California introduced a stronger measure, aimed at total prohibition of smoking opium imports.[73] Although both bills died in committee, they foreshadowed the strategy employed by later, successful legislation. Congressional efforts to do something about opium smoking were bound by a limited perception of federal police power, which did not permit a direct attack on social problems within the states. Briggs and Budd showed how this problem might be circumvented, by resorting to the taxing and commerce powers in an effort to restrict the supply.

Not all antiopium smoking measures involved the taxing and commerce powers, however; a variety of different approaches was tried. In 1887 Congress passed a bill designed to enforce provisions of an 1880 treaty with China. Article II of the treaty stipulated that U.S. citizens should not be allowed to import opium into China, and vice versa. But until enabling legislation was enacted, the article was essentially a dead letter. After years of delay and confusion, Congress finally managed to pass the appropriate legislation. The first section of the bill forbade "the importation of opium into any of the ports of the United States by any subject of the Emperor of China."[74] On paper a significant blow to the Chinese-dominated traffic, in reality the law had little effect; Chinese dealers in America either took the drug on consignment from legitimate white importers,[75] or continued to traffic in smuggled smoking opium.

A different tack was taken by New Hampshire's Senator Henry W. Blair. Informed that opium smoking had spread to the capital, Blair in 1886 introduced a strong measure designed to outlaw the practice in the District of Columbia and U.S. territories, where exercise of police power was possible. The bill failed. Blair, undaunted, reintroduced it in 1888, only to see it pass the Senate but die in the House Judiciary Committee. He tried again in 1889, with similar results.[76]

More successful was legislation designed to curtail opium smoking in the Philippines. When the United States assumed control of the Philippines in 1898, it also assumed responsibility for the 70,000 Chinese residents there, many of whom smoked opium. The displaced rulers, the Spanish, had sought to regulate the practice through a farming-out system: contracts to sell opium were auctioned to the highest bidders, with the proviso that opium could not be sold to Filipinos for smoking purposes. This system both raised revenue, about $600,000 per annum, and effectively checked the spread of opium smoking to the Filipino majority. But when the Americans first assumed control of the islands, the contract system was replaced by a tax on opium and a ban on opium dens. Unfortunately, there followed a marked increase in consumption, especially among the Filipinos. This was partly the result of a cholera epidemic in 1902, partly of the looser nature of the American system, which did not forbid the nonmedicinal use of opiates by native Filipinos.[77]

By 1903 the civil governing body of the islands, the Philippine Commission, and Governor William Howard Taft had become convinced that the contract system should be reinstated. Growing concern was, however, voiced by missionaries such as Homer Clyde Stuntz, Methodist Episcopal Bishop of Manila, that opiate use by natives was a serious evil and that it was immoral for any government to profit by taxing traffic in the drug. The Reverend Wilbur Crafts, head of the International Reform Bureau of the United States, organized domestic opposition to the contract plan; he arranged for 2,000 protests to be sent to the White House.[78] Bishop Charles Henry Brent, a distinguished and influential Episcopalian missionary who would later serve as president of the Shanghai Opium Commission, also voiced his opposition. The administration gave in; Secretary of War Elihu Root instructed Taft to withdraw the proposal. Although the contract plan was shelved, the Philippine Commission still opposed outright prohibition as unworkable.

Governor Taft next appointed an Opium Committee charged with studying how other Far Eastern governments dealt with their narcotic problems. The committee was composed of Dr. José Albert, a Filipino physician; Major Edward C. Carter, commissioner of public health of the Philippines; and Bishop Brent, long concerned with opiate abuse. Their investigation was thorough, covering Japan, Formosa, Shanghai, Singapore, Burma, and Java. The committee concluded that systems of regulation by taxation, especially as practiced by the British, were more concerned with revenue than reform, and that the Philippines would benefit from a policy of gradual prohibition, similar to that implemented by Japan in its recently acquired territory of Formosa. Congress received a draft of the Opium Committee's report and in March 1905 passed a law declaring that the importation of opium for other than medicinal purposes should cease in the Philippines as of March 1, 1908, and that henceforth it was illegal to sell non-medicinal opiates to native Filipinos.[79]

Concern over the Far Eastern opium situation, aroused by the Philippine controversy and sustained by the growing American involvement in that part of the world, continued after the passage of the 1905 measure. American missionaries pressed for action, especially for limitation of British exports from India to China. They were encouraged by the 1906 victory of the Liberal Party, which was opposed to continuation of the traffic, and by the growing anti-imperialist sentiment in China, which manifested itself in widespread support for a new government campaign against opium smoking. Brent wrote to Theodore Roosevelt in July 1906, urging the President to take the initiative in calling an international meeting. "From the earliest days of our diplomatic relations with the East," Brent commented, "the course of the United States of America has been so manifestly high in relation to the traffic in opium that it seems to me almost our duty, now that we have the responsibility of actually handling the matter in our own possessions, to promote some movement that would gather in its embrace representatives from all countries where the traffic in and use of opium is a matter of moment."[80] Roosevelt agreed, seeing in the propsed meeting an opportunity to improve Sino-American relations, which had been damaged by the exclusion controversy, as well as to achieve humanitarian ends. Invitations to an international opium commission were issued, although it was not until February 1, 1909, that the meeting got under way in Shanghai.[81]

The American delegates to the commission were Bishop Brent; Charles C. Tenney, a missionary and educator with long experience in China; and Hamilton Wright. Brent and Tenney were familiar with opiate addiction in China and the East; Wright, who made a survey of addiction in America shortly after his appointment, was conversant with the domestic situation. Wright and the State Department understood that the American delegation faced a special diplomatic problem, the almost complete lack of effective domestic antinarcotic legislation. Before the United States could assume leadership in the suppression of the Eastern opium traffic, it had to produce some tangible evidence that it was putting its own house in order; otherwise the American delegation was open to a charge of hypocrisy. Moreover, the United States collected a great deal of revenue on imported opiates, particularly smoking opium; it could hardly fault the British for profiting from the Sino-Indian traffic.[82] It was therefore expedient that some sort of domestic legislation be enacted before the Shanghai meeting convened.

Doubtless Wright would have preferred a comprehensive antinarcotic statute along the lines of the later Harrison Act, but time did not permit the passage of such a controversial bill. Elihu Root, now secretary of state, solved the problem by drafting and then submitting to Congress a bill "to prohibit the importation and use of opium for other than medicinal purposes," in other words, smoking opium.[83] Root patterned the bill on existing import bans and kept the measure short and simple. This was done, in his words, to ensure "legislation on this subject in time to save our face . . . at Shanghai."[84] Since smoking opium was identified with Chinese, gamblers, and prostitutes; since American firms had little financial interest in its importation;[85] and since physicians professed to see no therapeutic value in the drug; little opposition was anticipated.[86] Introduced January 4, 1909, the bill was signed into law on February 9, a little more than a week after the Shanghai Commission convened. Wright made the most of the occasion, reporting to the assembled nations that, with the passage of this bill, a "new era has dawned in the United States."[87]

Consequences of the Import Ban

Wright's grandiloquence aside, the 1909 act did represent the first national antiopium smoking policy, however indirectly or erratically derived. The law banned all importations of the drug, provided for fines ($50 to $5,000) and imprisonment (up to 2 years), and stipulated that mere possession of smoking opium was sufficient to warrant conviction "unless the defendant shall explain the possession to the satisfaction of the jury." What this meant, from the black marketeer's point of view, was great deal more trouble and risk. In the past, once smoking opium was smuggled into the country there was little danger of prosecution, for it was virtually impossible to prove that the drug had not been legitimately imported and the duty paid. But after 1909 the burden of proof was reversed; anyone caught with smoking opium was presumed guilty, because there were theoretically no more legitimate imports in circulation.[88] This did not prevent the illicit traffic—if anything, smuggling increased after 1909—but it did have pronounced market effects; as the legitimate supply dried up and the risk of smuggling increased, the price of smoking opium rose. By 1917 a 5-tael (6.67 oz.) tin of medium-quality smoking opium, which sold elsewhere for about $20, brought in the United States an average of $70; by 1924 the same size tin of high-quality smoking opium cost as much as $200. The retail price per grain, in the dens or on the streets, was even higher.[89]

By 1910 to 1915, then, addicted opium smokers were beginning to have second thoughts. Opium smoking was now dangerous and increasingly expensive. Had there been no alternative—that is, no other opiate available—they probably would have continued to pay the price. But there was always morphine and in some places heroin, both of which were considerably cheaper, especially before the Harrison Act went into effect on March 1, 1915. The decision was not an easy one; many smokers preferred the ambience and companionship of the dens and had doubts about the safety of hypodermic administration,[90] but the higher price and increased risk of prosecution eventually won out.

White smokers, who had the least cultural attachment to the drug, were among the first to switch. A Massachusetts study reported that of 78 addicts who had begun their careers as opium smokers, by 1917 all but 10 had taken up morphine, either alone or in combination with cocaine.[91] In Philadelphia there was, among "denizens of the 'tenderloin,'" a pronounced shift to heroin, and to a lesser extent morphine, after 1910.[92] A study of addicts in New York City's Tombs Prison revealed a similar pattern, with 80 to 90 percent of the white addicts using heroin in 1916.[93]

The relatively few white smokers who managed to avoid the needle were, for the most part, well-heeled. During the 1920s and 1930s there were enclaves of opium smokers in New York, Chicago, Miami, and other metropolitan areas. They were a diverse group—playboys, impresarios, show girls, high-class prostitutes, successful hustlers, and big-time gangsters—but the common denominators were money and style. "When you smoked the pipe," recalled one former smoker, now a methadone patient, "you kept yourself clean, you was meticulous . . . A pipe smoker . . . was neat about his clothes and everything." By the 1920s the squalid public den was passé; the fast set smoked its opium in private apartments or hotel rooms, with wet towels over the door to contain the odor.

Dorothy, another methadone patient, recalled her introduction to this glittering world in the early 1930s. A West Virginia miner's daughter, she left home and came to New York in 1924, at the age of 14. At first she was overwhelmed; she had never seen a movie or eaten in a restaurant. Because she was attractive, she was soon able to secure employment as an entertainer in a "high-class speakeasy." One night, at the suggestion of her boss, she went to a party to "have some fun." Entering a well-appointed apartment on Riverside Drive, she found

---

big stars . . . and gorgeous people there. And they looked at me and they said, "What kind of silk pajamas do you think she should wear?" And one says "blue," and one says "green." So the guy, Mervyn ———, he says "green, a light green" . . . We laid on a big satin mattress in the middle of the floor, and we had dishes of all sorts of fruits, and candies, and hard candies, in case you get dry. It was really lovely, [though] I had no idea I was going to that kind of a party . . . The first night that I was there, I was jumping around like crazy . . . I didn't [get sick]. They were amazed; they said, "This girl is going to be a junkie." And I said,

"What's a junkie?" And they said, "That's when you get on the white stuff." They thought that was terrible, you know.[94]

The "white stuff" was heroin, and opium smokers universally regarded heroin users as an inferior caste. Even if they were addicted to smoking opium, they never considered themselves "junkies." But, in the end, practically all the addicted white opium smokers — including Dorothy — were declassed; shrinking supplies of smoking opium, which was relatively bulky and hard to smuggle,[95] left them no choice.

The Chinese opium smokers underwent a similar experience. At first they remained loyal to the pipe; the 1916 Tombs Prison study yielded not a single Chinese "hypodermic fiend or sniffer."[96] In spite of stepped-up police activity,[97] smoking opium remained the opiate of choice through the 1910s and 1920s; as late as 1929, Walter L. Treadway, chief of the Narcotics Division of the U.S. Public Health Service, reported that Chinese addicts were still usually opium smokers.[98] In the long run, however, the Chinese addict also was forced to take up the syringe. From 1935 to 1964 officials at the Lexington Hospital in Kentucky observed that 90.5 percent of the Chinese addicts admitted were using heroin, even though more than half of this group had once used smoking opium.[99] Many of these patients undoubtedly switched during World War II, when smoking opium, even in such major drug-trafficking centers as New York City, was practically unavailable.[100]

Whether the Chinese had abandoned the practice or not, it is probable that the number of opium smokers per capita would have diminished because of the steady decrease in Chinese population. Immigration restrictions and racial antagonisms took their toll: the number of Chinese in America dropped from 103,620 in 1890; to 85,341 in 1900; to 53,891 in 1920.[101] Since the Chinese were the group most likely to use the drug, any sharp reduction in their numbers affected the overall rate of addiction to smoking opium. This was the primary reason that the per capita importation of smoking opium dropped off slightly in 1900 to 1909, even before the ban on imports took effect.

Two forces, one demographic, the other legal, brought about the decline and fall of opium smoking in America. The demographic force, the decrease in Chinese population from 1890 to 1920, reduced by one-half the group with the highest proportion of addicts. This in turn reduced the overall rate of addiction to smoking opium, though it did not of itself end the practice. More important was the steady accumulation of antiopium smoking statutes, culminating with the 1909 Smoking Opium Exclusion Act. From 1910 to 1915 most white smokers who had held out against a variety of state and local measures finally capitulated to the increased risk and higher price engendered by national legislation; the Chinese smokers remaining in America would follow in the 1920s, 1930s, and early 1940s. Capitulation did not take the form of the renunciation of opiates, as some reformers had hoped, but rather of the adoption of new and more potent varieties.

Addiction to Heroin

Heroin, today virtually synonymous in the public mind with opiate addiction, was unknown until the closing years of the nineteenth century. Introduced in 1898 as a cough suppressant, it was, like opium and morphine, employed as a therapeutic agent.[1] Also like opium and morphine, its liberal use led to a bout of iatrogenic addiction, although not on the scale of the morphine epidemic of the 1870s and 1880s. Unfortunately, just as physicians were becoming more circumspect in their use of the drug, heroin became popular among the young as a euphoric agent and as a substitute for smoking opium and cocaine. At first its use was concentrated in the New York City area, but because of fundamental changes in American narcotic laws, heroin spread throughout the country during the 1920s and 1930s.

More precise information is available about heroin addicts than about their predecessors, the opium smokers. The growing national debate over narcotic control stimulated medical interest in heroin addiction, as did the iatrogenic nature of the earliest reported cases. Another factor was World War I; any drug making inroads on draft-age youth was automatically a matter of concern, particularly for the new public health profession. Finally, when the Harrison Act went into effect on March 1, 1915, many heroin addicts sought or were forced to seek treatment in public institutions, thereby giving physicians an opportunity for firsthand observation. Their combined notes, reports, and articles yield sufficient epidemiologic data to fashion a detailed profile of the heroin addict, especially of the nonmedical user as he would appeared in the era 1910 to 1925.

Characteristics of Heroin Addicts

In contrast to nineteenth-century opium and morphine addicts, the vast majority of heroin addicts were men. Studies conducted by Clifford B. Farr in the Philadelphia General Hospital, by Harry Drysdale in the Cleveland City Hospital, and by Sylvester R. Leahy in the Brooklyn Kings County Hospital, all published in 1915, showed that 75.8, 80.0, and 95.0 percent of the heroin addicts treated at their respective institutions were male.[2] At the New York City narcotic clinic (1919–1920) 78.8 percent of the patients, most of whom used heroin, were male; among the cases studied by Lawrence Kolb in 1923, the percentage male was 82.5.[3] The only exception to the rule was Jacksonville, where in 1912 Charles Terry reported (on the basis of a relatively small sample) that 54.5 percent of the heroin addicts were women.[4]

Like opium smokers, heroin addicts typically became addicted in adolescence or early adulthood. In Brooklyn the average age of addiction was 19; in Cleveland, and among patients treated at Bellevue Hospital, in New York City, the average age was 20 years, 10 months.[5] At the Inebriate Hospital in Warwick, New York, the average age at the time of treatment (not addiction) was 22 years, 7 months; morphine addicts, by contrast, averaged 37 years, 5 months.[6] In 1919 army psychiatrist George C. McPherson and psychologist Joseph Cohen published case summaries of addicted draftees entering Camp Upton, New York, indicating an average age of addiction for heroin users of 19 years, 10 months.[7] The fact that these men were draftees may have biased the average downward, but it is still noteworthy that within the draft limits of ages 18 to 31, every one of the 37 heroin users listed was addicted by the time he was 26. Approximately three-quarters of the heroin cases examined by Lawrence Kolb were also addicted before age 26, with the average being 22 years, 3 months.[8] In addition to the purely statistical evidence, there are numerous allusions to the youth of heroin addicts. "Most of the addicts coming under our treatment," wrote Frank A. McGuire and Perry M. Lichtenstein, physicians at New York City's Tombs

Prison, "are young individuals. It is not uncommon to find boys and girls sixteen and eighteen years of age who give a history of having taken the drug for two years."[9] A similar description was offered by Lucius Brown, who characterized Tennessee's relatively few heroin addicts as "youngsters from 15 to 25 years of age."[10]

Heroin addiction was concentrated among whites, especially during the decade 1910 to 1920. The Chinese continued to smoke opium well into the 1920s and 1930s, and blacks, although they were known to use heroin, did not do so as frequently as whites.[11] In 1912 only 9.1 percent of Jacksonville's heroin addicts were black, although blacks constituted more than half the city's population.[12] Drysdale and Leahy recorded no black heroin users; McPherson and Cohen found some heroin addicts of "African" extraction, although they did not specify how many.[13] Blacks were not seriously afflicted with heroin addiction until they began migrating in large numbers to northern cities.

One of the few things heroin addicts had in common with opium and morphine addicts, aside from their racial background, was their nationality. The majority of heroin addicts were born in the United States. In New York City Leahy, Charles Stokes, and S. Dana Hubbard found that only 4.3, 16.7, and 30.6 percent of their respective cases were foreign-born, although in 1920 the foreign-born made up fully 36.1 percent of that city's population.[14] Of the draftee-addicts listed by McPherson and Cohen, only 2 of 37 heroin users were born outside the United States.[15]

If immigrants were relatively immune to heroin addiction, their children were not. Leahy went on to show that 41.7 percent of his sample was made up of second-generation Americans. While there were no heroin addicts born in either Ireland or Italy, 17 addicts of Irish parentage and 11 of Italian parentage were born in this country. Whereas there was only 1 addicted German and 1 addicted Russian Jew, there were 21 addicts of German parentage and 6 of Russian Jewish parentage born in the United States.[16]

Geographically, heroin addicts tended to cluster around New York City; by 1920 probably 9 out of 10 American heroin addicts were within 180 miles of Manhattan. The adjacent states of New York, New Jersey, Pennsylvania, and Delaware all had relatively high rates of heroin addiction.[17] From 1910 to 1916 a few distant cities, such as Cleveland,[18] seemed to be developing a significant heroin problem, but addicts in these places by and large had gone back to morphine by 1920. Morphine use persisted outside the New York City area for some time; in Boston, for example, it lasted well into the 1920s; in Chicago, well into the 1930s.[19]

The use of heroin, unlike that of opium or morphine, was concentrated in urban areas. In New York State virtually all of the heroin addicts resided in New York City.[20] Within the city itself the seamier neighborhoods, the "tenderloins," harbored the greatest number of addicts. The only figures available on this point, involving 100 addicts (93 heroin, 7 morphine) treated at Warwick, are sketchy. An excerpt from the report, compiled by Dr. E. W. Phillips, reads, "Neighborhood (always from the laborer's viewpoint.) Good, 21; fair, 28; bad, 51."[21] Exactly what, in Phillips' judgment, constituted "fair" or "bad" is difficult to say, but there is an abundance of other nonstatistical testimony affirming that heroin addiction was focused in impoverished and vice-ridden neighborhoods.[22]

Accordingly, heroin addicts tended to be of a lower-middle-class or lower-class background. "Us[ing] as a standard of comparison the ordinary laborer," Phillips continued, the addicts' social class could be described as "low normal for American communities."[23] Although precise statistics on income are not available, it is safe to assume that most heroin addicts grew up in relatively poor families, in many cases having been recently transplanted from Europe.[24] The cost of supporting their habit, especially after restrictive legislation drove up the price of heroin,[25] only exacerbated their poverty; drugs came first, necessities later. Hygiene and grooming were frequently neglected. As a group, then, heroin addicts would have struck the public as even worse than "low normal;" pale, emaciated, and shabbily dressed, they often looked more like down-and-outs than respectable laborers.[26]

When they were employed, heroin addicts generally held unskilled or semiskilled jobs: as drivers, conductors, elevator operators, factory workers, day laborers, longshoremen, painters, bellboys, peddlers, news dealers, soda jerks, and the like.[27] A few held skilled jobs, as plumbers or mechanics for instance, while others gave their occupation as salesman, clerk, or actor.[28] There were also gamblers and professional criminals, many of whom had a history of opium smoking.[29] Some of the female addicts gave their occupation as actress,[30] but a substantial number, possibly the majority, were prostitutes. Repeating a pattern observed among the opium smokers, some of these prostitutes lived with addicted lovers, who shared their heroin and their illicit earnings.[31]

The composite heroin addict was thus a young white male who lived in a slum neighborhood in New York or a neighboring eastern city. He was a citizen by birth, though his parents might have been immigrants. Poorly educated, when he worked at all he held a blue-collar job of an unskilled or semiskilled variety. He spent much time on the street, running with a gang, and it was often within the gang that his heroin use began. "Harold" typifies this new breed of addict. He was an orphan, or at least claimed to know nothing about his family. His youth was spent in abandoned houses "somewhere in Joisey," in the company of a juvenile gang that included escapees from various institutions. Group experimentation with opiates, smoking opium among them, was the order of the day. Harold soon became an opiate addict, using not only heroin, but any drug as long as it contained "any kind or quantity of Opium or Cocaine." A vagabond and a petty thief, Harold's appetite for drugs was as eclectic as it was voracious. "To what was he addicted?" wrote an awed physician, "I might answer in all sincerity, 'The Pharmacopoeia.' "[32]

Iatrogenic Heroin Addiction

Not all heroin addicts were as omniverous as Harold, nor did they owe their condition to association with other users. Between 1898 and 1910 there was another round of iatrogenic addiction, and a number of medical addicts were created. The key issue is one of extent: how significant a problem was therapeutically engendered heroin addiction, especially in comparison to street use?

The claim that iatrogenic heroin addiction was widespread was developed first and most forcefully in Charles Terry and Mildred Pellens' 1928 study, *The Opium Problem*. In this, as in all of their writings, Terry and Pellens stressed the prevalence of iatrogenic addiction, whether to opium, morphine, heroin, or codeine, and tended to portray the addict sympathetically, as the innocent victim of a careless practitioner.[33] Their argument regarding heroin ran as follows. Introduced in 1898 as a substitute for codeine and morphine, the drug was enthusiastically received by the European and American medical communities. It was recommended for every variety of complaint and enjoyed wide popularity as a therapeutic agent. Worse, it was touted as nonhabit-forming and was even endorsed as a cure for morphine addiction. Warnings that heroin was addictive accumulated gradually. It was not until 1910 that the profession fully awoke to the danger; by that time "a great many" heroin addicts had been created inadvertently.[34]

There are, however, several problems with this account. If the medical profession was as culpable as Terry and Pellens suggested, why was the iatrogenic heroin addict by 1914 clearly labeled as a minority type? Terry himself admitted that most of the Jacksonville heroin addicts owed their plight to dissipation.[35] "The present heroin habitué," wrote neuropsychiatrist Pearce Bailey in 1915, "rarely accuses a physician of being the one who introduced him to his cruel master. The first dose of heroin is neither pill nor hypodermic injection taken to alleviate some physical distress, but is a minute quantity of a fine powder 'blown' up the nose at the suggestion of an agreeable companion who has tried it and found it 'fine.' "[36]

Statistics bear out this interpretation. In 1912 Massachusetts physician Paul K. Sellew published an account of 9 cases of heroin addiction. Although he intended his article as a warning to the profession to avoid overprescribing the drug, only 2 of his cases were of therapeutic origin. The remaining 7 began using heroin through curiosity or dissipation, or as a substitute for smoking opium.[37] Of 18 heroin addicts treated by Stokes in 1917, 17 listed "companions" as the source of their addiction. Only 1 claimed medical reasons, citing a vague genitourinary ailment.[38] Finally, there was a retrospective study undertaken in 1927 by Lawrence Kolb and John H. Remig, inspector for the Pennsylvania Department of Health's Bureau of Drug Control. The sample was largely confined to opiate addicts who became addicted through medication or self-medication during the years 1898 to 1924, that is, after heroin was discovered and before its use was outlawed in the United States. Of the 150 cases examined, only 2 (1.3 percent) involved heroin, a woman addicted in 1906 and a man addicted in 1911. The remainder began with some form of morphine (94.0 percent), paregoric (2.7 percent), or tincture of opium (2.0 percent).[39] Something kept medically related heroin addiction to a minimum, in comparison to both medically related morphine addiction (itself a gradually disappearing phenomenon) and heroin addiction spread by association.

A reexamination of the literature on the therapeutic uses of heroin yields one important clue: heroin was indicated principally in respiratory disorders. Regarded as a specific, it was given for a limited range of diseases — unlike morphine, which in the nineteenth century served as a virtual panacea. Early work on the therapeutic applications of heroin, especially that of Heinrich

Dreser, emphasized its usefulness in suppressing cough and alleviating respiratory difficulties, a theme reiterated in most American discussions of the drug.[40] In 1900, for example, New York physician Bernard Lazarus reported favorably on the use of heroin in 9 cases. With the exception of a woman suffering from intercostal neuralgia, all of the patients had respiratory complaints.[41] In 1906 the *Journal of the American Medical Association* summarized the literature on heroin as follows:

[It is] recommended chiefly for the treatment of diseases of the air passages attended with cough, difficult breathing, and spasm, such as the different forms of bronchitis, pneumonia, consumption, asthma, whooping cough, laryngitis, and certain forms of hay fever. It has also been recommended as an analgesic, in the place of morphine in various painful affections.[42]

The last sentence refers to studies by Norman P. Geis, Samuel Horton Brown, Erle Duncan Tompkins, and others documenting heroin's analgesic potential.[43] Although these researchers were perfectly correct—heroin is at least as potent as morphine in relieving pain[44]—several dissenting opinions were expressed. An early German report indicated that heroin did not seem suitable as a general pain reliever (*Schmerzlindernd*), emphasizing instead its utility in cough.[45] Morris Manges, writing in the *New York Medical Journal,* described heroin as absolutely useless as a general analgesic in the usual dosage of 1/12 to 1/10 grain.[46] George E. Pettey also remarked that the drug was less powerful and less prompt than morphine as a pain reliever.[47] As misinformed as these critics were, they appear to have had an impact on the profession, for heroin continued to be used principally as a cough remedy.[48] This tendency was reinforced by the advertisements of the Bayer Pharmaceutical Company and other heroin distributors who promoted the drug as a specific for cough and respiratory disorders, and only rarely as an analgesic.[49]

The circumscribed use of heroin greatly reduced the number of potential iatrogenic addicts. Whereas virtually any complaint in the 1870s might have warranted an injection of morphine, a patient in the early 1900s suffering from rheumatism or dysentery or some other nonrespiratory ailment had a relatively remote chance of receiving heroin. The intimation of Terry and Pellens that the medical profession used heroin as indiscriminately as morphine obscured this important point.

Another weakness in the case for widespread iatrogenic heroin addiction involves the mode of administration. Heroin was given orally, in tablets, pills, and pastilles, or in an elixir or glycerin solution.[50] It was not generally injected, particularly in cases of cough, and the dosage was kept low.[51] Small amounts of opiates administered orally would not have been as dangerous as opiates injected hypodermically. Addiction via the oral route was still possible, of course, but at least the near-instantaneous relief and euphoria of an injection were absent.

This advantage was somewhat offset, however, by the fact that heroin was introduced as a nonaddictive drug. "Safe and reliable," "addiction can scarce be possible," and "absence of danger of acquiring the habit" were some of the early, misleading claims made about heroin.[52] More skeptical physicians soon began issuing warnings, however. In 1899 Horatio C. Wood, Jr., became the first American to urge caution; the following year Manges noted "habituation" as a consequence of treatment in 6 to 8 percent of his cases. Although he distinguished such habituation from full-blown morphine addiction, a condition he held to be much more serious, Manges nevertheless cautioned that "after all heroin is a derivative of morphine, and . . . is to be dispensed with the discrimination and judgment which are essential to all sedative drugs."[53] In 1903 George Pettey published a strong and unambiguous indictment, "The Heroin Habit Another Curse," in which he systematically rebutted the claims of safety advanced by heroin enthusiasts.[54] The aforementioned *Journal of the American Medical Association* article was equally clear on this point: "The habit is readily formed and leads to the most deplorable results."[55] Abstracts of European work on heroin addiction, which soon began appearing in English-language journals, were another source of information.[56] The significant point about these and other heroin warnings is that they appeared as early as they did, within a few years of the drug's introduction; physicians did not have to wait for 15 years, as was the case with the hypodermic injection of morphine. This relatively prompt response was another factor limiting the extent of iatrogenic heroin addiction.

The early heroin warnings also appeared in a period of growing professional concern over the excessive prescription of opiates and were therefore more likely to be heeded by the average practitioner, now highly sensitive to charges of narcotic overuse. It would be difficult to choose an exact date when iatrogenic heroin addiction ceased to be a problem (Terry and Pellens designated 1910); the situation is probably best described as a slow but steady abandonment of the drug. By 1920 Thomas Blair could announce that in Pennsylvania "there are literally thousands of physicians who have stopped the use of heroin altogether." Doctors prescribed an average of less than 16 grains apiece in 1919, and Blair anticipated that the average for 1920 would scarcely exceed 2 grains.[57] That same year the House of Delegates of the American Medical Association endorsed a resolution calling for a total ban on heroin.[58]

A final word must be said about heroin as a cure for morphine addiction. In 1899 a Berlin physician, Albert Eulenberg, suggested that heroin might be useful in treating morphine addiction, a proposal passed on to the American audience by Bernard Lazarus of New York.[59] How widespread this practice became is uncertain, but by 1903 Pettey reported that half (4 of 8) of the heroin cases coming under his care "had substituted Heroin for morphine with the idea that they were curing themselves of the habit, but after the substitution was made they were unable to leave off the Heroin."[60] After word spread that heroin was addictive, this practice was quickly abandoned.[61] From the standpoint of the overall prevalence of opiate addiction, the substitution cure was of little importance; no new opiate addicts were created, only old ones were fitted out with a new drug.

In summary, then, the therapeutic use of heroin led to the creation of some new addicts, and some older addicts were switched to heroin in a vain attempt at cure. Fortunately, there were several limiting factors. The most important was the fact that heroin, unlike morphine, was indicated principally for one category of disease, the respiratory disorders. It was never a panacea. Furthermore, heroin was given orally, rather than injected. The relatively early warnings of heroin's addictive potential, plus the profession's growing narcotic conservatism, also played a constraining role. By approximately 1910 iatrogenic addiction had been reduced to a trickle, and the heroin addict who could blame his condition on his physician was about to be eclipsed by a new and less sympathetic type. Enter the heroin sniffer.

The Origins of Nonmedical Heroin Addiction

"It is a notorious fact," remarked Congressman Joseph Holt Gaines of West Virginia, one of the few to speak against the 1909 Smoking Opium Exclusion Act, "that those who are addicted to the opium habit will secure the drug in some form . . . if they are prevented from getting it in the form in which it is preferred."[62]

Subsequent events proved Gaines correct; one of the earliest and most significant incentives to the use of heroin was the ban on imported smoking opium. This trend, according to Pearce Bailey, began about 1910, as veteran smokers and their recruits, deterred by the new crackdown on the dens, abandoned the pipe for more powerful and legal forms of opiates.[63] Smoking opium could still be had, of course, but it "became very expensive and could only be obtained in small quantities by those who could afford it at all."[64] Heroin, which was cheap and did not require the use of a hypodermic syringe, was an attractive alternative. The drug also appealed to curious neophytes who in years past would have experimented with smoking opium, but who now began sniffing heroin instead. The changing preference of these younger users helps to explain the low average age of heroin addicts.

Another factor behind the increasing popularity of heroin was the growing scarcity of cocaine. A popular underworld stimulant, cocaine was, like smoking opium, a target of restrictive legislation. Supplies diminished, prices rose, and substitutes were sought. In order to understand how this situation came about, and why cocaine users switched to heroin, it is necessary to digress briefly and explain something of the history of this controversial drug.

Coca leaves, chewed by South American natives for centuries, came to the attention of the western medical community in the mid-nineteenth century. Although the alkaloid cocaine was isolated as early as 1855, it was not until the mid-1880s that its therapeutic application became common. The major impetus to medical use of cocaine was a series of glowing reports, including articles by a then-obscure Viennese neurologist, Sigmund Freud.[65] Like morphine (but unlike heroin), cocaine was recommended for a wide variety of conditions. As one advertising brochure put it, an "enumeration of the diseases in which coca and cocaine have been found of service would include a category of almost all the maladies that flesh is heir to."[66] Cocaine was recommended as an antispasmodic, aphrodisiac, anodyne, and local anesthetic, as a specific for hay fever and asthma, and as a cure for alcoholism and opiate addiction, to name but a few of its proposed uses.[67] It was also recommended as an all-purpose tonic, for patients who exhibited "melancholy" or "the blues" or other less than precisely defined depressive symptoms. One especially popular product was Vin Mariani, a coca wine used and endorsed by Americans of no less stature than Thomas Edison and William McKinley.[68] Many physicians also tried cocaine on themselves, thereby worsening the profession's already serious addiction problem.[69]

The faddish use of such a powerful stimulant inevitably drew a counterattack. The suggestion, advanced by Freud and others, that cocaine be employed to alleviate withdrawal distress was vigorously condemned.[70] A growing number of critics chided the profession for overprescribing the drug in colds, hay fever, and other common ailments.[71] Equally important was the development of drugs like tropacocaine (1891), stovaine (1903), and novocaine (1904), synthetics that retained cocaine's valuable anesthetic properties but lacked its euphorigenic effects. Just as many practitioners put aside morphine for safer analgesics like aspirin, conscientious dentists and physicians began switching from cocaine to one of the new synthetics.[72] Unfortunately, patent-medicine vendors continued to promote self-medication with the drug, a key ingredient in many of their preparations. Cocaine was also available in a variety of soft drinks (some of which had medicinal pretensions, some not) or in pure form through the mails.[73]

The treatment or self-treatment of disease was only one factor in the spread of cocaine. Sometime in the late 1880s or early 1890s — the date is not certain — black stevedores in New Orleans began taking the drug in order to "perform more easily the extraordinarily severe work of loading and unloading steamboats," a task at which they toiled for up to "seventy hours at a stretch . . . without sleep or rest, in rain, in cold, and in heat."[74] It is likely that this practice had its origins in reports of similar use of coca leaves by South American natives, who were able to increase their nervous energy, forestall drowsiness, and "bear cold, wet, great bodily exertion, and even want of food to a surprising degree, with apparent ease and impunity."[75] The use of cocaine by black laborers spread from New Orleans to other parts of the South, to cotton plantations, railroad work camps, and levee construction sites.[76] "Well, that cocaine habit is might' bad," ran one work song, "It kill ev-ybody I know it to have had."[77] Others turned to the drug, not as a stimulus to work, but as a form of dissipation.[78] Some authorities charged that blacks, crazed by cocaine, went on superhuman rampages of violence, allegations that since have been denied.[79] Behavioral considerations aside, it is fair to say that cocaine was relatively popular in black communities, and that many blacks made at least occasional use of the drug as a euphoric agent. In 1912 Charles Terry found blacks significantly overrepresented among Jacksonville's regular cocaine users; their rate was 2.98 per thousand, in comparison to 1.61 for whites.[80]

Sometime between 1895 and 1900 cocaine became popular in the white underworld, in both northern and southern cities. "The classes of the community most addicted to the habitual use of cocaine," reported New York City Police Commissioner Theodore Bingham, "are the parasites who live on the earnings of prostitutes, prostitutes of the lowest order, and young degenerates who acquire the habit at an early age through their connection with prostitutes and parasites."[81] As a group they were quite similar to the white opium smokers; many, in fact, had a history of opium smoking, or had previously resorted to some other opiate.[82] As Bingham's remarks suggest, the practice was frequently acquired in brothels, where experienced prostitutes introduced their customers to the pleasures of the drug.[83]

Although cocaine as a medicine was inhaled, ingested, or injected, for euphoric purposes it was usually sniffed. George C. Biondi, of the Fordham University School of Medicine, commented that of approximately a thousand cases he had witnessed, he could recollect but "three or four instances of exclusive hypo users, and these were at the same time morphine-fiends."[84] Because of the vascularity of the mucous membrane, cocaine sniffed up the nostrils enters the bloodstream and produces its effects very quickly. Sniffing was also economical; only small amounts, when used in this manner, were required to produce stimulating effects. Sniffing also avoided the expense, unpleasantry, and possible sepsis involved in hypodermic administration.

Reaction to nonmedical cocaine use, among blacks as well as whites, was not long in coming. By 1915 most states had passed laws designed to restrict use of the drug to therapeutic purposes, mainly by limiting its purchase to those with a legitimate prescription.[85] New York passed a series of laws in 1907, 1908, 1910, and 1913, the last placing so many elaborate restrictions on cocaine that legal distribution was practically impossible.[86] While these laws did not prevent the illicit use of cocaine, they did succeed in stimulating higher black-market prices.

With the price of their favorite drug increasing, cocaine users in New York and elsewhere were forced to consider alternatives. Heroin was doubly attractive: it was cheap, and it was taken in the accustomed fashion, sniffing. Any unpleasant symptoms, particularly depression, that the regular cocaine user might experience on discontinuing use of the drug were alleviated by the tranquilizing and mood-elevating properties of heroin. From New York City, Philadelphia, and Boston came reports of heroin addicts with a prior history of cocaine use.[87] Newspapers and films also emphasized the link between the two drugs. One story, appearing in the *New York Times,* stated that heroin, "made by treating cocaine with acetic acid . . . is much cheaper than cocaine, [and] its use is proportionately greater." The slip is revealing; the reporter, aware that heroin and cocaine were taken in the same way and by the same type of people, assumed the one was a derivative of the other. "The Drug Terror," a silent movie of the era, made a similar error. The film opened with a shot of a heroin bottle; beneath it ran the caption, "This drug is identical with cocaine in effect." This, of course, is incorrect: heroin is a narcotic, cocaine a stimulant; prolonged heroin use will produce physical dependence, cocaine will not. But one can easily imagine how the filmmakers, intent on dramatizing the dangers of drug sniffing by a group who had a history of using both substances, could have mistakenly equated heroin and cocaine.[88]

Some users, however, had no previous experience with cocaine but began experimenting with heroin directly. Like "Harold," they might later sniff cocaine when it was available, but its use was relatively insignificant compared to the amount of heroin consumed once addiction was established.[89] Many of those who used heroin initially, as well as those who switched from other drugs, were members of juvenile gangs.[90] Gang members were susceptible for several reasons. If one of their number passed around some heroin and urged his peers to sample it, there was tremendous pressure to do so; turning it down was an act of cowardice, entailing loss of status or even expulsion from the gang. On the positive side, there was the tremendous curiosity — the quest for new adventure — that characterizes all such youthful groups. "The majority of the present takers are boys and young men whose easy sociability has been developed in the gangs," wrote Pearce Bailey. "A common story," he continued,

is of a group of boys being together at a dance, or a show, at some outdoor gathering in the summer. One of the number produces a "deck" or "package" of heroin and tells the others that the taking of it is wonderfully enjoyable; "try that and you won't have no trouble," he says; he sniffs it up his nose and has enough of it on hand or within reach to supply all the others who wish to try it. They, of course, all wish to follow exactly as the majority in any group of small boys will wish to imitate someone whom they see smoking tobacco. The first taking is generally not agreeable, but they try it again, and about twenty-five per cent become victims of the habit within a few months.[91]

Others described the same process in less sympathetic terms. "In many instances the patients [addicted to heroin] are members of gangs who congregate on street corners particularly at night, and make insulting remarks to people who pass," wrote Sylvester Leahy. "The histories as obtained from the patients and their relatives show that in practically every case the drug had been tried by one of the members of the gang who then induced the other members to try it."[92] New York City addiction specialist Alexander Lambert characterized heroin addiction as a "vice of the underworld," acquired by the young through "vicious associations and habits." He compared heroin addicts unfavorably to morphine users, most of whom were over 30 and taking the drug "to forget bodily pain and mental suffering."[93]

Is it appropriate to describe these youthful heroin users as criminals, or as representing a criminal class? The answer is a matter of definition. If by *criminal* is meant a hardened professional, a full-time lawbreaker, the answer is no. A boy's association with his gang and its activities was often casual, something he did after work or school. If, however, by *criminal* is meant engaging in criminal activities, the answer is a qualified yes. The typical urban street gang of the 1910s and 1920s engaged in a wide range of legal and illegal activities. It was, as Jacob Riis put it, a club gone wild. The same group that would organize a baseball game or a dance one day might be found pilfering boxcars or smashing windows the next. Fighting was an ever-popular activity, and beatings, knifings, and shootings, especially of rival gang members, were common. The gang was so structured that those who exhibited the most daring and pugilistic character quickly assumed leadership; hence members were quick to perform and brag about illegal feats.[94] Most gang members who began using drugs had a history of indulgence in destructive and dangerous pastimes, of which heroin sniffing was merely one manifestation.

Statistics on the age, sex, urban, and social background of the addicts fit well with this portrait of the heroin user as gang member. It would be misleading, however, to characterize heroin sniffing as strictly a juvenile gang activity. Many who took heroin were older—professional criminals, gamblers, and prostitutes who found it expedient to switch from smoking opium or cocaine. A few addicts came from respectable backgrounds.[95] Army barracks were also the scene of heroin sniffing. Nonmedical use of opiates in the armed services dates at least as far back as 1898, when soldiers stationed in the Philippines learned to smoke opium.[96] Somewhat later cocaine came into vogue, followed by heroin in the years 1912 to 1916. Soldiers were either introduced to the drug by their friends, who praised its ability to alleviate fatigue and induce euphoria, or by prostitutes who worked the nearby brothels. Heroin's appeal was enhanced by its reputation as an *aide d'amour* whose use prolonged the sexual act. Army officers took a dimmer view of the drug, however, and, on the ground that one addict might corrupt an entire company, soldiers caught using heroin or cocaine were punished and discharged.[97] Similarly, when the draft became a factor, recruits showing signs of drug addiction were summarily rejected. Supervision was especially strict during World War I; moreover, an addict shipped overseas, unless attached to a medical unit, would have found it almost impossible to secure a supply.[98] Because of these precautions and wartime conditions, heroin in the army remained an isolated and relatively insignificant problem, especially in comparison with growing civilian use. Not until the Vietnam War did the specter of heroin addiction again seriously trouble army physicians.[99]

The Spread of Heroin

In 1920 heroin sniffing was largely confined to New York and a few nearby cities, the most important of which was Philadelphia.[100] Other eastern and midwestern cities had their heroin addicts, but these were a decided minority. By 1940, however, heroin was the opiate of choice among underworld users in virtually every large American city. What effected this dramatic change?

To begin with a narrower question, why was heroin addiction concentrated in the New York City area in the first place? It was not always so; prior to 1916 outbreaks of nonmedical heroin use had been noted in Boston, Chicago, and other cities.[101] One story is that prisoners whose coughs were treated with heroin learned that the drug produced euphoria; they then passed this information along to friends on the outside, who in turn spread the news from one city to another. As a result, by 1915 heroin was known in tenderloin districts all over the country.[102] Heroin fell into disuse, however, except in New York and surrounding cities. Heroin's survival in that region was attributable largely to its continued availability. Many of the major heroin distributors, such as the Bayer, Merck, Schieffelin, and Martin H. Smith companies, were located in New York City. Retail druggists in the area would have been well stocked, and it would have been easier to divert large amounts of the drug into the illicit traffic (by rerouting orders, stealing from warehouses, spiriting imports past customs, and so forth) in New York than elsewhere.[103] In other places morphine was more abundant. In Boston, for example, much of the illicit traffic consisted of morphine legally exported to Canada, then smuggled back across the border.[104]

Addicts and their recruits adapted their requirements to suit the supply. One consequence of the temporary eclipse of heroin outside the New York City area was that morphine assumed new importance as a euphoric agent and as a substitute for smoking opium. In 1917 Leo L. Stanley, resident physician at California's San Quentin Prison, asked addicted inmates which form of opium they had first used. Of 100 prisoners interviewed, 58 indicated smoking opium, 20 morphine hypodermically, 8 morphine orally, 3 "yen shee" (ashes of smoking opium) orally, and 11 "cocaine and laudanum, or eating opium." But when asked which form of the drug they had last used, 48 replied morphine hypodermically, 8 morphine orally, 28 morphine and cocaine, 3 smoking opium, while the remaining 13 used "morphine by mouth and syringe together, according to circumstances" or took "heroin and laudanum." Morphine thus assumed the place of smoking opium in the California underworld.[105] By 1917 Massachusetts opium smokers had also largely switched to morphine, or morphine and cocaine.[106] In 1922 C. Edouard Sandoz, medical director of the Boston Municipal Court, published a detailed account of addiction in that city. Morphine was far and away the opiate of choice: "we rarely see a case of heroinism," he reported. Many of the Boston addicts had previously used smoking opium, cocaine, and heroin; others drank; still others took to morphine directly. Injection was the most common method of administration, and other drugs, especially cocaine, were used when available.[107] Like their heroin-sniffing counterparts, these addicts were young and were introduced to the drug by their associates. They were, in contrast to most nineteenth-century medical addicts, predominately male. To tie in a trend noted earlier, it may well be that the male majorities observed in Cleveland (1915), in Shreveport (1919–1923), and by Kolb (1923) reflect the increasing prevalence of this new type of morphine addict.[108] As "sporting" addicts were recruited in areas outside New York City, and as older female addicts died off, the shift in sex became more pronounced; a nationwide study of morphine addicts reported for violation of the narcotic laws between July 1 and October 31 of 1929 showed that fully 824 of 1,054 cases (78.2 percent) were male.[109]

This state of affairs — heroin sniffers in and around New York City, morphine addicts elsewhere — might have persisted were it not for yet another change in the legal status of the opiates and opiate addiction. The source of this change was the 1914 Harrison Narcotic Act. As detailed and scholarly accounts of the origin, passage, and interpretation of the Harrison Act are available elsewhere,[110] I shall confine myself here to a brief review of its legislative and judicial history.

When Hamilton Wright returned from the 1909 Shanghai Opium Commission, he had two basic goals in mind: the convening of an international opium conference, which, unlike a commission, would have treaty-drafting powers; and the passage of comprehensive domestic antinarcotic legislation. He achieved the first objective but not the second. Wright eventually was able to persuade Secretary of State Philander C. Knox of the value of an international opium conference, and on September 1, 1909, formal invitations and a tentative agenda were sent out to the nations that had participated in the Shanghai meeting.[111] The response was less than enthusiastic; many nations had a vested interest in the opium traffic and were reluctant to see international control imposed. After considerable delay the conference convened at the Hague on December 1, 1911.

Meanwhile Wright continued to push for more stringent domestic narcotic laws. His main efforts were devoted to the Foster bill, an elaborate measure which, like earlier smoking opium legislation, aimed at indirect control of the traffic through the long-recognized taxing and commerce powers. The Foster bill required those who dealt in narcotics to register, pay a tax, and carefully record all transactions, even of minute amounts. Drug containers, like liquor bottles, would bear a tax stamp, and persons who were not registered were barred from shipping narcotics across state lines. Penalties for violation were stiff, up to $5,000 and 5 years in prison. Further, state and loca. boards of pharmacy and law enforcement agencies would have access to the records. They could thus ascertain who sold how much of which drug to whom, information that could prove embarrassing to doctors and druggists who were little more than narcotics purveyors and that could lead to the better enforcement of existing narcotic laws. Wright also argued that the registration and record-keeping provisions would soon drive disreputable dealers, such as saloonkeepers and peddlers, out of interstate commerce, where they secured the bulk of their supplies.[112] But legitimate manufacturers and dealers countered that the elaborate regulations would hamstring their trade, and for this reason they strongly opposed the bill.[113] As we have seen, Wright's attempt to bluff the bill through in the face of this opposition was a failure.

So Wright set sail for the Hague without exemplary new narcotic legislation. He tried to put the best face on things; in a memorandum to the conference he explained that passage had been postponed "until all those affected shall have been heard. Besides this, there has been such a press of business before the Congress since the question of interstate control of cocaine, etc., was actively brought before it that action has been delayed."[114] The polite talk about delay fooled no one. The German delegate asked Wright point-blank what guarantee he could give that Congress would pass the necessary legislation to put the provisions of the treaty into force. This was twisting the knife in the wound, for Wright had done everything in his power to get the Foster bill through and had failed. Mortified, he nevertheless managed a lofty and dignified reply, "The good faith of the United States ought to be a sufficient guarantee that the government would carry out all that it had agreed to."[115]

Such incidents did not divert the conference for long, however, and by January 23, 1912, agreement was reached. The Hague Opium Convention dealt mainly with the international narcotic traffic, but it also pledged the contracting powers to promulgate and enforce laws to control the domestic manufacture and sale of medicinal opium, morphine, heroin, and cocaine, and to restrict their consumption to medical and legitimate uses only. Although some powers delayed signing the convention and it did not actually go into effect until 1914, Wright now believed that Congress had a moral and diplomatic obligation to honor the convention by regulating the domestic narcotic market.[116]

The campaign was renewed in June 1912, when a bill similar to the original Foster proposal was introduced into the House. Its sponsor was Congressman Francis Burton Harrison, a genteel New Yorker who agreed to take charge of the legislation after Foster's untimely death on March 21, 1912. Again the bill failed to get beyond the House Ways and Means Committee, primarily because Wright refused to incorporate changes demanded by the drug trades. Harrison tried again in January 1913, with similar results.[117]

Harrison eventually convinced Wright that he would have to negotiate directly with the National Drug Trade Conference

(NDTC), an ad hoc lobby charged with keeping careful watch on narcotic legislation. The legitimate organizations represented by the NDTC, such as the National Wholesale Druggists' Association, were not opposed in principle to government regulation of the narcotic market. Rather, they sought to eliminate the provisions of the Harrison bill they considered too stringent. The negotiations began inauspiciously; Wright became so incensed during the first session that he walked out of the meeting. He soon cooled off, however, and discussions resumed. Eventually they were broadened to include officials of the State and Treasury departments, as well as representatives of individual drug companies.

By May 1913 a compromise bill had been hammered out, and NDTC representatives John C. Wallace and Charles M. Woodruff signed a statement declaring that the new version had their thorough support and approval.[118] The concessions won by the drug trades and medical profession can be summarized as follows: chloral and cannabis were dropped from the list of controlled drugs, leaving opium and cocaine, their derivatives and salts; the amount of the proposed tax was reduced to a nominal one dollar; bookkeeping procedures were standardized and simplified; physicians in attendance upon a patient could dispense narcotics without making a record; and preparations containing small amounts of narcotics were exempted from the provisions of the bill. The basic scheme of the original Foster bill remained intact, however. All those who dealt in narcotic drugs were to register with and pay a small tax to their district internal revenue officer, and keep accurate records of their transactions.

In June 1913, one month after agreement with the NDTC was reached, Harrison introduced the compromise bill. It took this version less than a week to pass the House. On June 24, the day after it was introduced, it was reported back favorably from the Ways and Means Committee. The report bore witness to Wright's influence: his dramatic statistics were repeated, as well as his argument that "this government is bound to enact legislation to carry out its humanitarian, moral, and international obligations."[119] During the floor debate Harrison emphasized that the measure had at last received the imprimatur of the drug interests.[120] Even so, the measure came in for some sharp criticism, particularly section 6, which exempted nostrums containing small amounts of narcotics. Congressman James R. Mann acknowledged the criticism and allowed that narcotic patent medicines "probably ought to be abolished." Then he added candidly, "Unfortunately I am forced to believe that if we should attempt in this way to attack all the proprietary medicines which contain opium, the bill would have a rocky road to travel, and would be consigned to oblivion. That may not be a very good excuse, but, after all, it is practical."[121]

Mann was probably anticipating the bill's fate in the Senate when he uttered those words. As the measure made its none-too-rapid progress through the upper chamber, a variety of special-interest amendments were tacked on. Typical of these was an amendment raising the section 6 heroin limit from 1/12 grain per ounce to 1/4 grain per ounce. The House objected, a conference committee was appointed, and by late October 1914 a compromise had been worked out.[122] The bill was finally signed into law on December 17, 1914.

In many respects the Harrison Act was a classic piece of progressive legislation: reform effort (restrict the sale of narcotics) met business self-interest (rationalize the narcotic market) to produce a compromise measure. Large pharmaceutical firms were perfectly willing to see small-time, unregistered peddlers prosecuted; enlightened and professionalized pharmacists agreed to restrict sale to those possessing a prescription; and nostrum makers could go on merchandising their wares, provided they contained no more than the allowable amount of narcotics.

There was one issue, though, that could not be compromised, and that was maintenance. Either opiate addicts could obtain their supply legally, or they could not. The law was silent on this crucial point — the words *addict* and *addiction* appear nowhere in the statute — and there is frustratingly little in any of the hearings, floor debates, and committee reports to indicate congressional intent. Nevertheless, the agency first charged with enforcing the law, the Internal Revenue Bureau of the Treasury Department, assumed an aggressive antimaintenance stance. Alleging that a physician who issued a prescription to an addict for the sole purpose of maintenance was not acting within the bounds of the law, the bureau brought a number of indictments against doctors, druggists, and addicts for conspiracy to violate the Harrison Act. At first the bureau's efforts, notably in *United States* v. *Jin Fuey Moy* (1916), were unsuccessful; in that case Justice Oliver Wendell Holmes, Jr., speaking for the seven-man majority, rebuked the government for construing a revenue statute as a sweeping prohibition. In the 1919 *Webb* case, however, the government managed to reverse the earlier decision and obtain a ruling favorable to its antimaintenance policy.[123]

These laws and decisions had a marked impact on the addict in the street and on the kinds of drugs he used. After the Harrison Act went into effect addicts, as unregistered persons, had to obtain a prescription for their drugs. Increasingly these prescriptions were written by "dope doctors," licensed physicians who would for a fee provide the necessary service. During a single month one New York City doctor "wrote scrip" for 68,282 grains of heroin, 54,097 grains of morphine, and 30,280 grains of cocaine.[124] Although addicts might grumble at being gouged by the dope doctors, their only alternative was the black market. Black-market prices were up sharply, however, since unregistered dealers ran significant risks of prosecution and since it was now much more difficult to obtain sizable shipments from legitimate manufacturers.[125]

The situation deteriorated further during 1919 to 1921, in the wake of the *Webb* decision and the closure of many of the hastily organized narcotic clinics. Some addicts, particularly those in rural areas and those suffering from chronic and incurable diseases, were still able to obtain morphine on a legal or quasi-legal basis.[126] But a growing number of other users, particularly nonmedical addicts living in large cities, were forced to rely on illegal purchases.

Heroin was the illicit opiate par excellence. It spread throughout the country during the 1920s and 1930s because dealers and their customers came to appreciate its black-market virtues. From the dealer's point of view, the principal advantage was the ease with which heroin could be adulterated. Profits could be doubled or quadrupled by cutting heroin with milk sugar or a similar substance. "I have known of instances," wrote one New York official, "where the addict has paid at the rate of a dollar a grain and would get six-tenths of a grain, and many more instances where he would be sold nothing but pure sugar of milk."[127] By 1938 heroin sold in the United States was on average only 27.5 percent pure—very potent by today's standards, but considered highly diluted by a generation of addicts accustomed to purer drugs.[128] The fact that heroin, prior to adulteration, is a powerful yet compact substance also made it an ideal item for smuggling. In 1924 Congress, concerned with the youthfulness and alleged violence of heroin addicts and desiring to set an international precedent, effectively outlawed all domestic use of the drug;[129] yet even this drastic measure failed to stem the illicit traffic. "In fact," commented Narcotic Inspector Samuel L. Rakusin two years after the heroin ban, "it seems that it is more plentiful at this time than it ever was before."[130]

If dealers were eager to supply heroin, addicts were generally willing to purchase it. Heroin was, in the first place, considerably cheaper than morphine. A survey of illicit narcotic prices in fifteen major cities in 1934 showed that the wholesale price of morphine ranged from $50.00 to $150.00 per ounce, whereas heroin sold for $17.50 to $90.00. The per grain or street price of heroin was lower than that of morphine in every city where direct comparison was possible.[131] Not only was heroin less expensive, it was also stronger and faster acting than morphine when administered in a comparable manner.[132] Even though it was adulterated, heroin was "cheaper for the amount of kick in it," as one narcotic agent phrased it.[133] Finally, heroin could be injected or sniffed, the latter method appealing to new or potential users who might be needle-shy.[134]

In spite of these several advantages, the diffusion of heroin was a gradual process. Addicts, like everyone else, developed their preferences and idiosyncracies; changing to a new drug was not always casual or easy. Still, with the prospect of withdrawal before them and the price differential between morphine and heroin steadily increasing, even the most reluctant users eventually switched to the cheaper and more powerful opiate. In geographic terms, the diffusion of heroin is best described as radiation outward from New York City. By the mid-1920s growing numbers of users were observed in coastal cities running north and south of New York.[135] Heroin was also spreading westward, through Pennsylvania, Ohio, Illinois, and into the Midwest. Figure 7 maps heroin seizures for two calendar years, 1927 and 1928. The heaviest concentration was along the East Coast, from Washington, D.C., to Boston, but it can be seen that heroin use was extending through the Great Lakes region and beyond.[136] The process continued until, in 1932, the Bureau of Narcotics officially declared that "heroin has supplanted morphine to a considerable degree as the drug of addiction in every part of the United States except on the Pacific Coast."[137] That generalization was perhaps too sweeping—there were still in 1932 a great many southern morphine addicts—but on the whole the bureau had appraised the situation correctly.

Relative seizures of narcotic drugs are another index of heroin's growing importance. In fiscal 1927, 4.0 pounds of morphine for every pound of heroin were seized under federal internal revenue laws. By 1932, however, 3.4 pounds of heroin were seized for every pound of morphine, and by 1938 the heroin-to-morphine

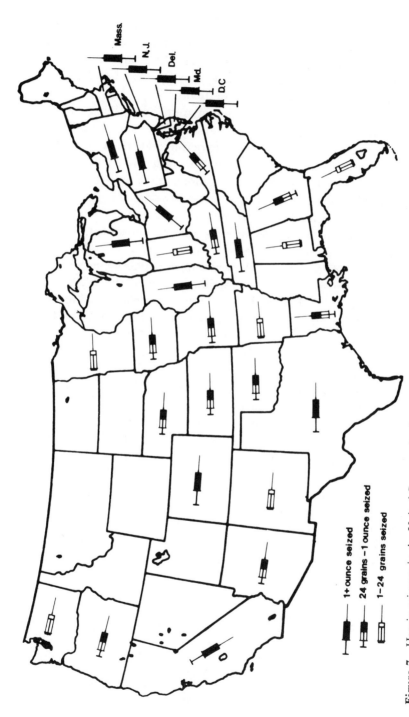

Figure 7 Heroin seizures in the United States, calendar years 1927 and 1928. Source: *Extracts from the Report of the Commissioner of Prohibition . . .*, 1927 and 1928, filed with Lawrence Kolb Papers, National Library of Medicine.

ratio[138] was 7.7 to 1. So scarce did morphine become that specialists in the pharmacology of opium alkaloids, who normally received a free supply of confiscated morphine for their experiments, began to run low. One prominent researcher, Lyndon F. Small, was warned that desperate addicts were beginning to raid legitimate supplies and that henceforth any morphine furnished for his research would be sent by Treasury Department courier, rather than through the mails.[139]

Another important development, paralleling the growing importance of heroin as a black-market opiate, was the diffusion of the hypodermic technique among heroin addicts. A user who had begun sniffing heroin in 1910 to 1915 would likely have been injecting it by 1920 to 1925. Continuous inhalation of heroin, particularly if taken with cocaine, seriously damages the nasal septum;[140] hence alternative routes must be sought. Addicts were also drawn to the hypodermic as a more convenient way of administering increasingly large doses and as a way of enhancing the drug's effect. The quickest and most euphorigenic route of all is the intravenous, and sometime in the early 1920s addicts learned to inject heroin directly into their veins. This technique probably began accidentally when an addict hit a vein and, after his initial fright wore off, discovered that this method was even more pleasurable than subcutaneous or intramuscular injection. He then passed this information on to his companions.[141]

Another motive for intravenous use was the steadily declining purity of street heroin during the 1930s. The official explanation for heavier adulteration was the tightening of international restrictions on heroin production in 1930 to 1932.[142] At the same time an aggressive new generation of Italian gangsters began infiltrating the drug traffic, replacing other groups, notably the Jews. The Jewish dealers had a reputation for being "businessmen," that is, they distributed a decent product, made a high but not exorbitant profit, and sought to maintain steady relations with their customers. However, they and other distributors were driven out of business through a variety of strong-arm tactics. Recalled one former Times Square dealer:

They'd find 'em in the East River if they kept selling it . . . We had a lot of kids on the East Side [killed] . . . . as soon as the wops found out that they was selling against their orders not to sell . . . They'd put you out, they wanted their man there, see, they had their man . . . They took your customer away; to get 'em, they'd say, "What does he charge ya? 10? Here, we give it to ya for 5."—You lost 'em! But the dopey bastard don't know that soon as

I'm out of business, they'll charge 'em 20 for what I give 'em for 10.[143]

Not only did the price increase, but the level of adulteration as well. "When the Chinese and the Jews had it, it was beautiful," remarked another former dealer. "But when the Italians got it—bah! They messed it all up . . . They started thinking people were just a herd of animals—just give them anything."[144] Precisely how much of this adulteration was due to growing Italian involvement and how much to new international restrictions is uncertain. It is certain, however, that many addicts, in order to derive maximum satisfaction from an increasingly diluted drug, began resorting to the most drastic and direct route of administration. As one addict, who turned to intravenous use around 1932, succinctly put it, "You didn't need no vein until they cut it." This user, described only as a white man from New York City, had a particularly interesting history, for he exemplified the changes the nonmedical opiate addict underwent in the early twentieth century. He learned to smoke opium fairly late, in 1912, at the age of 16. In 1914 he shifted briefly to oral use, then began to sniff heroin and cocaine in 1915. In 1922 he and his companions turned to subcutaneous injection, and then, 10 years later, to intravenous. The drug injected was heroin, or heroin with cocaine.[145]

The drift to the needle was in evidence as early as 1917, when Charles Stokes noted that 10 of 18 heroin patients treated at Bellevue in New York employed the hypodermic technique.[146] Of 37 heroin users examined in 1918 at Camp Upton, New York, 24 used a hypodermic, 8 sniffed the drug, and 5 used both routes.[147] A thorough study of 318 institutionalized addicts conducted in New York City in 1928-1929 showed that of 263 heroin cases, 251 used the drug subcutaneously, 11 intravenously, and 1 orally. Only 2 instances of sniffing were reported, even though sniffing was the most common manner in which the addict first used the drug.[148] A 1929 study of addicts in Philadelphia General Hospital's narcotic wards yielded similar findings: 80.0 percent of the patients used heroin prior to admission, the majority hypodermically, except for "several cases of sniffing and . . . two in which self-intravenous administration was employed."[149] The intravenous route continued to gain in popularity during the 1930s; by 1940 a majority of addicts admitted to the Lexington Hospital had a prior history of intravenous use.[150]

The transformation of the nonmedical user from opium smoker

to heroin mainliner was more than just a statistical trend, however; it was an event of incalculable physical and financial cost to the addict. Not only did he have to pay more for a drug of unknown strength and purity, but the health risks of injection — especially intravenous injection — were much greater than those involved with opium smoking. Too many addicts ended up like "Slim Wicket," an informer described in the memoirs of undercover narcotic agent Maurice Helbrant:

He shot himself every which way, in a vein sometimes, in any part of his body . . . He took his shots in my presence without any shame or modesty. It always made me wince, and still does: I never became hardened to the sight of it. He undressed for bed with equal indifference to what I saw — grimy underwear and an unwashed body (for addicts become indifferent to such things, even if they still try to keep up a decent appearance on the outside), and worse, the punctures in his skin, work of the needle, hundreds of them, some caked or festering, the skin of his upper arms literally in ribbons.[151]

Sepsis of every imaginable variety, hepatitis, endocarditis, emboli, tetanus, overdose, and early death; these were the consequences of the needle, and no small part of the damage done.[152]

Heroin addiction was originally iatrogenic in nature, the unexpected and unwanted by-product of treatment for respiratory disease. Although doctors eventually abandoned their use of the drug, it became popular after 1910 as a euphoric agent. Legal pressures on smoking opium and cocaine were important factors behind this early nonmedical use. Later, when the majority of addicts had been effectively denied access to legal opiates, heroin use spread — principally because it was the opiate most suitable for black-market distribution. In addition to a change in the geographic distribution of heroin addicts, from the New York City area to cities scattered throughout the country, there was a change in the method of administration: sniffing gave way to subcutaneous or intramuscular injection, which in turn gave way to intravenous. By 1940 the heroin mainliner had emerged as the dominant underworld addict type.

The Transformation of the Opiate Addict

5 During the nineteenth century the dominant addict type was a middle-aged, middle-class or upper-class female; the drugs most commonly used by addicts were morphine and opium; and the majority of cases were medical in origin. By 1940 the dominant addict type was a young, lower-class male; the drugs most commonly used by addicts were heroin and morphine; and the majority of cases were nonmedical in nature. The scope of this change can be described by the etymology of a single word, *junkie*. During the early 1920s a number of New York City addicts supported themselves by picking through industrial dumps for scraps of copper, lead, zinc, and iron, which they collected in a wagon and then sold to a dealer. Junkie, in its original sense, literally meant *junkman*.[1] The term was symbolically appropriate as well, since the locus of addiction had, within a single generation, shifted from the office and parlor to the desolate piles of urban debris.

The single most important cause of the transformation was the decline in iatrogenic opiate addiction. Reluctance to prescribe opiates to all but the incurably or terminally ill continued and even intensified after 1910. Conservative physicians were aided in their efforts by the passage of the Harrison Act and analogous state and local measures that tightened controls on opiates and made unauthorized prescription refill more difficult. Demographic forces were also at play, as the ranks of older and less conservative practitioners were thinned by death and retirement. Iatrogenic addicts, the bulk of them addicted in middle age between 1860 and 1895, were also aging. Moreover, addicts created by doctors after 1910 tended to die quickly, as they often suffered from terminal diseases such as cancer or advanced tuberculosis. Iatrogenic addicts thus were disappearing faster than they were being created, so that there ensued an absolute decline in their number and a sharp drop in their per capita rate. The same was true of those who became addicted through self-medication; fewer and fewer such addicts were in evidence, especially after the 1906 Pure Food and Drug Act exposed the contents of narcotic nostrums and drove many of them off the market. At the same time the number of nonmedical addicts was increasing relative to the total number of opiate addicts. Although the number of opium smokers dropped in the early twentieth century, new users, notably of heroin or morphine, were recruited to take their places. Many former opium smokers also continued as active opiate addicts, using a different form of the drug. As a result there was no marked reduction in the number of nonmedical addicts between 1895 and 1915 comparable to the decrease in medical addicts. After 1915 the number of nonmedical addicts continued to increase relative to the total, because of the progressive die-off of medical addicts and the continued recruitment of young users, especially in the slum areas of large cities.

Figure 8 illustrates this transformation. It is a heuristic device only, and the size of the areas represented should not be taken to correspond to exact numbers of addicts. In the late nineteenth century medical addicts (outer circle), defined as those who could trace their condition to a doctor's medication or self-medication with opiates, outnumbered nonmedical addicts (inner circle) by at least two to one, and probably more.[2] Medical addicts used opium and morphine; nonmedical addicts — those who began using opiates through curiosity, peer pressure, or bravado — were mainly opium smokers. By 1915, however, new patterns of nonmedical use had evolved, notably heroin in eastern cities and morphine (or morphine with cocaine) elsewhere. Only the Chinese and a few relatively wealthy whites remained steadfast opium smokers. Meanwhile the total number of opiate addicts had declined, with the result that nonmedical users made up a proportionately larger share. Graphically, Figure 8 begins to resemble an imploding star. The trend continued through the

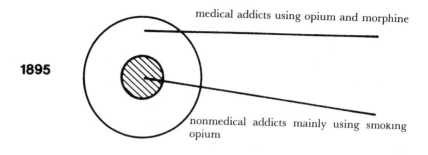

1895

medical addicts using opium and morphine

nonmedical addicts mainly using smoking opium

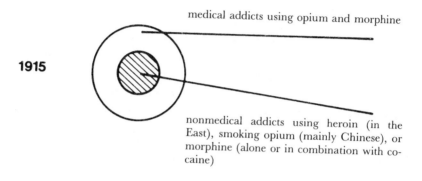

1915

medical addicts using opium and morphine

nonmedical addicts using heroin (in the East), smoking opium (mainly Chinese), or morphine (alone or in combination with cocaine)

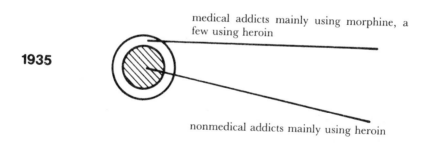

1935

medical addicts mainly using morphine, a few using heroin

nonmedical addicts mainly using heroin

Figure 8 Schematic representation of the transformation. Designated areas do not represent exact numbers of opiate addicts.

1920s and 1930s, as the generation of medical addicts created between 1860 and 1895 succumbed to old age. "The proportion of the delinquent type of addict is gradually increasing," summed up Lawrence Kolb and Andrew DuMez in 1924. "This is apparently not due to an increase in the number of this type, but to a gradual elimination of normal [medical] types."[3] At the same time, heroin, owing to its black-market virtues, was replacing smoking opium and morphine as the underworld opiate of choice.

The assumption, made explicit in Figure 8, that the number of nonmedical addicts remained constant during the 1920s and 1930s requires some explanation. I do not mean to imply that the number of nonmedical addicts remained absolutely fixed from year to year. There were definite fluctuations, with peak usage in 1921, 1928–1929, and 1934–1935. It is as though the core of the imploding star was pulsating, expanding and contracting in roughly seven-year cycles. However, this pattern did not persist indefinitely; there was an especially sharp drop in the number of nonmedical addicts during the early 1940s, just at the point in the cycle when an upswing would have been expected. The disruptive force was World War II, which had the twin effects of siphoning susceptible youths into the armed forces and abruptly cutting international smuggling routes. The supply situation became so tight that many addicts were reduced to injecting boiled-down paregoric or rifling medical supplies. Adulteration of opiates, especially heroin, reached an all-time high. In some parts of the country illicit opiates were simply not available.[4]

Figure 9A is a simplified representation of these events. The

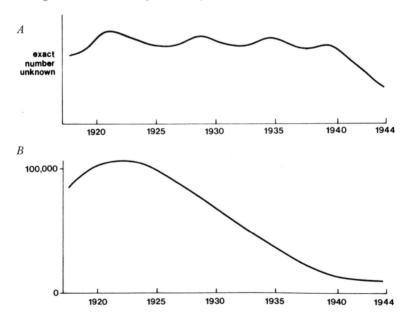

Figure 9 Prevalence of nonmedical addiction between 1917 and 1944. *A,* hypothesized; *B,* according to the Bureau of Narcotics.

effect of the periodic epidemics was not cumulative, that is, the prevalence curve did not undulate steadily upward, because of the high mortality of this type of user.[5] Figure 10, which plots federal and nonfederal narcotic prosecutions over time, corresponds to the hypothetical prevalence curve. The number of federal cases was down during the 1930s, but this coincided with a Depression-related cut in the budget and staff of the Bureau of Narcotics.[6] State and local cases increased during the same period, so the overall level of prosecution remained high. The first marked upswing in prosecutions, from 1921 to 1925, was related to an increase in the number of narcotic agents and other administrative improvements[7] and may therefore be regarded as artificial. It is more difficult to account for the increased prosecutions from 1928 to 1930 and again from 1934 to 1936, unless this activity reflected,

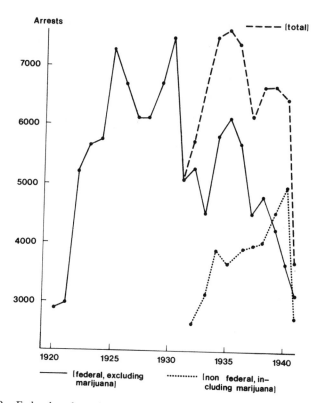

Figure 10　Federal and nonfederal narcotic prosecutions, 1920 to 1941. Nonfederal marijuana cases averaged no more than 10 to 15 percent of the total. Because of changes in reporting procedures and because the method of estimation was not made explicit, these data should be regarded as approximations only, not as exact totals. Source: Alfred R. Lindesmith, *The Addict and the Law* (Bloomington: Indiana University Press, 1965), 106–107.

with a slight allowance for lag, peaks in the epidemic cycle. It appears from the prosecution data that another peak was building, but was cut short by the war.

The idea of cyclic upswings is also supported by incidence data. (Incidence, as opposed to prevalence or total number, is a measure of new cases occurring during a certain time.) Figure 11 displays the year of onset of 76 cases of nonmedical addiction studied by Kolb in 1923. Although new cases were down somewhat in 1920, the general impression is that of an epidemic following the war, peaking in 1921. Thereafter new cases began to drop off, although not as quickly as it might at first seem, since there is a time lag built into all treatment data and recently created addicts are the least likely to be observed.[8] In New York City, among 318 nonmedical addicts treated in Bellevue Hospital in 1928-1929, 11 patients were listed as addicted for four years, 13 for three years, 16 for two years, and 19 for one year, statistics that point to a second peak at the close of the decade.[9] At the U.S. Public Health Service Hospital in Lexington, Kentucky, a study of the clinical records of 1,036 addicts admitted during fiscal 1937 showed that the modal length of addiction was two to three years, suggesting a third upswing in 1934–1935.[10] Finally, studies of heroin epidemics in our own time have also indicated a seven-year cycle, that being the calculated length of time required to expose all susceptibles within a community.[11] When demobilized soldiers scattered to cities throughout the country after World War I, they were the tinder for local outbreaks, which got under way at more or less the same time. The cycle went on repeating until World War II disrupted supplies and drew young men back out of the cities.[12]

It is interesting to note that seven-year cycles are observable in the Kolb data (Figure 11) even before World War I, with peaks in 1906 and again in 1912-1913.[13] The latter outbreak, in which

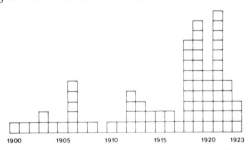

Figure 11 Onset of addiction for 76 cases of nonmedical addiction studied by Lawrence Kolb in 1923. Source: MS records, box 6, Lawrence Kolb Papers, National Library of Medicine.

118

heroin sniffing figured prominently, would also explain why the iatrogenic heroin addict was eclipsed so quickly after 1912. The idea of cyclic epidemics should not be pushed too far, however; opiate addiction is not the measles, and it would be naive to suppose that its pattern is completely regular and predictable. The important point is that in spite of periodic fluctuations, there was no pronounced decline in the long-term trend of nonmedical opiate addiction prior to September 1939.

Highly placed Treasury Department officials denied all of this, however, and took the position that both medical addiction and nonmedical addiction were steadily diminishing during the 1920s and 1930s. If the problem of lawmakers and government attorneys before 1919 was to play up the extent of addiction to secure more stringent legislation and rulings, the problem of bureaucrats after 1919 was just the opposite: they needed to show that the stringent laws and rulings had worked. The official stance was that there had been a temporary increase in nonmedical addiction during the early 1920s, but that the numbers of this type of addict thereafter began a sustained decline (Figure 9B). The evidence for this decline comprised, first, a 1926 survey which showed that the average age of nonmedical addicts known to field personnel was 34 years for men and 30 for women. One possible explanation, propounded by Narcotic Division Head Levi Nutt, was that nonmedical addicts were aging without being replaced. "The present [average age] of addicts," he concluded, "is evidence that few, if any, new recruits are now being made."[14] The same survey that produced this heartening news showed that there were about 91,000 nonmedical addicts in 1926, down from 106,000 in 1924. The decline continued; a second survey undertaken by the Bureau of Narcotics in 1938 indicated that there were less than 20,000 nonmedical addicts nationwide. Finally, bureau officials noted that during World War II only one of every 10,000 registrants examined at local selective service boards and induction centers was rejected for drug addiction. That rate, which extrapolated to a national total of no more than 14,000 addicts, seemed to clinch the argument that two decades of strict enforcement had nearly eradicated nonmedical addiction.

It was not so. Through a Freedom of Information Act request, I have been able to gain access to internal Treasury Department correspondence on the extent of addiction and to examine closely the methods and assumptions that went into these studies. In 1926 the Narcotic Division ordered its fifteen field supervisory officers to conduct a survey, method unspecified, and to provide an estimate of the number of addicts in their districts for the years 1924 and 1926. The final tabulation showed 106,025 addicts (0.93 per thousand) in 1924 and 91,245 (0.78 per thousand) in 1926.[15] The addicts enumerated were "considered almost entirely as non-medical cases in the sense that most of them were not obtaining their narcotic drugs directly or indirectly from a physician."[16] The phrase "most of them" was not elaborated. This definition, moreover, would have included an unknown number of bona fide but unlucky medical addicts who had lost their doctor connections and were forced to traffic with peddlers. Worse, some respondents either confused or ignored the distinction; otherwise it is hard to explain how states like Virginia and North Carolina managed to report the same number of nonmedical addicts for 1924 as did California. The disappearance of 14,780 users between 1924 and 1926 is also problematic—unless, of course, the sample contained sick and aging medical addicts. The possibility that the field officers fabricated the decline cannot be ruled out, since any decrease in the number of addicts reflected favorably on their work and since the Narcotic Division itself made no attempt to audit the results.

The likely inclusion of medical addicts also helps to explain why Nutt observed an average age between 30 and 34 years. Even if the reported users had consisted entirely in nonmedical addicts, this statistic would not of itself prove an end to recruitment. Average age at time of observation, which usually means age at last arrest or treatment, will always be higher than age at onset of addiction. Not only are younger users the least likely to be detected,[17] but their presence in a given sample will be balanced by older users who have been arrested or treated any number of times before—hence the higher average age. Incidence is the best index of recruitment, and several independent studies documented the continuing creation of addicts throughout the 1920s and 1930s. It is true, as Treasury Department officials insisted, that these new addicts were not usually teenagers;[18] gone were the days when decks of heroin were passed around clubhouses and dance halls like so many packages of cigarettes. But there were still many young males, usually in their twenties, who were introduced to opiates by their peers and who subsequently became addicted. From Figure 11 the average age of the 26 users addicted during or after 1920 was 22 years, 9 months, almost identical to the beginning age for the pre-1920 cases. The average age for all 76 cases *at time of treatment* was just under 30 years. The fact that 37.6 percent of these patients were addicted during the period

1920 to 1923 casts further doubt on Nutt's claim that few if any new addicts were being created. The increased incidence of addiction in New York City during 1928–1929 has already been noted; at Lexington, slightly over half of the patients admitted during fiscal 1937 had been addicted for less than ten years, over a quarter less than five years.[19] In Chicago sociologist Bingham Dai found that over a third of approximately 2,500 cases collected during 1928 to 1934 had been addicted for less than five years. Although he did not break down his data by year of onset, he thought that the number of recent recruits offered sufficient ground to reject the view, held by some, that opiate addiction was waning in Chicago. Instead, the continued appearance of new, mainly nonmedical cases raised in his mind "the important problem as to how far prohibitive measures could be relied upon as a means of preventing people from using narcotic drugs."[20]

Dissatisfaction with the 1926 survey — Bureau of Narcotics Commissioner Harry J. Anslinger himself privately admitted its inaccuracy[21] — coupled with a League of Nations request for current information on the extent of addiction in the United States, prompted a second survey in 1938. The league's request was communicated to the bureau by Assistant Secretary of the Treasury Stephen B. Gibbons, who was openly critical of the earlier estimate of approximately 100,000 addicts ("absolutely worthless," he called it) and who was convinced in advance that there had been a marked reduction in the extent of addiction.[22] It was clear to Anslinger and his staff that a reported decline would placate Gibbons, vindicate the bureau's performance, enhance American prestige in the eyes of the league, and underscore the effectiveness of American narcotic policies. There were, in short, powerful temptations to shade the results downward.

There were also serious methodological problems with the survey, the aim of which was to arrive at an estimate of strictly nonmedical addicts based on federal, state, and local records from selected areas. The final estimate of 19,885 addicts in 1938 (0.15 per thousand) was based on information received from fifteen states: Connecticut, Delaware, the District of Columbia, Georgia, Indiana, Kentucky, Michigan, Minnesota, Mississippi, Nevada, New York (excluding New York City), North Carolina, Oklahoma, Utah, and Washington. Conspicuously absent were data from California, Hawaii, Illinois, Pennsylvania, and, with the exception of Michigan, any large northern industrial states — that is, precisely those areas likely to have relatively large numbers of nonmedical addicts. The omission of New York City was especially questionable, since it had long been flooded with relatively cheap and abundant drugs[23] and had experienced an inordinately high rate of nonmedical addiction.

Within the bureau the findings were greeted, in some quarters, with surprise and disbelief. Undercover agent Maurice Helbrant was openly skeptical; in his opinion the bureau failed "to take into account the vast army of drug users of all kinds who live and die without ever appearing, as addicts, on any statistical lists."[24] Although he would later make use of it for public relations purposes, Anslinger too initially had reservations about the 1938 survey. Confronted with the preliminary returns, he concluded that there were "roughly about 35,000 and not more than 50,000 non-medical addicts in this country."[25] Barring an error in arithmetic, Anslinger was hedging, factoring in unrecorded addicts according to some intuitive formula. Perhaps he had in mind a recent memorandum from Alfred L. Tennyson, the bureau's legal counsel. Tennyson pointed out to Anslinger that the level of narcotic prosecutions, including both federal and independently made state cases, had not dropped appreciably; he suggested, very diplomatically, that the new survey was in error. "If," he wrote, "it is true . . . that the number of cases tried remains almost constant, and if it is true (as I believe it is) that most of these were peddler or conspiracy cases, it would seem that it took just as many peddlers to serve the addict trade in 1936 as it did in 1926 when the last estimate was made."[26] One has only to glance back at Figure 10 to see the thrust of Tennyson's argument; the level of federal and nonfederal prosecutions remained generally high throughout the 1920s and 1930s.

If the survey findings were unconvincing, the use of draft data was even more so. In his widely circulated 1953 book, *The Traffic in Narcotics* (coauthored with William F. Tompkins, former chairman of the New Jersey Legislative Committee on Narcotics), Anslinger argued that "roughly 1 man in 10,000 selective service registrants examined for military duty during World War II was rejected primarily because of drug addiction. This was a reliable indication of an impressive decrease . . . in comparison with World War I figures, when there [was] 1 man in 1,500."[27] The source of this information was a letter dated September 28, 1945, from Army Medical Statistics Division Director Harold F. Dorn. Contrary to Anslinger's statement, Dorn did not base the rejection rate on all draftees examined—only on those examined during 1944, other data being unavailable. This is significant, since by 1944 the country had been virtually without illicit narcotics for four years and the rate would naturally be low. Dorn, a distinguished epidemiologist who was among the first to note the correlation between smoking and lung cancer, also qualified his report carefully. "No information is available," he wrote, "as to the number of drug users (not addicts) who were found acceptable for service and inducted or who were rejected for other reasons. Moreover, some drug users and drug addicts undoubtedly escaped detection."[28]

Many, he might have added, were never examined in the first place. Felons were automatically and *without physical examination* placed in category IV-F, and of course by 1940 the overwhelming majority of male opiate addicts were both de jure and de facto felons. Some addicts were undoubtedly overlooked during 1917–1918 for similar reasons; the 1917 *Selective Service Regulations* disqualified anyone convicted of treason, felony, or an infamous crime. Still, there would have been proportionately fewer addicts rejected before examination: the *Webb* decision had not yet effectively cut off legal and relatively cheaper medical supplies; there were then more male medical addicts without criminal records; and many of the first-generation heroin sniffers were essentially youthful delinquents rather than harassed and hardened criminals.[29] Draft rejection ratios of 1917–1918 and 1944 are by no means directly comparable.

The weakness of the draft and survey data, the evidence of continued recruitment, and the generally high level of federal and nonfederal prosecutions throughout the 1920s and 1930s together make it impossible to infer any pronounced decline in the number of nonmedical addicts prior to 1940.[30] If Nutt and Anslinger had been more modest in their claims, if they had simply stated that prices were high and drugs were scarce, that teenage addicts were few, and that during a decade of unexcelled hedonism followed by a decade of unparalleled anxiety, strict enforcement had at least prevented an increase in nonmedical addiction, they would have been closer to the truth. Modest achievements, however, are not necessarily the best ways to justify bureaucratic performance. Moreover, it was easy to persuade Congress and the public of their case, since the overall rate of opiate addiction was then declining sharply. Medical addicts were dying off and the population as a whole was increasing: the imploding star was shrinking relative to an expanding universe. This fact proved a useful source of confusion for (and perhaps to) narcotic officials; when confronted with an undoubted and massive decrease in one major type of addiction, it was naturally easier to accept an across-the-board decline.[31]

Changes in the proportion of medical to nonmedical cases also meant changes in the sex, class, age, and geographic distribution of addicts. New Haven Police Chief Phillip T. Smith was among the first to notice this trend. Speaking before the 1914 meeting of the International Association of Chiefs of Police, he remarked, "Like everything else the style changes in drugs, and while years ago . . . [addicts] used opium, cocaine and morphine, usually acquiring the habit from having had these drugs prescribed for them during sickness, . . . nowadays drugs have become a regular diet with harlots and their pimps, and criminally inclined persons of all kinds."[32] Physicians practicing in large cities also were apt to comment on the changing pattern. Philadelphia neurologist Francis X. Dercum observed that the transformation was in evidence well before the Harrison Act, and that its essential characteristic was a marked diminution in the number of upper-class and middle-class addicts. These types were disappearing, he explained, because physicians had become much more conservative in their use of opiates, especially injections of morphine.[33] The time had passed when, in the words of one physician, "the plunger in our hypodermic syringe was never allowed to become dry from disuse."[34] The proportion of nonmedical addicts thus was increasing steadily; in New York City they constituted a clear majority as early as 1917.[35] In Chicago, too, the trend was unmistakable; Charles E. Sceleth and Sidney Kuh, looking back over the more than 5,000 cases they had treated from 1904 to 1924, remarked:

Fifteen or twenty years ago, most addicts acquired the habit through physical disease or discomfort. Today the number of new addictions through physicians' prescriptions is small. The great majority of cases now result from association with other addicts, following their advice in taking a "shot" or a "sniff" for "what ails you" and searching for new sensations. These are the pleasure users.[36]

The "pleasure users" were predominantly male, urban, and poor. It is noteworthy, however, that physicians and law enforcement officials who commented on this emerging type did not implicate or usually even mention blacks, a large and impoverished urban minority group widely associated with opiate addiction after 1945. The rate of opiate addiction among blacks, particularly those who had recently migrated to northern and western cities, increased during the 1920s and 1930s, but from a low initial level. In 1923 only 4.5 percent of Kolb's patients, described as representing a national cross section, were listed as black.[37] An investigation of

946 addicts known to the Bureau of Narcotics in 1935, however, showed a racial breakdown of 78 black, 88 Oriental, 3 American Indian, and 775 white, or a black share of 8.2 percent.[38] Other studies undertaken during 1929 to 1935 showed that 13.5 to 14.5 percent of all arrests for violations of federal narcotic laws involved blacks.[39] Racial prejudice may have inflated the arrest figures, but other independent studies confirmed the trend. Dai, for example, found that 17.3 percent of his sample was black, even though blacks made up only 6.9 percent of Chicago's 1930 population.[40] In absolute numbers, though, blacks were still in the minority—which is probably why officials persisted in thinking of the modal addict type as white.

Another significant feature of the transformation was that it did not proceed at the same pace in all parts of the country. In Iowa, a rural state largely untroubled by opium smokers and heroin sniffers, medical causes still accounted for the majority of opiate addicts in 1919,[41] and probably for some years thereafter. The same was true of the South,[42] although changes in the background of addicts from that region gradually became apparent in the 1920s and 1930s. John A. O'Donnell, in a study of narcotic addiction in Kentucky, noted that from 1914 to 1940 new cases of addiction were most common among males who took opiates for pleasure or as a means of sobering up after alcoholic sprees. Morphine remained the opiate of choice, principally because it could still be obtained, at least in Kentucky, from physicians.[43] Michael J. Pescor's study of addicts admitted to the Lexington Hospital during fiscal 1937 revealed a similar pattern. The patients, among whom Southerners were heavily overrepresented,[44] were for the most part younger men addicted as a consequence of curiosity and association with other users. Relief of hangover, as well as treatment or self-treatment of veneral disease, were other factors. A bare majority (50.7 percent) still used morphine,[45] a preference that reflects the southern bias of the sample.

Regional differences aside, at what point in time did the non-medical user emerge as the dominant type of American opiate addict? No definite answer can be given, but there is one suggestive study. Walter L. Treadway examined the records of 1,660 addicts reported for violation of the drug laws nationwide between July 1 and October 31, 1929. He found 563 cases deriving from the treatment or self-treatment of disease or emotional distress, 713 deriving from association or curiosity, 10 from relief of drunkenness, and 374 of unknown origin.[46] These figures would seem to indicate that by 1929 the national tipping point had been reached.[47]

In another sense, nonmedical addicts need not have constituted an absolute majority to give the impression that they had become the dominant type. Upper-class and middle-class medical addicts, particularly if they were supplied by a physician, were extremely secretive about their condition. Nonmedical users, while they did not advertise their plight to those outside the addict subculture, nevertheless were more likely to be observed in jails, public treatment centers, or clinic lines. Addicts queued up to register for the New York City clinic, for example, were regularly harassed by sightseeing buses, replete with gawking tourists and blaring megaphones.[48] "The only [ones] the general public knew anything about," complained Willis Butler, "were the riffraff, street addicts, and bums."[49] But appearances have a kind of reality, and it would be fair to say that, even in advance of the actual emergence of a nonmedical majority, a growing number of laymen and physicians perceived opiate addiction as essentially an underworld phenomenon.

Impact of the Transformation on Medical Theory and Practice

The actual and apparent changes in the characteristics of the addict population had important consequences for the medical profession's conception and treatment of opiate addiction. As the nonmedical addict emerged as the dominant type, an increasing number of physicians and public health officials came to view addiction as a manifestation of psychopathy or some other serious personality disorder, to support mandatory institutionalization of addicts, and to refuse to supply addicts (especially the nonmedical type) with drugs.

Prior to 1870 the prevailing view of opiate addiction was as a vice, a bad habit indulged in by weak-willed and sinful but otherwise normal persons. Although many addicts were first given an opiate in the course of an illness, they continued taking the drug, in the words of Methodist minister J. Townley Crane, because "they learned to love the excitement which it produces."[50] Addiction was thus a proper object of moral opprobrium. This attitude was opposed by a growing group of physicians who believed that opiate addiction was a species of a more general condition called *inebriety,* and that inebriety was a functional disease triggered by an underlying mental disturbance. The American Association for the Cure of Inebriates (established in 1870) and its official organ, the *Quarterly Journal of Inebriety,* provided a forum for these reformers, and a means of popularizing their views.[51]

The inebriety movement was influenced by two important nineteenth-century psychological theories, degeneration and neurasthenia. Degeneration, as the concept was originally developed by Benedict Augustin Morel in his 1857 *Traité des Dégénérescences Physiques, Intellectuelles et Morales de l'Espèce Humaine,* was a morbid deviation from the normal human type, transmissible by heredity and subject to progressive deterioration across generations. The first generation of an affected family might be nervous, the second neurotic, the third psychotic, the fourth idiotic, and so forth unto extinction. Environmental factors, among which Morel listed opium and alcohol, might be responsible for the original degeneration, but "hereditary predisposition" was equally important and served to explain how apparently unrelated nervous disorders, such as tic douloureux in the father and schizoid personality in the son, might be observed in the same family.[52] The interplay of environment and heredity was also central to neurasthenia, a concept described by George Miller Beard in 1869. Beard held that neurasthenia (literally, nervous weakness) was responsible for a variety of psychic and somatic ills from hysteria to hay fever. Those who had inherited an inadequate nervous system — the "nervous diathesis," corresponding to Morel's hereditary predisposition — were especially prone, but environmental influences played a role too. In particular, "brain workers," entrepreneurs, and others caught up in the hectic pace of industrial civilization were most likely to overtax their nervous systems.[53] Exhausted nerves in turn meant a greater susceptibility to opiate addiction.

Although Beard himself mentioned the connection between neurasthenia and addiction,[54] it fell to others to elaborate this aspect of his theory and to enshrine it in the canon of the inebriety movement. Thomas Crothers, editor of the *Quarterly Journal of Inebriety,* and Albert E. Sterne, an Indianapolis physician experienced in treating addiction, were representative of those who espoused the degeneration/neurasthenia thesis in its mature form. Crothers, in his influential 1902 treatise, *Morphinism and Narcomanias from Other Drugs,* argued that those who took morphine to relieve pain received a pathologic impression, the intensity and permanency of which varied with the individual. If the patient had inherited a neurotic tendency or predisposition to seek relief from every pain and discomfort or if he suffered from neurasthenia or some other nervous ailment, the pathologic impression was likely to be "more or less permanent," and repeated administration would intensify the impression into a morbid craving. Once the morbid craving or addiction was established, succeeding generations were especially vulnerable to inebriety. To illustrate the point, Crothers related the story of a Civil War soldier who became an opium addict because of a painful arm wound. He subsequently married, had two children, and managed until his death to conceal his addiction from his family. Nonetheless, his daughter became addicted to morphine following pregnancy and his son to morphine following a bout with drinking.[55]

Sterne, in a 1904 paper read before the Section on Nervous and Mental Diseases of the American Medical Association, noted the importance of heredity, reminding his audience of the "well-known fact that the progeny . . . develop the tendencies of ancestry to an augmented degree." He also called attention to the increased prevalence of alcoholism and drug use in the higher social strata. It was not that the wealthy and respectable were necessarily endowed with weaker nervous constitutions, but that the unending struggle for professional and social success drained them of what reserves they had. As a result, growing numbers were turning to drugs and alcohol to shore up their failing mental powers, with disastrous results for themselves and their class.[56]

The concepts of degeneration and neurasthenia dominated thinking about the etiology of opiate addiction from roughly 1880 to 1915. Lamarckian ideas were in the air, and it seemed plausible that a tendency to inebriety, like brown eyes or black hair, might be transmitted from generation to generation. Moreover, the terms of the hypothesis permitted easy proof, since an observer could always find some disease, habit, or peccadillo that tainted the ancestry of the addict in question. The discovery of a generalized and inherited nervous weakness, exacerbated by unavoidable environmental stresses, also provided a subtle means of defusing the intense guilt many addicts felt about their condition: nervous diathesis was a more respectable diagnosis than vice or sin.[57] Above all, the view that addiction was symptomatic of a mental disturbance, especialy when couched in terms of neurasthenia, seemed to explain certain observed characteristics of the addict population. Were not the majority of morphine addicts from the upper and middle classes, that is, those classes subjected to the greatest nervous strain? Did not brain workers, especially physicians, suffer an inordinately high rate of addiction? Blacks, on the other hand, had a low incidence of addiction because they lacked the "delicate nervous organization" of whites.[58] Moreover, many cases of addiction began in the course of treatment for a particular nervous disorder such as neuralgia, which, as Beard had taught, was but a physical manifestation of nervous exhaustion. The increase in the rate of addiction throughout the nineteenth century (or, if Hamilton Wright was to be believed, throughout the early twentieth as well) was readily explainable, given the accelerating tempo of American life and the simultaneous tendency for growing numbers of inebriates to pass on their weaknesses to their children.

Even this seemingly impressive fit between data and theory was not enough to persuade some physicians. Although they shared the essential belief that opiate addiction was a disease, they rejected the view that it was related to degeneration or neurasthenia. Two diverging lines of dissent were especially important. The first, pioneered by Jansen Mattison and later extended by Charles Terry, held that opiate addicts were basically normal personalities addicted iatrogenically. The second and diametrically opposed argument, ultimately associated with the work of Lawrence Kolb, held that addiction was most often a manifestation of psychopathy. When the degeneration/neurasthenia theory was largely abandoned after 1915, these two schools were left to dispute the role of personality in the addiction process.

The tenets of the first position were summarized by a Cleveland physician named Austin J. Pressey, who was present when Sterne read his paper on addiction and nervous weakness. Rising from the audience to launch a vigorous counterattack, Pressey denied that addicts were necessarily degenerates or neurasthenics and stated that most of the addicted patients who came under his care were born of parents of average health who manifested no traces of inebriety. The origin of their condition was instead the prolonged treatment of painful symptoms with opiates. "Persons only get . . . morphinism from morphine," was his pointed conclusion.[59] In making this critique, Pressey was echoing the opinions of Mattison, an early supporter of the inebriety movement who completely rethought his position on etiology during the 1880s and 1890s. In his early work he flirted with the idea of diathesis but, impressed with the extent of iatrogenic addiction in both the United States and abroad, he finally insisted that "morphinism is possible under any condition. I do not believe the person lives who, under certain conditions, can stand up against the power of morphine."[60] Mattison always believed that opiate addiction was a disease—he once publicly rebuked a physician who resurrected the old vice notion[61] — but rejected the assumption that it was rooted in personality disorder or some vague hereditary mental disturbance.

This was also the position of Terry, whose views on iatrogenic addiction, especially heroin addiction, have already been set forth. Small, wiry, and mustachioed, Terry was a remarkably energetic man, a nonstop public health reformer who regarded the human condition as something of a personal affront. Some idea of his determination can be gleaned from the fact that, during his seven years as Jacksonville's health officer, the infant mortality rate in that city dropped from 186.5 to just over 75 per thousand live births.[62] His thinking on opiate addiction, consistent with his lifelong goal of preventing disease and alleviating unnecessary suffering, was also shaped by his Jacksonville experiences. He observed, first, that detoxification seldom effected a permanent cure and that it was sometimes highly dangerous; he felt personally responsible for the deaths of an indigent woman and two physically dependent infants whose withdrawal he had either ordered or attempted. He also noted that many of the addicts he registered were physically ill persons addicted by careless physicians, and that underworld users were in a decided minority.[63] Far from being abnormal or defective, most addicts were blameless and pathetically misunderstood persons:

The psychology of the drug addict is the psychology of the average human being. It is the psychology of you and me when in pain, of you and me when desiring relief, of you and me when either of us finds himself incapacitated and quite innocently in a situation he has been taught to believe is degrading. It is the psychology of self-defense, of self-protection, and it is the psychology arising from persecution, intolerance and ignorance. It is the psychology engendered by the attitude of the man who has not suffered and who, without imaginative faculties or scientific knowledge, tries to explain the mental state of others. It is the psychology of the fear of death in one who knows what will avert his end. It is no less natural, this mental state, no more morbid than the psychology which prompts a thirsty man to drink, a hungry man to eat, a ravished woman to defend herself, an oppressed people to wage war.[64]

Terry concluded that addiction was a physical disease, a widespread and potentially fatal condition that might be checked through diligent efforts at prevention and through further scientific research, but for which no cure was currently available. The best course was therefore maintenance, until more effective treatment was discovered.

A somewhat different, though largely compatible, approach was taken by Willis Butler, whose Shreveport clinic Terry visited and greatly admired.[65] A pathologist by training, Butler's attention was drawn to the fact that most addicts suffered from a serious illness, such as syphilis or tuberculosis. Whether or not that was the precipitating cause of the addiction, something had to be done in the way of treatment; otherwise the detoxified addict was bound to relapse immediately. So addicts registered at Butler's clinic were divided into two categories: the incurables, mainly old and bedridden patients who were to be maintained indefinitely; and the curables, to be withdrawn from opiates as soon as any attendant illnesses were cleared up. Implicit in this approach was the concept that addiction was essentially a continuing response to pain, and only if the source of pain were removed did the addict stand a decent chance at abstinence. As a clinician Butler was little taken with abstract theories of predisposition; what he saw were men and women from all strata of society who injected morphine to alleviate their grief and pain. "No matter what different persons may call the condition," he wrote in 1921, "the patient is a sick person, and as such is entitled to and should have proper consideration, care, and treatment, either for the causes that are responsible for him being an addict, or for the addiction itself."[66]

If, as Mattison, Terry, and Butler believed, addiction was a disease of psychologically normal and usually blameless persons, precisely what sort of disease was it? What was its pathology, and how was it related to the phenomena of tolerance and withdrawal symptoms? Some answers to these questions seemed to be forthcoming during the decade 1910 to 1920, through the research of Ernest S. Bishop, George Pettey, and others. The antitoxin theory of Bishop, an eccentric New York City internist prone to monomania on the subject of addiction, was especially widely discussed. The origin of and initially favorable reaction to his work is best understood in the larger context of early-twentieth-century medical research, when the germ theory of disease held almost complete sway. It was an age when the American epidemiologist Joseph Goldberger had to administer to himself, his wife, and his colleagues the excreta of pellagrous patients to prove to skeptics that pellagra was not communicable, so strong was the presumption that any disease was of microbial origin.[67]

In this atmosphere Bishop popularized a seemingly powerful analogy between opiate addiction and the immune response. Drawing on the work of Carlo Gioffredi, Leo Hirschlaff, and other European researchers, Bishop postulated that the introduction of morphine into the body stimulated the production of antitoxins, just as bacteria brought forth specific antibodies. This explained the phenomenon of tolerance; addicts could withstand doses of opiates fatal to a dozen normal persons because they had built up a reserve of this antidotal substance. Full-blown addiction was defined as the point at which the manufacture of antitoxins was continuous, "an established pseudo-physiologic body-process." Unfortunately, these antitoxins had the Hyde-like property of turning toxic in the absence of fresh injections of morphine; they were really "toxic antidotal substances." This accounted for the occurrence of withdrawal symptoms. Finally, the antitoxin-turned-toxin lingered in the system for some time, which helped to explain the tendency to relapse. Two important conclusions followed: addicts were genuinely sick persons who ought not be denied the one substance, morphine, that could prevent a serious toxic reaction; and addiction was a disease that anyone, regardless of personality or heredity, could contract.[68]

These sentiments matched Terry's exactly, and it is not coincidental that he was an early supporter of Bishop's work.[69] In addition to the antitoxin thesis, George Pettey devised an autotoxin theory that gained some backing. Pettey, a Memphis addiction specialist who was among the first to sound the warning on heroin, hypothesized that opiates produced toxins of autogenous and intestinal origin. Increasing doses of morphine were required to offset these toxins, otherwise extreme irritation of nervous tissue and withdrawal symptoms ensued.[70] The implication again was that addiction was strictly a physiological disorder, and it seemed by 1920 that there were sound scientific reasons for rejecting the notion that addicts were in any way abnormal.

Within ten years this view was almost entirely discredited. During the 1920s and 1930s a variety of personality theories proliferated, none of which lent themselves to so benign an interpretation as normal persons addicted accidentally. Some of the new formulations were expressly Freudian,[71] but the more usual diagnosis was one of psychopathic personality. The term *psychopathic personality* was distressingly vague (one authority has called it a "psychiatric wastebasket"[72]) but some attempt can be made to winnow out its essential elements. During the early twentieth century a German term, *psychopathische Persönlichkeit,* was grafted to an older English concept called *moral insanity.* This phrase, coined by the Bristol physician James C. Prichard in 1835, described a state in which the moral faculty alone was disrupted or atrophied, the affected person retaining his reason but not the capacity to conduct himself "with decency and propriety in the business of life." Serious criminal acts, such as theft, sexual perversion, or murder, might be committed with blithe indifference, even though the morally insane or psychopathic patient was perfectly cognizant of the codes he was transgressing. It was widely regarded as an intractable and dangerous condition; upon release the patient could be expected to do the same or worse, no matter how many lectures he endured or how much punishment society meted out. The psychopath, though not overtly insane, was thus a stubborn and wholly irresponsible individual, completely unaffected by accepted moral and legal standards.[73]

The nonmedical opiate addict qualified on every count. Often from a criminal or delinquent background, his addiction was initiated in irresponsible and hedonic quest ("these are the *pleasure users*") and pursued, in spite of escalating legal pressure, continuously and without regard for his own well-being or that of society. Repeated relapse, an aspect of the problem that had baffled and frustrated physicians for generations, was explained as a function of the underlying personality disorder. The addict was still regarded as a mentally disturbed person, but not in the manner of the inebriety theorists, whose speculative etiologies had long since collapsed under repeated attack. If the neurasthenic model was that of a nervously inadequate person whose moral faculties were seriously impaired by the continued use of opiates — witness the proclivity of confirmed addicts to lie about their condition or source of supply — the psychopathic addict was someone whose moral sense was hopelessly perverted in the first place, and whose rapid descent to addiction was unchecked by the slightest ethical compunction.[74] While not intentionally pejorative, psychopathy was nevertheless a more serious and pessimistic label to attach to the addict and his condition.

Among the first to describe addicts in this way were Harry Drysdale, who concluded that all of the cases he saw in Cleveland were psychopathic; Sylvester Leahy of Brooklyn, who reported that all but two of his patients were of either inferior or psychopathic makeup; and John H. W. Rhein of Philadelphia, who contended that the addict is "a psychopath before he acquires the habit."[75] If fell to Lawrence Kolb, however, to systematize and popularize these views, and to discredit the thesis that addicts were normal persons suffering from a purely physiological disorder. Unlike Bishop the internist or Butler the pathologist,

Kolb was by training a psychiatrist and naturally inclined to view addiction from that perspective. Like Terry he was a public health official of considerable energy and wide-ranging interests, although there the similarities between the two men ended.

In 1923 Kolb found himself stationed at the U.S. Public Health Service Hygienic Laboratory in Washington, D.C., charged with investigating all phases of narcotic addiction. After studing a series of 230 cases, he devised a five-part scheme of classification. All addicts were either persons of normal nervous constitution addicted through medication; carefree, pleasure-seeking individuals (later abbreviated to "psychopathic diathesis"); cases with crystalized neuroses; habitual criminals who were always psychopaths; or inebriates. The first category, the normal medical addicts, Kolb regarded as a small and diminishing minority.[76] The inebriates as a rule were heavy drinkers who had switched to opiates; withdrawn from one drug, they could be counted on to return to the other. "I have seen a repeating visitor to the alcohol ward look over to the drug addict in the next bed," Kolb wryly noted, "and say with an air of finality, pity and superiority, 'I was a "doper" once but I was cured twenty-five years ago and have never taken any of the stuff since then.' "[77] The second and fourth categories, those suffering from psychopathic diathesis and psychopathic criminals, which together made up just over half of Kolb's original sample, were closely related types. Differentiated mainly by the seriousness of their infractions of social rules and customs, they were, as Kolb described them, individuals who knew it all but simply did not care. They were not, as some had suggested, mentally impaired or feebleminded; the problem lay instead with the emotive faculties.[78] Neurotic addicts were in many respects like the psychopaths, except that they usually had some pain, fixation, or disease on which they blamed their condition. "The psychopaths are more frank," he remarked. "They readily admit having fallen into addiction through associates and the pleasing effect that opium had upon them."[79] Pleasure was the key; the four abnormal types had in common a heightened receptivity to the euphoric effects of opiates, whereas normal persons experienced only relief of pain. The greater the degree of psychopathy, Kolb hypothesized, the more intense the euphoria. Opiates also had the effect of alleviating the feelings of inadequacy that plagued the abnormal or psychopathic user; they were a kind of psychic crutch that enabled inferior personalities to raise themselves temporarily to the posture of normal men. Feelings of inadequacy and unconscious pathological strivings persisted even after withdrawal, which explained why most nonmedical addicts speedily relapsed.[80]

Although his early writings were tinged with the slightest edge of contempt (a natural enough reaction for anyone, even a trained psychiatrist, suddenly exposed to over 200 assorted addicts), Kolb throughout his long career consistently defended the idea that addiction was a manifestation of true mental disease. Rejecting outright incarceration of addicts, as well as indefinite maintenance, he eventually settled upon extended treatment in a specialized institution as the least objectionable course of action.[81] Addicts needed to be "supervised rather than repressed," he once put it.[82] When he took charge of the Lexington Hospital, the first national center for the study and treatment of drug addiction, he was dismayed to learn that the physical structure had been conceived in terms of prison architecture. His characteristic response was to house addicts, as far as possible, in areas outside of the cell block.[83] Kolb also vigorously opposed propagandists like Richmond Hobson, who depicted the addict as a dangerous criminal and addiction as a widespread and worsening condition.[84] At a time when extremists were seriously proposing a bullet as the only final solution for addiction,[85] Kolb calmly and patiently, through articles and radio broadcasts, reiterated his view that addicts were mentally sick persons deserving of help. Nor was he averse to taking on the Bureau of Narcotics when he thought their enforcement activities got out of hand. The older he grew, the more critical he became of the punitive approach; "we should keep in mind," he protested in 1962, "that this country suffers less from the disease than from the misguided frenzy of suppressing it."[86]

Kolb's influence, especially in medical circles, was enormous. Called by one colleague "the Osler of drug addiction,"[87] he was instrumental in keeping alive in the United States the flickering belief that addiction was fundamentally a medical problem. Of more immediate concern, he was the single most important and frequently cited authority for the view that addicts were predominantly psychopathic. His classification scheme was adopted at the Lexington Hospital, and his fellow Public Health Service officers, notably Walter Treadway, Michael Pescor, William F. Ossenfort, and Robert H. Felix, gave wide circulation to his ideas.[88]

By the 1930s the psychopathy theory, in spite of the vagueness of its terminology and the circularity of its reasoning, had become a veritable cliché in the addiction literature.[89] At the same time, the view that addicts were normal persons addicted accidentally was all but abandoned, a reversal brought about by several factors. Undoubtedly the prestige of Kolb and his coworkers at the Public Health Service played a role; under their aegis psychopathy and kindred personality disorders became, for all intents and purposes, the official explanation of opiate addiction. Their opponents, moreover, fell on hard times during the 1920s. Ernest Bishop was indicted under the Harrison Act, continually harassed, and died a broken man in 1927. Willis Butler's Shreveport clinic was finally closed and he drifted off to other activities, only to be resurrected late in life as one of the early prophets of maintenance. Charles Terry held on for a while as executive secretary of the Committee on Addictions of the Bureau of Social Hygiene, a privately funded social research group, where he busied himself with compiling *The Opium Problem* and investigating the legal use of narcotics in Detroit and other cities. His eyesight beginning to fail, he was eased out of this position in the early 1930s, whereupon he retired to a turkey farm in his native Connecticut. (His parting shot: "It is a far cry from turkeys and bucolic peace to opium and the bickerings of pseudo-socio-scientists."[90]) Lacking institutional leverage, he was powerless to oppose Kolb's growing influence.

Kolb's position was enhanced by the fact that he was able to refute conclusively the antitoxin theory, thereby knocking the scientific underpinnings from beneath the normal personality thesis. In a 1925 paper coauthored with Andrew DuMez, he reported that a series of experimental injections of human-addict sera failed to confer any benefits of immunity on white mice, who died of morphine overdose at the same rate and at the same dosage as the controls.[91] The hypothesized antidotal substances were never found, and it was back to the drawing board for those who thought addiction was strictly a physiological disorder.

Perhaps the most important influence of all was one that was completely beyond Kolb's control: the ongoing transformation of the opiate addict population. It could be plausibly argued that the high-strung matron or exhausted clerk addicted to opium was basically neurasthenic, or that the invalid morphine addict was only the normal person in pain; but when the young tough snorting heroin on the street corner was perceived as the dominant addict type, new and more radical theories of addiction were in order. Psychopathy connoted irresponsible, deviant, and often criminal behavior, which fit the hustling style of the emerging nonmedical majority, but not at all the shame and reticence of previous generations of medical addicts. Not coincidentally, psychopathic addicts were described first in northern cities, where nonmedical users were especially abundant, while elements of the outmoded degeneration/neurasthenia theory lingered longest in the writings of southern physicians, who were still exposed to numerous medical cases.[92]

The transformation of the addict population also had an impact on attitudes toward mandatory institutionalization. During the nineteenth century four courses of treatment were available to the addict: outpatient withdrawal by a physician; the purchase of proprietary opium-habit cures, actually a disguised form of maintenance; voluntary commitment in a private asylum; and involuntary commitment in a state institution. The last alternative was seldom realized, since even those states with the facilities to do so seldom actively sought the confinement of opiate addicts. A growing body of expert opinion held that they were mentally disturbed and not to be trusted in matters of truthfulness and memory, but nevertheless they were clearly nonviolent and, unlike the alcoholic, could be counted on not to indulge in disruptive binges. One Ohio physician, James R. Black, was so struck by the differences between the two groups that he seriously proposed the mass conversion of incurable alcoholics to morphine addicts. Morphine addicts, he realized, were heavily tranquilized individuals who seldom presented a problem of social control.[93]

Some members of the inebriety movement, notably Crothers, agitated for compulsory treatment of inebriates, including opiate addicts, in publicly funded facilities, but these proposals were controversial and prior to 1910 were adopted in only a few states.[94] By 1930, however, a majority of physicians had come to support some form of mandatory institutionalization, even in the absence of specialized hospitals for the care and treatment of addicts (which had not yet been constructed in any sizable numbers). The plans differed in detail but had in common the idea that addicts, especially nonmedical addicts, were suitable subjects for involuntary commitment, whether in a prison, an asylum, or an elaborate narcotic farm far from the insalubrious city. Perry Lichtenstein, for example, proposed in 1914 that addicts be withdrawn from their drug and then shipped away to a farm "or some institution" outside the city, there to be "well fed, and made to work. This is the only positive way to cure a fiend. If you allow an habitué to go free at the end of two weeks treatment as cured, he will seek the first 'hop joint' that he can and make up for lost time."[95]

Ten years later another New York City physician, S. Adolphus Knopf, offered a more comprehensive solution. Prefacing his remarks with a spirited denial that physicians were responsible for most addiction, he endorsed the proposal that each municipality forcibly detoxify its addicts, index them, and send their records to an intercity identification bureau. There were, he allowed, some "higher types of unfortunates" who might be cured, but those who were both "chronic criminals and chronic narcotic addicts . . . should be chronically confined where they can no longer be a menace to society."[96] These thoughts were shared by Thomas Joyce, medial director of California's Spadra Hospital, the first state institution specially designed for the treatment of drug addiction. In 1935 he argued that while his institution might be of use to some inmates, there was a regrettably large class of uncooperative and incurable addicts, mainly criminal psychopaths, who should instead be "colonized" for periods of up to 15 years in a separate state narcotic farm. That would keep them off the streets and out of Spadra, where their presence was a waste of taxpayers' money as well as a source of discouragement to those genuinely seeking a cure.[97]

Joyce and the growing number of physicians who came to support involuntary, long-term institutionalization were neither arbitrary nor despotic; they were frustrated, disillusioned men who were seeing more and more of a less and less desirable type of addict. What David F. Musto has called "the cult of curability" — the collection of specific regimens for swift and sure cures offered by such addiction specialists as Pettey, Charles B. Towns, and Alexander Lambert — was by the 1920s thoroughly discredited.[98] Ambulatory treatment, the gradual reduction of opiates administered to outpatient addicts, had also fallen into disrepute. The New York City clinic had been a widely publicized failure; when their doses became too small, addicts simply supplemented their legal supply by purchasing from peddlers.[99] Reduction cures by private practitioners were open to the same objections or worse; many doubted the legitimacy of such treatment. One doctor, related Abraham C. Webber of the Boston district attorney's office, "started in with a full dram bottle prescription, and the second prescription was 59 grains, and the next was for 58 grains, and so on; and, after a while, when they were reducing too fast, he would cut down only half a grain . . . and if we had not interfered . . . only a quarter of a grain."[100]

The obvious solution to both subterfuge and supplementary supply was confinement in an institution, where all access to drugs could be carefully controlled.[101] Addicts of the new breed were the type who seemed to belong in institutions, anyway; in contrast to the sedate nineteenth-century medical addict, they were prone, by nature and circumstance, to irresponsible and criminal behavior. Ironically, this prejudice is nowhere clearer than in the work of Pettey, Bishop, and Terry, authorities who generally opposed involuntary commitment. All three made a sharp distinction between medical and nonmedial cases, the latter being mere dissipates who gave blameless addicts a bad name. The underworld addict was admittedly "a job for underworld control, and not for medical handling at all," as Bishop testified.[102] A 1920 report of the American Public Health Association's Committee on Habit Forming Drugs, signed by Bishop, Terry, and another promaintenance figure, Lucius Brown, was equally clear on this point: "Vicious, degenerate and criminal types should be handled on a basis of vice, degeneracy or criminality and treated for their addiction-disease in places suitable to their personal or class characteristics."[103] The authors could make such sweeping statements because they believed that medical addicts were heavily in the majority, and that the public could be persuaded that they at least deserved humanitarian treatment. But the passage of time and changes in medical practice eroded the medical majority upon which the entire argument rested, leaving the liberals hanging, as it were, by their own logic.

The double standard applied to medical and nonmedical addicts had a bearing on the issue of maintenance as well. After the closure of the narcotic clinics, physicians were essentially the only remaining legal source of opiates. Physicians, however, were increasingly reluctant to prescribe, not only because they risked prosecution, but because they had little sympathy for the average user who walked into their office looking for a fix. With few exceptions, concluded John O'Donnell, doctors viewed addicts as "a damn nuisance."[104] This was particularly true of the heroin addict, who was regarded as the lowliest sort of dissipate. Summing up the profession's attitude, one doctor remarked, "The morphinist has guts, while the heroinist has only bowels."[105]

The situation was different when the physician was dealing with a bona fide medical addict. If the patient was suffering from a painful and terminal disease, the course was clear: medical tradition and common humanity demanded maintenance until death. A 1920 American Medical Association report that condemned ambulatory treatment nevertheless emphasized that all who suffered from a condition requiring the use of opiates, "such as cancer, and other painful and distressing diseases," were not to be denied.[106] Unfortunately this proviso left uncertain the status

139

of an addict with a chronic but *non*terminal disease such as arthritis, or of one addicted long ago in the course of treatment for some minor and transitory ailment, but now a confirmed addict. It appears, however, that many of these patients were able to obtain opiates legally. Studies conducted by the Committee on Drug Addictions in Sioux City, Montgomery (Alabama), Tacoma, Gary (Indiana), Elmira (New York), El Paso, and Detroit between 1923 and 1927 showed that at least 1,019 addicts residing in those cities continued to be supplied by prescription, and an analysis of the prescription records indicated that many cases involved nonterminal diseases.[107] O'Donnell also reported that some physicians in Kentucky and other southern states practiced maintenance, at least until the late 1930s.[108]

On the other hand, there are documented cases of medical addicts who were unable to secure a legal supply and were forced to turn to the black market:

Dr Kolb Dear Sir . . . I am a working man of 5 Children in my care looking to me for food and I am a unfortuent man I was Put on Drugs Before this Haris narcotic law came in afect and the Doctor hoo Put me on it hee Died while I was away on a trip to Flordy so then I Came Back I had no Doctor that Knew me So you See I cant get my Medisun Without a Scrip and all I get now is just what I get from the Bootleger and that Robs My Babys from their their Bread and Clothes from my own back and is Robing my wife all So and if theres anny Way you Could help Me By writing a Letter to Some Doctor here I would More than apprechate you to the highest extent.[109]

How often the misfortune of this Bristol, Virginia, man was shared by others is impossible to say, since addicts were understandably tight-lipped about their suppliers, licit or otherwise. It seems that the position of the medical addict who was neither aged nor conspicuously infirm generally worsened after 1930, as older and more favorably disposed practitioners died or retired, and as narcotic officers kept up or intensified legal pressure.[110] The anti-maintenance attitude had become so ingrained that one agent seriously considered arresting an incredulous Lawrence Kolb for administering to addicts in the course of gradual withdrawal treatment.[111] Another factor was the long-delayed opening of the Lexington Hospital in 1935, which finally gave physicians — and the law-enforcement personnel who tacitly approved of such arrangements — an excuse to break off maintenance. While some doctors and policemen might balk at cutting an addict's supply when the only alternatives were prison or the black market, they did not hesitate to do so when specialized institutional treatment became available, provided always that the user was not afflicted with a grave and incurable ailment.[112]

Impact of the Transformation on Public Policy

If a growing number of physicians were inclined to view addicts as suffering from personality disorders, to support involuntary institutionalization, and to single out the nonmedical addict for harsher treatment, the same was true of public officials who sponsored and administered the narcotic laws. Harry Anslinger endorsed the psychopathy view,[113] as did his predecessor, Levi Nutt. Most drug addicts, Nutt wrote in 1928, were "mentally deficient or psychopathic characters," prone to repeated relapses:

It will be fruitless, therefore, as a permanent proposition, to proceed further with curing drug addicts of their habit, unless the source of supply for the drugs they now use is eliminated. Much in this country, however, may be done by individual states by creating institutions for the segregation, care and treatment of addicts. As long as addicts are permitted to remain at liberty on the streets of our cities where they have access to the drugs they will continue to create a demand for smuggled narcotics. The isolation and segregation of addicts for institutional treatment under restraint for a long period of time will greatly reduce the spreading of drug addiction among our people, and largely destroy the existing demand for smuggled drugs.[114]

The theme that addicts were dangerous and compulsive individuals, inclined to commit crimes and spread addiction, also dominated the 1928 congressional hearings on the establishment of two federal narcotic farms, which eventually became the Lexington and Fort Worth hospitals. Although they would accept some volunteer patients, the narcotic farms were conceived primarily as specialized prisons to siphon off the overflow of addicts from other federal penitentiaries. Wardens testified that their facilities were already badly overcrowded, and that addicts were troublesome prisoners constantly plotting to smuggle in drugs. They expressed fears that some of these drugs would find their way into the hands of nonaddicted inmates, worsening the narcotic problem. The solution was therefore to put all the bad apples into two capacious new barrels.[115]

The legislation's sponsor, Congressman Stephen G. Porter of

Pennsylvania, spoke of the need for quarantine, expanding it to society as a whole. Calling the addict "a serious menace" and "more dangerous than an insane person," he defended narcotic farms as a way of "taking the drug addict off the streets." Porter drew an analogy between the confinement of addicts and the confinement of the mentally ill. "It is just like the situation a long time ago," he later remarked, "when there was no provision made for lunatics, idiots, and feeble-minded people. Fortunately the humanity of that time brought about what is known as the insane asylum. Those people are confined for their own welfare and for the protection of society."[116] There was, moreover, a seemingly scientific basis for this analogy, since narcotic officials and the medical establishment by this time agreed that addiction was rooted in personality disorder. Porter's colleague, Congressman John Joseph Kindred of New York, testified before the House Judiciary Committee that addicts, as a class, were of psychopathic makeup. A physician who specialized in nervous and mental diseases, Kindred based his conclusion on personal experience, as well as on consultation with Lawrence Kolb, whose findings were entered into the official record.[117]

What was especially interesting about the narcotic farm hearings was the pronounced tendency to differentiate between the majority of nonmedical addicts and the diminishing minority of medical addicts. Congressman Porter, for example, noted that many morphine addicts "go on for years without the necessity of any control or restraint." He recalled, almost wistfully, "an old man who was wounded in the Civil War and who became an addict and lived to a ripe old age. He was a sufferer from sciatic rheumatism or something of that sort. He was not the menace to society that the heroin or cocaine addict is."[118] Rupert Blue, surgeon general of the United States, testified that

addicts should be divided into two general classes: First, legal or medical addicts should be defined as persons who habitually use narcotics because of disease, injury, or the infirmities of age, and for whom these drugs may be prescribed by physicians for the relief of pain . . . These addicts are few in number, and are provided for under the Harrison Act. The second class may be called "drug addicts" or dissipators, or persons who habitually use narcotics for other than medical reasons. These are the real addicts, and include psychopaths, neurotics, and criminals.[119]

Both Porter's and Blue's remarks convey the strong impression that had there been no transformation — had "the real addicts" not surfaced as the dominant type — then no one, least of all Congress, would have been concerned with confining them on publicly funded narcotic farms. Kindred made exactly this point when he noted that some cases of addiction persisted "among the so-called better classes, who do not belong to the psychopathic makeup, and many of these should receive proper medical treatment, if possible, outside of public institutions, and without the publicity of legal commitment, provided such legal detention is not absolutely necessary."[120] Here was a literal double standard: private care for one class of addicts, confinement in a public institution for the other.

In broader terms, the transformation of the addict population was a necessary condition for public support of the "police approach" to opiate addiction. During the nineteenth century, when medical addiction predominated, there was little sentiment for curtailing maintenance or for any other form of coercive legislation — with the notable and pregnant exception of ordinances against opium smoking. But attitudes changed as addiction became increasingly concentrated in the underworld. Americans were both angered and frightened by this emerging majority — angered because they were perceived as irresponsible and self-indulgent members of the lower classes (the undeserving poor in a new guise), frightened because they committed crimes and recruited new addicts.

Propagandists played upon and reinforced these fears. In 1928, for example, journalist Winifred Black published, with the assistance of William Randolph Hearst, a tract entitled *Dope: The Story of the Living Dead*. Black's primary goal was to mobilize public support for Porter's proposed narcotic farms. "A dope addict is a disease-carrier — and the disease he carries is worse than small pox, and more terrible than leprosy," she wrote. "Why not isolate him, as you would a leper?"[121] Why not, indeed? It was an effective and revealing rhetorical question. A generation previous, when the majority of addicts were docile, isolated, and disproportionately female, Black's leper metaphor would have been incomprehensible. But the changing characteristics of the addict population gave such sensational tropes a superficial plausibility and made it easier to frighten the public into supporting further restrictive measures.

The negative impact of these changing characteristics on public opinion may also provide a clue to an old puzzle. During the 1920s there were not one, but two prohibitions: on alcohol and narcotics. They were in many respects similar: both were generated by reform efforts concerned with the deleterious effects of these substances on the individual and society; both began with high expectations; and both were failures, in that they generated large and well-publicized black markets on which criminals fattened. Why, then, did the public withdraw its support for the prohibition of alcohol and, if anything, increase its support for the prohibition of narcotics? One factor (in addition to economic and political considerations) must have been that alcohol use was relatively widespread and cut across class lines. It seemed unreasonable for the government to deny a broad spectrum of otherwise normal persons access to drink. By 1930 opiate addiction, by contrast, was perceived to be concentrated in a small criminal subculture; it did not seem unreasonable for that same government to deny the morbid cravings of a deviant group. This dichotomous attitude toward prohibition was one of the reasons why in 1930 Porter sponsored legislation establishing a separate Bureau of Narcotics, instead of retaining supervision within the Treasury Department's Prohibition Unit. "We were all convinced of the wisdom of separating narcotics from [alcohol] prohibition," explained Porter, "for the simple reason that there is absolutely no relation between the two. The latter is highly controversial and the former is not."[122]

The Law, the Transformation, and the Behavior and Characteristics of Addicts

The assertion of Porter and others that addicts were responsible for a disproportionate amount of crime has proved to be highly controversial and has generated an ongoing, often heated debate. What has been at issue is not *whether* addicts commit crimes, but *why* they commit them. Critics of the government's antimaintenance policy have charged that the high incidence of crime among addicts is a function of the law and has nothing to do with alleged criminal tendencies of the users. Two basic arguments have been advanced: first, the law makes possession of the drug a crime in itself, so the user is a criminal by definition rather than by act; second, when the user does commit crimes such as theft, it is solely to obtain cash to pay for his drug, the price of which the law has driven beyond honest means.[123]

Those involved in enacting and enforcing narcotic laws, on the other hand, have tended to emphasize criminal behavior of the addicts prior to addiction, as a kind of implicit justification for a hard-line policy. This tradition dates back to Hamilton Wright and his 1910 *Report,* in which he claimed that 45.48 percent of "the general criminal population" was addicted, a rate more than 250 times that of the general adult population.[124] Other authorities picked up on the theme of personality disorder, alleging that addiction and criminal behavior derived from a common source. "Whether an addict becomes a criminal or a criminal becomes an addict the fact remains that they spring from the same soil — namely from the group of mental, moral and psychical inferiors," explained Carleton Simon, former special deputy commissioner of the New York City police.[125] The Bureau of Narcotics, always sensitive to charges that strict enforcement was creating criminals, took the stance that most of the addicts they prosecuted were offenders even before using drugs. Commented the bureau in its 1938 annual report, "The overwhelming majority of narcotic drug addicts which have come to the attention of the authorities recently in the United States belong to the criminal element . . . [a recent study of 225 cases showed that] every criminal among them had committed crime before the use of narcotics was begun."[126] The objectivity of the bureau's findings has been challenged, however, and other studies cited to the effect that only a minority of addicts had records before addiction.[127]

The use of police records to establish, one way or the other, an index of criminality prior to addiction is a technique fraught with peril. It is entirely possible that an addict may have committed crimes before using opiates and not been apprehended. Or it may be that crimes recorded prior to first arrest for violation of the narcotic laws were drug related, although mistakenly classified as committed before addiction. Add to this the difficulty of verifying addicts' statements about their pasts, and of collating scattered police files, and it becomes apparent that little reliance should be placed on this type of record.

It is still possible to describe, in a general way, what the transformation meant in relation to addict criminality. First, historical evidence supports the contention that the antimaintenance policy increased the amount of addict crime. If we set aside the issue of prior criminal activity, the fact remains that the street addict, once addicted, had to commit illegal acts on an almost daily basis to support his habit. Competent observers with a firsthand knowledge of the problem — men such as Perry Lichtenstein in New York City, Edouard Sandoz in Boston, Bingham

Dai in Chicago, Merrick W. Swords in New Orleans, and Leo Stanley in San Quentin — were unanimous in associating the addict's need for opiates with increased crime, particularly the sort designed to raise cash quickly. Summarized Sandoz, "Logically, criminality is bound to begin . . . the moment the economic margin above living expenses in not sufficient to cover the purchase of the habitual amount of the drug."[128]

The experience of "Jack," a young New York City addict, illustrates this principle. Jack grew up in a broken home in Jersey City; his father was an alcoholic, and his parents were divorced when he was 6 or 7 years old. His mother then married a German and the family moved to Hamburg. There, after dropping out of school, he learned to sniff heroin on the docks with a group of other boys. He was addicted by the time he returned to the United States in 1927. At first he was able to earn enough money by working for a cable company, but ultimately the rising price of the drug forced him to seek more lucrative means. In 1932 he made a connection with a higher-up and began selling heroin. "When I first started dealing . . . I was paying . . . 35 or 40 dollars an ounce (cut) and I was making 65 [one-] dollar packages out of it." But this arrangement did not last for long; he was seized by federal agents in 1933, along with 100 ounces of heroin he had stashed away in the Young Men's Hebrew Association. After 14 months in Leavenworth Penitentiary Jack was back on the street, back on heroin, and dealing again. "I didn't feel like stealing," he explained, "and you couldn't keep up a habit by working."[129]

Yet there is another aspect of the problem, generally overlooked by the narcotic law critics. Well before the anti-maintenance decisions were handed down, addiction was moving from the upperworld to the underworld, and the principal forces behind that shift were medical and demographic, rather than legal. Even if the government had failed to establish an anti-maintenance policy (if, for example, a single justice had switched his vote in the crucial *Webb* decision), the background of the typical opiate addict in 1940 would not have differed much from the one observed in historical actuality. He would have been a lower-class white male, living in a decaying urban area. He would have had a history of what contemporaries called vice (gambling, excessive drinking, or consorting with prostitutes), and perhaps would have committed more serious criminal acts. He would have been introduced to drugs by associates of similar background, rather than by a physician. The most important difference — and here the critique of the narcotic laws becomes relevant — is that the hypothetical addict would not have been compelled to commit *as much* crime; maintenance would have meant cheaper drugs. It is also likely that fewer addicts would have used adulterated heroin, the leading black-market opiate.

To state the argument another way, it is possible to distinguish between the characteristics and the behavior of addicts. The characteristics of the addict population were bound to change, given therapeutic reform; attrition in the ranks of older, medical addicts; and continuing recruitment of nonmedical users. The behavior of addicts, however, was very much influenced by the law. Legal changes had a direct or indirect bearing on the type of drug used and the method of administration — from morphine to heroin, from subcutaneous to intravenous injection. They also influenced the amount and type of crime committed by addicts, particularly those who could not secure a legal supply. A daily round of petty theft, drug peddling, or prostitution became the norm. The law did not create the underworld addict, but it did aggravate his behavior.

By 1940 the opiate addict population had undergone a marked transformation: the secretive, female morphine addict had given way to the hustling, mainlining male junkie. Medical addiction did not cease completely; a few patients continued to be addicted unnecessarily, and physicians themselves continued to suffer a relatively high rate of addiction. Most new users, however, were of the nonmedical type.

Judgment of the emerging nonmedical majority was harsh. They were held to suffer from psychopathy or some other form of twisted personality; they were denied a regular supply of legal opiates; and they were confined, often against their will, in prisons or in treatment centers that were quasi-penal in nature. More tolerant views had prevailed in the nineteenth and early twentieth centuries, but these were abandoned as the pattern of addiction shifted. The government's antimaintenance policy succeeded in making a bad situation worse: criminal activity was at least in part a function of black-market prices. Legal changes were not solely or even primarily responsible for the larger transformation of the addict population, however. That process had begun decades before, when the first, unknown physician thoughtfully laid aside his hypodermic syringe.

Appendix

Addiction Rate and City Size

Michigan, 1870

From Marshall's data, a regression of the addiction rate (A) on town population (P) yields

$$\hat{A} = 4.7780 + 0.23949 \times 10^{-3} P$$
$$(n = 96) \qquad (t = 1.13)$$

The coefficient is positive, but the correlation ($R^2 = 0.0135$) is exceedingly weak.

Clinic Data, 1919-1923

From the data of Table 2 (including the revised Shreveport estimate), plus a dummy variable (D, where South = 1, North and West = 0) to compensate for regional differences, a regression of the addiction rate on city population yields

$$\hat{A} = 1.1435 - 0.16357 \times 10^{-5} P + 0.84083 D$$
$$(n = 34) \qquad (t = -1.47) \qquad (t = 2.60)$$

In this case A and P are negatively related, but the t value and other tests of significance are weak. Adjusted R^2 for the regression is 0.1863. Some of the unexplained variance is undoubtedly due to the different policies and reporting procedures of the clinics, but on the whole it seems that city size was not a good predictor of the rate of addiction, at least prior to 1923.

Abbreviations

BI	Butler Interview
BMSJ	*Boston Medical and Surgical Journal*
BP	Butler Papers
CDA	Papers of the Committee on Drug Addictions of the Bureau of Social Hygiene
CHS	California Historical Society
CR	*Congressional Record*
G.P.O.	Government Printing Office
JAMA	*Journal of the American Medical Association*
JSC	*Report of the Joint Special Committee to Investigate Chinese Immigration*
KP	Kolb Papers
NLM	National Library of Medicine, History of Medicine Division
NYAM	New York Academy of Medicine, Rare Book Room
NYDSAS	New York State Division of Substance Abuse Services
RMML	Rudolph Matas Medical Library, Tulane University School of Medicine
SCP	Society of California Pioneers
TDF	Treasury Department Files
USIOC	Records of the United States Delegation to the International Opium Commission and Conference
USPHS	Records of the United States Public Health Service

Notes

Introduction

1. Oral history interview with Willis P. Butler (hereafter BI) conducted by the author November 11, 1978.

2. Sontag, *Illness as Metaphor,* 28.

3. For a recent report on the fate of addicts following discharge from methadone maintenance programs, see Dole and Joseph, *Methadone Maintenance Treatment.* On relapses in the nineteenth century see Chapter 2, n. 143.

4. A catalogue of all the personality theories of addiction would run to several pages. For representative examples see Radó, "Psychoanalysis of Pharmacothymia," 1–23; Hill, Haertzen, and Glaser, "Personality Characteristics of Narcotic Addicts," 127–139; and Overall, "MMPI Personality Patterns," 104–111.

5. Burroughs, "Kicking Drugs," 40. I do not mean to take the extreme position that personality has no bearing whatever; it simply seems to me to be a factor of minor importance in comparison to exposure. Certainly I have been unable to detect any common addictive personality among the hundreds of historical cases I have studied or among the dozens of older addicts I have interviewed.

6. See, for example, O'Donnell, "Rise and Decline of a Subculture," 77; and Zentner, "Prominent Features of Opiate Use," 103.

1   The Extent of Opiate Addiction

1. Simple increase/decrease surveys include Oliver, "Use and Abuse of Opium," 162–177, and Hartwell, "Opium in Massachusetts," 137–158.

2. There are earlier estimates (and references to estimates), but these tend to be unsystematic or difficult to verify. "Use of Opium," *Courant,* 56, mentions that a layman, a Mr. M'Gowan, presented statistics to the effect that 3,000 to 5,000 New York City residents were habitual opium users, a very high rate of 9.59 to 15.99 addicts per thousand. M'Gowan's forum, a meeting of the Temperance Society of the College of Physicians of the State of New York, casts some suspicion on his figures. On the other hand, New York City, as a principal port of entry for medicinal opiates throughout the nineteenth century, may have suffered an inordinately high rate of addiction. Without M'Gowan's original study there is

no way to evaluate the accuracy of his findings. A much lower figure was given by Stevens, "Opium," 120: "In every part of the country, I have found two or three persons of every thousand inhabitants using from a quarter to a half ounce of opium every week . . ." Again, it is impossible to determine precisely how diligent and wide-ranging Stevens was in his inquiry, and whether he overlooked any users.

3. Marshall, "Michigan," 63–73. The distribution of opium and morphine addicts is discussed in detail in Chapter 2.

4. Earle, "Opium Habit," 442–446. Two years later an Auburn, New York, physician, F. M. Hamlin, made inquiries among druggists and physicians in his community. Allowing that it was "difficult to obtain correct information concerning the number of habitués because of the secrecy preserved," Hamlin nevertheless ventured that "there are not far from 10 to 12 habitués per 1,000 of population." Hamlin's guarded language leads one to suspect that his method of inquiry, unlike Earle's, was rather unsystematic. Hamlin, "Opium Habit," 431.

5. Hull, "Opium Habit," 535–545.

6. Hynson et al., "Report of Committee," 569–570. The questionnaire asked for the number of persons with "drug habits," not just opium habits. The actual average recorded was 4 per pharmacist; suspicious of underreporting, the committee insisted that the actual figure was closer to 5 per pharmacist, which would yield a national rate of about 3.00 per thousand (p. 570). The committee also sent questionnaires to 100 physicians in Baltimore and an undisclosed number to physicians in Philadelphia. The respondents knew an average of 6 addicts each. According to R. L. Polk's directory of practitioners, cited on p. 344 of Rothstein, *American Physicians,* there were 119,749 physicians in the United States in 1900. Extrapolation yields a total of 718,494 addicts, a rate of 9.44 per thousand. But note that these figures include those who habitually used cocaine, chloroform, trional, sulfonal, and a host of other preparations, as well as opiates, and that overreporting is clearly a possibility, as many addicts trekked from one physician to another, vainly seeking a cure.

7. Sonnedecker's revision of Kremers and Urdang, *History of Pharmacy,* 306.

8. *Webb et al.* v. *United States,* 249 U.S. 96.

9. The standard account of the federal campaign against maintenance is Musto, *American Disease,* 147–182. See also Jaffe, "Addiction Reform," dissertation, 160–228.

10. The extent of this avoidance varied from program to program. In Los Angeles, for example, it was reported that many addicts stayed away, probably because the clinic treated predominantly lower-class, nonmedical addicts. (Treasury Department Files [hereafter TDF], case 73221, made available through the Freedom of Information Division of the Drug Enforcement Administration, Washington, D.C.) A similar pattern occurred in New York City, according to Davenport, "Drug Menace," 1–2. In Shreveport, however, Dr. Willis P. Butler's clinic

drew from all segments of the community, a fact he emphasized repeatedly in BI. See also Terry and Pellens, *Opium Problem,* 26.

11. Bailey, "Heroin Habit," 315, reports that when the Harrison Act went into effect on March 1, 1915, the price of street heroin rose from $0.85 to $7.50 per drachm (dram). Black-market prices are discussed further in Chapter 4.

12. Kolb and DuMez, "Prevalence and Trend of Drug Addiction," 1181–82.

13. Ibid., 1182.

14. Ibid., 1187–88; TDF, case 73790 (Houston); and Terry and Pellens, 40–41. For Butler's description of his clinic see "One American City," 154–162.

15. Terry, "Habit-Forming Drugs," *Annual Report for the Year 1913,* 55–58, and "Drug Addictions," 28–37; Terry and Pellens, 24–27. Terry's program was ultimately supplanted by a statute providing for the incarceration, rather than the maintenance, of addicts. See comments by Jacksonville's Police Chief Frederick C. Roach following Michael T. Long, "The Drug Evil," 48–49. Terry himself reduced the amounts prescribed prior to March 1, 1915, the day the Harrison Act went into effect. *1915 Annual Report,* 47.

16. Kolb and DuMez, 1201–2. In the privacy of a letter to his son, Kolb mentioned another possible source of error: "It is to be remembered . . . that Terry and Pellens were employed by a social organization [the Bureau of Social Hygiene's Committee on Drug Addictions], and, while they are perfectly honest, there would be an unconscious motive for them to exaggerate the findings, thus justifying the continued life of the committee." Lawrence Kolb to Lawrence C. Kolb, December 12, 1932, box 6, Lawrence Kolb Papers (hereafter KP), History of Medicine Division, National Library of Medicine, Bethesda, Maryland (hereafter NLM). I had dismissed this charge until I interviewed Willis Butler, who remarked that Terry "wasn't in a hurry to finish his job" with the Committee on Drug Addictions, implying that he drew things out to continue collecting his generous salary. Butler's comments are especially provocative in view of the fact that he was Terry's friend and ally. While I am sure that Terry never actually fabricated data to draw attention and money to his research, it is more than a little suspicious that he never mentioned the lower totals from the *1912 Annual Report.*

17. Terry and Pellens, 26; *1912 Annual Report,* 27.

18. Brown, "Enforcement," 323–333.

19. Blair, "Some Statistics," 608; and Kolb and DuMez, 1181. (From the context it is clear that most of the Pennsylvania "drug addicts" were opiate users.) In addition to the Pennsylvania and Tennessee studies, there is a Massachusetts document, *Report of the Special Commission to Investigate the Extent of the Use of Habit-Forming Drugs,* which, without hard evidence, estimated 60,000 drug addicts in the state.

20. The history of the New York City clinic is related in three articles

by Hubbard: "New York City Narcotic Clinic," 33–47; "Some Fallacies," 1439–41; and "Municipal Narcotic Dispensaries," 771–773. An attack on the inadequacies of the clinic is given in Terry, "Some Recent Experiments," 33–37. See also Jaffe, "Addiction Reform," dissertation, 204–228.

Not all studies of New York City addiction were based on the clinic data. State of New York, *Final Report,* 3, claims that "estimates were given the committee by persons in position to be able to gauge conditions with a fair degree of accuracy that from two to five percent of the entire population of the city of New York were victims of drug addiction." Precisely what was meant by "drug addiction" and how the experts arrived at their estimate were nowhere made clear. For an equally speculative estimate of the number of addicts in New York State as a whole, see State of New York, *Second Annual Report,* 5. See also note 75 below.

21. The base figure of 3,764,101 men examined is found in the U.S. Senate's *Digest of the Proceedings of the Council of National Defense,* 322. The number of addicts, 3,284, is reported in Bailey, "Nervous and Mental Disease," 195. An even smaller figure of 1,448 drug addicts is given in the War Department's *Defects Found in Drafted Men,* 107. This disparity arose because the compilers, Love and Davenport, did not study all American soldiers (p. 25).

There is also a study by McPherson and Cohen, "A Survey of 100 Cases of Drug Addiction Entering Camp Upton, N.Y.," 636, which found 178 addicts out of 53,000 recruits examined, a rate of 3.36 per thousand. McPherson and Cohen's relatively high rate was almost certainly a result of the camp's proximity to New York City, which had a relatively high rate of heroin addiction among draft-age youth.

22. Bailey, "Nervous and Mental Disease," 195. There was, however, some heroin and cocaine use in the armed forces before the United States entered the war, a point considered further in Chapter 4.

23. Domestic opium was cultivated during the War of 1812 and in the South during the Civil War when imports were disrupted. There were also a number of small-scale, peacetime experiments in opium cultivation. These undertakings were short-lived, however, owing to a lack of cheap labor to tend and collect the crop. Weiss, "California-China Trade," 522–526, suggested that opium could be grown as an export crop by exploiting Chinese labor in California; however, nothing came of this proposal. See also Shadrach Ricketson to John Coakley Lettson, June 15, 1801, MS 1329, Rare Book Room, New York Academy of Medicine (hereafter NYAM), New York City; U.S. Department of Agriculture, "The Opium Poppy," 206–210; Holder, "Opium Industry in America," 147; Bigelow, 218; Weschcke, "On Poppy Culture," 457–461; Cortlandt St. John to Hamilton Wright, August 13, 1908, Records of the United States Delegation to the International Opium Commission and Conference, 1909–1913 (hereafter USIOC), record group 43, National Ar-

chives, Washington, D.C.; and Randerson, *Cultivation of the Opium Poppy.*

24. Unfortunately, relatively few studies have taken this factor into account. To give some idea of the prevalence of this bias, I append here a partial list of books and articles that have made use of import data, but have failed to control for or have discounted altogether the possibility of smuggling: "Use of Opium in the United States," 476; Oliver, 163; Marshall, "Michigan," 67–69; Hubbard, *Opium Habit and Alcoholism,* vii; Kane, *Drugs That Enslave,* 6; Hartwell, 141; Watson, "Evil of Opium Eating," 671; Happel, "Morphinism," 407; Hynson et al., 568–569; Eberle et al., "Report of Committee," 473–474; Wilbert, "Number and Kind of Drug Addicts," 416; Kolb and DuMez, 1189–97; Isbell, "Historical Development of Attitudes," 158; Quinones, "Drug Abuse during the Civil War," 1008 and passim; and Helmer, *Drugs and Minority Oppression,* 23–24, 27–28.

25. "First Arrest Made in Smuggling Plot," *New York Times,* February 14, 1909, 8; "Two More Arrests in Smuggling Case," ibid., February 16, 1909, 3; and "Smugglers' Big Profits," ibid., February 17, 1909, 4. The doctor allegedly committed suicide because he "knew that the smuggling plot was about to be exposed, and he had also been accused of bigamy."

26. U.S. Senate, *A Report on the International Opium Commission,* 30–31.

27. " 'Opiokapnism,' " 719; Barth, *Bitter Strength,* 107.

28. U.S. Senate, *A Report on the International Opium Commission,* 39; Cortlandt St. John to Wright, August 13, 1908, USIOC. Ironically, the ship that conveyed Wright to the Shanghai Opium Commission, the *S.S. Siberia,* was implicated in a number of smuggling episodes. Enlow, in *Years of My Life,* 23–96, documents these incidents as well as several others involving smoking opium. A customs inspector in San Francisco from 1892 to 1919, Enlow was intimately familiar with both patterns of smuggling: duty avoidance prior to April 1, 1909, and circumvention of the congressional ban after that date.

29. Masters, "Opium Traffic," 58. See also Hynson et al., 573, and "Boston Notes" (TS, 1908), no pp., USIOC.

30. U.S. House of Representatives, *Letter from the Secretary of the Treasury,* 2.

31. "Opium Smuggling," 885. Cortlandt St. John, identified as "the best posted man on the opium trade," also stated that both crude and smoking opium were smuggled into the country. "New York Notes" (TS, 1908), 9, USIOC.

32. Marshall, " 'Uncle Sam,' " 12.

33. "Drug Smugglers Arrested," 12.

34. Cortlandt St. John to Wright, August 13, 1908, USIOC. There were some exceptions to this rule, however, especially when it was smoking opium that had been seized. Masters, "Opium Traffic in California," 60, and *Statutes at Large,* 54th Cong., 2nd sess. (1897), chap. 394.

35. Boynton, "Tales of a Smuggler," 512–513.

36. Masters, "Opium Traffic in California," 58–59. Hollow beams were later used in sea operations, according to Hasty, "Opium Smuggling," 687. See also Jaffe, "Addiction Reform," dissertation, 173.

37. U.S. House of Representatives, *Letter from the Secretary of the Treasury,* 1.

38. Excess morphine must be removed from crude opium containing more than 9 percent morphine before it is fit for the pipe; otherwise the smoker suffers skin eruptions and headaches. Masters, "Opium Traffic in California," 60.

39. This provision is part of the Tariff of 1890, *Statutes at Large,* 51st Cong., 1st sess. (1890), chap. 1244, secs. 36–40.

40. Holder, 147. See also Masters, "Opium and Its Votaries," 643; and Cortlandt St. John to Wright, August 13, 1908, USIOC.

41. Opiate use during the Civil War is, however, discussed at some length in Chapter 2.

42. For a detailed description of this traffic see Downs, "American Merchants," 418–442. The trade died out after 1838, when the Chinese attempted to put an end to the commerce. Thereafter most of the imports actually went to the domestic market. See also Stelle, "Americans and the China Opium Trade," dissertation.

43. Whether merchandise was dutiable or not, the law required that it be entered at the customhouse. Bruce, *Warehouse Manual,* 17. In years when there was no duty on opium, there would have been no point in attempting to circumvent customs and thereby risking a valuable cargo.

44. Chinese immigration statistics are found in the U.S. Census Bureau's *Historical Statistics,* 58–59.

45. It is necessary to anticipate an objection here. Helmer and Vietorisz, in *Drug Use, the Labor Market, and Class Conflict,* 3, assert that first-generation Chinese immigrants, being of the "better-off independent peasantry or the urban petty bourgeoisie . . . neither used opium in China nor brought the habit or the demand for the drug with them between 1850 and 1870." This claim is open to at least two serious objections. In the first place, the bulk of the early immigrants were in fact impoverished laborers. Barth, 57–58; "Slaves to Opium," 7. In the second place, smoking opium was clearly being imported prior to its separate listing in 1862. Wright, "Report from the U.S.A.," 40, gives $407,041 as the value of smoking opium imported in fiscal 1860 alone, with an undetermined amount in the 1850s. Who was consuming the imported smoking opium? It was not white Californians; Kane, in *Opium-Smoking,* 1–20, makes it perfectly clear that the practice spread from the immigrants to the natives, not vice versa. The inescapable conclusion is that there were opium smokers among the Chinese immigrants in the 1850s and 1860s, that they continued to smoke in America, and that they created a demand for the product that was reflected in the import statistics.

46. Crude opium contains an average of 10 percent anhydrous morphine. One part of anhydrous morphine will make 1.25 parts of mor-

phine sulfate. Therefore a pound of crude opium will yield, on average, 2 ounces of morphine sulfate. From this formula it is possible to combine crude opium imports, recorded in pounds, with imports of morphine or its salts, recorded in ounces. In fiscal 1890, for example, 380,621 pounds of crude opium and 19,953 ounces of morphine or its salts were (officially) imported. This may be expressed as 781,195 ounces ([380,621 × 2] + 19,953). Average duty for this quantity of "medicinal opiates" can then be easily computed. The source for the opium-morphine sulfate equivalency formula is Kolb and DuMez, 1193.

47. Some of the unexplained variance is attributable to the effect of the outlying observations for 1883 and 1884, years when the market was sharply distorted by speculation. When these two observations are dropped, the correlation between amount imported and duty becomes −0.51.

48. Note that in Figure 5 the decline was not so pronounced in fiscal years 1910 to 1914, even though the duty for those years was higher. This can be explained by the increased use of morphine and heroin by opium smokers who found it difficult to obtain their accustomed drug after 1909, a development discussed further in Chapters 3 and 4.

49. See the studies cited in Kolb and DuMez, 1189–91. Note that the 6 grains is an average figure; some individual addicts undoubtedly made do with less. The true average is probably higher; 6 grains is a highly conservative estimate, suitable only for computing the maximum number a given supply would support. Terry and Pellens challenged the average-dose approach, however, remarking that "so far as we know there has been made no study of a sufficiently large and representative number of individual cases under suitable conditions to permit of any definite statement as to an average daily dose" (p. 3). See also Terry to L. B. Dunham, September 22, 1929, ser. 3, box 5, folder 150, Papers of the Committee on Drug Addictions of the Bureau of Social Hygiene [hereafter CDA], Rockefeller Archive Center, North Tarrytown, N.Y. In view of the fact that Kolb and DuMez cited an impressive array of studies, some based on very large samples, to support their contention that 6 grains was the minimum average daily dose, this objection would seem to be unfounded. Kolb and DuMez erred, however, in applying their average-dose ratio to all import statistics, regardless of the likelihood of smuggling. Not realizing that high duty also led to smuggling (or not wanting to complicate their study), they stated that because opium was not proscribed, "there was no incentive to the smuggling trade as there is today" (p. 1193).

50. The base year for computing the 0.72 rate is 1835.

51. The base year for computing the 3.25 rate is 1894. Fiscal year 1897 was also duty free but, owing to the speculative importation mentioned earlier, its total was artificially high and is therefore not included in the annual average of 1,109,822 ounces. As a maximum rate for addiction to medicinal opiates, 3.25 per thousand is consistent with the sur-

veys of physicians and pharmacists discussed earlier, except for that of Marshall in Michigan. It is difficult to say why Michigan had such a high rate (5.8 per thousand) in comparison with the locations listed in Table 1. But the fact that one state survey produced a higher rate in no way falsifies the claim that the national *average* rate of addiction to medicinal opiates, computed on the basis of import statistics, was not more than 3.25 per thousand.

52. Obviously not all who received opiates became addicted. Estimates of the quantity of opium required for therapeutic purposes (other than maintenance) varied. Two leading authorities, Alonzo Calkins and E. R. Squibb, put the amount at about 20 percent of the total imported. ("General Facts about the Use of Opium," 215.) There would also have been a certain amount of wastage, up to 10 or 15 percent, according to Hamilton Wright. (U.S. House of Representatives, *Importation and Use of Opium: Hearings,* 94.)

53. According to the *Statistical Abstract of the United States,* issued annually by the Bureau of Statistics of the Department of the Treasury, the value of patent-medicine exports more than tripled from 1884 to 1914, reaching a peak of over $7,500,000 in 1912. Undoubtedly some of the exported nostrums contained opiates, although how many it is impossible to say.

54. Kolb and DuMez, 1190, cite a Formosan study that indicated a 2.5-pound-per-smoker annual average. This figure may be too low, however. "Opium in China," 186, states that "the average smoker consumes 3 mace or 6/15 of an ounce avoirdupois daily," or 9.13 pounds per annum. Kane, *Opium-Smoking,* 19, estimates that the average white smoker in America consumed 6.34 pounds per annum, the average Chinese smoker 3.8 pounds. Nevertheless, in the interest of establishing a maximum, it is better to err on the side of too small an average dose, so I have adopted the 2.5-pound estimate.

55. The base year for computing the 4.59 rate is 1894. Whether the national rate was ever higher than this is difficult to say. It is logically possible that in the late 1880s, just before the duty on crude opium was lifted, true per capita consumption (that is, legitimate plus smuggled opiates divided by population) was actually greater than in fiscal years 1891 to 1896 (see Figure 3). However, evidence will be presented in the next chapter that headway against iatrogenic addiction—the most common form—was not really made until the late 1890s, which in turn suggests that the rate peaked at that time, rather than during the late 1880s.

56. Figures 5 and 6 show imports of medicinal opiates and smoking opium per capita dropping by roughly half during 1900 to 1910, while population grew by less than a quarter during the same decade.

57. Wright made his reputation as a researcher of tropical diseases. His most celebrated "discovery" was that beriberi was an infectious disease, a finding soon demonstrated to be erroneous. For more on Wright's personality and career see *Dictionary of American Biography,* vol.

20 (New York: Charles Scribner's Sons, 1936), 552–553; *National Cyclopaedia of American Biography,* vol. 22 (New York: James T. White & Company, 1932), 430–431; Musto, *American Disease,* 33–62; and Taylor, *American Diplomacy,* 54–56.

58. *Statutes at Large,* 60th Cong., 2nd sess. (1909), chap. 100.

59. The Foster bill is discussed in more detail in Chapter 4.

60. Musto, *American Disease,* 43–44; U.S. Senate, *Report on the International Opium Commission,* 48–50; U.S. House, *Importation and Use of Opium: Hearings,* 83.

61. H. B. Rosengarten to Wright, August 5, 1908; Jay Schieffelin to Wright, September 4, 1908; and N. B. French to Wright, September 17, 1908; all USIOC.

62. U.S. Senate, *Report on the International Opium Commission,* 42 (emphasis added). A few pages earlier, Wright sought to anticipate this objection by claiming that duty-free opium imported speculatively in the 1890s was only then being released for consumption. This makes no economic sense unless one is prepared to believe that an importer would pay for 15 years of storage in the hopes of realizing a $1 per pound profit. Indeed, it is improbable that imports would have continued at all if the warehouses had been as glutted as Wright suggested. In all likelihood the speculative importation to which he referred — the 1,073,999 pounds entered in fiscal 1897 — for the most part was consumed the following year, during which a scant 72,287 pounds was brought into the country. See also Rosengarten to Wright, August 5, 1908, and Charles B. Dunlop to Wright, August 7, 1908, USIOC.

63. U.S. Senate, *The Opium Traffic: Message from the President of the United States, Transmitting Report of the Secretary of State Relative to the Control of the Opium Traffic,* 5; Wilbert and Motter, *Digest of Laws and Regulations* (Public Health Bulletin No. 56), 14; Sollmann, *Manual of Pharmacology,* 232; "Prevalence of Morphin," (*JAMA*), 1363; and Marshall, "Uncle Sam," 12.

64. *Registration of Producers,* 2. Wright's statistics are still circulating; see, for instance, Ashley, *Cocaine,* 61.

65. Taylor, 59 n. 29.

66. DuMez, "Some Facts Concerning Drug Addiction" (TS, 1918), Records of the United States Public Health Service (hereafter USPHS), record group 90, file 2123, National Archives, Washington, D.C.

67. U.S. Treasury Department, *Traffic in Narcotic Drugs,* 10.

68. B. U. Richards to Rupert Blue, June 24, 1919, USPHS, file 2123.

69. *Brief on Behalf of the United States, W. S. Webb and Jacob Goldbaum v. The United States of America* (Washington, D.C.: G.P.O., 1919), 33–34; *Brief on Behalf of the United States, The United States of America, Plaintiff in Error, v. C. T. Doremus* (Washington, D.C.: G.P.O., 1919), 29. As a matter of fact, Congress did not have these statistics, or anything remotely similar, when it passed the Harrison Act. All it had was Wright's

intimation that the per capita consumption of opiates was steadily on the increase. I am indebeted to Ruth Whiteside for help in obtaining copies of these briefs.

70. *Webb et al.* v. *United States,* 249 U.S. 96; *United States* v. *Doremus,* 249 U.S. 86.

71. *Traffic in Narcotic Drugs,* 20. For another version of how this figure was derived, see "Introduction: Narcotic Problem — Historical Aspects" (TS, 1927), 19, ser. 3, box 4, folder 136, CDA. This document accuses the report of "very flagrant errors," particularly the redundant counting of addicts.

72. Reid Hunt to Surgeon General H. S. Cumming, September 21, 1926, KP, box 3. Hunt went on to add, "A person gets the impression that there has been an extraordinary improvement in the situation in the last 10 or 15 years."

73. Kolb and DuMez, 1192.

74. Lawrence Kolb to Lawrence C. Kolb, December 12, 1932, KP, box 6. It is noteworthy that one of the committee members who did not repudiate the findings, Benjamin Rhees, was later appointed head of the Washington, D.C., office of the Prohibition Unit's Narcotic Division.

75. *Congressional Record* (hereafter *CR*), 65th Cong., 2nd sess. (1918), 10466–69, 10674–75, quotation at 10467. See also *Revenue Bill of 1918,* House report no. 767, 65th Cong., 2nd sess. (1918), 36–37, and Musto, *American Disease,* 134–138. Carleton Simon, a physician and former special deputy commissioner of the New York City Police Department, denounced the statement that there were 200,000 addicts in that city as "preposterous." Simon to Kolb, July 21, 1926, box 5, KP. Nevertheless, the 200,000 figure continued to circulate, for instance in Wallis, "Menace of the Drug Addict," 743; and Black, *Dope,* 3. Rainey's character and career are described in Waller, *Rainey of Illinois.*

76. *Statutes at Large,* 65th Cong., 3rd sess. (1919), chap. 18, secs. 1007–9. Rainey's tactics, though successful, were not strictly original. The Bureau of Internal Revenue's *Annual Report for the Fiscal Year Ended June 30, 1915* (Washington, D.C.: G.P.O., 1915), 29–30, prefaced a slate of amendments to the Harrison Act with the claim that there were up to 130,000 addicts in a single (unnamed) industrial state.

77. "A Million Drug Fiends," 10; and Blair, "Relation of Drug Addiction to Industry," 284.

78. "A Million Drug Fiends," 10; "8,000 Lads," 24. According to Black, *Dope,* 9, "When we made the draft at the beginning of our entrance into the World War, we discovered that we had a quarter of an available army rotten with dope."

79. Hobson, "One Million Americans," 4; Epstein, *Agency of Fear,* 25.

80. Epstein, 23–34; "Dope," 52–53; Hobson file, box 3, KP, especially Kolb to Surgeon General [Hugh Smith Cumming], May 26 and August 20, 1924; Cumming to assistant secretary of the treasury, De-

cember 30, 1925; and undated memorandum from L. G. Nutt to secretary of the treasury, "Concerning Richmond P. Hobson and Drug Addiction." A revised version of Hobson's "Peril of Narcotic Drugs" appears in *CR,* 68th Cong., 2nd sess. (1925), 4088–91. See also Musto, *American Disease,* 190–193, 321–323 nn. 32, 33.

2   Addiction to Opium and Morphine

1. Useful guides to official preparations containing opium and morphine include Bolles, "Opium," vol. 5, pp. 324–325, and Wilbert, "Opium in the Pharmacopoeia," 688–693. For unofficial preparations see Oleson, *Secret Nostrums.*

2. Marshall, "Michigan," 67; Earle, "Statistical," 442–443; and Hull, 539. Terry and Pellens, 17 n. 10, note that the phrase "129 females" on p. 539 of Hull's report is a typographical error and should read "149 females" in order to be arithmetically correct.

3. "Michigan," 66. It is possible that this difference reflects the preference of male Civil War veterans for opium, the type of opiate given most commonly in the army.

4. Cited in Nolan, 835. Todd Savitt has called to my attention the address by H. B. Pierce, 75, which estimates five female addicts for every male. Dr. Pierce was speaking generally, however, and did not specify a place or elaborate on his admittedly small sample.

5. Terry, *1912 Annual Report,* 27; *1913 Annual Report,* 57. Percentages do not include combination opiate-cocaine users.

6. Brown, "Enforcement," 327.

7. "Drug Addicts in the South," 147–148.

8. Drysdale, 354-357. Altogether, 62 cases are described in this article: 34 morphine, 20 heroin, 7 smoking opium, and 1 cocaine. I define morphine cases as those where the initial use of an opiate was morphine, even if cocaine was involved and even if the user later switched to another drug. Similarly, opium smokers are those who started with smoking opium, and heroin addicts are those who started with heroin. There are some cases where the patient began using morphine and heroin simultaneously or near-simultaneously; these are counted with the heroin addicts.

9. MS case records on oversize sheets, box 6, KP. Kolb used these data sheets in preparing a series of articles that appeared between 1925 and 1928. In one of these studies, "Types and Characteristics of Drug Addicts," 300–313, he described the material as "representing . . . addicts in various situations, from various walks of life, and in widely separated sections of the country, [and] . . . fairly representative of the addict population as a whole." All told, there are 230 decipherable cases: 174 opium and morphine, 40 heroin, 7 smoking opium, 7 cocaine only, and 2 veronal. Most of the cases in the first category began with and con-

tinued on morphine, although I also number in this group those who used cocaine prior to or concurrently with opium or morphine, or who later switched to another opiate. Thus users whose drug history was described by Kolb as cocaine and morphine, or cocaine to morphine, or morphine to heroin, are regarded here as morphine addicts. (Those few users whose history is given as morphine and heroin to straight heroin or cocaine, and morphine and heroin to straight heroin are considered with the heroin group; see note 8 above.) I infer that the records were compiled in late 1923 or shortly thereafter, since that was the year Kolb began his addiction work for the Public Health Service and since 1923 is the last date of addiction listed in the records.

10. Waldorf et al., 28–29. More than 98 percent of the patients at the clinic used morphine. Cuskey et al., 9, apparently discounted or overlooked the Drysdale, Kolb, and Waldorf data in reaching the unqualified conclusion that as late as 1920 female addicts outnumbered male addicts two to one.

11. See Chapter 1, note 14. For an account of one addict's odyssey from Oregon to Shreveport, see Howard, "Inside Story," 118–119.

12. Massachusetts, *Special Commission,* 10, and McIver and Price, 477, also indicate a majority of male addicts. Unfortunately their sample included heroin, cocaine, and combination users, and the sex of those addicted strictly to morphine is not clear from context. Kolb and DuMez, 1186, state that "the percentage of females among 2,455 [out of 4,123] cases at the clinics was 44.25." This percentage is inaccurate, however. The data summary sheet from which these authors took their information contained an undetected error in arithmetic; the figures should have read: male, 58.09 percent; female, 41.91. Even the correct totals are misleading, since the clinics without age and sex data were mainly in the South, a region with a large number of female opium and morphine addicts. (EKR to Nutt, May 4, 1921, and "Data on Clinics" [TS, 1923], no pp., both TDF. These documents were found among the remnants of the Shreveport file, for which I could find no case number. The clinic records are decaying badly, and need organization and professional archival care.)

Another possible source of bias is the tendency of clinics with large numbers of male underworld users to frighten away upper-class addicts, which would have included many potential female clients (for instance, Los Angeles file, case no. 73221, TDF; see also Musto and Ramos, 1074). To complicate matters further, there was another brief report on the clinic data, "Survey of Drug Addicts," 1655, which stated that of "several thousand" registrants, women slightly outnumbered men. The possibility of an emerging majority of male morphine users from 1915 to 1923 is discussed further in Chapter 4.

13. Calkins, *Opium and the Opium Appetite,* 164; Earle, "Statistical," 443.

14. Brown, "Enforcement," 327, and table IV, 328. Altogether 98.3

percent of the Tennessee addicts used some form of opium or morphine.

15. Butler, 158, gives the average age of Shreveport patients as 41 years and their average length of addiction as 13 years. Drysdale's morphine patients began at an average of 26 years, 11 months (n = 32); Kolb's at 28 years, 2 months (n = 170). Drysdale, 354–357; MS records, box 6, KP. Other writers sorted opium and morphine addicts into age brackets. The distributions recorded in Earle, "Statistical," 443; Hull, 539; Josselyn, 195; and "Drug Addicts in the South," 147, all support the view of opium and morphine addiction as a condition of middle age. Also of interest are the frequency polygons in Bloedorn, 313–314, esp. chart 7.

16. Roberts, 206–207.

17. The exact percentages are 72.9 percent white for 1912, 74.0 percent for 1913 (not counting combination opiate-cocaine users). Terry, *1912 Annual Report,* 27; *1913 Annual Report,* 57.

18. "Enforcement," 330–331.

19. Waldorf et al., 28; memorandum to L. G. Nutt, March 26, 1920, Houston file, TDF.

20. MS cases, box 6, KP; see note 9, above. Another clinical study (Drysdale, 354–357) reported no blacks among 34 morphine addicts.

21. Earle, "Statistical," 443. The author stated that 12 of 235 addicts (5.1 percent) were "colored." According to the 1880 census only 6,480 of 503,185 Chicagoans (1.3 percent) were colored. This disproportion is probably related to the large number of prostitutes (56, or 23.8 percent) in Earle's sample — larger, in fact, than in any comparable study. It is known that in 1872 in St. Louis 16.2 percent of all prostitutes were colored, even though coloreds made up only 7.1 percent of the population. (Jordan, 137; 1870 census.) Assuming that blacks also made up a disproportionate share of prostitutes in Chicago in 1880, and bearing in mind that Earle's urban sample contained an unusually large number of prostitutes, then the relatively high addiction rate for Chicago blacks is understandable. Note that the large number of prostitutes, black or otherwise, also helps to explain why Earle reported a very high percentage (71.9) of females.

22. Earle, "Statistical," 443; 1880 census. In arriving at these figures I have counted Earle's 12 coloreds as Americans.

23. Josselyn, 195.

24. Drysdale, 354–357. Of 34 morphine addicts, only 7 (20.6 percent) were evidently foreign; 3 "Hebrew" and 1 each Finnish, "Scotch," Assyrian, and German. Foreign-born whites, by contrast, made up fully 34.9 percent of Cleveland's population in 1910.

25. Including Houston and Clarksburg, and using Butler's revised estimate of 211 addicts for Shreveport.

26. Eaton, 665.

27. Thirty of 100 randomly selected entries in the prescription record book of George D. Feldner, Rudolph Matas Medical Library, Tulane University School of Medicine (hereafter RMML), contained opiates;

the same is true of 19 of 100 randomly selected entries in the prescription record book of Erich Brand, Historical Pharmacy Museum of New Orleans. The Feldner sample falls in the years 1886 to 1889; the Brand sample, 1877 to 1878. Both druggists were situated on Magazine Street. The fact that a larger percentage of Feldner's prescriptions contained opiates than Brand's may indicate that opium and morphine addiction increased in New Orleans during the 1880s. This interpretation would certainly be consistent with the national increase in opium importations during that decade (Figure 6). See also the comments in the House by Levi Nutt, *Exportation of Opium: Hearings,* 133.

28. According to census data, the black share of southern population ranged between 36.4 percent in 1870 and 26.9 percent in 1920.

29. Frost, 145.

30. Blair, "Relation of Drug Addiction to Industry," 291. For more on small-town and rural drug use see Lathrop, 421; Wright, "Report from the United States," 20; and Morgan, 11.

31. Blair, "Dope Doctor," 19–20. Note, however, that Philadelphia did have a growing heroin problem, a point to which I shall return in Chapter 4.

32. Marshall, "Michigan," 64–66.

33. Pearson, "Is Morphine 'Happy Dust'?" 919. The word *class,* used repeatedly throughout this study, should not be taken to mean a self-conscious group of people banded together in the exercise of political or economic power, as in the phrase *class conflict.* It refers instead to a group of people with similar incomes and social status. While I regret the vagueness of the term, I am forced to employ it, for my sources, with rare exceptions, use nothing else. Different types of addicts were described, for example, as belonging to the upper or better classes, or to the lower class, without any qualification or detail, such as exact income levels.

34. Sigma, 408–409; "The Opium Habit's Power," 8; Nolan, 827; Kane, *Drugs that Enslave,* 25; Keeley, 22; Hamlin, 427; Hull, 537; Aikin, 332; Sterne, 610; Douglas, "Morphinism," 436; and Rountree, 305, all emphasize the frequency of opium and morphine addiction in the upper classes, defined variously and vaguely in terms of education, "cultivation," income, or occupation. Sources that refer to addicts as coming from all classes include Ludlow, 387; Calkins, "Opium and Its Victims," 35; Lathrop, 422; Lichtenstein, "Truth," 523; Morgan, 10; and Waldorf et al., 19.

35. Hartwell, 139–140.

36. Eaton, 665.

37. See also Blair, "Relation of Drug Addiction to Industry," which argues that relatively few American workers used opium or morphine. Compare the descriptions of English working-class opiate use in "The Narcotics We Indulge In," 608; Calkins, *Opium and the Opium Appetite,* 34–35, 162; and Hayter, 32–33. However, Berridge, "Victorian Opium

Eating," 446–448, notes that working-class opiate use in England may have been exaggerated for political reasons.

38. Towns, 581.

39. D. Percy Hickling, comment on Somerville, 112; Mattison, "Genesis," 304; Sell, 17; and Eddy, "One Million Drug Addicts," 639–640.

40. Keyes, 293; Johnson, *Randolph of Roanoke,* 261; and Wilson, *Crusader in Crinoline,* 569.

41. Mary Lucinda Mitchell to Lucinda Bradford, February 9, 1845, Mitchell Family Papers, Special Collections Division, Howard-Tilton Memorial Library, Tulane University, New Orleans; Varina Davis to Margaret K. Howell, December 13, 1847, Jefferson Davis Papers, University of Alabama, Tuscaloosa; Varina Davis to Jefferson Davis, January 24, 1849, cited in Strode, 207; Chesnut, 84, 504–506; Ballinger diary, Archives Department, Rosenberg Library, Galveston, Texas, entry dated February 2, 1866. I am grateful to John Collinge, Walter Buenger, and the staff of the Jefferson Davis Association for calling these sources to my attention.

42. Barringer, 404. There is a similar reference to morphine for "cramp cholic" in the Civil War diary of Confederate artilleryman Miles S. Bennet, p. 79, Eugene C. Barker Texas History Center, University of Texas, Austin.

43. Earle, "Statistical," 444; Martin, 231. Drysdale, 354–357; Kebler, "Present Status," 20; and memorandum to T. E. Middlebrooks, March 21, 1928, file 0120–9, TDF, contain some statistical information on occupations and marital status of female addicts. Massachusetts, *Report of the Special Commission,* 10–11, provides some information on occupational status, with the qualification that not all of the addicts studied used opium or morphine. There are also several letters indicating heavy use by prostitutes to Hamilton Wright from authorities in the eastern United States, including New York Fourth Deputy Police Commissioner Arthur Woods, August 11, 1908; Boston physician E. W. Taylor, August 28, 1908; Connecticut Hospital for the Insane Superintendent Henry S. Noble, September 2, 1908; and W. Gilman [?] Thompson, September 20, 1908; all USIOC. Thompson was a New York physician with long experience at Bellevue Hospital. The date and origin of these letters are significant; as the pattern of addiction shifted after 1900, and iatrogenic addiction became less common, prostitutes made up an increasingly larger share of female addicts, particularly in eastern cities.

44. Smith, *Inaugural Dissertation,* 21; Calkins, "Opium and Its Victims," 35, and *Opium and the Opium Appetite,* 163; Brown, *An Opium Cure,* 15; Bartholow, 5th ed., 251; Meylert, 9; Cobbe, 173; and Happel, "Morphinism," 408. Robert T. Edes to Hamilton Wright, August 7, 1908, USIOC, claims that addiction among society women may have been exaggerated, however.

45. Leartus Connor, comment on Wilson, "Causes and Prevention,"

817; FWR [full signature indecipherable] to Wright, September 4, 1908, and Cortlandt St. John to Wright, August 13, 1908, both USIOC; Rountree, 306; Chase et al., 15; and Bauguss, 24.

46. Crothers, "Morphinism Among Physicians," *Medical Record*, 784. Crothers defended his findings in an article with the same title in *Quarterly Journal of Inebriety*, 98–100. A similar conclusion was reached by Faxton E. Gardner, a New York physician who had studied opiate addiction extensively while in Paris. Observing the 95 physicians who practiced in his building, he estimated that 5 or 6 were addicted to morphine. Gardner to Wright, August 29, 1908, USIOC. See also Musto, *American Disease*, 275 n. 35.

47. "Morphinism," 409.

48. "Say Drug Habit Grips the Nation," 8. The nature of the evidence for this estimate is unknown, and I have not been able to locate Keister's original paper.

49. Mattison, "Ethics," 297–298, and "Morphinism in Medical Men," 186; Dewey, 324; Burr, 1588; Ashworth, "Increasing Frequency," 36; and Kebler, "Present Status," 21. Scheffel, 854, notes that of 50 volunteer patients, 11 were doctors. Physicians, like laymen, tended to become addicted in middle age. The average age at addiction for 25 physician cases studied by Kolb was 32 years, 11 months; the average age at time of treatment was 52 years, 8 months. (MS cases, box 6, KP.)

50. Cobbe, 189–190; Aikin, 332.

51. Penfield, 2214–18; Olch, 479–486.

52. Inglis, 392; Kebler, "Present Status," 20–21; Chase et al., 15; Bauguss, 24.

53. Ludlow, 387; Calkins, "Opium and Its Victims," 35; Brown, *An Opium Cure*, 13–14; Parrish, "Opium Intoxication," 363; Josselyn, 195; Bartholow, 5th ed., 251; Phenix, 206; Crothers, *Morphinism and Narcomanias*, 44; Burnett, 329; Rountree, 305.

54. See, for example, Earle, "Statistical," 444; Kebler, "Present Status," 20–21.

55. Calkins, *Opium and the Opium Appetite*, 164, lists mariners as "universally" exempt from addiction. This conforms to my experience; among the hundreds of case histories I have examined, I noted only one sailor whom I suspected of addiction. His name was John Rose, and he suffered from chronic rheumatism for which he took "large doses of sulphate of morphia." U.S. Treasury Department, Public Health Service, "Public Health Service Hospital, Portland, Me., Case Reports," 3 (MS, 1870–1871), 328, NLM. If the records of New Bedford druggist Thomas Otis are any guide, sailing ships did not routinely carry large amounts of opiates. Otis, who regularly furnished the armamentaria of departing ships, seldom provided more than an ounce or a half-ounce of opium and a few ounces of laudanum or paregoric. Thomas Otis, Day Books, 2 (MS, 1854–1867), passim, NLM.

56. Oliver, 168; Cobbe, 160; Blair, "Relation of Drug Addiction to

Industry," 291 and passim. Only Oliver thought use common among the manufacturing classes, and he allowed that American workers consumed less than English. Waldorf et al., 20, provide figures that show skilled and semiskilled workers to have been well represented among Shreveport addicts, but the authors caution that these data "undoubtedly reflect the economic life of the community," oriented toward oil and agriculture.

57. Lee, *To Kill a Mockingbird,* 108–121. Contrast the male addict, Martin Jocelyn, in Roe, *Without a Home.*

58. Weatherly, 67; Parrish, "Opium Intoxication," 362; McFarland, 290; Mattison, "Clinical Notes," 66; Duncan, 247; Bancroft, 326; Walker, 692; Cobbe, 40; Comings, 366; Hyde, 227; Boggess, 881; Nickerson, 50; Adams, "Morphinomania," 14; Kebler, "Present Status," 16–17; Wholey, 723; Kennedy, 20; Terry, "Drug Addictions," 32; Brown, "Enforcement," 329; Sceleth, 862; McIver and Price, 477; Butler, 160; and Lambert, 7.

59. Kett, 105; Rothstein, 155–156. Blair, "Relative Usage," 1630, notes unsurprisingly that homeopathic hospitals used fewer narcotics than regular hospitals. See also George S. Adams to Wright, September 9, 1908, USIOC. Hyde, 227, admitted that on occasion a homeopathic physician might, out of ignorance of lazinesss, use morphine excessively. See also Shipman, 74. Such instances were rare, however. Eclectic texts gave some indications for opiates (such as for dysentery or cancer of the uterus), but only in conjunction with other drugs or as a last resort. See, for example, Paine, 84–85, and King, *Woman,* 196.

60. Rothstein, 159, 323 n. 62.

61. Barnes, 3. Nineteenth-century therapeutic skepticism and therapeutic nihilism did indeed win some converts in the regular medical profession, but as Ackerknecht, *Therapeutics,* 120, points out, such scruples were held by only a small elite. See also Rothstein, 180–181, 184–185.

62. It is not my intent to discuss at length the early use of opium. Readers interested in the subject should consult Sonnedecker, 276–280. Other accounts, which differ in some particulars from Sonnedecker, include Macht, "History of Opium," 477–480; Terry and Pellens, *Opium Problem,* 53–60; Ellis, 44–52; Kritkos and Papadaki, 17–38; Wright, "History of Opium," 64–65; Fields and Tararin, 371–373; Krikorian, 95–114; and Sapira, 379–399.

63. Ackerknecht, *Therapeutics,* 37, 68, 78; Wright, "History of Opium," 62, 70; Sigerist, 530–544; and Mildred Pellens, "Notes on the History of Opium" (TS, n.d.), NLM.

64. Holmes, 202–203.

65. Duffy, *Epidemics,* 8; Gill, 35; Blanton, 114, 117, 118.

66. Leigh, 133–143; Handy, passim; Carter, 26; Shafer, 141; Blanton, 129.

67. Leigh, 143.

68. Betts, 1. [Brown,] *Pharmacopeia,* 10, 21, 22–23, 26, 27–28;

Handy, 18-19; Gill, 47; Cash, 5-8; and Griffenhagen, 30, 32, all cite American military use. Chapman, vol. 2, p. 190, mentions British use in the Revolutionary War.

69. Thacher, 309.

70. Wilson, *Inaugural Dissertation,* 30-32.

71. "Effects of Opium Eating," 130; R, 157; Perry, 319. The first article, "Effects," does not specify the origin in the eighteenth-century cases.

72. Wilson, *Inaugural Dissertation,* 30-32.

73. [Coleman,] 21.

74. Vine Utley, "History of a mortal Epidemic" (MS, 1814), 24, Connecticut Historical Society, Hartford.

75. Chapman, *Elements,* 4th ed., vol. 2, p. 162. The first edition appeared in 1817; the description of Chapman's work as the first systematic treatise on materia medica is that of John Shaw Billings. Chapman's judgment was seconded by Carpenter, 17, who accorded opium "perhaps the most conspicuous place in the materia medica."

76. A concise account of Brown's system is Risse, 45-51. Brown himself took opium and alcohol for his "asthenic" gout (p. 49). On Brown's influence in America see Kett, 101, 156, 159.

77. Seaman, passim. For more on the sedative-stimulant controversy, see Handy, passim; Coxe, 471; Eberle, vol. 2, p. 9; and Murray, 83.

78. Wood and Bache, 486. Further evidence of opium's wide use is found in other pharmacology texts of the day, with their long lists of indications for the drug—for example, Coxe, 471-472; Murray, 84-87; Pereira, 1046-52; and Wood, *Treatise on Therapeutics,* vol. 1, pp. 739-762.

79. The best English-language article on the discovery and early development of opium alkaloids is Hanzlik, 375-384.

80. See Wood and Bache, 477, on the impurities found in imported opium.

81. Smith, *Inaugural Dissertation,* 16.

82. Carpenter, 17; Smith, *Inaugural Dissertation,* 23; and "Destructive Practices," 19. The record book of Dr. John McNeil Stewart of Brazoria County, Texas (MS, 1836-1837), Woodson Research Center, Fondren Library, Rice University, Houston, typifies the penchant for opium prescription to which Carpenter and Smith referred. Stewart, it should be added, had one of the finest medical educations of the day, at the University of Pennsylvania Medical School. Parrish, *Treatise,* 172, notes that many alcoholics, as well as opium addicts, were created by prescription of Brownian stimulants. Benjamin Rush concurred. Apropos spirits he told his students, "It is better to die of your disease, than to rely on this detestable Brunonian remidy." Austin, "Notes on the Lectures of Benjamin Rush" (MS, 1809), 322, RMML. Significantly, Rush was much less cautious about opium; at several points in his lecture on therapeutics he commended it as a useful stimulant. Utley also strongly favored opium over alcohol.

83. The concern with overdose derived largely from opium's long-standing popularity as a euthanasic suicide agent: "From the *New England Weekly Journal*," 1; Awsiter, 51; Calkins, "Statistics," 738; and Courtright, "Report," 961. Doctors were often called upon to treat such overdoses, accidental or otherwise; hence the interest in opium toxicology reflected in the literature. Examples of post-1830 discussions of addiction include "Effects of Opium Eating," 128–130; "Opium Eating," 66–67; Seeger, 117–119; "Narcotics," 400–401; and Parrish, *Treatise*, 172–173.

84. See Chapter 1, note 2.

85. See note 105 below. The dates for these epidemics are from Ackerknecht, *History and Geography*, 25–26, 48. Ackerknecht states further that American troops fighting in the Mexican War (1846 to 1848) were seriously afflicted with dysentery. Like their counterparts in the Civil War, some of these soldiers may have become addicted to opium given to check their discharges. There is one such veteran in Turner, 215, although otherwise the evidence is sketchy. Finally, Musto, *American Disease*, 26, notes a reported increase in opium use among Filipinos following the 1902 cholera epidemic, so there is at least one parallel case to support the idea of increased use following a cholera outbreak in the United States.

86. Bartholow, 1st ed., 17–18. Some condemned use of the hypodermic syringe as dangerous—for example, Beck, *Lectures*, 367.

87. In 1860 Antoine Ruppaner of Boston published the first important article on hypodermic medication in an American journal, "Researches upon the Treatment of Neuralgia by the Injection of Narcotics and Sedatives, with Cases." Five years later he authored the first American text on the subject, *Hypodermic Injections in the Treatment of Neuralgia, Rheumatism, Gout and Other Diseases*. Roberts Bartholow's *Manual of Hypodermic Medication*, 1st ed., was published later (1869) but was also very influential, going through five editions by 1891.

88. Gallagher, 535.

89. Bartholow, 1st ed., 18, remarks that as late as 1869 only a minority of Americans physicians used the hypodermic syringe. However, a survey taken by Ingals, 491, indicates that use of the instrument was common by the late 1870s. See also Kane, *Drugs That Enslave*, 29–30.

90. G. V. Lafargue, F. Rynd, Alexander Wood, and other early pioneers of hypodermic medication were all seeking a way of injecting morphine; the best account of their efforts is Howard-Jones, "Critical Study," 201–249. See also, Macht, "History of Intravenous and Subcutaneous Administration," 859. For an account of the early injection of drugs other than morphine, see Bartholow, 1st ed., 73–88, 99–144.

91. Mattison, "Responsibility," 103.

92. Schuppert, "Notes, Case Records and Observations" (MS, 1875–1879), 54, RMML. See also Fülöp-Miller, 378–389, for a good description of the impact of morphine on a suffering patient. Physicians replying to Kebler, "Present Status," 16, overwhelmingly indicated that

the hypodermic method was the one most likely to produce addiction. See also Dole, 146, 148, 150, 154.

93. Personality theories of addiction are discussed in Chapter 5. Recent research has shown the presence of morphine-like substances within the body called endorphins. It has been speculated that persons naturally deficient in endorphins are especially prone to addiction; see Goldstein, 1085, as an example. If we assume a random distribution of endorphin deficiency in the population, there is nothing in the epidemiology of nineteenth-century opiate addiction to support this hypothesis. Addiction was a disease of exposure; persons suffering from chronic illnesses with access to drugs and doctors were at the highest risk. If, on the other hand, it should be proved—and this would be a fascinating and significant finding—that endorphin deficiency *is* correlated with chronic diseases like neuralgia, then the epidemiologic data might be made to fit Goldstein's hypothesis. Such proof has not yet been forthcoming.

94. The 10-to-14-day period is an approximate one, chosen for purposes of illustration. The actual span varies with the individual, his expectations, the form of opium used, method of administration, and circumstances under which the drug is taken. Some addicts I have interviewed claimed that they were dependent (on heroin) after 3 days of regular use, while others stated that it took months before they became dependent on smoking opium.

95. The exception, of course, would be if the physician were treating a painful, terminal illness such as cancer and elected deliberately to addict the patient.

96. The practice of leaving the hypodermic syringe with the patient was frequently remarked upon. See, for example, McFarland, 289–290; Kane, *Drugs That Enslave,* 18; and Bartholow, 5th ed., 252.

97. Lindesmith, *Addiction and Opiates,* 47–67, argues that full-blown addiction, which includes psychological dependence or craving, cannot occur unless the patient recognizes the connection between withdrawal symptoms and the absence of the drug. For an excellent illustration of this principle, see Morris, 69.

98. Keeley, 8–9; Pettey, *Narcotic Drug Diseases,* 312–314.

99. Frost, 144–145; Brown, *An Opium Cure,* 12–13. There is an excellent account of this process in Hughes, 35–36. Hughes was a physician who treated himself for sciatica.

100. Englehardt, 19; Vandergriff, "Dosimetric Medication" (MS, 1846), 104–105, RMML; H. H. Kane, cited in Terry and Pellens, *Opium Problem,* 72; Wilson, "Notes on Subcutaneous Injection," 256.

101. Defining what contemporaries meant by *neuralgia* is a difficult task. Today the term is reserved for cyclic attacks of acute pain of a peripheral sensory nerve, where no pathological change in the nerve itself is discernible, such as trigeminal neuralgia. However doctors in the nineteenth and early twentieth centuries used the term in a looser sense, to include virtually any acute pain following the course of a nerve, from

whatever cause. Rothstein, 191, goes even further in arguing that neuralgia was merely a catchall term for any pain of obscure origin — that the disease was invented so doctors would have something else to treat with opiates. This is perhaps too sweeping a generalization. If one examines, for example, the pioneering article of Wood, "New Method of Treating Neuralgia," 265–281, it is clear that the concept of neuralgia antedates the hypodermic administration of morphine and that the term is used in a strict sense. On the other hand, Rothstein is undoubtedly correct that some physicians, out of laziness or ignorance, dubbed all obscure painful symptoms neuralgic and proceeded to treat them with opium or morphine.

For more on the definition of neuralgia, see Dunglison, 631–632, and Mo[tt], vol. 19, pp. 427–428. On the use of morphine to treat neuralgic attacks, see Musser, "Principles and Practice of Medicine" (MS, 1843–1844; some entries postdate 1844), 80, RMML; Ruppaner, "Researches," 193–194; Gibbons, 483–485, 490–491, 493; Mattison, "Impending Danger," 70; Marshall, "Michigan," 70; Osler, 1005–7; Reber, 393; and Burr, 1588. See also "Hypodermic Use of Opium," 7–9; Calkins, *Opium and the Opium Appetite,* 56; Pepper, 87–88; Whittaker, 147–148; Josselyn, 196–197; and Shipman, 74, for cases of neuralgia sufferers turned addicts.

102. Mattison, "Prevention," 113–115; McKay, 466–467; and Scheffel, 853, speak respectively of "neuralgic headache," "nervous headache," and "chronic headache" in connection with addiction.

103. Hubbard, *Opium Habit,* 17; W. P. Crumbacker to Wright, September 3, 1908, USIOC. See also the comment by Dr. Goodell in Evans, 265. In addition to dysmenorrhea, opiates were used to treat morning sickness, uterine colic, difficult or protracted labor, and various other unspecified female disorders. See "Notes on Dudley's Lectures Taken in 1830" (MS), 163–164, RMML; Bennet, "On Hypodermic Treatment," 302–304; [Kormann,] 325; Hendrick, 397–399; Hudson, 102; Calkins, *Opium and the Opium Appetite,* 152, 155, 239; Marshall, "Michigan," 70; Earle, "Statistical," 444; Papin, 18–23; Goodwin, 314–316; Byford, *Practice of Medicine,* 96–97; Crothers, "New Sources of Danger," 339; Witherspoon, 1591; and Brown, "Enforcement," 329.

104. Russell, "Opium: Its Use and Abuse," 315; Beck, 375; Lathrop, 421; Mattison, "Genesis," 304; Frese, 60; Douglas, "Morphinism," 436; Pettey, *Narcotic Drug Diseases,* 317–319; Earle, *Confessions,* 27; and Sandoz, 37. In some cases the switch from alcoholic excess to morphine addiction may have been deliberate. See Black, "Advantages," 537–541, and Fox, 701.

105. For respiratory diseases see Gibbons, 483; Marshall, "Michigan," 70; Sell, 18–19; Cheadle, 349; and Anders, 6–7. For diarrhea and dysentery see "Notes on Dudley's Lectures," 153; Barnes, 3; Oliver, 167; the second and sixth cases in Fitch, "Case Records, Charity Hospital, New Orleans" (MS, 1881), RMML; Cheadle, 350; and

Duffy, *New York City,* 592. Opium and morphine, of course, have useful constipating, as well as analgesic properties. Note that *diarrhea* and *dysentery* signified in the nineteenth century practically any disease in which the chief symptom was a loose stool (diarrhea) or a loose stool with blood and pus (dysentery).

Other diseases in which diarrhea was a symptom, such as cholera, or in which diarrhea was sometimes present, such as typhoid fever, were also treated with opium and morphine. Ashe, 644; Kennon, "Notes on the Lectures of Drs. Chaillé, Nott, Jones and Stone," vol. 1 (MS, 1866), no pp., RMML; case 5 in Fitch; Comings, 369; Shryock, 54; Howard-Jones, "Cholera Therapy," 380. "Dr Labadie's Cholera Remedy" (MS, n.d.), Dr. Nicholas D. Labadie Papers, Archives Department, Rosenberg Library, Galveston, Texas, illustrates the tendency to use opium, often in conjunction with other drugs, in the treatment of cholera. New York City's Metropolitan Board of Health, faced with the prospect of a cholera epidemic, also advised citizens to treat the diarrheal symptoms of the disease with frequent doses of laudanum and camphor. (*Annual Report, 1866,* Appendix "N," 429.) In the case of malaria, opium and morphine were given to "arrest or modify the [intermittent] paroxysm." Reynold Webb, Jr., "Medical Notebook" (MS, 1819), vol. 1, p. 98, Connecticut Historical Society, Hartford; Beck, *Lectures,* 368; and "Opium in Fevers," 265. See also Lodwick, dissertation, 21.

For syphilis and other venereal diseases see Coxe, 498; Terry, *1913 Annual Report,* 57–58; and Blair, "Some Statistics," 608. Waldorf et al., 23, comment that over one-quarter (27.2 percent) of the Shreveport cases they analyzed cited venereal disease as the reason for initial addiction. But in our interview Butler observed that some users may have acquired the disease after addiction, so the Waldorf figure may be high. Note also that Butler was an early pioneer in the treatment of venereal disease, and a syphilitic addict would have had a double incentive to come to Shreveport for treatment. (BI.)

The use of opium and morphine to combat diarrhea, dysentery, malaria, cholera, and typhoid fever also receives scattered mention in Vandergriff, "Pharmaceutical Preparations and Select Prescriptions" (MS, 1850), RMML; Bowers, "Notebook on Practice of Medicine, Materia Medica" (MS, 1882), Eugene C. Barker Texas History Center, University of Texas, Austin; and Bemiss, "Clinical Lectures" (MS, 1882–1883), RMML. See also the table of indications in Charles Hunter's popular 1865 manual, *On the Speedy Relief of Pain and Other Nervous Affections, by Means of the Hypodermic Method,* 27; and Gallagher, 546.

106. Marshall, "Michigan," 70; Earle, "Statistical," 444; Waldorf et al., 23.

107. Earle; "Statistical," 444; Morris, 69; Blair, "Some Statistics," 608.

108. As the species name of the opium poppy, *Papaver somniferum,* suggests, opiates have sleep-inducing and tranquilizing properties, in

addition to their analgesic qualities. Their use in treating insomnia, anxiety, and other nervous conditions was common. Musser, 77; Kane, *Drugs That Enslave,* 17–18; Hubbard, *Opium Habit,* 71; Mattison, "Genesis," 304; Bancroft, 326; "Confessions of a Cocainist," 1769b; Sterne, 610; Crothers, "Criminality and Morphinism," 163; Scheffel, 853; and Musto, *American Disease,* 1.

I have deliberately omitted cancer from the list of diseases most likely to lead to addiction. It is not that opium and morphine were denied to cancer patients, but rather that victims of this disease were unlikely to survive as addicts for long. See Scranton, "Case Book" (MS, 1873–1874), 6–7, RMML. Thomas H. Nott, "Notes, Long Island Col. Hosp. Brooklyn N.Y." (MS, 1874), no pp. Thomas H. Nott Papers, Eugene C. Barker Texas History Center, University of Texas, Austin, remarks apropos stomach cancer, "Make an opium eater of yr [sic] patient as early as possible." William Osler's case notes show that he also eased the sufferings of a cancer patient with morphine. See his "Case Histories at the University of Pennsylvania Hospital" (MS, 1887–1888), 250–251, MS, film 13, NLM. See also Gordon, "Insanities," 100.

109. Kane, *Drugs That Enslave,* 25; Hamlin, 427; Whitwell, 17; Gosling, dissertation, 164–169. For more detail on the association between gynecological and nervous disorders and female addiction see Courtwright, "Female Opiate Addict."

110. In 1890, for example, the median age of blacks was 18.1 years; of whites, 22.5 years. (*Historical Statistics,* 11.) Another factor, not related to age, was the partial immunity of blacks to malaria. It is now known that blacks, for a variety of complex genetic reasons, suffered fewer and less severe cases of malaria. (Savitt, 17–35.) Since malaria was one of the chronic diseases treated with opiates, this conferred a slight advantage on blacks from the standpoint of avoiding addiction.

111. Conrad, 505, 507; DuBois, 110; Morais, 85–86; Legan, 267.

112. "Opium and Its Consumers," 2; Kolb and DuMez, 1184; Deaderick and Thompson, 21, 399. Kolb and DuMez also mention endemic hookworm as a factor, but I have found little evidence that this condition was routinely treated with opiates. The prevalence of diarrheal diseases in the South is reflected in "Record of Cases Attended at Charity Hospital, New Orleans, October 1868–February 1875" (MS), compiled by Samuel Merrifield Bemiss, RMML. Campbell, 78, notes that in 1907 paregoric "was being 'abused in Mississippi most grievously.' " This is a significant clue, for paregoric is the form of opium commonly given for diarrhea. Finally, there is an interesting parallel between the addiction experience of the American South and that of the English Fenland. The Fens were one of the unhealthiest areas in nineteenth-century England, the residents allegedly "prone to the ague, 'painful rheumatisms,' and neuralgia." The presence of these endemic diseases was one important reason the region had an exceedingly high rate of opium consumption. Lomax, 175; and Berridge, "Fenland Opium Eating," 275–284.

113. Handlin, *The Uprooted*, 55, and *Immigration as a Factor in American History*, 31–41. Roughly 60 percent of nineteenth-century immigrants were male; see *Historical Statistics*, 62.

114. The two best contemporary accounts of the pressures and attitudes leading to a high rate of addiction among physicians are Mattison, "Opium Addiction in Medical Men," 621–623, and Ashworth, "Increasing Frequency," 36–39. A physician with ready access to opium and morphine might use them to treat similar conditions in his own family, hence the high rate of addiction for doctors' wives.

115. The figure of 12,000 is obtained by using Crothers' 6 to 10 percent estimate and assuming that there were roughly 120,000 physicians at the turn of the century. (Rothstein, 344.) On ironic justice see Foot, 459; and Knerr, 344.

116. American physicians were well aware of "opium eating" before 1870, but morphine addiction as a consequence of hypodermic injection was not well publicized until the near simultaneous appearance in 1870 of Sewall, 137; Gibbons, 481–495; and Albutt, 327–331. Bartholow, 1st ed. (1869), 71–73, also discusses morphine addiction, but erroneously suggests that the condition is easily treated. An 1869 article, "Hypodermic Use of Opium," 7–9, documents a case of morphine addiction via the hypodermic route; Terry and Pellens, in *Opium Problem*, 67, give the author as Joseph Parrish, but I have found nothing to confirm this attribution.

117. See, for example, McFarland, 289–292; Wilson, 816–817; Pressey, 614; Barr, 161–162; Phenix, 210; Nickerson, 50–52; and Witherspoon, 1591–92.

118. Books and articles pertaining to the European situation then available in English included Levinstein, "On Morphinomania," 55–58, and his classic *Morbid Craving for Morphia*; Kane, "Rapid Spread of the Morphia Habit [taken from an 1878 paper by A. Loose of Bremen]," 337–341; Lewin, 142–147; "Morphia Abuse," 771; Ball, *Morphine Habit*; Sharkey, 335–342; and Kerr, *Inebriety or Narcomania*.

119. Brown, *An Opium Cure*, 18–19; J. N. Upshur, comment on Crothers, "New Sources of Danger," 341; Ashworth, "Increasing Frequency," 36–39; Hughes, 30; Scott, 608; and Duffy, *The Healers*, 232–233. An assessment of the weaknesses of nineteenth-century medical education is Kaufman, *American Medical Education: The Formative Years, 1765–1910*.

120. Faxton E. Gardner to Wright, August 29, 1908, USIOC; Kenniston's comment on Crothers, "Medicolegal Relations," 413.

121. Nickerson, 49, also ties the local rate of addiction to the carelessness of the local practitioner. Others pointed out that a physician who was both incompetent and addicted was especially dangerous to his patients. See, for example, Charles Hill to Wright, September 4, 1908, USIOC; Brown, "Enforcement," 322.

122. Eberle et al., 472.

123. Burnett, 328. Compare Hughes, 36.

124. Douglas, "Morphine in General Practice," 882.

125. Gibbons, 487.

126. Frost, 144; Steensen, 165–167; Pettey, "Narcotic Drug Addictions," 25; Howard-Jones, "Critical Study," 233.

127. Phenix, 210. Commented Corbus, 15, "It is almost as easy to get opium as epsom salts."

128. "Opium Habit's Power," 8. The problem of unauthorized refills was much discussed. See Brown, *An Opium Cure,* 12–13; Kane, *Drugs That Enslave,* 219–220; Duncan, 248; Whitwell, 17; Nickerson, 50–51; and Terry, "Drug Addictions," 34–35. Statistics on the volume of opium and morphine sales by druggists are found in Grinnell, 594–595; data on the frequent refilling of prescriptions containing opiates are in Eaton, 665. Hypodermic syringes were also easily obtained. Towns, 582; Morgan, 6.

129. Richmond, 428–454, dates the reception of the germ theory in America to the early 1880s, but Rothstein, 272–278, argues persuasively that it was the success of diphtheria antitoxin in 1895 that really won over the rank and file of the profession.

130. Wain, 264–280. The declining importance of gastrointestinal disease in the formation of opium and morphine addiction is shown in a 1927 study undertaken by Dr. John H. Remig at the behest of Lawrence Kolb. Remig furnished Kolb with 150 case summaries of medical addicts addicted between 1898 and 1927. In contrast to earlier, nineteenth-century addicts, only two of these cases listed diarrhea as the disease initially treated with opiates. Kolb to Remig, November 14, 1927, box 4, KP. The TS case summaries are in box 6, "Questionaire [*sic*] re Drug Habit." The original purpose of this study had been to assess the extent of iatrogenic heroin addiction.

131. "Substitutes for Opium in Chronic Disease," 351–356. Adams also emphasized that agents other than opiates could be used to induce sleep and check diarrhea. A few years later Henry B. Hynson, an influential member of the American Pharmaceutical Association, pointed out that the use of coal-tar anodynes was contributing to the declining use of morphine. "Baltimore Notes" (TS, 1908), no pp., USIOC.

132. Robb, 680; Reber, 393. One physician, E. V. Swing, 505–508, was so alarmed at the shift to synthetic analgesics that he felt compelled to reassert the propriety of opium for certain conditions. A few physicians, such as Barr, 161–162, advocated another opium alkaloid, codeine, as a substitute. This course was not safe as substituting antipyretics; codeine, although weaker than morphine, can still lead to physical dependence.

133. Byford, 96–97.

134. Byford et al., 105. Charles Terry, a lifelong critic of medical education vis à vis opiates, remarked in *The Opium Problem,* 72, "From the earliest warnings until 1900 the great majority of textbooks . . . failed to

issue any warning of the dangers of the hypodermic use of morphine." Terry's statement was true, as far as it went, but it obscured the fact that the new texts issued in the 1890s (the "minority") were much more conservative, signaling the growing sensitivity of the profession.

135. Herdman, comment on Burr, 1592. Happel, "Opium Curse," 728, shows that Herdman's stance was not unusual. "The teaching of today," wrote Happel, "is, when in doubt as to the propriety of an opiate, do not give it." The problem of medical addiction, remarked Los Angeles Assistant Police Surgeon C. W. Bonyge, "is probably becoming less and less as all teachers of Materia Medica and the text books are very persistent in their warnings of the danger." (Bonyge to Wright, August 12, 1908, USIOC.) Concerned instructors like Herdman also had more time to make their point; the length of medical education expanded significantly in the 1890s. (Rothstein, 288.)

136. Boggess, 883. Opium and morphine should only be administered, Boggess further cautioned, when the physician was in direct attendance on the patient. See also Mattison, "Morphinism in Medical Men," 188; Towns, 580; Douglas, "Morphine in General Practice," 882; and Diner, 317. Advertisers of opiate-free preparations picked up on this trend as well, announcing in bold face that their products contained no dangerous drugs (see, for example, *JAMA,* June 14, 1902, adv. sec., 24).

137. Houston's ordinance, passed August 8, 1898, was typical: "All persons in the City of Houston are hereby prohibited from selling cocaine, morphine or any opium in any quantity unless by order of some reputable physician residing in the City of Houston." The fine was $25 to $100 for each unauthorized sale. City of Houston, *Revised Code and Ordinances of 1904.* I am indebted to Michael Ours for calling this ordinance to my attention.

138. On inadequate enforcement see Wilbert, "Efforts to Curb Misuse," 898. However, Kebler, "Habit-Forming Agents," 3, attributed the 1900 to 1910 decline in per capita opium imports to "anti-narcotic legislation and publicity." He also remarked that "most physicians are using greater circumspection than formerly when prescribing opium."

139. Chas. B. Whilden, secretary, California State Board of Pharmacy, to Wright, September 17, 1908. A résumé of Wright's extensive correspondence on opiates reached the following conclusion: "Physicians almost unanimous in their opinion that use of opium and its derivatives is much less by the profession than it was ten years ago." (Hawkins Taylor to Wright, October 5, 1908.) See also John K. Mitchell to Wright, August 7, 1908, and F. X. Dercum to Wright, September 8, 1908. All correspondence USIOC.

140. Blair, "Is Opium the 'Sheet Anchor of Treatment'?" 829–834. See also Webster, 345. Berridge, "Victorian Opium Eating," 453, notes a similar development in Britain.

141. Young, "On the Use of Opiates," 154.

142. This trend was noted as early as 1908, when a District of Colum-

bia official reported that the "morphine, laudanum, and kindred drug users . . . have been greatly reduced in number through the efforts of the medical profession." U.S. Senate, *Reports of the President's Homes Commission,* 255. Alexander Lambert, in *Importation and Use of Opium: Hearings,* 144–145, also testified in the House that the dangers of iatrogenic addiction "have been greatly eliminated in the last years."

143. For the per capita decline, see Figure 5. In absolute terms, medicinal opiate imports (in equivalent ounces of morphine sulfate) dropped from an average of 1,083,476 ounces per annum in fiscal 1900 to 1904 to 900,075 ounces per annum in fiscal 1905 to 1909. The duty was the same for both periods. This analysis assumes that death was a more potent factor than voluntary renunciation in decreasing the total number of addicts; the rate of relapse was very high. (Eaton, 665–666; "Practical Notes on the Morphine Habit," 308–310; Hinckley, 39; and Lichtenstein, "Truth," 522.) The fact that, unlike today, most users were taking relatively high doses of pure drugs, plus the tendency of chronic ailments to worsen with age, helps to explain why few opium and morphine addicts managed to achieve permanent abstinence before death. On the connection between pain and relapse see also Jerome B. Thomas to General C. R. Edwards, April 16, 1907, USIOC.

144. Representative of this traditional view are Dai, 35, 153; Eldridge, 4–5; Simrell, 23; and Maurer and Vogel, 8.

145. Complete documentation for these and other assertions in this section may be found in Courtwright, "Opiate Addiction as a Consequence of the Civil War," 101–111.

146. Quinones, 1019. See also Musto, *American Disease,* 251 n. 2.

147. Courtwright, "Opiate Addiction as a Consequence of the Civil War," 106–108.

148. *Opium Eating,* esp. 50–60.

149. Keeley, 163.

150. Russell, "Opium Inebriety," 148–149.

151. For the figure 63,000, see Adams, "Substitutes," 355. Woodward, 259–260, indicates that not every Union physician made liberal use of opiates, but that there were some who did so "with a freedom which borders on recklessness."

152. Crothers, *Morphinism and Narcomanias,* 75–76.

153. As an illustration of this principle, the only Civil War veteran to be found in the records of the Shreveport clinic, W. O. Johnson, was 81 years of age. Case no. 115, Willis P. Butler Papers, hereafter BP, Department of Archives, Louisiana State University in Shreveport. Soldiers who were in their twenties, thirties, and forties in 1861 to 1865 would have been reaching their sixties, seventies, and eighties in 1900 to 1905.

154. Watson, 673; Parrish, *Treatise,* 172. "Recipes" for various opium preparations were also published in newspapers or shared among friends; an example is Anna G. McKenney, "Mrs. McKenney's Cook

Book" (MS, 1830?–1860?), Daughters of the Republic of Texas History Research Library, San Antonio, 77, 83, 88, 91, 92. Official opium preparations were also available in commercial medicine chests, complete with guides for self-medication. Wilson, *Drugs and Pharmacy*, 77–80.

155. Sometimes patent medicines were also prescribed by physicians, but this practice became increasingly rare as professional opposition to nostrums mounted. Dykstra, 402.

156. The best account of patent medicines in America remains James Harvey Young, *The Toadstool Millionaires*. Patent medicines of British extraction were common in eighteenth-century America, but the golden age for such nostrums was the nineteenth century, particularly the last 35 years.

157. Mason, 5–6; Oleson, 167; and Hartwell, 150.

158. Terry, *Annual Reports* for 1912 and 1913, and MS case records, box 6, KP. Of 171 opium or morphine addicts of known background, Kolb listed the causes as 41.5 percent "physician," 25.1 percent "self-medication," and 22.2 percent "associates." Another category, totaling 11.1 percent, consisted in those who were introduced to the drug by a physician but continued on their own initiative. Thus physicians were directly or indirectly involved in over half the cases. Terry (1912) also found doctors implicated in slightly more than half the cases. There is also a survey of sanitariums in Kebler, "Present Status," 15, which indicated that physicians were far more important than self-medication; but because sanitarium patients were apt to be wealthier than average, the sample may have been biased.

159. Dykstra, 402.

160. Griffin, 1584, adds that once the victim discovered that the active ingredient in his nostrum was morphine he would simply "buy . . . the drug direct."

161. Cited in Adams, "Morphinomania," 14. Dosing infants with soothing syrups was a much-decried abuse. See Webb, "Medical note book," vol. 1, p. 188; "Death of a Child from Laudanum," 33–34; Beck, "Effects of Opium"; Stevens, 120–121; Hubbard, *Opium Habit and Alcoholism*, 151–152; Fischer, 197–199; "Opium Habit in Infant from Kopp's Baby's Friend," 1540; S. Solis Cohen to Wright, September 3, 1908, USIOC; and Kebler, "Habit-Forming Agents," 4–6.

162. Some contemporaries, such as Brown, *An Opium Cure*, 13, or Crothers, "Danger of Opium in Infancy," 1173, held that the use of soothing syrups made the child more prone to addiction in later life. This hypothesis, actually a variant of the theory of degeneration (Chapter 5), was never substantiated, in the sense that no study of matched adult groups (one given soothing syrups as children, the other not) was ever forthcoming.

163. Wiley and Pierce, 394. See also Oliver, 167; Chaillé, 1–8; McFarland, 290–291; Hull, 538–539; Adams, *Great American Fraud*, 112–122; Kebler, "Habit Forming Agents," 15–18; Swatos, 750.

164. Street, "Patent Medicine Situation," 1037–38. See also "Boston Notes" (TS, 1908), no pp., USIOC.

165. Street, "Patent Medicine Situation," 1038. Wright, "Report from the United States," 19, states, "Since the passage of our National Pure Food Law, and the State and City Laws modeled upon it, there has been a reduction of 40 per cent in the sale of proprietary medicines containing opiates." Any Wright statistic is suspect, but this one seems to be corroborated by other evidence, particularly Wilbert et al., 1379. See also Jay Schieffelin to Wright, September 4, 1908, and Hawkins Taylor to Wright, October 5, 1908, both USIOC; and comments by Lyman F. Kebler in Perkins et al., 1071–72.

166. De Quincey, *Confessions,* edited and introduced by Alethea Hayter, 7–8, 21.

167. For example, Colton, 421–423; and Blair, "An Opium-Eater in America," 47–57.

168. Calkins, *Opium and the Opium Appetite,* 91–92, 158–160; *Opium Eating,* 70–76, 124–130; Keeley, 11–13; Nolan, 827; Mattison, "Genesis," 304; Cobbe, 184; Frese, 60; and Crothers, *Morphinism and Narcomanias,* 204, all comment on De Quincey's influence, but only as one of several relevant factors, most notably physicians' prescriptions.

169. Smith, *Inaugural Dissertation,* 21; Parrish, *Treatise,* 172; Oliver, 169–170; Hamlin, 427; Happel, "Opium Curse," 731; Wright, "Report from the United States," 20; De Crèvecoeur, 149–150; and Haller and Haller, 302. Some sources, such as "Opium and the Opium Trade," 298–299; Kendall, comment on McFarland, 293; Friends for New England, 13; and Cobbe, 172–173, speculated that opium use was higher among both sexes in "dry" areas. I find no evidence to substantiate this claim. In fact, Michigan and Jacksonville, places with relatively high rates of addiction, were both "wet" at the time of their respective surveys. It may be that recurring hangovers and other alcohol-related disorders treated with opiates more than compensated for the unavailability of drink, or it may be that drink was not unavailable in supposedly dry areas. See also Ernest G. Swift, general manager of Parke, Davis & Company, to Wright, September 9, 1908, USIOC; Sceleth and Kuh, 679; and the statement by Congressman Stephen G. Porter in *Prohibiting the Importation of Opium for the Manufacture of Heroin: Hearings,* 21.

170. For most persons opium and morphine serve, like alcohol, to elevate mood. This effect is strongest in the early stages of use; later, after dependence has been established, the drug is consumed primarily to stave off withdrawal and maintain a feeling of normality. This phenomenon is often termed *reversal of effects.* (An analogy may be useful here: young smokers puff on cigarettes because, among other things, they enjoy the effects of nicotine; confirmed smokers keep on smoking mainly because they fear the effects of quitting — in other words, they are "hooked." The principal difference between opiates and nicotine in this regard is that with opiates the reversal of effects sets in much more

quickly.) Those who dabbled with the drug for euphoric or experimental purposes thus might end up in the same predicament as those who took the drug to relieve the effects of chronic disease. For a good, contemporary account of the reversal of effects phenomenon, see Hughes, 173.

171. Collins and Day, vol. 5 (November 1909), 4–5. Even though one of the authors admitted that this series of articles was virtually devoid of "solidly scientific information" (Collins to Wright, December 1, 1909, USIOC), it does contain some interesting anecdotal and interview material, including a conversation with Jane Addams.

172. Female addicts who have reached a high level of tolerance are the most likely to experience amenorrhea. Magid, 308.

173. Howard, "Some Facts," 128.

174. Earle, "Statistical," 443; Phenix, 206; and Terry, *1913 Annual Report*, 57–58. Terry noted that many of the prostitutes also suffered from venereal disease. Marshall, "Michigan," 71; Hull, 539–540; and Lawrence Kolb, *Drug Addiction*, 10, concur that the prostitute-addict was largely confined to cities. The one exception is Sanger, *The History of Prostitution*. Sanger's statistical chapter on New York City prostitutes makes no mention of opiate use. This, however, was probably because he inquired only about alcohol, omitting other drugs from his schedule of questions (pp. 450–451).

---

3   Addiction to Smoking Opium

1. Mattison, "Genesis," 305; " 'Opium Smoking as a Therapeutic Means,' " 100–101; Carman, 501; Bancroft, 326; " 'Opiokapnism,' " 719–720; Walker, 692; and comments by Carleton Simon in U.S. House, *Bureau of Narcotics: Hearings,* 103.

2. The most notable exception to this rule is Kane, *Opium-Smoking in America and China.* Harry Hubbell Kane was a New York physician who specialized in treating addiction. This study, although book length, unfortunately is often impressionistic and contains relatively little information about opium smoking in the Chinese immigrant community.

3. Sandmeyer, table 3, 17.

4. U.S. Senate, *Report of the Joint Special Committee to Investigate Chinese Immigration* (hereafter *JSC*), vii, 22–23, and passim; Seward, 286–287; Barth, 84–85, 155.

5. "The Opium Habit," clipping in California Historical Society (hereafter CHS) scrapbooks.

6. Chang, 35.

7. *JSC,* 489.

8. Examples are Kane, *Opium-Smoking,* 41; and "The Opium Habit." In 1908 the Reverend Frederic Poole of the Christian League of Philadelphia wrote to Wright that smoking opium "appears to be confined largely to the older and more indolent class of Chinese." By this time,

however, the age structure of the Chinese population in America had changed; many young Chinese who had begun smoking in 1850 to 1880 were old men by 1908. Poole to Wright, July 27, 1908, USIOC.

9. Sandmeyer, 20–21, provides useful data on the geographic distribution of Chinese immigrants.

10. California Senate, Special Committee on Chinese Immigration, 220; Kane, *Opium-Smoking*, 8–9, 66; Whitwell, 9; "Opium 'Joints,'" 654–655; Barth, 111.

11. Kane, *Opium-Smoking*, 1; "Closure of the Opium 'Joints,'" 26; Earle, "Opium-Smoking in Chicago," 109; Byrnes, 385; Masters, "Opium and Its Votaries," 641; "'Opiokapnism,'" 719; Crothers, *Morphinism and Narcomanias*, 215; "Boston Notes," no pp., USIOC; Cortlandt St. John to Wright, August 13, 1908, USIOC; and Nascher, 175, 178. Williams, *Demon*, 20–21, alludes to prostitutes and "kept women" in the opium dens. Actors and actresses, bartenders, traveling salesmen, and telegraph operators were some other occupations mentioned in connection with opium smoking, although there was a consensus that the criminal or "vicious" element predominated.

12. Mattison, "Genesis," 305. See also Arthur Woods to Wright, August 11, 1908, USIOC, and Gavit, 13, 32. After 1900 there were a few references to lower-class, urban blacks smoking opium, for instance, *Reports of the President's Homes Commission*, 255; "New York Notes," 6, and Poole to Wright, July 27, 1908, both USIOC. The problem never assumed serious dimensions, however, as most blacks continued to reside outside cities with substantial Chinese populations. By the time blacks did migrate to cities in large numbers, smoking opium had been superseded by morphine and heroin.

13. The cases include 7 from Earle, "Opium-Smoking in Chicago," 106–108; 7 from Drysdale, 354–357; 2 from Stanley, "Drug Addictions," 62–65, 67–69; 7 from Kolb, MS records, box 6, KP; and 4 from Richardson, passim. The cases cited in Drysdale, Kolb, and Richardson were all former opium smokers, in the sense that they had switched to other opiates by the time they were studied. There are other accounts (such as Kane, *Opium-Smoking;* Williams, *Demon;* and Whitwell, *The Opium Habit*) that mention white men and women smoking together, but when they come to particular cases, they usually discuss men. Most of the former or active opium smokers interviewed by Dai, 124–184, were male, although several interviewees claimed they were introduced to the drug by female acquaintances.

14. Dobie, 247. References to upper-class use include Lloyd, 262; *JSC,* 133; Keeley, 176; Kane, *Opium-Smoking,* 11–12, 72; Liggins, 5; Williams, *Demon,* 20, 48–49; Earle, "Opium-Smoking," Case no. 3, 107–108; "Growth of the Opium Habit in Denver," 5; Crothers, *Morphinism and Narcomanias,* 215–216; "Fighting to Save Women from Chinese Opium Traffic," clipping, n.d., USIOC; "Boston Notes," no pp., USIOC; McGuire and Lichtenstein, 185. Two sources—Byrnes, 385,

and "Waifs and Strays," 215—deny the presence of respectable or wealthy women in the dens.

15. "The Golden 'Yen Hock,' " 2. It is possible, however, that some upper-class addicts smoked undetected in their homes or private dens. See Kane, *Opium-Smoking,* 11, 43; "Philadelphia Notes" (TS, 1908), no pp., USIOC; and T. O'Leary, assistant superintendent of the Philadelphia Department of Public Safety, to Wright, August 5, 1908, USIOC.

16. Earle, "Opium-Smoking," 107–108. Average age at time of treatment was 28.7 years.

17. Drysdale, 354–357 (6 cases); McPherson and Cohen, 638 (4 cases).

18. Kolb, MS records, box 6, KP (5 male cases); Richardson, passim (4 male cases).

19. Williams, *Demon,* 20. The female addict mentioned in Earle, "Opium-Smoking," 106–107, was also described as young. The 2 female cases in Kolb, MS records, box 6, started at ages 28 and 30.

20. Whitwell, 11; Masters, "Opium Traffic," 56; Shoemaker, 1407.

21. Robertson, 227; Shoemaker, 1407; and Faxton E. Gardner to Wright, August 29, 1908, USIOC, stress the importance of the Chinese in spreading the practice, an attitude shared by virtually everyone who wrote on the subject.

22. Williams, *The Middle Kingdom,* vol. 2, pp. 380–382, offers a good description of this process, as does Samuel Russell's MS notebook in the Records of Russell & Company, Manuscript Division, Library of Congress, Washington, D.C. The opium used, whether imported from India or native to China, contained less than 9 percent morphine. Opium containing more than that amount, unless specially treated to remove the excess morphine, produces headaches and skin rashes. (Kane, *Opium-Smoking,* 25; Masters, "Opium Traffic," 60.) United States tariff law generally classified all opium containing less than 9 percent morphine, prepared or otherwise, as smoking opium.

23. Allen, 21. See also Chang, 34; Hsü, 223; and Lodwick, dissertation, 22–29.

24. Spence, 144–145. See also Fay, 43. I take exception to the statement in Lodwick, dissertation, 22, that "there is no evidence that opium smoking was ever adopted by the Chinese for any reason other than medicinal." It is true that smoking opium had more therapeutic purposes in China than it did in the West, but there is nothing in any of the sources I have examined, including Spence, to indicate that the problem was basically a by-product of treatment or self-treatment for disease.

25. These estimates are cited in Chang, 35, 34. See also Lodwick, dissertation, 19–20.

26. The principal sources for this account of opium smoking in China are Great Britain, Royal Commission on Opium, 5–63; Clementi, passim; "Memorandum on Opium from China," 44–45; Chang, 17–50; Fields and Tararin, 373–377; and Spence, 143–173. Spence's essay is the

most thorough; still, there are many conflicting details and unanswered questions, especially concerning the early spread of opium smoking and the ultimate extent of addiction. On heavy use in Canton, see "The Cruelty of Avarice," 314–320. For a well-written and carefully researched account of the Opium War, see Fay, passim.

27. Most of these details of early Chinese immigration are drawn from Barth, 1–108, but see also Sandmeyer, 12–15, and Wood, thesis. For more on the coercive function of the district companies, see *JSC*, 23–24 and passim; on the credit-ticket system see U.S. House, *Chinese Immigration*, 1–2.

28. The dens in San Francisco's Chinatown were located mainly in the area bound by Stockton, Washington, Dupont, and Pacific streets, in close proximity to Chinese gambling resorts and houses of prostitution. Of 26 dens cited in San Francisco Board of Supervisors, 181, only 6 were described as being above ground. The dens contained an average of about 12 bunks; given 2 smokers per bunk (Lloyd, 261), they could have supported a maximum of 24 customers. They apparently did not operate to capacity; "The Opium Habit" reported that "nearly all the dens visited in Chinatown had from five to fifteen smokers." The Board of Supervisors' report also noted that there was a great deal of smoking in private lodgings (pp. 180–181). Outside cities like San Francisco, dens tended to be smaller and were often an appendage to a restaurant, laundry, gambling resort, or virtually any other establishment run by Chinese.

29. Barth, 109–128; "Slaves to Opium," 7.

30. Kane, *Opium-Smoking*, 81; Sandmeyer, table 7, 22. Masters, "Opium and Its Votaries," 638; and Condit, 60, all comment on the pauperizing tendency of opium smoking. There was a similar situation in Hawaii, according to the Hawaii Legislature's Special Committee on Opium, 6. (The Chinese also had introduced opium smoking there.)

31. Calkins, *Opium and the Opium Appetite*, 38.

32. There are at least two documented cases of immigrants familiar with smoking opium before landing in America. The first, a 39-year-old Chinese named Joe Fat, worked in a restaurant in Shreveport. He had become addicted in China, before emigrating to the United States. (Case no. 2, BP.) The second, Wong Foon, was arrested in 1936 at age 90. He stated that he had been smoking since age 18 and had resided in the United States since he was 20. (Dobie, 252–253.)

33. St. John to Wright, August 13, 1908, USIOC.

34. Speer, 635; *JSC*, 133. Masters, "Opium and Its Votaries," 641, remarks that opium couches were frequently found in the homes of well-to-do Chinese, another indication that merchants smoked. "Slaves to Opium," 7, concurs that the majority of merchants smoked, but notes that they generally restricted their consumption.

35. "The Chinese New Year," 5; "Boston Notes," no pp., and "Baltimore Notes," no pp., both USIOC; Barth, 120, 123.

36. Browne, 274; Hesse, 25; Wright, "History of Opium," 67.

37. Masters, "Opium Traffic," 56.

38. *JSC*, 60; California Senate, *Chinese Immigration*, 114.

39. "The Opium Habit."

40. Wright, "Report from the United States," 8. According to Wright's definitions, heavy smokers (6 lb per year) and light smokers (1.5 lb per year) were likely to be either addicts, or, in the case of "light" smokers, well on their way to addiction.

41. Masters, "Opium and Its Votaries," 640. The author added that about a third of the addicts were "confirmed opium sots"—evidently the equivalent of Wright's heavy smokers. Masters' estimate was cited six years later by Holder, 147.

42. Condit, 61.

43. Kane, *Opium-Smoking*, 17. There is another estimate, of no more than 10 percent total, made by "J.F.M." in a letter to Collins, 64, but again no hard evidence was presented.

44. The use of pre-1870 smoking opium import statistics to work out a rate of addiction for the Chinese in America is problematic, because of uncertainty about the level of smuggling and uncertainty about the average dose (see Chapter 1, note 54).

45. There is one exception, Dobie, 252, who claimed that true addiction was rare among Chinese smokers. Dobie did not substantiate this, however, and his explanation—"Something in the racial set-up of the Chinaman made moderate indulgence possible"—is suspect at best.

46. Bryce, vol. 2, p. 428. For more on the anti-Chinese movement see Sandmeyer, passim; Barth, 129–156; Wortman, 275–291; and Miller, passim.

47. Kane, *Opium-Smoking*, 1. M. K. Swingle, reference librarian for the CHS, has kindly checked the San Francisco city directories for me and reports that there was no resident with the surname Clendenyn. There was, however, an entry in the 1869–70 volume for "D. R. Clendening Major USA dwelling cor Market & Stockton." It is possible, given the phonetic similarity of the two surnames, that Clendening was actually the first smoker.

48. Collins, 43.

49. But see Kane, *Opium-Smoking*, 3, for a different version of the spread of opium smoking to Nevada. There is also an offhand allusion to whites smoking opium in New York City in the 1860s, in a den run by one Wah Kee. But the source, Alvin F. Harlow (p. 392), is rather gossipy, and it is hard to accept this story at face value. All other accounts concur that opium smoking among whites began in the West.

None of them explained, however, why the white underworld took up opium smoking in the early 1870s, rather than the 1850s or 1860s. It seems likely, however, that the accelerating geographic dispersion of the Chinese, increasing the frequency of contact, plus the growing familiarity of the Chinese with the English language, increasing the intimacy of contact, had some relevance. Moreover, as Mark Haller remarked June 2, 1981, at the Conference on the Historical Context of Opium Use, Philadelphia, the Chinese, when they began settling in the cities, almost invariably lived in or near the red-light district. The proximity of the two groups encouraged a certain amount of cultural borrowing. Not only did white prostitutes take up opium smoking, Haller noted, but they also began sending out for Chinese food.

50. D. F. MacMartin's *Thirty Years in Hell* is a vivid account of under-world morphine use in the late nineteenth and early twentieth centuries. MacMartin, a shyster lawyer and rakehell, became addicted after he began using morphine to relieve his frequent hangovers. That was in 1889, in Oklahoma. D. C. Van Slyke (see *The Wail of a Drug Addict,* 29) also began by using morphine to sober up. If MacMartin and Van Slyke had been offered pipes, rather than syringes, they might well have become opium smokers. Both Kane, *Opium-Smoking,* 50–51, and Crothers, *Morphinism and Narcomanias,* 215, mention that many smokers previously drank to excess.

51. Crothers, *Morphinism and Narcomanias,* 208.

52. Kane, *Opium-Smoking,* 70.

53. According to Byrnes, 384, some veteran smokers also offered their services as "professional cooks," who received "so much for every twenty-five cents worth of opium" they helped to prepare. Or the cook might take every other smoke for his fee. Williams, *Demon,* 19.

54. On New York see Byrnes, 381–385; quotation at 385. On Denver see "The Golden 'Yen Hock,'" 2. See also Kane, *Opium-Smoking,* 43.

55. Williams, *Demon,* 60; Jordan, 31, 132.

56. "The Golden 'Yen Hock,'" 2.

57. Byrnes, 386–387. The conclusion of the story is somewhat ambiguous, but it appears that the smoker quit before becoming addicted.

58. Case 14 in Dai, 142–149.

59. Commented Pittsburgh Police Superintendent Thomas A. McQuaide, "The inmates of Bawdy houses hit the pipe to bring on forgetfulness of their present, and to bring on dreams of a former and better life." (McQuaide to Wright, June 29, 1909, USIOC.) In Baltimore street walkers and their pimps reportedly retired after a long night's work and smoked themselves "into oblivion." ("Baltimore Notes," no pp., USIOC.) See also "New York Notes," 2, USIOC.

60. Kane, *Opium-Smoking,* 66–68, 71; Keeley, 176.

61. Kane, *Opium-Smoking,* 93.

62. Poole to Wright, July 27, 1908, USIOC. See also "Baltimore Notes," no pp., and "New York Notes," 2, 6, 8, both USIOC. "One of the most unfortunate phases of the habit of opium smoking in this country is the large number of women who have become involved and were living as common-law wives of or cohabiting with Chinese in the Chinatowns of our various cities," commented Wright in U.S. Senate, *Report on the International Opium Commission,* 45.

63. "The Opium Habit in San Francisco," 784. See also "Chinese in New York," 3; Earle, "Opium-Smoking," 111; Williams, *Demon,* 19–20, 30; Riis, 95; résumé of clippings attached to M. I. Wilbert to J. W. Kerr, March 6, 1913, file 2123, USPHS, especially "Kansas City"; *Importation and Use of Opium: Hearings,* 71; and Chase et al., 14–15. The miscegenation theme was even the basis for doggerel verse such as "Chung Hi Lo and Mary" in Clem Yore, *Songs of the Underworld,* 8–9.

64. "J.F.M." in Collins, 64; and "New York Notes," 3, USIOC. Conversely, when the Chinese smokers kept to themselves, they were generally left alone. See T. O'Leary to Wright, August 5, 1908, and C. W. Bonyge to Wright, August 12, 1908, both USIOC. Compare Bennett, *Sixth Report,* 93–94, and *Seventh Report,* 206–207, which express concern over opium smoking only as it threatened to spread to whites. See also Whiteside, 47–68, who aptly describes the white attitude toward opium smoking among the Chinese as "contemptuous tolerance" (p. 57).

65. Whitwell, 10. See also "The Opium Habit," and A. L. Bennett to Wright, August 14, 1908, USIOC.

66. Dobie, 248.

67. See "Opium Smoking," 306, 376, on the Philadelphia case. There was a parallel case in 1880 involving a Denver youth; see "Deadly Opium," 8; "Celestials Corraled," 1; "The Opium Case," 8; and "Well Done," 3. Yet six years later another Denver paper complained that the muncipal laws against opium smoking were practically never enforced. ("The Golden 'Yen Hock,' " 2.)

68. Kane, *Opium-Smoking,* 2, and 1–14 generally. See also Williams, *Demon,* 21–24, 46–49; Whitwell, 10–11; Masters, "Opium and Its Votaries," 641; and McGuire and Lichtenstein, 185, for more on the private dens and their supply. Byrnes, 385, mentions that most public dens, even those patronized primarily by whites, had a Chinese proprietor.

69. *California Statutes* (1881), sec. 307, 34.

70. Wilbert, "Efforts to Curb Misuse," 901–925.

71. Hartwell, 156.

72. *CR,* 46th Cong., 2nd sess. (1880), 1772. This particular bill failed, but in 1883 the duty was raised from $6 a pound to $10 a pound.

73. *CR,* 48th Cong., 1st sess. (1884), 1982.

74. For the legislative history of this measure, see *CR,* 48th Cong., 1st sess. (1884), 475, 4742; U.S. Senate, *Message from the President of the United States, Transmitting a Report of the Secretary of State Relative to Legislation Touching the Treaty of 1880 with China; CR,* 49th Cong., 2nd sess. (1886–1887), 326, 392, 1512–13, 2249; and U.S. Senate, *Report to Accompany Bill S.3044.* Few Chinese in America desired (or could legally obtain) citizenship; hence they could not legitimately import the drug as U.S. citizens.

75. "Opium Smoking," 306. U.S. Senate, *Opium Habit in the District of Columbia,* 3, notes that Chinese merchants continued to retail the bulk of the drug. This was also the case in Baltimore, Philadelphia, and Boise.

See "Baltimore Notes," no pp., and Idaho State Penitentiary Warden E. L. Whitney to Wright, August 28, 1908, both USIOC.

76. *CR,* 49th Cong., 1st sess. (1886), 6105; 50th Cong., 1st sess. (1888), 27, 3549, 4879, 4953; and 51st Cong., 1st sess. (1889–1890), 124, 5118, 9979, 10072. The last version contained some clarifying amendments, designed to avoid interference with legitimate prescription of opiates. One imagines that Blair would have gone right on reintroducing the bill, had he not lost his Senate seat in 1891. During the 51st Congress, Congressman William W. Morrow of California also introduced a pair of antiopium smoking bills, although these resorted to the more familiar tactics of controlling importation and manufacture of the drug. He got no further than Blair. *CR,* 51st Cong., 1st sess. (1889), 229, 1789.

77. U.S. Senate, *Report of the Committee Appointed by the Philippine Commission to Investigate the Use of Opium . . . ,* 49; Taylor, 32; Musto, *American Disease,* 26.

78. Crafts, "Diplomacy and Agitation as International Forces," address dated September 16, 1909, USIOC. Crafts had 2,000 telegraphic blanks printed in rubric, "Undersigned earnestly petition you to overrule Philippine opium monopoly, and substitute Japan's effective prohibition." They were then distributed to "men of large influence" for signature.

79. The law is actually in the form of a proviso to the 1905 Philippine Tariff Act. See *Report of the Philippine Commission,* esp. 4, 54–55; *CR,* 58th Cong., 3rd sess. (1905), 2999–3001, 3528, 3714–18, 4033; Taylor, 33–43. There was one earlier law that dealt with American involvement in the Eastern opium traffic, a minor statute prohibiting Americans from selling guns, opium, and liquor to the natives of certain Pacific islands. *CR,* 57th Cong., 1st sess. (1902), 1202–3, 1810.

80. U.S. State Department, *Papers Relating to the Foreign Relations of the United States with the Annual Message of the President Transmitted to Congress December 3, 1906* (hereafter *Foreign Relations*), pt. 1, 361–362. See also Zabriskie, 97–111. Brent was not aware of, or chose not to mention, the Sino-American opium trade before 1840. He was also not the only missionary to ask the President to do something about the China traffic. See U.S. Senate, *Opium in China,* 1–4.

81. Details of the invitation process and a summary of the aims of the commission may be found in a State Department memorandum from acting secretary Alvey A. Adee, *Foreign Relations, 1908,* 98–100. Taylor, 47–60, and Musto, *American Disease,* 28–35, both have useful accounts of the events leading up to the Shanghai Commission and of that meeting's bearing on the 1909 Smoking Opium Exclusion Act.

82. In 1907 alone the United States collected approximately $1,900,000 in duties on opiates, of which $1,460,000 was derived from smoking opium.

83. *CR,* 60th Cong., 2nd sess. (1909), 449, 1396–1400, 1681–84, 1716,

2098. Henry Cabot Lodge, the bill's manager in the Senate, and Sereno Elisha Payne, manager in the House, emphasized, in connection with the upcoming Shanghai Opium Commission, the need for speedy passage. Relatively little time was spent discussing the nature or extent of the opium smoking problem in America, an omission which underscores the diplomatic and symbolic intention of the bill.

84. Root to Congressman James S. Sherman, December 26, 1908, USIOC. See also the confidential "Report to the Department of State by the American Delegation . . . at Shanghai" (TS, 1909), 27, USIOC.

85. Schieffelin to Wright, September 4, 1908, USIOC, stated categorically, "We do not see why the importation of any smoking opium should be permitted." Schieffelin & Co. was one of the largest pharmaceutical houses in the nation. In general, large drug companies confined their imports to crude opium and its alkaloids and derivatives.

86. Some opposition did emerge, however, often from unexpected quarters. Senator Joseph W. Bailey of Texas attacked the bill as a disguised and unconstitutional exercise of police power. "The government has no right to regulate through a tax a matter which it has no right to regulate directly," he asserted. *CR,* 60th Cong., 2nd sess. (1909), 1398. Unfortunately for Bailey, the Supreme Court, in *Champion* v. *Ames,* 188 U.S. 321, had previously ruled in favor of such indirect exercises of federal police power. Albert Beveridge cited the precedent and managed to persuade the Senate that Bailey's constitutional qualms were misplaced. In the House questions were raised about the cost of the bill in lost revenue, the efficacy of the bill, and whether or not the enforcement section violated the rules of criminal evidence. The measure survived these objections, only to be held up by a remarkable contretemps. It was decided that since the bill was ostensibly a revenue measue, it had to originate in the House, so the bill was sent back to the Senate with a House number to be, in effect, repassed. In view of the time pressure, such rigid adherence to the rules is difficult to understand. It is almost as if Congress never took the issue seriously. *CR,* 60th Cong., 2nd sess (1909), 1683–84.

87. Wright, "Report from the United States," 20.

88. Some dealers cleverly exploited a technicality. Under the 1909 act smoking opium imported before April 1, 1909 (the day the law went into effect) was not liable to seizure. By saving the revenue stamps from this smoking opium and carefully affixing them to containers filled with the smuggled drug, the dealers usually were able to avoid conviction. However, this and other loopholes in the 1909 act were closed by an amendment approved January 17, 1914. The reasons for this amendment are spelled out in U.S. House, *Reenactment of Opium-Exclusion Act,* 1–5. There was also concern that the demand for the drug would be met by large-scale domestic cultivation of opium poppies, which in turn would be converted to smoking opium. This eventuality was met by the authorization, also on January 17, 1914, of a law placing a prohibitive tax on the

domestic manufacture of smoking opium. See U.S. Senate, *Manufacture of Smoking Opium,* esp. 5–6. For the texts of the amendment to the 1909 act and the statute placing a prohibitive tax on the manufacture of smoking opium, see *Statutes at Large,* 63rd Cong., 2nd sess. (1914), chaps. 9–10.

89. Hasty, 689; Agent W. H. Wouters to L. G. Nutt, May 7, 1924, file 0120-9, TDF; and U.S. Treasury Department, Bureau of Narcotics, *Traffic in Opium for 1931,* 68. See also U.S. Senate, *Report on International Opium Commission,* 57; U.S. House, *Importation and Use of Opium: Hearings,* 88.

90. The loyalty of opium smokers to their drug was widespread, but evidently not universal. Kane, *Opium-Smoking,* 44, 59; Crothers, *Morphinism and Narcomanias,* 211; Helbrant, 26; and Lindesmith, *Addiction and Opiates,* 215, indicate a preference among opium smokers for their accustomed drug and fear of opiates injected hypodermically. However, at least one source (Robertson, 227, 232) reported that many whites switched to morphine well before the 1909 legislation. John M. Scott, a detective who was also a morphine addict, observed that when "it is not convenient for smokers to smoke, they tide over with morphine or gum opium." They evidently shifted back to the pipe as circumstances permitted. ("Boston Notes," no pp., USIOC.)

91. *Report of the Special Commission to Investigate Habit-Forming Drugs,* 10.

92. McIver and Price, 477, 478.

93. McGuire and Lichtenstein, 189.

94. Oral History interview with Dorothy ———, June 27, 1980. This is part of a series of interviews taped with the cooperation of the New York State Division of Substance Abuse Services (hereafter NYDSAS). The NYDSAS oral history project is ongoing, but ultimately these tapes will be housed at Columbia University's Oral History Center. To help ensure confidentiality, the tapes will be restricted for 10 years. All names used here are either truncated or are aliases. Other NYDSAS interviews which refer to the persistence of this elite opium smoking subculture include Patrick C———, May 2, 1980; Abe D———, May 5, 1980; Edith D———, May 16, 1980; "Frieda," May 30, 1980; "Henry," June 9, 1980; "Mel," July 3, 1980; Nicholina ———, July 15, 1980; and "Jerry," July 23, 1980. See also Larner and Tefferteller, 159–160.

95. Patrick C———, May 28, 1980, and "Jack," July 2, 1980, NYDSAS interviews.

96. McGuire and Lichtenstein, 189.

97. In California, for example, the State Board of Pharmacy mounted a sustained, 18-month campaign ending in February 1914. Approximately 1,500 cases were prosecuted, with 1,200 convictions. The drive culminated with the public burning of $20,000 to $25,000 worth of seized narcotics, together with hundreds of opium pipes, "some of them 200 or 300 years old, . . . wrought in ebony, mahogany, bamboo and precious hardwood decked with silver mountings and ivory

mouth pieces, . . . [worth up to] $200 to $300, according to its age and the consequent degree to which it had become impregnated with opium." Some of the pipes were Chinese family heirlooms. ("Opium Pipes Fed to Flames," clipping in "Chinatown" folder, Society of California Pioneers [hereafter SCP], San Francisco.)

From the point of view of the user, the great drawback of smoking opium, aside from the drug's rapidly increasing price, was the ease with which it could be detected. The layout was bulky, smoking opium gave off a distinctive odor, and the locations of dens were usually known to police. In the case of San Francisco, Jesse Cook, police chief from 1908 to 1910, was able to compile an extensive list of dens; he had the option of moving in on them anytime he chose. ("Data given to Mrs. M. G. Foster by Jesse Cook . . ." [MS, n.d.], "Chinatown" folder, SCP.) The addict using morphine or heroin, however, was a less conspicuous and more mobile target. (Helbrant, 26.)

98. Treadway, "Further Observations," 546. See also Simon, 676.

99. Ball and Lau, 243. Chinese addicts in Hawaii also held out for a time; they threatened to withhold their labor on plantations unless "assured that they [would] not be disturbed in their habit of smoking opium." (1926 memorandum and data sheet signed S. L. Rakusin, file 0120–9, TDF.) During the 1930s, however, aging Chinese opium smokers there either died off, returned or were deported to China, were forced into abstinence, or presumably switched to other opiates; by 1939 opium dens had "practically ceased to exist" in Hawaii. (C. T. Stevenson to H. J. Anslinger, March 8, 1940, file 0120–9, TDF.) Dillon, 68, also comments on the declining use of smoking opium by Chinese: "It was the change in mores of the Americanizing Chinese rather than the crackdown by officials—or even the physical destruction of the dens by the [1906] holocaust—which brought an end to the opium evil." That may be partially true for second-generation and third-generation Chinese born in the United States, but Dillon underestimates the significance of the switch to other opiates, the continuation of "the opium evil" in other forms. As another San Franciscan, Fritz Simmons, 3, put it, "Chinese dope addicts . . . adopted the needle along with other western habits."

100. Mr. "Li," June 5, 1980, NYDSAS interview. In San Francisco a 5-tael tin of high-quality smoking opium had reached $600 to $700 by 1940. U.S. Treasury Department, Bureau of Narcotics, *Traffic in Opium for 1940*, 19, and *Traffic in Opium for 1945*, 16.

101. *Historical Statistics*, 9.

---

4 Addiction to Heroin

1. Heroin was first produced in 1874, but did not come into general use until some years after its discovery. The most important early proponent of heroin was H. Dreser, "Pharmakologisches über einige Mor-

phinderivate" and "Ueber die Wirkung einiger Derivate des Morphins auf die Athmung." English-language summaries of Dreser's work on heroin (and that of others) soon appeared in American and British journals. See also "History of Heroin," 3–6; and Musto, "Early History," 175.

2. Farr, 893; Drysdale, 354–357; Leahy, 251.

3. Hubbard, "New York City Narcotic Clinic," 44–45; MS records, box 6, KP. Kolb listed 40 heroin users altogether, defined here as those who either moved from cocaine to heroin, or who began with heroin, either alone or in combination with cocaine and/or morphine. (Cases whose histories are listed as morphine to heroin, or as cocaine and morphine to heroin, are counted as morphine addicts. See Chapter 2, note 9.)

4. Terry, *1912 Annual Report,* 27. This situation was reversed by the influx of itinerant addicts the following year; the *1913 Annual Report,* 57, listed 67.9 percent of the heroin users as male. One possible reason that females predominated in the first report is that in 1912 Terry was registering mainly local medical addicts; at that time heroin was only beginning to spread among largely male, nonmedical users. See also notes 37 and 63 below.

5. Leahy, 260, 256, gives the age of the Brooklyn patients as 20, the length of their addiction as "about one year," yielding an approximate beginning age of 19 years. For Cleveland see Drysdale, 354–357. The Bellevue average is derived from the ward notes of Dr. Charles Stokes (TS, 1917), file 2123, USPHS, based on 18 cases where the apparent first use of an opiate was heroin. (One case, that of "Frank Pare," has been deleted because I could not determine which opiate was used initially.)

6. Stokes, "Problem of Narcotic Addiction," 756.

7. McPherson and Cohen, 638–639.

8. MS records, box 6, KP, for the 38 heroin cases of known length of addiction.

9. McGuire and Lichtenstein, 189.

10. Brown, "Enforcement," 332. See also "Caught Using Heroin," 18; Bailey, "Heroin Habit," 315; Farr, 893; Stokes, "Features of Narcotic Addiction," 766–768; Hubbard, "New York City Narcotic Clinic," 36; and *Traffic in Narcotic Drugs,* 24.

11. Lichtenstein, "Narcotic Addiction," 964.

12. Terry, *1912 Annual Report,* 27. These users evidently moved, died, or were cured, because the following year no black heroin users were listed.

13. Drysdale, 354–357; Leahy, 260; and McPherson and Cohen, 637.

14. Leahy, 260; Stokes, ward notes, file 2123, USPHS (18 cases); Hubbard, "New York City Narcotic Clinic," 45; 1920 census. See also McGuire and Lichtenstein, 189.

15. McPherson and Cohen, 638. Overall, 10 of the 100 cases studied

were foreign-born, although this would include some nonheroin users (p. 637).

16. Leahy, 260. Drysdale, 354–357, indicates that there were several (6 of 20) "Hebrew" heroin users, but does not indicate their country of birth.

17. Kolb, "Drug Addiction in its Relation to Crime," 86–87.

18. Phillips, "Prevalence of the Heroin Habit," 2147; Drysdale, passim. The reasons why heroin use fell into abeyance outside the New York City area are discussed further below.

19. Sandoz, 12; Dai, 60–61. According to Sceleth and Kuh, 679, less than 4 percent of Chicago's addicts used heroin in 1924.

20. New York, *Second Annual Report,* 5–6; "Survey of Drug Addicts," 1655.

21. Stokes, "Problem of Addiction," 756. Italics deleted from the original.

22. Sources that refer to heroin addicts concentrating in tenderloin districts and/or large cities include: Phillips, "Prevalence of the Heroin Habit," 2147; Brown, "Enforcement," 332; Farr, 893; Bloedorn, 309; McPherson and Cohen, 637; and MacMartin, 112.

23. Stokes, "Problem of Addiction," 756.

24. This was a theme that surfaced often in the NYDSAS interviews— for example, "Frieda," May 30, 1980, and "Lillie," June 27, 1980.

25. Bailey, "Heroin Habit," 315; New York, *Second Annual Report,* 18. See also note 125 below.

26. Descriptions of the appearance and behavior of heroin addicts are found in Stokes, "Problem of Addiction," 756, and Hubbard, "New York City Narcotic Clinic," 36–39. "In our opinion," wrote Hubbard, "drug addiction is simply a degrading, debasing habit, and it is not necessary to consider this indulgence in any other light than an anti-social one." McIver and Price, 478, in words strikingly similar to those applied to opium smokers, refer to heroin addiction spreading among "the dissipated and vicious."

27. Leahy, 257; Stokes, "Problem of Addiction," 756; and McPherson and Cohen, 637.

28. The most thorough list of occupations is found in Hubbard, "New York City Narcotic Clinic," 46–47. It is impossible, however, to tell how many of the addicts in Hubbard's occupational categories used opium or morphine. Another problem is that some of his figures are at variance with those given in New York, *Second Annual Report,* 19. See also Phillips, "Prevalence of the Heroin Habit," 2147; Drysdale, 354–357; McGuire and Lichtenstein, 189; and Stokes, "Problem of Addiction," 756.

29. Sellew, 1673–74 (cases 5 through 9); and McIver and Price, 477, "notorious crooks and thieves." Not all of McIver and Price's cases used heroin; unfortunately they are vague about the kinds of opiates used. It is certain, however, that a minority (38 of 147) used morphine exclusively.

30. McGuire and Lichtenstein, 189; and Hubbard, "New York City

Narcotic Clinic," 46. Presumably some of the female heroin addicts were housewives. Drysdale, 354–357, lists the occupations of the 4 female heroin users in his sample as "housework," wife, and prostitute (2). Leahy, 260, states that 3 of 7 females in his sample were married, but did not specify their occupation. The majority of the male heroin addicts were single, separated, or divorced.

31. Leahy, 257. See also "The Opium Habit"; McIver and Price, 477; and Kane et al., 503.

32. Hawkins, 71–75. Dr. Hawkins was himself an opiate addict.

33. In 1921 Terry published an apologia for maintenance, "Some Recent Experiments in Narcotic Control," 32–44, in which he indicated more clearly than in any other work his essential sympathy for the addict and support for maintenance programs. See also Terry to L. B. Dunham, March 11, 1929, ser. 3, box 5, folder 150, and L. B. Dunham to Colonel [Arthur] Woods, January 22, 1930, ser. 3, box 6, folder 152, both CDA. Terry's views on maintenance are discussed further in Chapter 5. For the views of Terry and Pellens on iatrogenic addiction, see Terry et al., 85–86; Terry and Pellens, 53–156; and Terry, Pellens, and Cox, 21. As late as 1931 Terry was still fuming about the "needless use of opium"; see his "Development and Causes of Opium Addiction," 343.

34. Terry and Pellens, 76–86, 484. "Legal Heroin," 6, takes Terry and Pellens' argument as a given and then further exaggerates the problem, claiming "literally millions" of medical heroin addicts.

35. Ibid., 85. Brown, "Enforcement," 332, reaches a similar conclusion. Only 2 of 20 heroin cases in Drysdale, 354–357, list medical causes. When Alexander Lambert read the draft of *The Opium Problem,* he specifically criticized its failure to "differentiate between the heroin and morphine groups of narcotic users" and indicated that heroin use was essentially a "sociologic," rather than a medical, phenomenon. Mildred Pellens, "Report on Survey of Scientific Opinion Concerning Proposed Activities to the Committee on Drug Addictions" (TS, 1926), 35, ser. 4, box 1, folder 554, CDA.

36. Bailey, "Heroin Habit," 315.

37. Sellew, 1670–78. It is not certain, however, that by 1912 medical heroin addicts were outnumbered by nonmedical types. See Kebler, "Present Status," 15, for evidence that medical heroin addicts were still in the majority in 1911. The swing to heroin in urban slums was only then getting under way.

38. Stokes, ward notes, file 2123, USPHS. See also Drysdale, 354–357.

39. "Questionaire [*sic*] re Drug Habit," box 6, KP; Kolb to John H. Remig, November 14, 1927, box 4, KP. Kolb expressed his hypothesis to Remig as follows: "My idea has been that the use of heroin in medical practice seldom resulted in addiction, although when used in the underworld for dissipation only it doubtless has produced numerous addicts." To my knowledge, the results of the Kolb-Remig survey were never

published. Kolb, on the basis of other data in his possession, later noted that only 1 of a group of 119 medical addicts was originally addicted to heroin. ("Drug Addiction: A Study of Some Medical Cases," 171–183; MS records, box 6, KP.)

40. Dreser's articles are cited in note 1 above. Among the early American reports discussing heroin's usefulness in respiratory disease are Manges, "Treatment of Coughs," 768–770; Wood, "Newer Substitutes," 89–90; Fulton, 960–961; Herwirsch, 728–730; Coblentz, 70; Lang, 79–80; Daly, 190–192; and Stewart, 86–88. Towns, 586, also notes that a number of commercial cough and asthma preparations contained heroin.

41. Lazarus, 600–602. The neuralgia case is of interest because the following year Stewart, 88, stated, "My results with heroin in several cases of neuralgia . . . have been negative." Both cases of addiction reported in Brooks and Mixwell, 386–387, involved heroin for cough. These authors also commented on the growing nonmedical use of heroin on the extreme East Side and West Side of New York City. For an unusual case of tuberculosis phobia leading to addiction, see Fauntleroy, 930.

42. "Heroin Hydrochloride," 1303.

43. Geis, 929–930; Brown and Tompkins, 519–520; Johnson, "A Few Remarks," 413–415.

44. Platt and Labate, 51–52.

45. Floret, 512.

46. Manges, "Treatment," 770.

47. Pettey, "Heroin Habit," 180. See also Wood, "Newer Substitutes," 90, and Patterson, 166.

48. *Merck's 1907 Index,* 216. Charles W. Richardson, testifying before the House on behalf of the AMA in *Prohibiting the Importation of Opium for the Manufacture of Heroin: Hearings,* 11, stated that "in my work in medicine it [heroin] was largely used to allay cough." Charles Stokes, a former navy surgeon general who became interested in and wrote several articles on opiate addiction, described heroin as "a palliative in respiratory infections." ("Drug Addiction, the Drug Made Criminal and the Remedy" [TS, n.d.], file 2123, USPHS.) Phillips, 2146, recounts a case of addiction stemming from the administration of heroin as an analgesic, but otherwise stresses its frequent use in cough, as does Stieren, 870. Musto, "Early History," 175–176, also emphasizes the drug's use as a cough suppressant. See also Street, *I Was a Drug Addict,* 14.

Others dissent from this view, but without good evidence. There is an undocumented claim in McCoy et al., 4: "Hailed as a 'miracle drug' by medical experts around the globe, heroin was widely prescribed as a nonaddicting cure-all for whatever ails you, and soon became one of the most popular patent medicines on the market." Another unsubstantiated statement is the one in Barber, 26, that heroin was "touted as 'great for children.' " There is also a remark in "History of Heroin," 3, that heroin was prescribed "for almost all illnesses in which codeine and morphine had been found." This inference seems to be unfounded, however, as the primary medical sources cited in the article are almost exclusively concerned with the use of heroin in treating respiratory disease. Altogether I have found only one contemporary source (Johnson, "A Few Remarks," 414) that claimed for heroin widespread popularity as an analgesic agent—and that claim is suspect, since Johnson was one of the most irresponsible and uncritical of all the heroin enthusiasts.

49. See, for example, the advertisements in the December 2, 1899, February 2, 1901, April 12, 1902, and April 19, 1902 issues of *JAMA* (adv. secs., pp. 47, 25 and 31, 36, and 34, respectively).

50. Lang, 19; Coblentz, 70; and *JAMA* ads cited above.

51. It was sometimes injected, however, when given as an analgesic. Brown and Tompkins, 520. On the significance of small doses see Kolb, "Drug Addiction: A Study of Some Medical Cases," 172.

52. Brown and Tompkins, 520; Floeckinger, 644; Daly, 190. See also Floret, 512, and Johnson, "A Few Remarks," 413. Claims about heroin's safety led some to try the drug who otherwise might not have—for example, case 1 in Sellew, 1671.

53. "Newer Substitutes," 90. Wood's exact words were, "Of course, it is hardly possible to say as yet whether these remedies [dionin and heroin] are likely to cause drug-habits." Manges, "Second Report," 82. Stewart, 88, is ambivalent: claiming that heroin did not "tend to produce habit," he nevertheless warned that "it is very unwise to place this drug in the hands of your patients for their indiscriminate use as it will likely be abused, and may lead to toxic symptoms."

54. Pettey, "Heroin Habit," 174–180.

55. "Heroin Hydrochloride," 1303.

56. See, for instance, "Heroin and the Results of Its Abuse as a Drug," 91; "Heroin and the Heroin Habit," 576. Another and ruder type of warning was the lawsuit brought by an outraged patient. See "Defective Complaint," 1969.

57. Comment by Blair in "Symposium on 'The Doctor and the Drug Addict,' " 1591. Testifying before the House in 1923, Dr. Amos O. Squire remarked that "years ago we did use heroin frequently in chest conditions, but I have not prescribed heroin in 20 years, and I do not think the average practitioner of medicine has." Squire's testimony is reprinted in *Establishment of Two Federal Narcotic Farms: Hearings,* 169.

58. Upham et al., 1328, 1318.

59. Eulenberg, 187; Lazarus, 600. See also Manges, "Second Report," 53, and Ahlborn, 235–236. One historian of heroin, John Kramer, 18, comments as follows: "Though the story has been told often, and has even been dignified by appearing in print, I have found no evidence for the contention that heroin was introduced as a cure for the morphine habit." The key word is *introduced.* True, heroin was not intended primarily or even secondarily for use in morphine addiction, nor was it advertised as such; Eulenberg's and the others' point was simply that here was another, unanticipated benefit of the drug.

60. Pettey, "Heroin Habit," 176. Heroin was also the active ingredient in at least one habit cure, "Habitina." (Stieren, 869–870.)

61. Of 151 physicians surveyed in 1911 none recommended heroin to "remove the craving and cure addiction." (Kebler, "Present Status," 22.) The use of heroin to treat morphine addiction was not an isolated episode; other drugs, such as cocaine, codeine, and dionin (ethylmorphine hydrochloride) were also tried. Cocaine in morphine addiction is discussed below; for codeine see Lindenberger, 219, and Barr, 161–162; for dionin see Fromme, 302. This article was abstracted as "Dionin in Chronic Morphinism," *JAMA*, 32 (1899), 1400. Several advertisements (for example, *JAMA*, April 19, 1902, adv. sec., pp. 14, 34) also recommended the use of this drug in morphine addiction.

62. *CR*, 60th Cong., 2nd sess. (1909), 1683.

63. Bailey, "Heroin Habit," 314. Bailey's dating of the problem to 1910 is corroborated by Bloedorn, chart 6, 312, and Street, *I Was a Drug Addict*, 11, 37. Farr, 893, gives the date for the first case treated at Philadelphia General Hospital as 1911, with a sharp increase in admissions beginning in 1913. McIver and Price, 478, suggest 1912 as the date underworld heroin use began. See also U.S. House, *Prohibiting the Importation of Opium for the Manufacture of Heroin: Hearings*, 46.

64. McIver and Price, 478.

65. Freud's work on cocaine has been conveniently collected in an annotated volume entitled *Cocaine Papers*, Robert Byck and Anna Freud, eds.

66. "Coca Erythroxylon and Its Derivatives," cited in Freud, 128.

67. Stockwell, 402–404; Huse, 256–257; Stimmel, 252–253; LeForger, 458; Marsh, "A Case of the Opium Habit," 359; Freud, 63–73; Whittaker, 145, 148; Bolles, "Coca," 218–219; and Hammond, 754–759. Hammond, a vigorous advocate of the drug, even noted that cocaine-soaked lint had been used to numb the genitals of female masturbators. Exotic applications aside, it appears that the most common origin of medically related cocaine addiction was the use of the drug to treat catarrh (inflammation of a mucous membrane resulting in discharge). See, for example, Mattison, "Cocainism," 34–36, and the case of self-treatment reviewed in Gilbert, 119. Cocaine is not addicting in the same sense that the opiates are—that is, there are no physical withdrawal symptoms. Cessation can bring on a train of psychological symptoms, however, including marked depression and craving for the drug.

68. Helfand, 13. See also Stockwell, 403; "Coca Erythroxylon and Its Derivatives," cited in Freud, 133; and Musto, *American Disease*, 7.

69. Ten of 17 cases in Mattison, "Cocainism," 34–36, involve physicians, and 4 of 6 in Brainerd, 193–201. See also Hunter, "Evils of Cocaine," 331–338. William S. Halsted and Ernst von Fleischl-Marxow are other well-known examples.

70. Lewin, *Phantastica*, 80; Jones, 64; Freud, xxxii. One of the more

trenchant American critics of cocaine in morphine addiction was Jansen Mattison, who took up the cause in 1887. See his article, "Cocainism," 474. See also Meylert, 51–52.

71. Haynes, 14; and Scheppegrell, 421. W. Golden Mortimer defended cocaine in his massive *Peru: History of Coca,* 20–21, arguing that the drug was perfectly safe when used in the treatment of normal patients. He failed, however, to convince an increasingly wary profession.

72. C[rouch], 909; Simon, 677; Keys, 42, 136; and Musto, *American Disease,* 8.

73. Kebler, "Habit Forming Agents," 6–12, for nostrums and soft drinks containing cocaine. Meister, 344, and Kempner, 48–49, for cases of cocaine through the mail. In answer to a frequently asked question, Coca-Cola at one time did contain cocaine, although only a minute quantity. Kahn, 99.

74. "Negro Cocaine Fiends," 895, abstracted as "The Cocaine Habit Among Negroes," 1729. See also Pettey, *Narcotic Drug Diseases,* 426. There were also isolated episodes of white workers (such as mill operatives in Maine and miners in Colorado) resorting to cocaine. Rev. Harry N. Pringle to Wright, December 3, 1909, USIOC; and Whiteside, 64.

75. Whittaker, 148. See also Stockwell, 401.

76. "The Cocaine Habit Among Negroes," 1729; Harris Dickson to Wright, December 7, 1909, USIOC.

77. Cited in Levine, 283.

78. "Cocaine Alley," 337–338; "The Cocain Habit," *JAMA,* 34 (1900), 1637.

79. The question of the behavior of black cocaine users is extremely troublesome; more research, especially in primary sources such as police and coroners' records, is clearly needed. Numerous printed sources mention violent crimes by black cocaine users, performed with unusual strength and desperation. See, for example, the statement of Col. J. W. Watson in "Cocaine Sniffers," 11; the statement of District Attorney St. Clair Adams in "Aaron Martin Sold 470 Ounces of Cocaine in Nine Months," *New Orleans Item,* n.d., no pp., clipping, USIOC; the statement of Judge Harris Dickson in Collins and Day, vol. 4 (July 1909), 4, 29; Werner, 84–86; Wright's remarks in U.S. Senate, *Report on the International Opium Commission,* 48–50; U.S. House, *Importation and Use of Opium: Hearings,* 83; "10 Killed," 1; Williams, "Negro Cocaine 'Fiends,' " 12, and "Drug Habit Menace," 247–249. Williams and Werner were more concerned about assault and murder, Wright about the rape of white women.

Several of the police chiefs who corresponded with Wright (such as J. J. Reagan of Lexington, Ky., June 17, 1909; W. P. Ford of Norfolk, Va., June 18, 1909; E. E. Creecy of St. Louis, June 21, 1909; A. G. Miller of Des Moines, June 21, 1909; and W. J. O'Connor of New Orleans, June 22, 1909; all USIOC) stated that cocaine was "an incentive to crime," without going into particulars; Louisville Police Chief J. H. Haager wrote, "When negroes get too much of it they are inclined to go on the war-path, and when in this condition they give a police officer who attempts to arrest them . . . a hard time." (Haager to Wright, July 9, 1909, USIOC.) During the period when it was freely available, noted Pittsburgh's Superintendent of Police Thomas A. McQuaide, "Cocaine produced nearly as many court cases as alcohol." (McQuaide to Wright, June 29, 1909, USIOC.)

Wright, as Musto observes, had ulterior, political motives for playing up the rape stories, so his testimony should be discounted. Williams may also have had ulterior motives, in the sense that he was an anti-prohibitionist and believed that the public would tolerate alcohol if it perceived the alternative — cocaine — to be more dangerous. (Musto, *American Disease*, 256 n. 20.) Interestingly, Williams extended his antiprohibition philosophy to narcotics; he was bitterly opposed to the government's antimaintenance policy. See his illustrations in Henry Smith Williams, *Drug Addicts are Human Beings.* But the other authorities — Colonel Watson, Judge Dickson, District Attorney Adams, Chiefs Werner, Haager, McQuaide, and the other police officials — had no apparent motive for distortion. Moreover, Williams, Werner, and the "10 Killed" story provided detailed accounts of the alleged violent incidents.

Musto, *American Disease*, 7, followed by Ashley, *Cocaine*, 67–72, Zentner, "Cocaine," 97–98, Phillips and Wynne, 64–71, and others debunk stories of black cocaine rampages. To quote Musto, "These fantasies characterized white fear, not the reality of cocaine's effects, and gave one more reason for the repression of blacks." Ashley's rebuke is even sharper, "Of course all these fearmongering fantasies were just that, fantasies and nothing more." Phillips and Wynne view the episode as a "media" fabrication, adding that "no reputable researchers have uncovered any statistical or other type of evidence to indicate that the use of cocaine resulted in a massive (black) crime wave."

While I share these authors' essential skepticism and doubt that black cocaine rampages were commonplace, I nevertheless feel it is important to offer some plausible explanation of why so many contemporaries were convinced of the link between black cocaine use and crime. Musto suggests that the stories were used as an excuse to repress and disfranchise blacks, and as a convenient explanation for crime waves (*American Disease*, 255 n. 15). Ashley thinks the police used them as an excuse to obtain heavier weapons. Less conspiratorially, it may have been that the police were simply repeating a legend based on a few actual incidents and embellished with the passage of time. It is not difficult to imagine how a "hitherto inoffensive, law-abiding negro," as Williams described him, chafing under accumulated slurs and outrages, might under the influence of cocaine vent his rage on a white person, especially a white policeman. Such an attack might represent genuine cocaine psychosis, or simply relaxed inhibitions combined with long-standing grievances.

(Significantly, white cocaine users as well were observed to seek revenge "for some real or imaginary insult." Crothers, "Cocainism," 80. See also the "Aaron Martin" clipping; Whiteside, 64; and Phillips and Wynne, 162–163.) Whatever the motive of the attack, a few such incidents would be more than enough material from which to fashion a cocaine "menace." The fear of cocaine-sniffing blacks was thus not unlike the fear of slave rebellion that swept the South after Nat Turner's short-lived foray; both were exaggerated reactions to isolated but potently symbolic deeds.

Another possible explanation involves the background of black cocaine users, especially those who lived in cities. They belonged, as Chiefs O'Connor and Werner put it, to the "immoral and lower" and "illiterate and troublesome" elements of the black community. Some were, in other words, already engaged in criminal activity, and a white policeman, aware that they also sniffed cocaine, might well have inferred that cocaine caused the crime: *post hoc ergo propter hoc.*

Finally, there is a sense in which cocaine indirectly contributed to crimes against property. Regular cocaine use could be expensive, especially after restrictive state legislation increased its price; therefore many impoverished black users would have had to resort to petty crime if they wanted to obtain the drug. Once again an observer—particularly one who had heard other cocaine-crime stories—could well have drawn the inference that the action of the drug itself, rather than the lack of money to purchase it, had inspired the deed. (A similar mistake was made during the early 1920s, when it was commonly held that heroin, rather than the compulsion to obtain it, was a direct incentive to crime.)

So the belief that cocaine caused blacks to commit crimes, which perhaps originated in one or two genuine episodes, was sustained and expanded by a false sense of causation. The legend grew even further when Wright and Williams, both physicians with impeccable credentials, played it up to suit their own political ends.

80. Terry, *1912 Annual Report,* 27, not counting combination opiate-cocaine users, or occasional users who failed to find their way into Terry's program. The following year the situation was reversed, but only, as repeatedly noted, after a large influx of outside users. It is my view that the original 1912 data best represent the Jacksonville situation. Several of the police chiefs who were consulted by Wright or his assistants (for example, Colonel Swan in "Baltimore Notes," no pp.; W. P. Ford of Norfolk, Va., June 18, 1909; J. J. Donahue of Omaha, June 21, 1909; A. G. Miller of Des Moines, June 21, 1909; and Thomas A. McQuaide of Pittsburgh, June 29, 1909; all USIOC) stated that there were proportionately more black cocaine users than white. This was also the opinion of two prison physicians, O. J. Bennett at the Western Penitentiary of Pennsylvania and Frank A. McGuire at the City Prison of New York. Bennett found that 7 of 682 inmates examined over a two-year period admitted the use of cocaine, and all of these were black. "My candid

opinion of the matter," he was quoted as saying, "is that use of . . . [cocaine] is increasing rapidly, especially among the black population." (Simonton, 558; McGuire to Wright, August 4, 1908, USIOC.)

Years later blacks were still overrepresented among federal prisoners who used only cocaine; of 11 such cases listed in U.S. House, *Establishment of Two Federal Narcotic Farms: Hearings*, 140–147, 151–160, there were 4 blacks, 6 whites, and 1 Mexican. Finally, of 7 cocaine-only cases listed in MS records, box 6, KP, 3 were black. The exception to the rule seems to have been California, where cocaine was confined largely to whites. (Memorandum to San Francisco Police Captain Thomas S. Duke, forwarded to Wright, July 26, 1909, USIOC.) California, it should be added, had only a small black population and was geographically removed from the regions of greatest black cocaine use, the South and East. Compare Eberle et al., 468.

There is one contrary article, Green, 702, to the effect that cocaine was a factor in only 2 of 2,119 black cases admitted to the Georgia State Sanitarium between January 1, 1909, and January 1, 1914. Green thought cocaine sufficiently expensive and (surprisingly) disruptive of working ability that few blacks could afford its habitual use, hence few psychoses resulted. He conducted his study, however, well after adverse legislation had driven up the price of the drug. Green's statistics, moreover, do not of themselves prove a low incidence of cocaine use among Georgia blacks—only that cocaine-using blacks were not confined in Georgia sanitariums. Either cocaine psychosis was uncommon or, when it occurred, some other agency dealt with it. Incidents involving theft or violence would be more likely to terminate in prison, or at the end of a rope, than in an asylum. (Compare the places of confinement for the medical and the criminal cases in Simonton, 558.)

Finally, I have been in correspondence with Lawrence W. Levine, whose *Black Culture and Black Consciousness* is cited above. On the basis of his study of black music, Levine feels that cocaine use was common, although he doubts that the drug provoked interracial violence. I am indebted to Eugene Genovese for calling my attention to Levine's work.

81. Bingham to Wright, June 23, 1909, USIOC; also "Cocaine Alley," 337–338; "The Cocain Habit," *JAMA*, 36 (1900), 330; "Cocaine Sniffers," 11; "Growing Menace," 1; J. J. Donahue to Wright, June 21, 1909, and Thomas S. Duke to Wright, June 26, 1909, both USIOC; and Werner, 84. Just as the proximity of the Chinese to the red-light district helps to explain the spread of opium smoking to the white underworld (Chapter 3, note 49), the fact that recently arrived blacks also settled in or near the tenderloin district provides a clue to understanding why cocaine sniffing was adopted by white prostitutes and criminals in several different cities at approximately the same time. (Significantly, one of the earliest references to white cocaine use, that of Waterhouse, 464–465, describes black and white prostitutes in St. Louis sniffing together.)

Several journal articles published from 1898 to 1910 convey a feeling of transition: medically related cocainism, the authors suggested, was still a problem, but the practice was also spreading rapidly among blacks and lower-class, urban whites who took the drug for euphoric purposes. Compare Crothers, "Cocaine-Inebriety," 370; Simonton, passim; Hunter, "Evils of Cocaine," 334; and Crothers, "Cocainism," 79, 81. Statistics in *Reports of the Presidents' Homes Commission,* 254, also point to growing use by criminals; 15 of 175 prisoners studied in the Washington workhouse "had intimate knowledge of the use of cocaine." This rate, 85.7 per thousand, is much higher than the 2.3 per thousand rate observed for the Jacksonville population at large. Unfortunately, I have been unable to determine the exact date the survey was made, or the nature of the charges against these prisoners, or their race. Finally, it should be noted that cocaine became popular among underworld users in Europe and elsewhere. Lewin, 80; and Woods, 25.

82. Poole to Wright, July 27, 1908, USIOC. Eberle et al., 476, comment, "The use of cocaine seems to be rapidly supplanting in part the use of morphine among men and women of the 'underworld.'" It is more likely, however, that underworld users, rather than abandoning opiates, simply used them in conjunction with morphine. Compare Vice Commission of Chicago, 84–87.

83. Chase et al., 18; Eberle et al., 476; Meister, 345; *Traffic in Narcotic Drugs,* 23; and Charles Terry to Lawrence Dunham, July 24, 1932, ser. 3, box 4, folder 133, CDA. Block, "The Snowman Cometh," 88, notes use by prostitutes, as well as by actors and actresses with underworld connections.

84. Biondi, 466. See also Scheppegrell, 421; Simonton, 559; Owens, "Signs and Symptoms," 329; Meister, 346; Drysdale, 354–357; and Reynolds, 62. Douglas, "Cocainism," 115, reports that among his patients the hypodermic route was more common. He was dealing, however, with morphine addicts who had turned to cocaine in an attempt at cure, only to become addicted to both drugs—a type of user already familiar with the hypodermic method.

85. Wilbert, "Efforts to Curb Misuse," 901–923.

86. *Laws of New York, 1907,* chap. 424, 879–880; *1908,* chap. 277, 764–765; *1910,* chap. 131, 231–233; and *1913,* chap. 470, 984–991. Musto, *American Disease,* 103–104.

87. Stokes, "Problem of Narcotic Addiction," 756, 757; Chase et al., 9; Farr, 893, 894; Wilbert, "Efforts to Curb Misuse," 898. MS records, box 6, KP, show that 26 of 40 heroin addicts used cocaine prior to or concurrently with the first use of heroin. See also note 3 above.

88. "15,000 Drug Victims," 20; and Hughes, 181. Cocaine is sometimes classed as a "narcotic" for legal purposes, although its true action is that of a stimulant.

89. Stokes, "Problem of Narcotic Addiction," 756. Farr, 893, mentions that heroin and cocaine were sometimes sniffed together.

90. On the prior use of cocaine by juvenile gangs see "Boy Cocaine Snuffers," 6, and Collins and Day, vol. 5 (November 1909), 4–5. Nick J————, June 3, 1980, NYDSAS interview, gives a good description of cocaine sniffing by members of a juvenile gang.

91. Bailey, "Heroin Habit," 315. Charles Schultz, in Lambert et al., 469, added that many of those who passed heroin about "in poolrooms, dance halls, street corners, etc." misrepresented it as nonaddicting. Several other sources also made use of the tobacco analogy, for instance, Hubbard, "New York City Narcotic Clinic," 36; Stokes, "Problem of Narcotic Addiction," 757, and Lambert, 6. Jane Addams remarked that "boys of the city streets . . . whose instinctive craving for excitement is directed into forbidden channels by the social conditions under which they live, are prone to experiment with drugs, as well as the other evils of drink and cigarettes." (Collins and Day, vol. 5 [November 1909], 4–5.) For an excellent first-person account of the role of peer influence, with respect to both initial use and relapse, see Street, *I Was a Drug Addict,* passim.

92. Leahy, 256–257.

93. Lambert to Miss Shimer, December 6, 1924, box 3, KP. Stokes, "Drug Addiction, the Drug Made Criminal and the Remedy," USPHS, notes that "heroinism" was a "gang or crowd addiction," in contrast to the "solitary habit" of opium and morphine addiction.

94. Good descriptions of the gangs and their activities can be found in "New York's Junior Gangland," 16, and Thrasher, *The Gang.* Thrasher's study was first published in 1927 and contains information on gangs in New York and other eastern cities, in addition to those in Chicago. Asbury's *Gangs of New York* furnishes some useful information, but deals mainly with gangs of professional criminals in an earlier era.

95. The student-addicts mentioned by Lambert, 144, are examples.

96. Wright denied this, reporting to the Shanghai Opium Commission that "among the personnel of our Army and Navy there is not the slightest evidence that the use of opium or its derivatives has been introduced except for purely medical purposes." ("Report from the United States," 20.) Luckily for Wright the assembled delegates lacked access to his files, else they might have found a letter from an Illinois physician, George A. Zeller, who had served for three years in the Philippines. "In our isolated posts in the provinces," Zeller wrote, "the tiendas or stores of the Chinese were places wherein the soldiers liked to congregate. Every place of this sort had an opium joint and the proprietor would lie down on his bamboo bunk and proceed with his smoke, using from one to five pipes in the presence of the visitor with absolute unconcern, perhaps in the next bunk some Chinaman would be lying in a stupor. The soldier[s] became interested in and later tolerant and it was found that probably an average of three American soldiers to the company became addicted to the opium habit. I had several such in the post hospitals at various times." (Zeller to Wright, September 7, 1908, USIOC.) "Portland,

Maine, Notes" (TS, 1908), 2, USIOC, also speaks of cocaine use by soldiers returning from the Philippines. See also Eberle et al., 475; Musto, *American Disease,* 33; and Block, 88.

97. Owens, "Importance of Eliminating the Cocaine Habitué," 204–205; Blanchard, 140–143; Meister, 344–351; King, "Use of Habit-Forming Drugs," 273–281, 380–384; Blair, "Relation of Drug Addiction to Industry," 294; "Report of Committee on Drug Addiction" (TS, 1926), 9, file 0120-9, TDF; and Richardson, case 26–3, pp. 3–4. The idea that heroin prolonged intercourse was also common among civilians. (McIver and Price, 478.) In the long run, of course, heroin addiction drastically reduces sexual desire and function.

98. Bailey, "Nervous and Mental Disease," 195.

99. Perkins, 116.

100. See McIver and Price, 478, and Farr, 893–894, on Philadelphia's heroin problem. Block, "The Snowman Cometh," 87, notes "well-established" criminal connections between New York and Philadelphia, which may help to explain the continued availability of heroin in the latter city. Wilmington, Delaware, a city not far from Philadelphia, also had a high incidence of heroin addiction, judging from case summaries in McPherson and Cohen, 638–639.

101. See Blanchard, 142, and Chase et al., 9, for Boston; Sceleth and Kuh, 681 (entries under heroin in table entitled "Deaths from Narcotics in Cook County"), for Chicago.

102. Kane et al., "Drugs and Crime," 503. There is a similar story in Street, *I Was a Drug Addict,* 37.

103. Another factor was that the New York City narcotic clinic (1919–1920) supplied heroin or morphine, whereas most other clinics furnished only the latter. Thus New York addicts were not induced to switch to morphine during the city's brief clinic era.

104. U.S. House, *Exportation of Opium: Hearings,* 25–26, 132. See also National Drug Trade Conference, "Special Meeting of the National Drug Trade Conference, New Willard Hotel, Washington, D.C., Tuesday, May 1, 1917" (TS, 1917), 53, 61, NLM. Heroin was so scarce in Boston that one female user paid a dollar for 1/12 grain. Similar conditions prevailed in Minneapolis–St. Paul, where, according to retail druggist Charles T. Heller, "we find in the underworld that their entire supply . . . consists of morphine. Heroin we do not hear of." (Ibid., 94.) Heller also reported that the morphine was smuggled from Canada (p. 95).

105. Stanley, "Morphinism and Crime," 751. In an earlier article, "Morphinism," 587, Stanley emphasized heroin's medical applications, particularly in bronchial and pulmonary affections, rather than its use as a euphoric agent.

106. Massachusetts, *Report of the Special Commission to Investigate Habit-Forming Drugs,* 10.

107. Sandoz, "Report on Morphinism," esp. 12, 34–37. Morphine

and cocaine were used together to generate a stronger feeling of euphoria, particularly by those who had undergone a reversal of effects and no longer derived much pleasure from morphine alone. Terry remarked that "those using the combined drugs are the most depraved class of whites," in contrast to the straight opium or morphine users, whose addiction generally was medically related. ("Drug Addictions," 30.) This generalization seems to hold up elsewhere, with the exception of opium and morphine addicts who were treated with cocaine in the 1880s, only to form a "twin habit."

108. See Chapter 2. Significantly, males made up a larger percentage of the Cleveland morphine cases attributed to indulgence (80.0 percent) than they did of the cases attributed to illness (61.1 percent); Drysdale, 354–357. The difference is even more pronounced in MS records, box 6, KP. Of 93 undoubted cases of medical morphine addiction (excluding doctors) studied by Kolb, slightly less than half (48.4 percent) were men. Of 41 cases of morphine addiction attributed to association, however, males made up 87.8 percent. Age of addiction also varied. The medical morphine addicts (n = 133, including doctors and all cases claiming medical origins) averaged 29 years, 10 months; the association cases of known onset (n = 37) averaged 22 years, 4 months. The overall picture of morphine addiction thus was changing, especially after 1909, when the ban on imported smoking opium went into effect. There had always been some young, male, nonmedical morphine users, but now their numbers were rapidly increasing. This was particularly true in areas outside New York City, where heroin was not so readily available.

109. Treadway, "Further Observations," 550. It should be noted, however, that this percentage is somewhat biased, as surviving female morphine addicts with chronic diseases were not likely to be arrested by narcotic agents. The term *sporting* comes from Sandoz.

110. Taylor, *American Diplomacy,* 82–132; Musto, *American Disease,* 37–65, 121–132; and Jaffe, "Addiction Reform," dissertation, 160–196.

111. *Foreign Relations, 1909,* 107–111.

112. U.S. Senate, *Report on the International Opium Commission,* 60–61. The text of the Foster bill is appended to this document.

113. U.S. House, *Importation and Use of Opium: Hearings,* esp. 109–164.

114. Wright, "Memoranda," in *Conference Internationale de l'Opium, Actes et Documents,* vol. 2, p. 12.

115. Ibid., vol. 1, pp. 184–185. See also Wright's confidential report to the secretary of state, February 12, 1912, pp. 22–23, USIOC.

116. Wright stressed this theme repeatedly; see, for example, his confidential report to the secretary of state, February 12, 1912, p. 9; his letter to Francis Burton Harrison, May 24, 1913; and his memorandum to the secretary of state, March 11, 1913, p. 10; all USIOC. Secretary of State William Jennings Bryan did not accept Wright's argument that the United States was required to pass such legislation, but he supported do-

mestic narcotic laws as a model for other nations to emulate. (U.S. House, *Bureau of Narcotics: Hearings,* 85.)

117. *CR,* 62nd Cong., 2nd sess. (1912), 7947; and 3rd sess. (1913), 1812. A copy of the latter bill (H.R. 28277) is attached to M. I. Wilbert to J. W. Kerr, March 6, 1913, file 2123, USPHS.

118. See Harrison's remarks on the evolution of the bill, *CR,* 63rd Cong., 1st sess. (1913), 2202.

119. U.S. House, *Registration of Producers and Importers,* 1–2.

120. *CR,* 63rd Cong., 1st sess. (1913), 2201.

121. Ibid., 2210.

122. U.S. House, *Traffic in Opium; Statutes at Large,* 63rd Cong., 3rd sess. (1914), chap. 1. See also Wiley and Pierce, 396–397.

123. The government lost some later cases, however, notably *Linder* v. *United States,* 268 U.S. 5. Linder was a reputable physician who gave one tablet of morphine and three tablets of cocaine to an addict. The Supreme Court unanimously reversed his conviction. Convictions in which defendants had indiscriminately issued prescriptions for large quantities of drugs (for example, *Webb; Jin Fuey Moy* v. *United States,* 254 U.S. 189; and *United States* v. *Behrman,* 258 U.S. 280), were upheld, however, and Treasury Department regulations continued to refer to *Webb* as the basic ruling affecting the situation.

124. Graham-Mulhall, 107. See also New York, *Second Annual Report,* 27–29. Even prior to the Harrison Act many states required prescriptions for the purchase of narcotics, but these laws were not always vigorously enforced.

125. Phillips, 2147, notes that a bottle of 100 heroin tablets (1/12 grain) could be obtained for $0.60 in 1912. By March 16, 1915, the price of that same bottle was $1.25 to $1.50; by April 1, $4.50. (Farr, 893; Drysdale, 361.) In Chicago the price of drugs worth $0.30 rose to $4.00 by March 11, $6.00 by March 12, and $8.00 by March 14. ("Beds for 1,600," 1.) The disruption of trade engendered by World War I may also have stimulated higher prices; see the Bureau of Internal Revenue, *Annual Report for 1915,* 16. Some addicts attempted to solve the problem by consuming large amounts of paregoric, an exempt preparation under the Harrison Act that could still be purchased with relative ease. But, as Ernest Bishop noted, drinking paregoric made "wrecks" of many addicts, because of its high alcohol content. ("Special Meeting of the National Drug Trade Conference," 30, 102–103.)

126. Maintenance for rural and medical addicts is discussed further in Chapter 5.

127. [Walter R. Herrick,] New York, *Second Annual Report,* 14. Street, *I Was a Drug Addict,* 203, notes adulteration "in a big way" around 1917–1918, and that it got even worse in later years.

128. "History of Heroin," 8. NYDSAS interviewees addicted in the 1920s were almost unanimous in commenting on the declining purity of heroin during the 1930s.

129. *Statutes at Large,* 68th Cong., 1st sess. (1924), chap. 352. The measure amended the 1909 Smoking Opium Exclusion Act to prohibit the importation of crude opium for the manufacture of heroin. See Committee on Traffic in Opium of the Foreign Policy Association; also U.S. House, *Prohibiting the Importation of Crude Opium for the Manufacture of Heroin;* the 1924 Ways and Means Committee hearings of the same title; and Musto, "Early History," 181–184.

130. S. L. Rakusin, 1926 memorandum and data sheet, file 0120-9, TDF. For references to the advantages of heroin's compactness, see Chief City Magistrate William McAdoo of New York to Surgeon General Rupert Blue, April 22, 1917, USPHS; and Kolb to Surgeon General [H. S. Cumming], May 26, 1924, p. 5, box 3, KP.

131. U.S. Treasury Department, Bureau of Narcotics, *Traffic in Opium for 1934,* 31. For further evidence of the high cost of morphine see Spillard, 15; U.S. House, *Exportation of Opium: Hearings,* 26; and Terry and Pellens, 485. Large numbers of Chicago morphine addicts began switching to heroin around 1935. "One reason given to us by addicts . . . is the exacting price of morphine [$90–$110 per ounce] compared with that of heroin [$38–$40]." (Dai, 61.)

Several factors contributed to morphine's high price. After the 1919 *Webb* ruling undercut maintenance by physicians, it became more dangerous to divert "scrip" morphine into the illicit traffic. In 1922 Congress passed the Narcotic Drugs Import and Export Act, which made it more difficult to export bulk morphine to Canada and other places, for later smuggling back into the United States. (U.S. House, *Exportation of Opium: Hearings* and *Prohibit Importation of Opium; Statutes at Large,* 67th Cong., 2nd sess. [1922], chap. 202.) However, the most important reason for the relative scarcity and high price of morphine after 1920 was the growing preference of dealers for handling heroin, a drug whose compactness and ease of adulteration translated into less risk and greater profits.

132. Simon, "Survey," 676; Terry and Pellens, 484; Eddy, 133; and Platt and Labate, 52. Furthermore, heroin was less likely to produce nausea, according to Kane et al., 504, and Charles W. Richardson, in *Prohibiting the Importation of Opium: Hearings,* 11.

133. Helbrant, 30.

134. Woods, 14; "History of Heroin," 7.

135. Kolb to Surgeon General [H. S. Cumming], May 26, 1924, p. 5, box 3, KP; Simon, "Survey," 675; and Levi Nutt, "The National Narcotic Drug Situation Today" (TS, 1928), p. 1, ser. 3, box 5, folder 150, CDA.

136. It is interesting to note in this context that the gradual diffusion of heroin outward from New York followed an apparent exodus of addicts from that city in the early 1920s. Carleton Simon wrote to Kolb (July 21, 1926, box 5, KP) that many New York City addicts left (or were forced to leave) town when the clinic closed down. Some had been

drifters in the first place, with no particular ties to the area. It is tempting to suppose that these fleeing addicts acted as agents of transmission, explaining and introducing (or in some cases, reintroducing) heroin to local users and their dealers. In this sense Figure 7 is like the spot map of an infectious disease, with local outbreaks marking the progress of travelers from the original site of infection.

137. U.S. Treasury Department, Bureau of Narcotics, *Traffic in Opium for 1932,* 11.

138. Ibid., *for 1932* and *1938*, pp. 59 and 80 respectively. Also U.S. Treasury Department, *Traffic in Opium for 1927,* 6.

139. W. L. Treadway to Small, September 22, 1932, Lyndon Frederick Small Papers, NLM. Small later offered to reconvert seized heroin to morphine, if no morphine was available. (Small to H. J. Anslinger, December 10, 1932, Small Papers.)

140. Phillips, 1147; McGuire and Lichtenstein, 186; Lichtenstein, *A Doctor Studies Crime,* 43; Hesse, 56-57; and "Red," June 26, 1980, NYDSAS interview.

141. O'Donnell and Jones, 155-162. Geech W———, May 30, 1980, NYDSAS interview, contains a description of what one addict felt when he accidentally hit a vein. Consistent with O'Donnell and Jones' account, he was frightened at first, but then felt good and decided to continue injecting heroin in that way. Street, *I Was A Drug Addict,* 140-141, 237-283, went to the needle for reasons of efficiency and later discovered he required less of the drug when he injected into a vein. In "The Heroin Epidemic in Cairo Between the World Wars," a paper delivered at the Conference on the Historical Context of Opium Use, Philadelphia, June 3, 1981, Gregory Austin reiterated the story, mentioned by O'Donnell and Jones, that intravenous use was brought to the United States in the 1920s by Egyptian sailors familiar with the technique. At the same conference John Crellin noted that intravenous medication had become accepted by this time; therefore it is possible that some addicts picked up the practice from observing doctors or nurses. The important point is that these hypotheses are not mutually exlusive. Just as opium smoking may have been transmitted to whites by several different Chinese smokers in different places at roughly the same time, it is conceivable that during the early to middle 1920s heroin users began acquiring the intravenous technique independently — some by accident, some from foreign sailors, and some from knowledge or observation of medical practice. Intravenous use did not seem to become widespread, however, until the 1930s, when the declining quality of heroin provided an incentive for many nonmedical addicts to switch to a more direct route, in an effort to recapture the pleasurable sensations that purer drugs had once provided.

142. "History of Heroin," 8.

143. Patrick C———, May 28, 1980, NYDSAS interview.

144. "Mel," July 3 and July 15, 1980, NYDSAS interview. These

remarks should be carefully qualified. In the first place, they apply mainly to New York City in the 1930s; whether and to what extent Italians dominated the traffic elsewhere has yet to be established. Second, as Mark Haller has pointed out to me, it is unlikely that the Italians achieved a total monopoly, at least during the 1930s; entry into the illicit market was still possible for some rival traffickers, especially in the South and West. Nevertheless, these and other NYDSAS interviewees addicted at this time (for example, "Jack," July 2, 1980; "Nicholina," July 15, 1980; and "Otha Williams," July 29, 1980) were virtually unanimous in asserting that the Italians had enough leverage to boost prices, while at the same time decreasing quality. The Italian takeover is discussed further in David T. Courtwright, Herman Joseph, and Don Des Jarlais, "Oral Histories of Elderly Methadone Patients," forthcoming in the 1981 *Oral History Review.*

145. O'Donnell and Jones, 158.

146. Stokes, ward notes, file 2123, USPHS. Two patients switched to straight morphine, but the others who adopted the hypodermic were still using heroin. See note 5 above.

147. McPherson and Cohen, 638–639.

148. Lambert et al., 470–471. These figures add up to more than 263, indicating that some addicts used more than one route. It is of interest that many of these cases had a prior history of opium smoking or cocaine sniffing.

149. Light et al., 9. See also Kolb, "Pleasure and Deterioration," 706.

150. O'Donnell and Jones, 150.

151. Helbrant, 68. See also Berg, 65.

152. A number of the older NYDSAS interviewees managed to avoid these dangers by taking pains to sterilize their needles before each use. However, the mere fact of their survival (relatively few twentieth-century addicts live beyond 60 years) may indicate that such precautions were not universal, or even usual. In the 1870s and 1880s even the most cautious needle addict would have had trouble avoiding sepsis, for the role of bacteria in transmitting infections was not yet generally understood. See, for example, "Habit of Taking Opium," 572.

5 The Transformation of the Opiate Addict

1. Nick J———, June 3, 1980, NYDSAS interview.

2. The two-to-one ratio is based on the analysis of the maximum number of addicts that respective levels of medicinal and smoking opium imports could support, but because the calculated maximum for smoking opium was very liberal (Chapter 1, note 54), it seems likely that the true ratio of medical to nonmedical addicts in 1895 was higher. Kane, *Opium-Smoking,* 19, estimated that there were only 26,000 opium smokers in 1882, yielding a ratio closer to ten to one. The number of

opium smokers had increased by 1895, however, and allowance must also be made for the fact that some opium and morphine addicts (prostitutes, for example, or curious writers) should be classed as nonmedical types.

3. Kolb and DuMez, 1203. See also Kolb, "Drug Addiction: A Study of Some Medical Cases," 171. I wish to emphasize that there are pronounced differences between this model and the one proposed by Helmer in *Drugs and Minority Oppression*. Writing from a radical perspective, Helmer argues that "narcotics use in America has always, both before and after the Harrison Act, been predominantly a *working-class* phenomenon. This has been a specific *cause*, not a general consequence, of narcotics prohibition when it has been enacted" (p. 7; italics in original). He sees narcotic laws as a vehicle of oppression, especially against minority workers in times of economic distress when there is increased competition for jobs.

First, the assertion that narcotic use prior to the Harrison Act was a "working-class" phenomenon is (with the possible exception of cocaine) demonstrably false. Although heroin (after 1910) and smoking opium were associated with the lower classes, addicts of this type, from both quantitative and qualitative evidence, were outnumbered by opium and morphine addicts in most regions of the country before 1900 and probably for some years thereafter. Helmer himself acknowledges that middle-class and upper-class addicts used morphine (p. 15); given that the level of medicinal opium and morphine imported during the nineteenth century was consistently greater than the level of imported smoking opium, it is difficult to discern the basis for the alleged working-class dominance. Even more compelling is the fact that virtually no knowledgeable nineteenth-century authority detected working-class overrepresentation — although Helmer either ignores or dismisses such contrary testimony as so much mythmaking (pp. 4–7).

Second, while I shall later argue that there are linkages between the social class of addicts and public and scientific attitudes toward opiate addiction, they are nevertheless of a more subtle and less conspiratorial nature than those propounded by Helmer. The contention that narcotic laws were essentially a way of repressing certain groups of workers ("the conflict over social justice is what the story of narcotics in America is about," p. 53) is both reductionistic and unsupported by the historical evidence, especially by such key MS collections as USIOC, USPHS, and KP.

4. U.S. Treasury Department, Bureau of Narcotics, *Traffic in Opium for 1939*, 23–27, and *for 1940*, 16–19. An acute shortage was first noted in the last months of 1939. For a discussion of the situation in Hawaii, see p. 3 of C. T. Stevenson's report to Anslinger, March 8, 1940, file 0120-9, TDF.

5. On high mortality see Kane et al., 505; Street, *I Was a Drug Addict*, 40, 209–210, 242.

6. H. J. Anslinger to Lawrence B. Dunham, April 10, 1933, ser. 3, box 4, folder 134, CDA; and Musto, *American Disease,* 214.

7. "Report of Committee on Drug Addiction," 1, file 0120-9, TDF.

8. For a general discussion of treatment-program data lags, see Hunt and Chambers, 35–41.

9. Lambert et al., 467.

10. Pescor, 24. Time of onset was not given for patients addicted more than five years, and not all of these cases were nonmedical.

11. Hunt and Chambers, 3–26.

12. In a sense the timing of World War II was fortunate, at least with respect to opiate addiction. Not only was an epidemic due in 1941, but the number of new cases would have been unusually large. There had been a baby boom following World War I, which meant that in 1940 a disproportionate number of males were entering their early twenties—the age of greatest susceptibility. (Coale and Zelnik, 25.)

13. There was a similar pattern among 138 nonmedical addicts confined in the Atlanta penitentiary as of April 1, 1928. Peak usage, in terms of the reported year of onset of addiction, occurred in 1907, 1912-1913, and 1920-1921, with another peak building at the end of 1927. (U.S. House, *Establishment of Two Federal Narcotic Farms: Hearings,* 140-147.) It may be only coincidental, but it is interesting that the Harrison Narcotic Act was debated and passed shortly after the 1912-1913 epidemic of nonmedical addiction, when public and professional concern over opiates (particularly heroin) was running high. The outcry may have made legislators more susceptible to Wright's exaggerated claims and more willing to pass restrictive legislation.

14. Memorandum from Nutt to W. Blanchard, assistant head, Narcotic Division, July 7, 1926, file 0120-9, TDF. The temporary increase of nonmedical addiction in the early 1920s is acknowledged in Anslinger and Tompkins, 165.

15. Undated [1926] memorandum and data sheet signed S. L. Rakusin, file 0120-9, TDF. The returns on which these totals are based were expressed mainly in round hundreds and thousands, an indication of the casualness of the undertaking.

16. Unsigned memorandum, March 8, 1932, file 0120-9, TDF. The same statement with only minor changes in wording, appeared in *Traffic in Opium for 1931,* 9-10.

17. They tend to have smaller habits, a better chance of escaping police notice, and often are not yet disillusioned with opiates. In Michigan, for example, the average age of 83 addicts at the time of first conviction was 31 years, but their average age at time of addiction was only 24 years—a 7-year difference. (L. A. Koepfgen to John D. Farnham, August 26, 1932, ser. 3, box 4, folder 133, CDA.)

18. Anslinger and Tompkins, 166.

19. Lambert et al., 467; Pescor, 24.

20. Dai, 65-66. See also Treadway, "Drug Addiction," 372, 374.

Although Treadway had previously observed a high average age of arrest for a mixed group of medical and nonmedical addicts ("Further Observations," 543–544), in this article he reported that 25 percent of the narcotic drug addicts sentenced to prison for the first time had been addicted for six years or less. He also noted that half of all addicts (excluding doctors and druggists) were addicted by age 25, two-thirds by 30.

21. Memorandum from Stephen B. Gibbons, December 2, 1937, file 0120–9, TDF.

22. Memorandum from Gibbons, January 12, 1937, file 0120–9, TDF.

23. U.S. House, *Establishment of Two Federal Narcotic Farms: Hearings*, 40. The relative cheapness of drugs in New York City was confirmed by several of the NYDSAS interviews (for instance, with "Russ," June 6, 1980). The bureau's final estimate of the number of nonmedical addicts appears in Anslinger and Tompkins, 266.

24. Helbrant, 85.

25. Memorandum and data sheet signed by Anslinger, March 16, 1938, file 0120–9, TDF.

26. Tennyson to Anslinger, February 24, 1938, file 0120–9, TDF.

27. Anslinger and Tompkins, 265.

28. The full text of this letter appears in U.S. Treasury Department, Bureau of Narcotics, *Traffic in Opium for 1945*, 13. One NYDSAS interviewee, John B———, December 10, 1980, was admitted into the army on a trial basis in spite of his addiction, but this was clearly exceptional.

29. U.S. War Department, *Selective Service Regulations*, sec. 79, rule XII, subpar. (h), p. 53; Petersen and Stewart, par. 104b and 362a, pp. 104 and 116; and Stokes, "Features of Narcotic Addiction," 766.

30. One critic of the Bureau of Narcotics, Alfred R. Lindesmith, has gone so far as to suggest that the total number of opiate addicts actually increased during this period. "When new and younger addicts are not being recruited in sufficient numbers to replace older addicts who die or quit the habit," he argued, "it necessarily follows that the average age of the addicted population must increase. However, it is well known that between 1915 and 1945 the average age of known addicts declined considerably, and this demonstrates that we must assume a constant stream of new addicts being added each year." (*The Addict and the Law*, 105.) What Lindesmith overlooked, however, was that a long-term reduction in age was also consistent with the process diagrammed in Figure 8, namely, older medical addicts shrinking in number relative to younger nonmedical addicts.

I must also take exception to Lindesmith's claim, appearing in an article coauthored with Gagnon, 166–169, that underworld opiate use was essentially a consequence of legal developments. The Harrison Act, the argument runs, caused an illicit traffic to spring up, a traffic run by underworld figures and centered in large cities. Groups in proximity to or having connections with these black marketeers—delinquents, criminals, and slum dwellers—subsequently developed a high rate of addiction. The problem with this theory is that it ignores the heavy use of opiates by the underworld prior to 1914, when the pattern of distribution allegedly shifted. Opiate addiction, as shown in Chapters 3 and 4, was well established in tenderloin districts before regulation. (The statement made by Lindesmith and Gagnon in table 1 [p. 169] that drug use by "white criminals and delinquents . . . up to 1914" was "low" is completely at variance with the facts.) It is true that exposure to opiates has a great deal to do with the addiction rate of a given group; the point is that delinquents, criminals, and slum dwellers were well exposed prior to the Harrison Act, and their high incidence of addiction was not simply a concomitant of that law. For an analysis similar to that of Lindesmith and Gagnon, with similar limitations, see Ashley, *Heroin*, 55–56.

31. I should especially like to call attention to the well-known "ski-jump curve," which has appeared in numerous Bureau of Narcotics publications and which can be found on p. 105 of Lindesmith, *The Addict and the Law*. The graph, labeled "History of Narcotic Addiction in the United States," shows a sharp decline between 1922 and 1942; does not differentiate between medical and nonmedical addicts; and seems to imply that the prevalence of addiction, both medical and nonmedical, was entirely a function of federal narcotic legislation. There was in truth a decline, but it was only partially caused by the Harrison and Pure Food and Drug acts; was not at all related to the government's anti-maintenance policy; and, given state reform and the changing attitude of the medical profession, would have occurred to some degree even in the absence of federal legislation.

32. Smith, "Drugs—Use and Sale," 63. Other early references to proportionately greater nonmedical use are Alfred S. Warthin to Wright, August 28, 1908, and Chas. B. Whilden to Wright, September 17, 1908, both USIOC. Warthin was a pathologist at the University of Michigan, Whilden the secretary of the California State Board of Pharmacy.

33. Dercum, 362, also abstracted in *JAMA*, 67 (1916), 1965. See also Doane, 480; Kane et al., 503; and Light et al., 8, on the transformation in Philadelphia.

34. Webster, 345. For evidence of continued narcotic conservatism see the statement of the Council on Pharmacy and Chemistry of the American Medical Association in Emerson et al., 1609.

35. Bloedorn, 309–310; Joyce, 220. See also Prentice, 1551; Knopf, 135–139; Lambert et al., 461, 469; and New York District Supervisor Garland Williams to Anslinger, February 9, 1940, file 0120-9, TDF. Williams stated that the medical addict was by 1940 a rarity, with the exception of some aging addicts who attributed their condition to injuries sustained during World War I.

36. Sceleth and Kuh, 679. See also Dai, 36, 42–43, and Downs, "Relation to Life Insurance," 125. For statistics on the increasingly ur-

ban background of opiate addicts see Treadway, "Further Observations," 545, and Lindesmith, *The Addict and the Law,* 112.

37. MS records, box 6, KP (n = 221). By contrast 25.0 percent (23 of 92) of the users supplied at the Syracuse clinic, case 15566, TDF, were black. This was a profit-type clinic that sold both morphine and cocaine, however, and it is not clear from context which drug the black patients used.

38. U.S. Treasury Department, Bureau of Narcotics, *Traffic in Opium for 1935,* 3.

39. Treadway, "Further Observations," 543–544; California Senate, *Report on Drug Addiction in California,* 75. There is one earlier source that deals with conviction and imprisonment rather than arrest: U.S. House, *Establishment of Two Federal Narcotic Farms: Hearings,* 140–147, 150–160, shows that 75 of 788 (9.5 percent) of the opiate addicts in the Atlanta and Leavenworth penitentiaries in 1928 were black.

40. Dai, 46. There is also an earlier New York City study (Lambert et al., 437), which reported that only 8 of 318 male patients (2.5 percent) treated in 1928–1929 were black. Dai's cases dated from 1928 to 1934, and it would be interesting to know if most of the black Chicago addicts commenced using drugs in the early 1930s, as the New York City study would suggest, or whether the increase in the rate of black addiction was more gradual and sustained. Possibly the black rate accelerated as the Depression deepened, but, lacking more detailed race and incidence data, this hypothesis cannot be tested.

Pescor's study of addicts committed to the Lexington (Ky.) Hospital in fiscal 1937 showed that 8.9 percent of the patients were black, a percentage that exactly matched the black share of the national population (p. 10). Caution is required in interpreting this finding, however, since Southerners were heavily overrepresented at Lexington (note 44 below), and southern blacks still had a very low rate of addiction in the 1920s and 1930s. See also report to T. E. Middlebrooks, narcotic agent in charge, Atlanta, Georgia, March 21, 1928, file 0120-9, TDF.

Finally, Perry M. Lichtenstein, a New York City physician experienced in forensic medicine, mentioned that in the early 1930s there was also a great increase in the number of Puerto Rican and Cuban addicts. Many of these had been marijuana smokers who switched to opiates when they immigrated to the United States. Lichtenstein did not furnish any statistics, however. (*A Doctor Studies Crime,* 36.)

41. Mackin, 174.

42. In Mississippi as late as 1908 an estimated 90 to 95 percent of all cases of addiction were iatrogenic in nature. (O. W. Bethea, secretary of the Mississippi State Pharmaceutical Association, to Wright, September 5, 1908, USIOC.) Medical cases still predominated in Atlanta in 1928. (Report to T. E. Middlebrooks, narcotic agent in charge, March 21, 1928, file 0120-9, TDF.)

43. O'Donnell, *Narcotic Addicts in Kentucky,* 136–137, 240–243.

O'Donnell is not explicit about what percentage of drinkers-turned-morphine-addicts first received the drug from their physician, but suggests that association with other morphine users was an important factor.

44. Although a number of authors have treated Pescor's study as if it represented a national cross section (an error Pescor did little to avert), a closer look at the patients reveals a distinct regional bias. For example, New York and California, two states that had serious addiction problems, contributed to Lexington in fiscal 1937 only 1.5 and 1.0 patients per 100,000 males 21 years of age or older. By comparison Louisiana had 13.9; Texas, 8.2; Kentucky, 8.0; District of Columbia, 7.0; Oklahoma, 5.2; Georgia, 4.5; Tennessee, 4.2; Arkansas, 3.9; Florida, 3.6; Missouri, 3.6; South Carolina, 3.3; and Alabama, 3.1 (Pescor, table 2, 26; 1940 census; Ball, "Two Patterns," 89 n. 18.) Granted the South had a higher rate of opiate addiction, but the difference was closer to 64.5 percent (Chapter 2) than to the several hundred percentage points suggested by the figures above. The reason for the bias is almost certainly that the Lexington Hospital, located in Kentucky, drew most heavily from the southern region, at least during the first years of its operation.

45. Pescor, 3–4, 15, table 1, 24.

46. Treadway, "Further Observations," 552. See also U.S. House, *Establishment of Two Federal Narcotic Farms: Hearings,* 140–147. These tables show 130 medical cases, 138 nonmedical, and 36 cases where no opiate was involved or the origin was unknown. Treadway also remarked, in "Some Epidemiological Features," 50, "that 80 percent of the present-day addiction occurs in the land of 'Hobohemia,' or the underworld." In 1932 L. A. Koepfgen, managing director of the Narcotic Educational Association of Michigan, made an analysis of 83 cases treated at the association's narcotic farm. The causes of addiction were listed as army service (5), sickness or accident (19), overwork (3), drinking (10), and ignorance, curiosity, or association with addicts (46). (Koepfgen to John D. Farnham, August 26, 1932, ser. 3, box 4, folder 133, CDA.) See also U.S. Treasury Department, Bureau of Narcotics, *Traffic in Opium for 1935,* 3–4, chart 16, 82.

A recent study by Musto and Ramos, 1071–77, is also suggestive. Of 88 morphine addicts registered at the New Haven narcotic clinic who had verifiable addresses, 68 (77.3 percent) lived in commercial or lower-class neighborhoods — "an overrepresentation from lower socioeconomic levels" (p. 1074). Federal agents who investigated the clinic also noted that a majority of the patients were petty criminals (p. 1073). These findings should be carefully qualified: a number of white women shunned the clinic (p. 1074), and the data do not show whether an individual's addiction was medical or nonmedical in origin, or whether morphine was the initial opiate of choice. Nevertheless, the lower-class background of the New Haven patients is certainly consistent with the process diagrammed in Figure 8 and may indicate that the transformation of the addict population was largely complete (at least in the Northeast) by 1919–1920.

47. There is, however, some bias in Treadway's data, since wealthy medical addicts were among the least likely to be arrested. On the other hand, young and recently created nonmedical addicts, especially those addicted during 1928–1929, were also likely to have escaped notice; it is possible that the two factors balanced out.

48. Terry, "Some Recent Experiments," 33. Davenport, 1, displayed photographs of the "line of unfortunates waiting for relief" outside of the New York City clinic. See also Pearson, "Police Powers," 37–38, and Street, *I Was a Drug Addict,* 207.

49. BI. Dr. John Hughes made a similar point about legislators, who derived their limited knowledge of drugs from Chinese opium smokers, or from "hopheads" and "coke fiends" of the tenderloin districts. "Hence, they look upon all such addictions as merely vicious habits, persisted in for the physical pleasures to be derived therefrom; and, therefore, catalogue them along with afflictions *a la* Oscar Wilde, and other abnormalities." (Hughes, 113.)

50. Crane, 562. See also Berridge, "Victorian Opium Eating," 456. Buerki, 7, reports that moral overtones lingered in some discussions of addiction well into the 1890s.

51. Jaffe, "Addiction Reform," dissertation, 1–79. Jaffe has consolidated his work on the inebriety movement in an article, "Reform in American Medical Science: The Inebriety Movement," 139–147.

52. The history of the degeneration theory is discussed in Dain, 111; Ackerknecht, *Short History,* 54–59; Hale, 76; and Pichot's excellent essay, "Psychopathic Behaviour," 57–61. Morel's own exposition is in the *Traité,* esp. 1–7, 81.

53. A brief but highly useful account of Beard's thought is Rosenberg, "Beard in Nineteenth-Century Psychiatry." See also Rosenberg's "Factors in the Development of Genetics," 32–33, and Sicherman, 25–38.

54. See Beard's *Stimulants and Narcotics,* 19–20; *American Nervousness,* 308; and "Relation of Inebriety," 1–2. In the last article Beard stressed that sufferers of mild forms of neurasthenia were the most likely to succumb, total nervous wrecks being unable to tolerate large doses of opium or alcohol.

55. Crothers, *Morphinism and Narcomanias,* 48–49, 64. Crothers' base of operations was the Walnut Lodge Hospital, a private asylum for inebriates established in Hartford, Connecticut, in 1880 and not closed until approximately 1918. He enjoyed a world-wide reputation, delivering papers in London and Paris, as well as in the United States. For further biographical details, see "Thomas Davison Crothers, M.D.," 277–278.

Crothers' views were paralleled, in many respects, by those of Leslie E. Keeley, one of the best-known of the nineteenth-century "cure doctors." Keeley postulated that inebriety was a disease, and he treated both alcoholics and opiate addicts in his national chain of Keeley Institutes. He also believed that individuals inherited varying degrees of nervous susceptibility, and that opium and alcohol changed or "educated" impressionable nerve cells. What set Keeley apart was his advocacy of a mysterious specific, the Bichloride of Gold formula, for treatment of both species of inebriety. (Keeley, 91 ff.) This opened him to charges of quackery and generated a long controversy. H. Wayne Morgan has a very thorough account of Keeley and his battles in a forthcoming work, tentatively titled *Pursuing the Genie: Drug Use in America since 1800.*

56. Sterne, 609–611. Other expressions of the concepts of degeneration and/or neurasthenia in relation to opiate addiction include Brown, *An Opium Cure,* 13–14; Morris, 65–70; Hamlin, 426; Sudduth, 796–798; Phenix, 206; Robertson, 226–229; Boggess, 882; Happel, "Morphinism," 409; Paulson, 416; "Modern Life and Sedatives," 572; Sprague, 585; Griffin, 1584; Gordon, "Relation of Legislative Acts," 214; and Doane, 480. Hutchins, 132, relies heavily on the concept of neurasthenia but uses a different terminology, namely, "brain cell exhaustion." Block, "Drug Habitues," 406, thought there were some addicts "whose trouble is like a neurasthenia, if there is such a sickness," but that the majority had a "definite hysteria." The earliest attempt I have found to link addiction to nervous stress, antedating even Beard, is [Day,] 7.

57. Compare Sicherman, 27. See also the statement of Henry G. Cole, cited in Frisch, 203.

58. Roberts, 207.

59. Sterne, 612. See also Marsh, "Morphinism," 461.

60. Mattison, "Morphinism in Women," 1400. His early expressions of the nervous diathesis view include "Impending Danger," 71, and "Responsibility of the Profession," 102. The turning point seems to have come when Mattison encountered the work of Eduard Levinstein (1875–1877; translated into English, 1878), a Berlin physician who argued on the basis of considerable clinical experience that morphine addiction was generally an iatrogenic disease that could be contracted by anyone, "whether of a strong or weak constitution." See also Mattison, "Genesis," 303.

61. Mattison, "Ethics," 297.

62. Smith, "Seven Years of Pioneering," 725–728. Comments on Terry's personality are based on BI and personal correspondence from Dr. Edward Smith, who kindly furnished me with a reprint of his article on Terry's career as health officer. Terry divorced his first wife, Marian, and subsequently married Mildred Pellens, his coworker and coauthor of *The Opium Problem.*

63. U.S. House, *Exportation of Opium: Hearings,* 107; and Terry, "Narcotic Drug Addiction," 30, 31.

64. Terry, "Some Recent Experiments," 41.

65. BI; Terry to Butler, November 27, 1928, BP; and J. D. Farnham's file memorandum of October 27, 1931, ser. 3, box 6, folder 157, CDA. "The only criticism that I would make is that you did this work about twenty years ahead of the time in which it could be appreciated," wrote Terry, "and I have little doubt but that within the next ten or fifteen years your plan will be in widespread operation in this country." Here, as in so many other matters, he was to be disappointed.

66. "Louisiana State Board of Health Narcotic Dispensary" (TS, 1921), 9, BP. Also Butler, "One American City," 159.

67. Goldberger, 3159–73.

68. Bishop outlined his theory in several articles, but the most convenient summary is his book, *The Narcotic Drug Problem,* esp. 35–49. His views were popularized in such articles as Eddy, 638. Bishop's personality is discussed in BI.

69. See Terry's comments on Bishop, "Narcotic Drug Addiction," 489–490; and Terry, "Narcotic Drug Addiction," 32. Bishop also carried on a somewhat one-sided correspondence with Butler, in which he raved about his indictment under the Harrison Act and his suspicions of other addiction experts in New York. See, for example, Bishop to Butler, January 5, 1923, and May 19, 1923, BP. Bishop's legal problems are sympathetically discussed in King, *The Drug Hang-Up,* 59–60.

70. Pettey's theories are summarized in his book, *The Narcotic Drug Diseases.* His views were concurred in by Pittsburgh addiction specialist C. C. Wholey. A convenient précis of early twentieth-century addiction research is A. G. DuMez, "Increased Tolerance," 1069–72. On the relationship between Bishop and Pettey see Musto, *American Disease,* 279–281 n. 23.

71. See, for instance, Radó, 1–23.

72. Pichot, 55.

73. Prichard, *A Treatise on Insanity;* Maughs, 330–356, 465–499; Tuke, vol. 2, pp. 813–816; Dain, 73–75; Cleckley, 113; and Pichot, 56–57, 67.

74. Lawrence Kolb, "The Opium Addict and His Treatment" (TS, 1938), 3–4, box 8, KP.

75. Drysdale, 363–364; Leahy, 258–259; "Symposium on the 'The Doctor and the Drug Addict,'" 1589. The idea that opiate addiction was a form of moral insanity also gained currency in early-twentieth-century Britain, although it was not embodied in the important Rolleston Committee's report of 1926. (Parssinen and Kerner, 283, 289.)

76. Kolb acknowledged that there were still a large number of medical addicts, in the broad sense of any users introduced to opiates as a medication; but, consistent with his theory, he denied that there were a majority of nervously normal persons even among the medical group. ("Drug Addiction: A Study of Some Medical Cases," 174.)

77. "The Opium Addict and His Treatment" (TS, 1938), 4–5, box 8, KP.

78. Feeblemindedness as a cause of opiate addiction was an idea that gained some currency during the decade 1910 to 1920, but died shortly thereafter. See for example Stokes, "Problem," 756; Anderson, 756–757; and Hubbard, "New York City Narcotic Clinic," 42. Jaffe, "Addiction Reform," dissertation, 237–238, also has a useful discussion. Kolb's objections to the feeblemindedness theory are outlined in his article, "Relation of Intelligence," 163–167. Feeblemindedness, it should be added, like the concept of psychopathy, probably would not have been advanced as a hypothesis unless there had been a fundamental shift in the addict population.

79. "The Opium Addict and His Treatment" (TS, 1938), 5, box 8, KP.

80. Kolb's thesis was expressed and refined in a series of articles he published in the mid-1920s, including "Types and Characteristics," 300–313; "Drug Addiction in Its Relation to Crime," 74–89; "Pleasure and Deterioration," 699–724; and "Clinical Contribution," 22–43.

81. Jaffe, "Addiction Reform," dissertation, 202, relates that Kolb was generally skeptical of the prospects of extended institutional care during the 1920s, given his belief in the relative intractability of the psychological disorders underlying addiction. When appointed head of the Lexington Hospital, however, he altered his views, stating in a 1938 article coauthored with W. F. Ossenfort, "The Treatment of Drug Addicts at the Lexington Hospital," 914, that "in the absence of organic deterioration one should never despair of effecting cure." In "Drug Addiction in Relation to Crime" (TS, 1939), 12, box 8, KP, Kolb further stated that the large category of users suffering from psychopathic diathesis had a relatively good chance of cure, although he remained pessimistic about neurotics and full-blown psychopaths. Late in life he changed his mind yet again and seemed to be leaning toward a modified maintenance scheme when in 1962 he published *Drug Addiction: A Medical Problem.* See also note 86 below.

82. Kolb and Ossenfort, 917.

83. Comment by Dr. S. W. Hamilton on Kolb, "The Opium Addict and His Treatment," *Archives of Neurology and Psychiatry,* 40 (1938), 199.

84. See the Hobson file in box 3, KP. I am convinced that one reason Kolb largely ignored or discounted Terry's work is that Terry believed that opiate addiction was a widespread problem, even accepting the Treasury Department's million addict estimate that Kolb so despised. (U.S. House, *Exportation of Opium: Hearings,* 105.) After the unpleasantry of the Hobson affair, any outside authority who posited a large number of addicts was bound to raise Kolb's suspicions. Conversely, the entire first chapter of Terry and Pellen's *Opium Problem* can be read as a rebuttal to Kolb and DuMez's 1924 article, "Prevalence and Trend."

85. Proposals to kill off addicts are mentioned in Kolb, "The Opium Addict and His Treatment" (TS, 1938), 2, box 8, KP; Helbrant, 85–86; Jaffe, "Addiction Reform," dissertation, 236; and Curtiss, 93. Dr. and

Mrs. Curtiss, cofounders of the Order of Christian Mystics, objected to the killing of addicts on the ground that "we simply send them out into the astral world where they can prey upon humanity, ten, a hundred, yes a thousand times more viciously than if they were set free while still in the flesh."

86. Kolb, *Drug Addiction: A Medical Problem,* 169. By 1965 his disillusionment had progressed so far that he had taken to writing long and sympathetic letters to Dr. Marie Nyswander, one of the pioneers of methadone maintenance. "Even if addicts can be stabilized or satisfied with small doses of methadone substituted for heroin or morphine," he cautioned her, "the Narcotics Bureau will still be penitentiary minded." See also Kolb to S. Spafford Ackerley, medical director, Louisville Mental Hygiene Clinic, September 4, 1956, box 2, KP. Kolb's son, Lawrence C. Kolb, himself a distinguished psychiatrist, also took up the attack in "Drug Addiction: A Statement Before a Committee of the United States Senate," 306–309.

87. Comment by Dr. William Ossenfort in Livingston, 45. See also Harris Isbell's remarks, ibid., 114–115.

88. Treadway, "Drug Addiction," 373–374; Pescor, 17, 22; Kolb and Ossenfort, 916–917; and Felix, "Some Comments," 569. A sixth category, drug addiction associated with psychoses, was added in the 1930s. See also Felix, "Lawrence Kolb," 718–719.

89. See Jaffe, "Addiction Reform," dissertation, 240–242, on the weaknesses of Kolb's reasoning and on its continuities with the earlier inebriety theories. Kolb himself conceded the inexactitude of his terminology: "The whole thing, of course, of psychopathic personality is more or less vague. It is a classification we put everything in when we do not know where else to put it." (Kolb and Ossenfort, 921.) Other expressions of the psychopathic personality theory and its variants include Lambert et al., 449–452; Pohlisch, 31; Lichtenstein, *A Doctor Studies Crime,* 59; Adams, *Drug Addiction,* 54–55; and Hall, 338–339. Of the report by Lambert et al., Nutt wrote to Kolb, "It fully supports your opinion given to us a long time prior hereto." (Nutt to Kolb, December 19, 1929, box 4, KP.) Nutt's views on the psychopathic tendencies of addicts will be discussed further.

90. Terry to John Farnham, April 27, 1932, ser. 3, box 4, folder 133. See also Jaffe, "Addiction Reform," dissertation, 186, 330–331 n. 154, 257–284, on Bishop's fate and the work of the Committee on Drug Addictions. Butler, a tough political infighter who always seemed to land on his feet, continued his career as Caddo Parish coroner and later was an early supporter of Huey Long. (BI.)

91. DuMez and Kolb, 548–558. Filed with KP is a document from the New York State Commission of Prisons, *Special Report on Drug Addiction.* Kolb's marginalia, on p. 5 opposite a summary of Bishop's views, consists of a single word, "rot."

92. Compare note 75 above with Davis, 276–278; Ashworth,

"Etiology of Habit Disease," 720; and Dr. W. D. Partlow's comments on Kolb and Ossenfort, 919–920.

93. Black, "Advantages," 537–541. C. A. Drew, medical director of the Bridgewater, Massachusetts, State Asylum for Insane Criminals to Wright, August 27, 1908, and E. W. Scribner, superintendent of the Worcester, Massachusetts, Insane Asylum to Wright, September 2, 1908 (both USIOC), and Whiteside, 67, all indicate that alcohol was much more likely to produce insanity than drug use. Whiteside, 63, also notes that indigent addicts could not be sent to Colorado institutions unless they had agreed to accept treatment. Nor could addicts, once hospitalized, usually be detained. J. W. Steere, for example, was a traveling salesman admitted to the Hartford Hospital on August 20, 1901, for treatment of "morphinism." He was discharged two days later, "before time for any improvement according to his own wishes." (Case 30671, G. L. Towne et al., Hartford Hospital Medical Records [MS, 1901–1902], Connecticut Historical Society, Hartford.)

94. Jaffe, "Addiction Reform." dissertation, 46–79, 81. On the critical reaction to Crothers, see Musto, *American Disease,* 78. One problem with Jaffe's work, which turns out to be at least partially a problem inherent to his sources, is that it is seldom clear what the proposed confinement of "inebriates" really involved. Were the inebriety reformers primarily concerned with the unruly and more numerous alcoholics, or were they, as Jaffe seems to imply, equally dedicated to the involuntary confinement and treatment of the relatively harmless and secretive opiate addicts? Most nineteenth-century medical articles specifically about opiate addiction published outside the *Quarterly Journal of Inebriety* do not even raise the issue of state commitment, their authors concentrating instead on the need to restrict sale to prescription only. See also Clark, 220.

95. Lichtenstein, "Narcotic Addiction," 965–966. He still held similar views in 1934, in *A Doctor Studies Crime,* 67–68. Like Kolb, he was opposed to simply slapping the addict in prison; nevertheless he favored involuntary treatment followed by parole. See also Baldi, 1965; Kane et al., 506; Dana, 177–178; and Graham-Mulhall, 111.

96. Knopf, 135–138. Similar sentiments were expressed by Dr. D. Percy Hickling in U.S. House, *Establishment of Two Federal Narcotic Farms: Hearings,* 37. Commented Assistant Surgeon General Treadway, "there is no hard and fast rule governing the parole of drug addict prisoners, except that it is desirable to keep them in prison as long as possible." (Treadway to L. B. Dunham, February 23, 1932, ser. 3, box 4, folder 132, CDA.)

97. California Senate, *Report on Drug Addiction in California,* 49–51.

98. Musto, "American Antinarcotic Movement," 605. Duffy, *New York City,* 599–602, also comments on the frustration of physicians as a cause for abandoning addiction as a medical problem.

99. Hubbard, "New York City Narcotic Clinic," 40. The reduction

might have gone more smoothly had treatment facilities been available, but as Jaffe, "Addiction Reform," dissertation, 208–222, relates, New York City Health Commissioner Royal S. Copeland was unable to secure adequate bed space.

100. "Special Meeting of the National Drug Trade Conference," 48–49, NLM.

101. New York, *Second Annual Report*, 31–36; Copeland, 18; U.S. Treasury Department, Bureau of Internal Revenue, *Annual Report for 1920*, 34. Anslinger was throughout his career an unyielding opponent of ambulatory treatment, as he made clear in an interview with Kenneth W. Chapman. See Anslinger and Chapman, 182–191; also Anslinger and Tompkins, 227.

102. "Special Meeting of the National Drug Trade Conference," 40, NLM; and Davenport, 2. See also Pettey, *Narcotic Drug Diseases*, 319.

103. Terry et al., "Report of Committee on Habit Forming Drugs," 85, and the outline for the medical and historical chapters of *The Opium Problem* found in Pellen's "Notes on the History of Opium," NLM. Compare Lambert et al., 461. This was actually a very old distinction. "When we allude to opium eaters," wrote an anonymous contributor to the *Boston Medical and Surgical Journal* in 1833, "we mean those only who took it originally as a medicine for some nervous affection, and continue it from necessity, rather than from choice; — who take it, not to intoxicate, but to strengthen and balance the nervous system and to enable them to attend to business, and appear like other people. Of those who take opium for purposes of unnatural excitement and inebriation, we have no knowledge. They need less our sympathy, and would excite us less to exertions in their behalf." ("Opium Eating," 66.) The idea that medical addicts were essentially blameless while nonmedical addicts, especially opium smokers, were essentially vicious was also clearly marked in Mattison's work (for example, "Genesis," 305). Butler also reserved the right to turn away undesirables: "We go thoroughly into their history and finger print them in order that we may not knowingly care for some individual who is not worthy of our assistance." ("Louisiana State Board of Health Narcotic Dispensary," 4, BP.) Scattered fingerprints and mug shots of addicts survive in BP. Other examples of the medical/nonmedical double standard include Perkins et al., 1066; Simon, 675; and the published address of L. A. Koepfgen, *Our Association* (Detroit: n.p., 1932), 6, in ser. 3, box 4, folder 133, CDA.

104. O'Donnell, 223–229.

105. Hubbard, "Some Fallacies," 1439. Blair, "Some Statistics," 608, also remarks that most physicians refused to treat cases of "pure" (nonmedical) addiction. The major exception to this rule was the dope doctor, who risked legal difficulties in exchange for exorbitant prescription fees.

106. Upham et al., 1326. By the late 1930s, however, some physicians had become so morphine-shy that they were even questioning the wisdom of administering opiates to cancer patients. See, for example,

Daland, 1–5. Lee, "Medication," 216–219, argued that opiates were contraindicated in terminal cancer because they might lead to addiction.

107. Terry and Cox, 60–61; Terry, Pellens, and Cox, 19–20. Kolb thought Terry and his coworkers again exaggerated the number of addicts, this time by using too low a dosage as an index of addiction. See his uncirculated memorandum of June 14, 1927, box 8, KP.

108. O'Donnell, 223–227, 243; further remarks cited in Brecher et al., 131–132. The physicians who wrote prescriptions for addicts in Kentucky supplied some nonmedical as well as medical types, although in the latter citation O'Donnell noted that they were on safer ground if they had some medical pretext.

109. Claud S——— to Kolb, May 30, 1934, box 6, KP. See also Butler to "Whom It May Concern," January 13, 1930, Butler to narcotic agent in charge, Shreveport, La., April 19, 1930, and Butler to Catherine Simpson, April 12, 1933, all BP; and case 3, Dai, 103–105.

110. Statistical data on the fate of medical addicts during the 1920s are scant, but suggest at least some opportunity for licit supply. In addition to the studies cited in note 107, the 1927 TS survey in box 6, KP, shows that only 5 of 150 medical cases were listed as having switched from morphine to heroin, a sure sign that they had been forced to the black market. Similarly a memorandum to Agent T. E. Middlebrooks, March 21, 1928, file 0120–9, TDF, shows no apparent alarm that 195 Atlanta addicts continued to receive opiates by prescription, even though it was admitted that the maintenance of so large a number was unusual. Many of the causes listed for addiction, moreover, include nonterminal diseases.

During the 1930s the climate changed and uprooted medical addicts were observed trekking from city to city, seeking out a willing physician or pharmacist. (Memorandum from Assistant Secretary Gibbons, December 2, 1937, file 0120–9, TDF.) Another sign that conditions were deteriorating in the 1930s is found in L. A. Koepfgen's study of 83 Michigan addicts. Although approximately a third of these cases were of medical origin, by mid-1932 practically all of them were supporting themselves by criminal means. (Koepfgen to John D. Farnham, August 26, 1932, ser. 3, box 4, folder 133, CDA.)

111. Kolb to Nyswander, August 6, 1965, box 4, KP. See also Williams, *Drug Addicts are Human Beings,* 65–110.

112. O'Donnell, 243.

113. Anslinger and Tompkins, 223–226. The official adoption of the psychopathy view gave rise to an embarrassing paradox, pointed out by Congressman Harry A. Estep of Pennsylvania. If addicts were psychopaths and therefore notorious liars, how could they be trusted to give accurate testimony in cases against doctors who had sold them the drug? (U.S. House, *Bureau of Narcotics: Hearings,* 94–95.)

114. "The National Narcotic Drug Situation Today," 3, ser. 3, box 5,

folder 149, CDA. See also Nutt's statement in U.S. House, *Establishment of Two Federal Narcotic Farms: Hearings,* esp. 38, 42.

115. U.S. House, *Establishment of Two Federal Narcotic Farms: Hearings,* 10, 22, 119–120, and passim.

116. Ibid., 2, 105; and U.S. House, *Bureau of Narcotics: Hearings,* 52.

117. U.S. House, *Establishment of Two Federal Narcotic Farms: Hearings,* 62–86.

118. Ibid., 49, 105.

119. Ibid., 102. Compare California Senate, *Report on Drug Addiction in California,* 11. Blue's assertion that medical addicts were provided for under the Harrison Act is only half true. As noted earlier, some medical addicts were not able to obtain supplies through a physician, especially during the 1930s.

120. Ibid., 76. Hollingshead and Redlich, 284–285, note a similar pattern among alcoholics: "The lower the class, the greater the probability that an alcoholic patient will be cared for in the state hospital; the higher the class, the greater the tendency for alcoholics to be treated by private practitioners."

121. Black, *Dope,* 57. Less sensationally, newspaper editorials across the country reiterated the quarantine theme and stressed the need to isolate addicts in the name of public safety. See the editorials in U.S. House, *Establishment of Two Federal Narcotic Farms: Hearings,* 216–224.

122. U.S. House, *Bureau of Narcotics: Hearings,* 13.

123. Proponents of this view include Schur, 135–140; Lindesmith, *The Addict and the Law,* 124–128; Eldridge, 24–28; Ploscowe, 64–68; Nyswander, 4–5, 164; Brecher et al., 58, 133, 142–143, 152; King, "Narcotics Bureau," 748–749, and *The Drug Hang-Up,* 163, 351; and Clark, 222–223. There is also a documentary film by Julia Reichert and James Klein, "Methadone: An American Way of Dealing," which perpetuates the idea that the 1919 rulings transformed addicts into criminals "overnight."

124. U.S. Senate, *Report on the International Opium Commission,* 47. Wright also noted that 6 percent of those "who entered our large jails and state prisons" were addicted. The discrepancy between the figures of 45.48 and 6 percent is at first puzzling; one would expect the population of large jails and state prisons would be representative of the "general criminal population." In reexamining Wright's papers, I discovered that he was using a distinction proposed by one of his correspondents, Charles B. Whilden, who noted that most criminal addicts committed misdemeanors and were hence confined in city and county jails, rather than state penitentiaries. (Whilden to Wright, September 17, 1908, USIOC.)

125. Simon to Kolb, July 21, 1926, box 6, KP. See also Hubbard, "Some Fallacies," 1440, and "Report of Committee on Drug Addiction," 2, file 0120-9, TDF.

126. U.S. Treasury Department, Bureau of Narcotics, *Traffic in Opium for 1938,* 6–7. See also *Traffic in Opium for 1939,* 16–17; Helbrant, 6, 82; Wolff, 45–46; and Anslinger and Tompkins, 267–278. The study of 225 addicts was actually undertaken by Kolb, although not credited to him in the bureau's reports. ("Drug Addictions in Relation to Crime" [TS, 1939], 6–7, box 8, KP.) Kolb always maintained, however, that addicts were not prone to violent crime, because of the tranquilizing properties of opiates. See also Hughes, 186.

127. Ausubel, 68; and Inciardi, 246–250.

128. Sandoz, 42 (original in italics). See also Stanley, "Morphinism and Crime," 756; Swords, 26, 29; Williams, *Opiate Addiction,* ix; Pearson, "Police Powers," 37; Lichtenstein, "Truth," 521–522; U.S. House, *Establishment of Two Federal Narcotic Farms: Hearings,* 61, 88, 98, 104, 134, 162; Dai, 188; and Hawkins, 110–111. For critiques by contemporary drug users, see Crowley, *Cocaine* (first published in 1917), and Street, *I Was a Drug Addict,* 104, 137, 153, 209.

129. "Jack," July 2, 1980, NYDSAS interview. Jack had had one previous arrest in 1928, for possession.

Bibliography

Knowing how to read the literature on opiate addiction is as important as knowing where to find it. A great deal of confusion can be avoided if careful note is made of the date, the background of the author(s), the context of the cases presented, and above all the type of opiate addiction being discussed. Otherwise it is difficult to account for apparently contradictory findings.

Of the manuscript collections I have examined, six are most extensive and useful: the Treasury Department Files, the Kolb Papers, the Records of the U.S. Delegation to the International Opium Commission and Conference, the Records of the U.S. Public Health Service, the Records of the Committee on Drug Addictions of the Bureau of Social Hygiene, and the Butler Papers. Other manuscript sources, particularly the impressive collection of notes and clinical records at the Rudolph Matas Medical Library in New Orleans, have been consulted to gain insight into contemporary medical practice; they would not be of interest to scholars focusing only on legal aspects of the problem.

Beginning researchers will first want to consult the standard accounts, Arnold H. Taylor's *American Diplomacy and the Narcotics Traffic, 1900–1939* (1969) and David F. Musto's *American Disease* (1973). Although neither book contains a significant amount of epidemiologic data, both provide useful chronological and conceptual frameworks, especially for legal, diplomatic, and political developments. *The Opium Problem,* by Charles E. Terry and Mildred Pellens (1928; 1970 reprint ed.), does contain statistical material but, as I have stressed in the text, it is an occasionally misleading work.

The best guide to primary printed sources is Hugo Krueger, Nathan B. Eddy, and Margaret Sumwalt, *The Pharmacology of the Opium Alkaloids,* pt. 2, *Public Health Reports,* suppl. no. 165 (1943). An account of how this monumental bibliography was assembled is contained in an oral history interview with Eddy conducted by W. D. Miles, January 18, 1972, NLM. The five series of the *Index-Catalogue of the Library of the Surgeon-General's Office* also list numerous references, many not found in the *Pharmacology of the Opium Alkaloids.* Gregory Austin, *Perspectives on the History of Psychoactive Substance Use* (Rockville, Md.: National Institute on

Drug Abuse, 1978) contains a selected bibliography of mainly secondary sources, as well as chronological information on the opiates and numerous other drugs. Researchers particularly interested in the history of cocaine should consult Joël L. Phillips, *A Cocaine Bibliography* (Rockville, Md.: National Institute on Drug Abuse, 1974). Finally, the Fitz Hugh Ludlow Memorial Library in San Francisco has a substantial collection of printed material, including many rare items, on both the opiates and cocaine.

The sources cited in this book are divided into five categories: manuscripts and typescripts; government documents; oral history interviews; unpublished theses and dissertations; and books and articles (including signed articles appearing in government serials). All are organized alphabetically, except that the manuscripts and typescripts are alphabetical under the institution in which they are housed.

Manuscripts and Typescripts

Connecticut Historical Society, Hartford
  Towne, G. L., et al. Hartford Hospital Medical Records.
  Utley, Vine. "History of a mortal Epidemic that appeared in the Towns of Lyme and Waterford, County of New London, Connecticut, in Dec. AD 1812 and during the winter and spring of the year 1813."
  Webb, Reynold, Jr. "Medical note book." 2 vols.
Drug Enforcement Administration, Freedom of Information Division, Washington, D.C.
  Treasury Department Files 0120-1, 0120-9, and Clinic Records.
Historical Pharmacy Museum, New Orleans, Louisiana
  Brand, Erich. Prescription Record Book.
Library of Congress, Manuscript Division, Washington, D.C.
  Records of Russell & Company.
Louisiana State University in Shreveport, Department of Archives
  Willis P. Butler Papers.
National Archives, Washington, D.C.
  Records of the United States Delegation to the International Opium Commission and Conference, 1909–1913. Record Group 43.
  Records of the United States Public Health Service. Record Group 90. File 2123.
National Library of Medicine, History of Medicine Division, Washington, D.C.
  Lawrence Kolb Papers.
  Lyndon Frederick Small Papers.
  National Drug Trade Conference. "Special Meeting of the National Drug Trade Conference, New Willard Hotel, Washington, D.C.,

Tuesday, May 1, 1917."

Osler, William. "Case Histories at the University of Pennsylvania Hospital." MS film 13.

Otis, Thomas. Day Books.

Pellens, Mildred. "Notes on the History of Opium."

U.S. Department of the Treasury, Public Health Service. "Public Health Service Hospital, Portland, Me., Case Reports." 3 vols.

New York Academy of Medicine, Rare Book Room, New York, New York

Ricketson, Shadrach. Letter. MS 1329.

Rice University, Fondren Library, Woodson Research Center, Houston, Texas

Stewart, John McNeil. Record Book.

Rockefeller Archive Center, North Tarrytown, New York

Papers of the Committee on Drug Addictions of the Bureau of Social Hygiene.

Rosenberg Library, Archives Division, Galveston, Texas

Ballinger, William Pitt. Diary.

Dr. Nicholas D. Labadie Papers.

Society of California Pioneers, San Francisco

Cook, Jesse. "Data given to Mrs. M. G. Foster by Jesse Cook, former Chief of Police in S.F."

Texas History Research Library, San Antonio

McKenney, Anna G. "Mrs. McKenney's Cook Book."

Tulane University, Howard-Tilton Memorial Library, New Orleans, Louisiana

Mitchell Family Papers.

Tulane University School of Medicine, Rudolph Matas Medical Library, New Orleans, Louisiana

Austin, John. "Notes on the Lectures of Benjamin Rush by John Austin."

Bemiss, Samuel Merrifield. "Clinical Lectures, Charity Hospital, 1882–83."

———. "Record of Cases Attended at Charity Hospital, New Orleans, October 1868–February 1875."

Feldner, George D. Prescription Record Book.

Fitch, Jacob Everett. "Case Records, Charity Hospital, New Orleans."

Kennon, Charles E. "Notes on the Lectures of Drs. Chaillé, Nott, Jones and Stone on Obstetrics, Pharmacology, and Therapeutics, Medical College, University of Louisiana, New Orleans, January 15, 1866–February 6, 1866." 2 vols.

Musser, Benjamin. "Principles and Practice of Medicine, Notes on Lectures of Dr. John Kearsley Mitchell, 1843–1844, Jefferson Medical School."

"Notes on Dudley's Lectures Taken in 1830."

Schuppert, Charles. "Notes, Case Records, and Observations, Charity Hospital Medical College."

Scranton, G. W. "Case Book, Case Sessions, 1873–1874, Charity Hospital."

Vandergriff, John B. "Dosimetric Medication arranged by Jno. B. Vandergriff, M.D., Graduate of La University at New Orleans."

———. "Pharmaceutical Preparations and Select Prescriptions."

University of Alabama, Library, Tuscaloosa
Jefferson Davis Papers.

University of Texas, Eugene C. Barker Research Center, Austin
Bennet, Miles S. Diary.

Bowers, Harry. "Notebook on Practice of Medicine, Materia Medica."

Nott, Thomas H. "Notes, Long Island Col. Hosp. Brooklyn, N.Y."

Government Documents

California Senate. Interim Narcotic Committee. *Report on Drug Addiction in California.* Sacramento: California State Printing Office, 1936.

———. Special Committee on Chinese Immigration. *Chinese Immigration: Its Social, Moral, and Political Effect.* Sacramento: State Office, 1878.

Great Britain. Royal Commission on Opium. *Final Report: Historical Appendices.* Vol. 7, pt. 2. London: Her Majesty's Stationery Office, 1895.

Hawaii Legislature. Special Committee on Opium. *Report.* Honolulu: n.p., 1892.

Massachusetts House of Representatives. *Report of the Special Commission to Investigate the Extent of the Use of Habit-Forming Drugs.* Boston: Wright & Potter Printing Co., 1917.

New York City. Metropolitan Board of Health. *Annual Report, 1866.* New York: C. S. Wescott & Co.'s Union Printing-House, 1867.

New York State. *Final Report of the Joint Legislative Committee Appointed to Investigate the Laws in Relation to the Distribution and Sale of Narcotic Drugs, Transmitted to the Legislature March 1, 1917.* Albany: J. B. Lyon Co., 1918.

———. Narcotic Drug Control Commission. *Second Annual Report.* Albany: J. B. Lyon Co., 1920.

San Francisco Board of Supervisors. "Report of Special Committee on the Condition of the Chinese Quarter." *Municipal Reports for the Fiscal Year 1884–85, Ending June 30, 1885.* San Francisco: Wm. Hinton & Co., 1885.

U.S. Department of Agriculture. "The Opium Poppy." *United States Department of Agriculture Report, 1870.* Washington, D.C.: G.P.O., 1871.

U.S. Department of Commerce. Bureau of the Census. *Historical Statistics of the United States: Colonial Times to 1957.* Washington, D.C.: G.P.O., 1960.

U.S. Department of State. *Papers Relating to the Foreign Relations of the United States with the Annual Message of the President Transmitted to Congress December 3, 1906.* 2 parts. Washington, D.C.: G.P.O., 1909. Volumes for subsequent years are also cited in the text.

U.S. Department of the Treasury. *Traffic in Narcotic Drugs: Report of Special Committee of Investigation Appointed March 25, 1918, by the Secretary of the Treasury.* Washington, D.C.: G.P.O., 1919.

_____. *Traffic in Opium and Other Dangerous Drugs for the Year Ended June 30, 1927.* Washington, D.C.: G.P.O., 1928.

_____. Bureau of Internal Revenue. *Annual Report for the Fiscal Year Ended June 30, 1915.* Washington, D.C.: G.P.O., 1915. Reports for subsequent years are also cited in the text.

_____. Bureau of Narcotics. *Traffic in Opium and Other Dangerous Drugs for the Year Ended December 31, 1931.* Washington, D.C.: G.P.O., 1932. Reports for subsequent years are also cited in the text.

_____. Customs Division. *The Tariff Act of October 3, 1913, on Imports into the United States.* Washington, D.C.: G.P.O., 1913.

U.S. House of Representatives. *Bureau of Narcotics: Hearings before the Committee on Ways and Means.* 71st Cong., 2nd sess. (1930).

_____. *Chinese Immigration.* House Report no. 240, 45th Cong., 2nd sess. (1878).

_____. *Establishment of Two Federal Narcotic Farms: Hearings before the Committee on the Judiciary.* 70th Cong., 1st sess. (1928).

_____. *Exportation of Opium: Hearings before a Subcommittee of the Committee on Ways and Means.* 66th Cong., 3rd sess. (1920–1921).

_____. *Importation and Use of Opium: Hearings before the Committee on Ways and Means.* 61st Cong., 3rd sess. (1910–1911).

_____. *Letter from the Secretary of the Treasury Submitting A Draught and Recommending the Passage of a Bill to Prohibit the Importation of Opium in Certain Forms.* House Ex. Document no. 79, 50th Cong., 1st sess. (1888).

_____. *Prohibit Importation of Opium.* House Report no. 1345, 66th Cong., 3rd sess. (1921).

_____. *Prohibiting the Importation of Crude Opium for the Manufacture of Heroin.* House Report no. 525, 68th Cong., 1st sess. (1924).

_____. *Prohibiting the Importation of Opium for the Manufacture of Heroin: Hearings before the Committee on Ways and Means.* 68th Cong., 1st sess. (1924).

_____. *Reenactment of Opium-Exclusion Act.* House Report no. 24, 63rd Cong., 1st sess. (1913).

_____. *Registration of Producers and Importers of Opium, Etc.* House Report no. 23, 63rd Cong., 1st sess. (1913).

_____. *Revenue Bill of 1918.* House Report no. 767, 65th Cong., 2nd sess. (1918).

_____. *Tariff Acts Passed by the Congress of the United States from 1789 to 1909.* House Document no. 671, 61st Cong., 2nd sess. (1909).

_____. *Traffic in Opium.* House Report no. 1196, 63rd Cong., 2nd sess. (1914).

U.S. Senate. *Digest of the Proceedings of the Council of National Defense during the World War.* Franklin H. Martin, compiler. Senate Document no. 193, 73rd Cong., 2nd sess. (1934).

_____. *Manufacture of Smoking Opium.* Senate Report no. 130, 63rd Cong., 1st sess. (1913).

_____. *Message from the President of the United States, Transmitting a Report of the Secretary of State Relative to Legislation Touching the Treaty of 1880 with China.* Senate Ex. Document no. 148, 49th Cong., 1st sess. (1886).

_____. *Opium Habit in the District of Columbia.* Senate Document no. 74, 54th Cong., 2nd sess. (1897).

_____. *Opium in China: Report of the Hearings at the American State Department on Petitions to the President to Use His Good Offices for the Release of China from Treaty Compulsion to Tolerate the Opium Traffic, with Additional Papers.* Senate Document no. 135, 58th Cong., 3rd sess. (1905).

_____. *The Opium Traffic: Message from the President of the United States, Transmitting Report of the Secretary of State Relative to the Control of the Opium Traffic.* Senate Document no. 736, 61st Cong., 3rd sess. (1911).

_____. *Report of the Committee Appointed by the Philippine Commission to Investigate the Use of Opium . . .* Senate Document no. 265, 59th Cong., 1st sess. (1906).

_____. *Report of the Joint Special Committee to Investigate Chinese Immigration.* Senate Report no. 680, 44th Cong., 2nd sess. (1877).

_____. *A Report on the International Opium Commission and on the Opium Problem as Seen within the United States and Its Possessions.* Hamilton Wright, compiler. Senate Document no. 377, 61st Cong., 2nd sess. (1910).

_____. *Reports of the President's Homes Commission.* Senate Document no. 644, 60th Cong., 2nd sess. (1909).

_____. *Report to Accompany Bill S. 3044.* Senate Report no. 1621, 49th Cong., 2nd sess. (1886).

U.S. Supreme Court. *Brief on Behalf of the United States, The United States of America, Plaintiff in Error, v. C. T. Doremus.* Washington, D.C.: G.P.O., 1919.

_____. *Brief on Behalf of the United States, W. S. Webb and Jacob Goldbaum v. The United States of America.* Washington, D.C.: G.P.O., 1919.

U.S. War Department. *Defects Found in Drafted Men.* Albert G. Love and Charles B. Davenport, compilers. Washington, D.C.: G.P.O., 1920.

_____. *Selective Service Regulations.* Washington, D.C.: G.P.O., 1917.

Oral History Interviews

Anonymous elderly methadone patients. Conducted by the author and Herman Joseph, under the auspices of the New York State Division of

Substance Abuse Services. Tapes (restricted until 1990) to be housed at the Columbia University Oral History Center.

Butler, Willis P. Conducted by the author, November 11, 1978.

Eddy, Nathan B. Conducted by W. D. Miles, January 18, 1972. NLM.

Unpublished Theses and Dissertations

Gosling, Francis George, III. "American Nervousness: A Study of Medicine and Social Values in the Gilded Age, 1870-1900." Ph.D. dissertation, University of Oklahoma, 1976.

Jaffe, Arnold. "Addiction Reform in the Progressive Age: Scientific and Social Responses to Drug Dependence in the United States, 1870-1930." Ph.D. dissertation, University of Kentucky, 1976.

Lodwick, Kathleen Lorraine. "Chinese, Missionary, and International Efforts to End the Use of Opium in China." Ph.D. dissertation, University of Arizona, 1976.

Stelle, Charles Clarkson. "Americans and the China Opium Trade in the Nineteenth Century." Ph.D. dissertation, University of Chicago, 1938.

Wood, Ellen Rawson. "Californians and Chinese: The First Decade." Master's thesis, University of California, 1958.

Books and Articles, Including Signed Articles in Government Serials

Ackerknecht, Erwin H. *History and Geography of the Most Important Diseases.* New York: Hafner Publishing Co., 1965.

————. *A Short History of Psychiatry,* Sula Wolff, trans., 2nd rev. ed. New York: Hafner Publishing Co., 1968.

————. *Therapeutics: From the Primitives to the 20th Century,* F. E. Verlag, trans. New York: Hafner Press, 1973.

Adams, E. W. *Drug Addiction.* Oxford: Oxford University Press, 1937.

Adams, J. F. A. "Substitutes for Opium in Chronic Disease," *BMSJ,* 121 (1889), 351-356.

Adams, J. Howe. "Morphinomania and Kindred Habits." *Medical Times,* 35 (1907), 13-16.

Adams, Samuel Hopkins. *The Great American Fraud,* 4th ed. Chicago: Press of the American Medical Association, 1907.

Ahlborn, Maurice B. "Heroin in the Morphine Habit." *New York Medical Journal,* 74 (1901), 235-236.

Aikin, Joseph M. "The Drug Habit; Its Cause and Restriction." *Medical News,* 79 (1901), 332-333.

Albutt, Clifford. "On the Abuse of Hypodermic Injections of Morphia." *Practitioner,* 5 (1870), 327-331.

Algren, Nelson. *The Man with the Golden Arm.* New York: Doubleday & Co., 1950.

Allen, Nathan. *An Essay on the Opium Trade. Including a Sketch of Its History, Extent, Effects, Etc. As Carried on in India and China.* Boston: John P. Jewett & Co., 1850.

Anders, J. M. "The Morphine Habit." *Medical Bulletin,* 21 (1899), 6–8.

Anderson, V. V. "Drug Users in Court." *BMSJ,* 176 (1917), 755–757.

Anslinger, H. J., and Tompkins, William F. *The Traffic in Narcotics.* New York: Funk & Wagnalls Co., 1953.

Anslinger, Harry, and Chapman, Kenneth W. "Narcotic Addiction [interview]." *Modern Medicine,* 25 (1957), 170–175, 182–191.

Asbury, Herbert. *The Gangs of New York: An Informal History of the Underworld.* Garden City, N.Y.: Garden City Publishing Co., 1928.

Ashe, Isaac. "The Subcutaneous Injection of Morphia in Cholera." *Medical Times and Gazette,* 25 n.s. (1862), 644.

Ashley, Richard. *Cocaine: Its History, Uses and Effects.* New York: St. Martin's Press, 1975.

————. *Heroin: The Myths and the Facts.* New York: St. Martin's Press, 1972.

Ashworth, W. C. "The Etiology of Habit Disease." *Southern Medicine and Surgery,* 92 (1930), 519–520.

————. "The Increasing Frequency of the Use of Narcotic Drugs by Members of the Medical Profession and the Probable Reasons for It." *Atlanta Journal–Record of Medicine,* 56 (1910), 36–39.

Ausubel, D. P. *Drug Addiction: Physiological, Psychological, and Sociological Aspects.* New York: Random House, 1966.

Awsiter, John. "An Account of the Effects of Opium as a Poison; with the Method of Cure; and proper Directions what to do when medinal [*sic*] Assistance is not at hand." *Gentleman's Magazine,* 33 (1763), 51–54.

Bailey, Pearce. "The Heroin Habit." *New Republic,* 6 (1916), 314–316.

————. "Nervous and Mental Disease in United States Troops." *Medical Progress,* 36 (1920), 193–197.

Baldi, Frederick S. "The Drug Habit and the Underworld." *JAMA,* 67 (1916), 1965.

Ball, B. *The Morphine Habit (Morphinomania).* New York: J. Fitzgerald, 1887.

Ball, John C. "Two Patterns of Opiate Addiction." In *The Epidemiology of Opiate Addiction in the United States,* John C. Ball and Carl D. Chambers, eds. Springfield, Ill.: Charles C Thomas, 1970.

Ball, John C., and Chambers, Carl D., eds. *The Epidemiology of Opiate Addiction in the United States.* Springfield, Ill.: Charles C Thomas, 1970.

Bancroft, Charles P. "The Opium Habit." In *Reference Handbook of the Medical Sciences,* vol. 5. New York: William Wood & Co., 1887.

Barber, Charles. "Drugs: A Study in Politics, Law and Bureaucracy." *ALSA Forum,* 3 (1978), 23–35.

Barnes, L. *Opium — Its Wonderful Fascination — Overwhelming Power — Transient Joys and Lasting Sorrows. The Fearful End. Case of Rev. G. W. Brush and Others.* Cleveland: Beckwith & Co., 1868.

Barr, G. Walter. "The Therapeutic Abuse of Opium." *JAMA,* 26 (1896), 161–162.

Barringer, Graham A., ed. "The Mexican War Journal of Henry S. Lane." *Indiana Magazine of History,* 53 (1957), 382–434.

Barth, Gunther. *Bitter Strength: A History of the Chinese in the United States, 1850–1870.* Cambridge, Mass.: Harvard University Press, 1964.

Bartholow, Roberts. *A Manual of Hypodermic Medication,* 1st ed. Philadelphia: J. B. Lippincott, 1869.

———. *A Manual of Hypodermatic Medication: The Treatment of Diseases by the Hypodermatic or Subcutaneous Method,* 5th ed. Philadelphia: J. B. Lippincott, 1891.

Bauguss, J. B. "Drug Addiction." *U.S. Veterans' Bureau Medical Bulletin,* 1 (1925), 24–28.

Beard, George M. *American Nervousness: Its Causes and Consequences.* New York: G. P. Putnam's Sons, 1881.

———. "The Relation of Inebriety to Other Nervous Diseases." *American Journal of Stimulants and Narcotics,* 1 (1882), 1–2.

———. *Stimulants and Narcotics; Medically, Philosophically, and Morally Considered.* New York: G. P. Putnam & Sons, 1871.

Beck, John B. "The Effects of Opium on the Infant Subject." Reprint from *New York Journal of Medicine* (January 1844), NYAM.

———. *Lectures on Materia Medica and Therapeutics, Delivered in the College of Physicians and Surgeons of the University of the State of New York,* C. R. Gilman, ed., 3rd ed. New York: Samuel S. & William Wood, 1861.

"Beds for 1,600 are Offered to Victims of Drugs." *Chicago Daily Tribune,* March 12, 1915, 1.

Bennet, J. Henry. "On the Hypodermic Treatment of Uterine Pain." *BMSJ,* 70 (1864), 302–304.

Bennett, A. L. "Report of State Medical Inspector of Chinese." Colorado State Board of Health. *Seventh Report* (1902–1904).

———. "Report of State Medical Inspector of Chinese." Colorado State Board of Health. *Sixth Report* (1900–1902).

Berg, Louis. *Prison Doctor.* New York: Brentano's, 1932.

Berridge, Virginia. "Fenland Opium Eating in the Nineteenth Century." *British Journal of Addiction,* 72 (1977), 275–284.

———. "Victorian Opium Eating: Responses to Opiate Use in Nineteenth-century England." *Victorian Studies,* 21 (1978), 437–461.

Betts, Thaddeus. "To the Public." *Connecticut Journal,* April 21, 1778, 1.

Biddle, J. B. "Value of Opium Imported and Exported from 1827 to 1845." *American Journal of Pharmacy,* 13 (1847), 18.

Bigelow, Walter Scott. "The Drug Trade in the United States." *Chautauquan,* 29 (1899), 217–221.

Biondi, G. C. "A Few Remarks on Cocainism." *American Medicine,* n.s. 6 (1911), 465–468.

Bishop, Ernest S. "Narcotic Drug Addiction: A Public Health Problem." *American Journal of Public Health,* 9 (1919), 481–490.

————. *The Narcotic Drug Problem.* New York: MacMillan Co., 1920.

Black, J. R. "Advantages of Substituting the Morphia Habit for the Incurably Alcoholic." *Cincinnati Lancet-Clinic,* n.s. 22 (1889), 537–541.

Black, Winifred. *Dope: The Story of the Living Dead.* New York: Star Co., 1928.

Blair, Thomas S. "The Dope Doctor and Other City Cousins of the Moonshiner." *Survey,* 44 (1920), 16–20, 55.

————. "Is Opium the 'Sheet-Anchor of Treatment'?" *American Journal of Clinical Medicine,* 26 (1919), 829–834.

————. "The Relation of Drug Addiction to Industry." *Journal of Industrial Hygiene,* 1 (1919), 284–296.

————. "The Relative Usage of Narcotic Drugs in Hospital Service and Private Practice." *JAMA,* 75 (1920), 1630–32.

————. "Some Statistics on Drug Addicts Under the Care of Physicians in Pennsylvania." *JAMA,* 76 (1921), 608.

Blair, William. "An Opium-Eater in America." *Knickerbocker,* 20 (1842), 47–57.

Blanchard, R. M. "Heroin and Soldiers." *Military Surgeon,* 33 (1913), 140–143.

Blanton, Wyndham B. *Medicine in Virginia in the Seventeenth Century,* reprint ed. New York: Arno Press, 1972.

Block, Alan A. "The Snowman Cometh." *Criminology,* 17 (1979), 75–99.

Block, Siegfried. "Drug Habitues." *New York Medical Journal,* 101 (1915), 405–407.

Bloedorn, W. A. "Studies of Drug Addiction." *U.S. Naval Medical Bulletin,* 11 (1917), 305–318.

Boggess, Walter F. "Morphinism." *Medical Age,* 17 (1899), 881–886.

Bolles, W. P. "Coca." In *Reference Handbook of the Medical Sciences,* vol. 2. New York: William Wood & Co., 1886.

————. "Opium." In *Reference Handbook of the Medical Sciences,* vol. 5. New York: William Wood & Co., 1887.

"Boy Cocaine Snuffers Hunted by Police." *New York Times,* January 8, 1907, 6.

Boynton, S. S. "Tales of a Smuggler." *Overland Monthly,* 22 (1893), 511–516.

Brainerd, H. G. "Report of Committee on Diseases of the Mind and Nervous System: Cocaine Addiction." *Transactions of the Medical Society of the State of California,* n.s. 20 (1891), 193–201.

Brecher, Edward M., et al. *Licit and Illicit Drugs.* Boston: Little, Brown and Co., 1972.

Brooks, Harlow, and Mixwell, H. R. "Two Cases of Heroin Habituation." *New York State Journal of Medicine,* 11 (1911), 386–387.

Brown, H. James. *An Opium Cure: Based Upon Science, Skill and Matured Experience; Not an Invariable Nostrum, but an Enlightened Treatment, Constituting a Sovereign Antidote and Restorative for the Opium Disease,* 2nd ed. New York: Fred. M. Brown & Co., 1872.

Brown, Lucius P. "Enforcement of the Tennessee Anti-Narcotics Law." *American Journal of Public Health,* 5 (1915), 323–333.

Brown, Samuel Horton, and Tompkins, Erle Duncan. "Heroin as an Analgesic—A Report of Fifty Administrations of Heroin in the Howard Hospital." *Therapeutic Gazette,* n.s. 16 (1900), 519–520.

[Brown, William.] *Pharmacopoeia simpliciorum et efficaciorum in usum nosocomii militaris, ad exercitum Foederatarum Americae Civitatum pertinentis; Hodiernae nostrae inopiae rerum angustiis, feroci hostium saevitiae, belloque crudeli ex inopinato patriae nostrae illato debitis, maxime accommodata.* Philadelphia: Styner & Cist, 1778.

Browne, Frank. "Some Constituents of Opium Smoke." *Pharmaceutical Journal and Record,* ser. 4, 104 (1920), 274.

Bruce, Hamilton. *The Warehouse Manual and General Custom House Guide* . . . New York: the author, 1862.

Bryce, James. *The American Commonwealth,* 3rd ed. 2 vols. New York: MacMillan and Co., 1895.

Buerki, Robert A. "Medical Views on Narcotics and their effects in the mid-1890s." *Pharmacy in History,* 17 (1975), 3–12.

Burnett, S. Grover. "Why the Indifference of the Profession to Morphinism Should Be Changed." *Medical Herald,* n.s. 29 (1910), 327–337.

Burr, C. B. "Concerning Morphine Addiction and Its Treatment." *JAMA,* 39 (1902), 1588–92.

Burroughs, William S. "Kicking Drugs: A Very Personal Story." *Harper's,* 235 (July 1967), 39–42.

Butler, Willis P. "How One American City is Meeting the Public Health Problems of Narcotic Drug Addiction." *American Medicine,* 28 (1922), 154–162.

Byford, Henry T., et al. *An American Text-Book of Gynecology, Medical and Surgical, for Practitioners and Students,* 2nd ed. J. M. Baldy, editor. Philadelphia: W. B. Saunders, 1898.

Byford, William H. *The Practice of Medicine and Surgery Applied to the Diseases and Accidents Incident to Women.* Philadelphia: Lindsay & Blakiston, 1865.

Byrnes, Thomas. *1886: Professional Criminals of America,* reprint ed. New York: Chelsea House Publishers, 1969.

Calkins, Alonzo. "Opium and Its Victims." *Galaxy,* 4 (1867), 25–36.

————. *Opium and the Opium Appetite.* Philadelphia: J. B. Lippincott & Co., 1871.

————. "Statistics of Opium-poisoning." *Quarterly Journal of Psychological Medicine and Medical Jurisprudence,* 2 (1868), 738–752.

Campbell, Leslie Caine. *Two Hundred Years of Pharmacy in Mississippi.* Jackson: University Press of Mississippi, 1974.

Carman, J. H. "The Danger of Opium Smoking as a Therapeutic Measure." *Medical Record,* 26 (1884), 501.

Carpenter, George W. "Observations and Experiments on Opium."

American Journal of Science and Arts, 13 (1828), 17–32.

Carter, Robert. *An Inaugural Essay, Being a Comparative Inquiry into the Properties and Uses of Opium.* Philadelphia: Office of the Gazette of the United States, 1803.

Cash, Philip. *Medical Men at the Siege of Boston, April, 1775–April, 1776: Problems of the Massachusetts and Continental Armies.* Philadelphia: American Philosophical Society, 1973.

"Caught Using Heroin." *New York Times,* June 3, 1913, 18.

"Celestials Corraled." *Rocky Mountain News,* October 12, 1880, 1.

Chaillé, Stanford E. "The Opium Habit, and 'Opium-Mania Cures.' With Chemical Analysis of Dr. Beck's 'Opiumania Cure,' by J. Johnson." Reprint from *New Orleans Medical and Surgical Journal* (May 1876), RMML.

Chang, Hsin-pao. *Commissioner Lin and the Opium War.* Cambridge, Mass.: Harvard University Press, 1964.

Chapman, Nathaniel. *Elements of Therapeutics and Materia Medica,* 4th ed. 2 vols. Philadelphia: H. C. Carey and I. Lea, 1825.

Chase, J. Frank, et al. *The Dope Evil.* Boston: New England Watch and Ward Society, 1912.

Cheadle, W. B. "The Clinical Uses of Opium." *Clinical Journal,* 4 (1894), 345–351.

Chesnut, Mary Boykin. *A Diary from Dixie,* Ben Ames Williams, ed. Boston: Houghton Mifflin Co., 1949.

"Chinese in New York." *New York Times,* December 26, 1873, 3.

"The Chinese New Year." *New York Times,* February 16, 1874, 5.

Clark, Norman H. *Deliver Us From Evil: An Interpretation of American Prohibition.* New York: W. W. Norton & Co., 1976.

Cleckley, Hervey M. "Psychopathic Personality." In *International Encyclopedia of the Social Sciences,* David L. Sills, ed., vol. 13. New York: Macmillan Co., 1968.

Clementi, C., trans. *Article on the Poppy from the Compendium of Literature and Illustrations, Ancient and Modern, . . .* Hong Kong: Noronha & Co., 1908.

"Closure of the Opium 'Joints' in New York." *American Journal of Stimulants and Narcotics,* 1 (1882), 26.

Coale, Ansley J., and Zelnik, Melvin. *New Estimates of Fertility and Population in the United States: A Study of Annual White Births from 1885 to 1960 and of Completeness of Enumeration in the Censuses from 1880 to 1960.* Princeton: Princeton University Press, 1963.

Cobbe, William Rosser. *Doctor Judas: A Portrayal of the Opium Habit.* Chicago: S. C. Griggs and Co., 1895.

Coblentz, Virgil. *The Newer Remedies: A Reference Manual for Physicians, Pharmacists, and Students,* 3rd ed. Philadelphia: P. Blakiston's Son & Co., 1899.

" 'Cocaine Alley.' " *American Druggist and Pharmaceutical Record,* 37 (1900), 337–338.

"The Cocaine Habit Among Negroes." *British Medical Journal,* pt. 2 (1902), 1729.

"Cocaine Sniffers." *New York Tribune,* June 21, 1903, 11.

"The Cocain Habit." *JAMA,* 34 (1900), 1637.

"The Cocain Habit." *JAMA,* 36 (1900), 330.

[Coleman, William.] *A Collection of the Facts and Documents, Relative to the Death of Major-General Alexander Hamilton; with Comments: together with the Various Orations, Sermons, and Eulogies, that have been published or written on his Life and Character,* facsimile ed. Austin, Texas: Shoal Creek Publishers, 1972.

Collins, Charles W., and Day, John. "Dope, the New Vice." *Everyday Life,* vol. 4 (1909), no. 10, 3-4, 29; no. 11, 6-7; no. 12, 4-5; vol. 5 (1909), no. 1, 10-11; no. 2, 4-5.

Collins, Samuel B. *Theriaki: A Treatise on the Habitual Use of Narcotic Poison: How the Habit is Formed, Its Consequences and Cure.* Laporte, Ind.: n.p., 1887.

Colton, Walter. "Effects of Opium." *Knickerbocker,* 7 (1836), 421-423.

Comings, F. W. "Opium. Its Uses and Abuses." *Transactions of the Vermont State Medical Society* (1895-1896), 359-371.

Committee on Traffic in Opium of the Foreign Policy Association. *The Case Against Heroin.* New York: Foreign Policy Association, 1924.

Condit, Ira M. *The Chinaman as We See Him and Fifty Years of Work for Him.* Chicago: Fleming H. Revell Co., 1900.

"The Confessions of a Cocainist." *Scientific American,* suppl. no. 1107, 43 (1897), 17695-96.

Conrad, Horace W. "The Health of Negroes in the South: The Great Mortality Among Them; The Causes and Remedies." *Sanitarian,* 18 (1887), 502-510.

Copeland, Royal S. "The Narcotic Drug Evil and the New York City Health Department." *American Medicine,* 26 (1920), 17-23.

Corbus, Burton R. "Some Factors in the Causation of Drug Habits." *Medical Standard,* 27 (1904), 14-15.

Courtright, George S. "Report of a Case of Poisoning, by Tinct. Gelsemium. Treated by the Hypodermic Injection of Morphia." *Cincinnati Lancet and Observer,* 19 (1876), 961-966.

Courtwright, David T. "The Female Opiate Addict in Nineteenth-Century America." *Essays in Arts and Sciences,* 10 (1981, in press).

————. "Opiate Addiction as a Consequence of the Civil War." *Civil War History,* 24 (1978), 101-111.

Coxe, John Redman. *The American Dispensatory, Containing the Operations of Pharmacy; together with the Natural, Chemical, Pharmaceutical and Medical History of the Different Substances employed in Medicine . . . ,* 3rd ed. Philadelphia: Thomas Dobson, 1814.

Crane, J. Townley. "Drugs as an Indulgence." *Methodist Quarterly Review,* 40 (1858), 551-566.

Crothers, T. D. "Cocaine-Inebriety." *Quarterly Journal of Inebriety,* 20 (1898), 369–376.

––––––. "Cocainism." *Quarterly Journal of Inebriety,* 32 (1910), 78–84.

––––––. "Criminality and Morphinism." *New York Medical Journal,* 95 (1912), 163–165.

––––––. "The Danger of the Use of Opium in Infancy." *Medical News,* 84 (1904), 1173–1174.

––––––. "Medicolegal Relations of Opium Inebriety and the Necessity for Legal Recognition." *JAMA,* 35 (1900), 409–413.

––––––. "Morphinism Among Physicians." *Medical Record,* 56 (1899), 784–786.

––––––. "Morphinism Among Physicians." *Quarterly Journal of Inebriety,* 22 (1900), 98–100.

––––––. *Morphinism and Narcomanias from Other Drugs: Their Etiology, Treatment, and Medicolegal Relations.* Philadelphia: W. B. Saunders & Co., 1902.

––––––. "New Sources of Danger in the Use of Opium." *JAMA,* 35 (1900), 338–342.

C[rouch], H[erbert] C[hallice]. "Anaesthesia." In *Encyclopaedia Britannica,* 11th ed., vol. 1. Cambridge: Cambridge University Press, 1910.

Crowley, Aleister. *Cocaine.* San Francisco: Level Press, 1973.

"The Cruelty of Avarice." *National Magazine,* 5 [?] (March 1855), 314–320.

Curtiss, Homer F. "Some Fundamentals in the Psychology of Drug Addiction." In *Narcotic Education: Edited Report of the Proceedings of the First World Conference on Narcotic Education, Philadelphia, Pennsylvania, July 5, 6, 7, 8, and 9, 1926,* H. S. Middlemiss, ed. Washington, D.C.: the editor, 1926.

Cuskey, Walter R., et al. "Survey of Opiate Addiction Among Females in the United States Between 1850 and 1970." *Public Health Reviews,* 1 (1972), 6–39.

Dai, Bingham. *Opium Addiction in Chicago,* reprint ed. Montclair, N.J.: Patterson Smith, 1970.

Dain, Norman. *Concepts of Insanity in the United States, 1789–1865.* New Brunswick, N.J.: Rutgers University Press, 1964.

Daland, Ernest M. "The Relief of Pain in Cancer Patients." *Public Health Reports,* suppl. no. 121 (1936).

Daly, James R. L. "A Clinical Study of Heroin." *BMSJ,* 142 (1900), 190–192.

Dana, Charles L. "The Problems of Drug Addiction." *Medical Record,* 93 (1918), 177–178.

Davenport, Walter A. "The Drug Menace and What It Means to New York." *New York Sun,* July 27, 1919, sec. 3, pp. 1, 2, 5.

Davis, M. T. "Some Observations on the Use and Abuse of Opium." *Atlanta Journal-Record of Medicine,* 62 (1915), 276–281.

[Day, Horace B., ed.] *The Opium Habit, with Suggestions as to the Remedy.* New York: Harper & Brothers, 1868.

Deaderick, William H., and Thompson, Loyd. *The Endemic Diseases of the Southern States.* Philadelphia: W. B. Saunders Co., 1916.

"Deadly Opium." *Rocky Mountain News,* October 9, 1880, 8.

"Death of a Child from Laudanum." *BMSJ,* 20 (1839), 33–34.

De Crèvecoeur, Hector St. John. *Letters from an American Farmer,* Ernest Rhys, ed. No. 640 of Everyman's Library. London: J. M. Dent & Sons, 1945.

"Defective Complaint in Action for Malpractice in Prescribing Heroin." *JAMA,* 58 (1912), 1969.

De Quincey, Thomas. *Confessions of an English Opium Eater,* edited and introduced by Alethea Hayter. Hammondsworth, Middlesex: Penguin Books, 1975.

Dercum, Francis X. "Relative Infrequency of the Drug Habit Among the Middle and Upper Classes. Treatment and Final Results." *Pennsylvania Medical Journal,* 20 (1917), 362–364. Abstracted in *JAMA,* 67 (1916), 1965.

"Destructive Practices." *Boston Medical Intelligencer,* 1 (June 1823), 19.

Dewey, Richard. "Addiction to Drugs, Especially in Reference to the Medical Profession." *Medical Age,* 18 (1900), 321–325.

Dillon, Richard H. *The Hatchet Men: The Story of the Tong Wars in San Francisco's Chinatown.* New York: Coward-McCann, 1962.

Diner, Jacob. "Drug Addiction and Its Treatment." *Medical Record,* 94 (1918), 316–319.

Doane, Joseph C. "Drug Toxemias, Their Nature, Etiology and Symptomatology." *Archives of Neurology and Psychiatry,* 2 (1919), 480–481.

Dobie, Charles Caldwell. *San Francisco's Chinatown.* New York: D. Appleton-Century Co., 1936.

Dole, Vincent P. "Addictive Behavior." *Scientific American,* 243 (December 1980), 138–140, 142, 144, 146, 148, 150, 154.

Dole, Vincent P., and Joseph, Herman. *The Long-Term Consequences of Methadone Maintenance Treatment.* New York: Rockefeller University and the Community Treatment Foundation, 1979.

"Dope." *Time,* 17 (March 2, 1931), 52–53.

Douglas, Charles J. "Cocainism." *Medical News,* 35 (1904), 115–116.

——. "Morphine in General Practice." *New York Medical Journal,* 97 (1913), 882–883.

——. "Morphinism." *Medical Record,* 72 (1907), 435–437.

Downs, Jacques M. "American Merchants and the China Opium Trade, 1800–1840." *Business History Review,* 42 (1968), 418–442.

Downs, James T. "The Relation of Narcotic Drug Addiction to Life Insurance." In *Narcotic Education: Edited Report of the Proceedings of the First World Conference on Narcotic Education, Philadelphia, Pennsylvania,*

July 5, 6, 7, 8, and 9, 1926, H. S. Middlemiss, ed. Washington, D.C.: the editor, 1926.

Dreser, H. "Pharmakologisches über einige Morphinderivate." *Therapeutische Monatshefte,* 12 (1898), 509–512.

_____. "Ueber die Wirkung einiger Derivate des Morphins auf die Athmung." *Archiv fuer die Gesammte Physiologie des Menschen und der Tiere,* 72 (1898), 485–520.

"Drug Addicts in the South." *Survey,* 42 (1919), 147–148.

"Drug Smugglers Arrested." *New York Times,* May 16, 1899, 12.

Drysdale, H. H. "Some of the Effects of the Harrison Anti-Narcotic Law in Cleveland. (Analysis of Cases of Drug Addiction Treated in the Observation Department of the Cleveland City Hospital)." *Cleveland Medical Journal,* 14 (1915), 353–364.

Du Bois, W. E. Burghardt, ed. *The Health and Physique of the Negro American: Report of a Social Study made under the direction of Atlanta University; together with the Proceedings of the Eleventh Conference for the Study of the Negro Problems, held at Atlanta University, on May the 29th, 1906.* Atlanta: Atlanta University Press, 1906.

Duffy, John. *Epidemics in Colonial America.* Baton Rouge: Louisiana State University Press, 1953.

_____. *The Healers: The Rise of the Medical Establishment.* New York: McGraw-Hill, 1976.

_____. *A History of Public Health in New York City, 1866–1966.* New York: Russell Sage Foundation, 1974.

DuMez, A. G. "Increased Tolerance and Withdrawal Phenomena in Chronic Morphinism: A Review of the Literature." *JAMA,* 72 (1919), 1069–72.

DuMez, A. G., and Kolb, Lawrence. "Absence of Transferable Immunizing Substances in the Blood of Morphine and Heroin Addicts." *Public Health Reports,* 40 (1925), 548–558.

Duncan, H. S. "The Morphia Habit—How Is It Most Usually Contracted, and What Is the Best Means to Diminish It?" *Nashville Journal of Medicine and Surgery,* n.s. 35 (1885), 246–248.

Dunglison, Robley. *A Dictionary of Medical Science . . . ,* rev. ed. Philadelphia: Blanchard and Lea, 1860.

Dykstra, David L. "The Medical Profession and Patent and Proprietary Medicines During the Nineteenth Century." *Bulletin of the History of Medicine,* 29 (1955), 401–419.

Earle, Charles Warrington. "The Opium Habit: A Statistical and Clinical Lecture." *Chicago Medical Review,* 2 (1880), 442–446.

_____. "Opium-Smoking in Chicago." *Chicago Medical Journal and Examiner,* 52 (1886), 104–112.

Earle, James H. *Confessions of an American Opium Eater: From Bondage to Freedom.* Boston: the author, 1895.

Eaton, Virgil G. "How the Opium Habit is Acquired." *Popular Science Monthly,* 33 (1888), 663–667.

Eberle, E. G., et al. "Report of Committee on the Acquirement of Drug Habits." *Proceedings of the American Pharmaceutical Association,* 51 (1903), 446-487.

Eberle, John. *A Treatise of the Materia Medica and Therapeutics,* 1st ed. 2 vols. Philadelphia: James Webster, 1822.

Eddy, Clyde Langston. "One Million Drug Addicts in the United States." *Current History,* 18 (1923), 637-643.

Eddy, Nathan B. "The Search for a Non-Addicting Analgesic." In *Narcotic Drug Addiction Problems,* Robert B. Livingston, ed. Public Health Service Publication no. 1050. Washington, D.C.: G.P.O., 1963.

"Effects of Opium Eating." *BMSJ,* 6 (1832), 128-131.

"8,000 Lads in City Are Drug Addicts." *New York Times,* April 15, 1919, 24.

Eldridge, William Butler. *Narcotics and the Law: A Critique of the American Experiment in Narcotic Drug Control,* 2nd ed. Chicago: University of Chicago Press, 1967.

Ellis, E. S. *Ancient Anodynes: Primitive Anaesthesia and Allied Conditions.* London: Wm. Heinemann, 1946.

Emerson, Haven, et al. "Report of Committee on Narcotic Drugs of the Council on Health and Public Instruction." *JAMA,* 76 (1921), 1669-71.

Englehardt, H. Tristram, Jr. "The Disease of Masturbation: Values and the Concept of Disease." In *Sickness and Health in America: Readings in the History of Medicine and Public Health in America,* Judith Walzer Leavitt and Ronald L. Numbers, eds. Madison: University of Wisconsin Press, 1978.

Enlow, E. E. *Recalling the Years of My Life.* Sebastopol, Calif.: n.p., 1946.

Epstein, Edward Jay. *Agency of Fear: Opiates and Political Power in America.* New York: G. P. Putnam's Sons, 1977.

Eulenberg, A. "Ueber subcutane Injectionem von Heroinum muriaticum." *Deutsche Medicinische Wochenschrift,* 25 (1899), 187-188.

Evans, H. Y. "The Hypodermic Employment of the Sulphate of Morphia, in fifty distinct cases." *Medical Times,* 1 (1871), 264-265.

Farr, Clifford B. "The Relative Frequency of the Morphine and Heroin Habits: Based Upon Some Observations at the Philadelphia General Hospital." *New York Medical Journal,* 101 (1915), 892-895.

Fauntleroy, C. M. "A Case of Heroinism." *New York Medical Journal,* 86 (1907), 930.

Fay, Peter Ward. *The Opium War, 1840-1842: Barbarians in the Celestial Empire in the Early Part of the Nineteenth Century and the War by Which They Forced Her Gates Ajar.* Chapel Hill: University of North Carolina Press, 1975.

Felix, Robert H. "Lawrence Kolb, 1881-1972." *American Journal of Psychiatry,* 130 (1973), 718-719.

――――――. "Some Comments on the Psychopathology of Drug Addiction." *Mental Hygiene,* 23 (1939), 567-592.

Fields, Albert, and Tararin, Peter A. "Opium in China." *British Journal of Addiction*, 64 (1970), 371-382.

"15,000 Drug Victims . . ." *New York Times*, January 22, 1914, 20.

"First Arrest Made in Smuggling Plot." *New Yorks Times*, February 14, 1909, 8.

Fischer, Louis. "The Opium Habit in Children." *Medical Record*, 45 (1894), 197-199.

Floeckinger, F. C. "Clinical Observations on Heroin and Heroin Hydrochloride, as Compared with Codein and Morphin." *New Orleans Medical and Surgical Journal*, 52 (1900), 636-646.

Floret, [Theobald]. "Klinische Versuche über die Wirkung und Anwendung des Heroins." *Therapeutische Monatshefte*, 12 (1898), 512.

Foot, Arthur Wynne. "On Morphinism." *Dublin Journal of Medical Science*, 88, ser. 3 (1889), 457-472.

Fox, A. C. "Morphinism." *Alkaloidal Clinic*, 4 (1897), 701-702.

Frese, Carl. "Drug Habits." In *An American Text-Book of Applied Therapeutics for the Use of Practitioners and Students*, J. C. Wilson, ed. Philadelphia: W. B. Saunders, 1897.

Freud, Sigmund. *Cocaine Papers*, Robert Byck and Anna Freud, eds. New York: Stonehill, 1974.

Friends for New England. *The Traffic in and Use of Opium in Our Own and Other Countries*. Providence: Rhode Island Printing Co., 1882.

Frisch, John R. "Our Years in Hell: American Addicts Tell Their Story, 1829-1914." *Journal of Psychedelic Drugs*, 9 (1977), 199-207.

"From the New England *Weekly Journal*." *Pennsylvania Gazette*, June 25, 1741, 1.

Fromme, A. "Dionin und seine Anwendung bei der Abstinenzkur des chonischen Morphinisimus." *Berliner Klinische Wochenschrift*, 36 (1899), 302.

Frost, C. R. "Opium: Its Uses and Abuses." *Transactions of the Vermont State Medical Society* (1869-1870), 131-147.

Fülöp-Miller, René. *Triumph Over Pain*, Eden and Cedar Paul, trans. New York: Literary Guild of America, 1938.

Fulton, Henry D. "Heroin in Affections of the Respiratory Organs." *New York Medical Journal*, 70 (1899), 960-961.

Gallagher, Thomas J. "On Hypodermic Injections." *New York Medical Journal*, 13 (1871), 532-550.

Gavit, John Palmer. *Opium*. New York: Brentano's, 1927.

Geis, Norman P. "Heroin as an Analgetic." *New York Medical Journal*, 72 (1900), 929-930.

"General Facts about the Use of Opium in this Country." *Quarterly Journal of Inebriety*, 2 (1878), 214-217.

Gibbons, H. "Letheomania: The Result of the Hypodermic Injection of Morphia." *Pacific Medical and Surgical Journal*, 12 (1870), 481-495.

Gilbert, D. D. "The Cocaine Habit from Snuff." *BMSJ*, 138 (1898), 119.

Gill, Harold B., Jr. *The Apothecary in Colonial Virginia.* Williamsburg, Va.: Colonial Williamsburg Foundation, 1972.

Goldberger, Joseph. "The Transmissibility of Pellagra. Experimental Attempts at Transmission to the Human Subject." *Public Health Reports,* 31 (1916), 3159-73.

"The Golden 'Yen Hock.'" *Rocky Mountain News,* October 10, 1886, 2.

Goldstein, Avram. "Opioid Peptides (Endorphins) in Pituitary and Brain." *Science,* 193 (1976), 1081-86.

Goodwin, Charles H. *Treatment of Diseases of Women, Puerperal and Non-Puerperal.* New York: the author, 1884.

Gordon, Alfred. "Insanities Caused by Acute and Chronic Intoxication with Opium and Cocain." *JAMA,* 51 (1908), 97-101.

———. The Relation of Legislative Acts to the Problem of Drug Addiction." *Journal of Criminal Law, Criminology, and Police Science,* 8 (1917), 211-215.

Graham-Mulhall, Sara. "Experiences in Narcotic Drug Control in the State of New York." *New York Medical Journal,* 113 (1921), 106-111.

Green, E. M. "Psychoses among Negroes—A Comparative Study." *Journal of Nervous and Mental Disease,* 41 (1914), 697-708.

Griffenhagen, George B. "Medicines in the American Revolution." In *American Pharmacy in the Colonial and Revolutionary Periods,* George A. Bender and John Parascandola, eds. Madison: American Institute of the History of Pharmacy, 1977.

Griffin, R. E. "Morphine—Its Uses and Abuses." *Kentucky Medical Journal,* 8 (1910), 1583-85.

Grinnell, Ashbel Parmelee. "A Review of Drug Consumption and Alcohol as Found in Proprietary Medicine." *Medico-Legal Journal,* 6 (1906), 589-611.

"The Growing Menace of the Use of Cocaine." *New York Times,* August 2, 1907, pt. 5, 1-2.

"Growth of the Opium Habit in Denver." *Denver Times,* Feb. 1, 1899, 5.

"Habit of Taking Opium—Inordinate Use of the Hypodermic Syringe." *Medical Record,* 11 (1876), 572.

Hale, Nathan G., Jr. *Freud and the Americans: The Beginnings of Psychoanalysis in the United States, 1876–1917.* New York: Oxford University Press, 1971.

Hall, Margaret E. "Mental and Physical Efficiency of Women Drug Addicts." *Journal of Abnormal and Social Psychology,* 33 (1938), 332-345.

Haller, John S., and Haller, Robin M. *The Physician and Sexuality in Victorian America.* Urbana: University of Illinois Press, 1974.

Hamlin, F. M. "The Opium Habit." *Medical Gazette,* 9 (1882), 426-431.

Hammond, W. A. "Remarks on Cocaine and the So-called Cocaine Habit." *Journal of Nervous and Mental Disease,* 13 (1886), 754-759.

Handlin, Oscar. *The Uprooted,* 2nd ed. Boston: Little, Brown and Co., 1973.

————, ed. *Immigration as a Factor in American History.* Englewood Cliffs, N.J.: Prentice-Hall, 1959.

Handy, Hast[ings]. *An Inaugural Dissertation on Opium.* Philadelphia: T. Lang, 1791.

Hanzlik, P. J. "125th Anniversary of the Discovery of Morphine by Sertürner." *Journal of the American Pharmaceutical Association,* 18 (1929), 375–384.

Happel, T. J. "Morphinism from the Standpoint of the General Practitioner." *JAMA,* 35 (1900), 407–409.

————. "The Opium Curse and Its Prevention." *Medical and Surgical Reporter,* 72 (1895), 727–731.

Harlow, Alvin F. *Old Bowery Days: The Chronicle of a Famous Street.* New York: D. Appleton and Co., 1931.

Hartwell, B. H. "The Sale and Use of Opium in Massachusetts." Massachusetts State Board of Health. *Annual Report,* 20 (1889), 137–158.

Hasty, J. E. "Opium Smuggling." *Illustrated World,* 26 (1917), 687–690.

Hawkins, John A. *Opium Addicts and Addictions.* Boston: Bruce Humphries, 1937.

Haynes, Robert W. "The Dangers of Cocaine." *Medical News,* 65 (1894), 14.

Hayter, Alethea. *Opium and the Romantic Imagination.* Berkeley: University of California Press, 1968.

Helbrant, Maurice. *Narcotic Agent.* New York: Vanguard Press, 1941.

Helfand, William H. "Vin Mariani." *Pharmacy in History,* 22 (1980), 11–19.

Helmer, John. *Drugs and Minority Oppression.* New York: Seabury Press, 1975.

Helmer, John, and Vietorisz, Thomas. *Drug Use, the Labor Market, and Class Conflict.* Washington, D.C.: Drug Abuse Council, 1974.

Hendrick, O. "On the Value of Hypodermic Injections of Morphia in Obstetric Pratice." *Richmond and Louisville Medical Journal,* 8 (1869), 397–399.

"Heroin and the Heroin Habit." *American Journal of Pharmacy,* 79 (1907), 576.

"Heroin and the Results of Its Abuse as a Drug." *British Medical Journal* (1902), epitome sec., 91.

"Heroin Hydrochloride." *JAMA,* 47 (1906), 1303.

Herwirsch, Charles. "Heroin in Cough." *Therapeutic Gazette,* 23 (1899), 728–730.

Hesse, Erich. *Narcotics and Drug Addiction,* Frank Gaynor, trans. New York: Philosophical Library, 1946.

Hill, Harris E., Haertzen, Charles A., and Glaser, Robert. "Personality Characteristics of Narcotic Addicts as Indicated by the *MMPI*." *Journal of General Psychology,* 62 (1960), 127–139.

Hinckley, Livingston S. *Narcotic Drug Addiction: The Modern Scourge.* Newark, N.J.: the author, 1918.

"History of Heroin." *Bulletin on Narcotics,* 5 (1953), 3–16.

Hobson, Richmond Pearson. "One Million Americans Victims of Drug Habits." *New York Times,* November 9, 1924, pt. 9, 4.

Holder, C. F. "The Opium Industry in America." *Scientific American,* 78 (1898), 147.

Hollingshead, August B., and Redlich, Frederick C. *Social Class and Mental Illness: A Community Study.* New York: John Wiley & Sons, 1964.

Holmes, Oliver Wendell, Sr. *Medical Essays: 1842–1882.* Boston: Houghton Mifflin Co., 1891.

Howard, Sidney. "The Inside Story of Dope in this Country." *Hearst's International,* 43 (1923), 24–28, 116, 118–120.

Howard, William Lee. "Some Facts Regarding the Morphine Victim." *Quarterly Journal of Inebriety,* 26 (1904), 128–136.

Howard-Jones, Norman. "Cholera Therapy in the Nineteenth Century." *Journal of the History of Medicine and Allied Sciences,* 27 (1972), 373–395.

––––––. "A Critical Study of the Origins and Early Development of Hypodermic Medication." *Journal of the History of Medicine and Allied Sciences,* 2 (1947), 201–249.

Hsü, Immanuel C. Y. *The Rise of Modern China,* 2nd ed. New York: Oxford University Press, 1975.

Hubbard, Fred. Heman. *The Opium Habit and Alcoholism.* New York: A. S. Barnes & Co., 1881.

Hubbard, S. Dana. "Municipal Narcotic Dispensaries." *Public Health Reports,* 35 (1920), 771–773.

––––––. "The New York City Narcotic Clinic and Differing Points of View on Narcotic Addiction." New York City Department of Health. *Monthly Bulletin,* 10 (1920), 33–47.

––––––. "Some Fallacies Regarding Drug Addiction." *JAMA,* 74 (1920), 1439–41.

Hudson, William L. "Opium Cure." *American Medical Weekly,* 1 (1874), 102.

Hughes, John Harrison. "The Autobiography of a Drug Fiend." *Medical Review of Reviews,* 22 (1916), 27–43, 105–120, 173–190.

Hull, J. M. "The Opium Habit." Iowa State Board of Health. *Biennial Report,* 3 (1885), 535–545.

Hunt, Leon Gibson, and Chambers, Carl D. *The Heroin Epidemics: A Study of Heroin Use in the United States, 1965–75.* New York: Spectrum Publications, 1976.

Hunter, Charles. *On the Speedy Relief of Pain and Other Nervous Affections, by Means of the Hypodermic Method.* London: John Churchill & Sons, 1865.

Hunter, Q. W. "The Evils of Cocaine." *Medical Age,* 24 (1906), 331–338.

Huse, Edward C. "Coca-Erythroxylon – A New Cure for the Opium Habit." *Therapeutic Gazette,* n.s. 1 (1880), 256–257.

Hutchins, Frank F. "The Psychological Aspect of the Drug Habit." *Medical and Surgical Monitor,* 8 (1905), 131–134.

Hyde, Louis D. "A Contribution to the Study of the Morphine Habit."

Transactions of the Homeopathic Society of New York, 33 (1898), 227–230.

Hynson, Henry B., et al. "Report of Committee on Acquirement of the Drug Habit." *Proceedings of the American Pharmaceutical Association,* 50 (1902), 567–575.

"Hypodermic Use of Opium." *Probe,* 1 (1869), 7–9.

Inciardi, James A. "The Villification of Euphoria: Some Perspectives on an Elusive Issue." *Addictive Diseases,* 1 (1974), 241–267.

Ingals, E. Fletcher. "Danger from the Hypodermic Injection of Morphia." *Chicago Medical Journal and Examiner,* 36 (1878), 491–496.

Inglis, John. "Morphinism." *Denver Medical Times,* 22 (1903), 391–395.

Isbell, Harris. "Historical Development of Attitudes Toward Opiate Addiction in the United States." In *Conflict and Creativity,* R. H. L. Wilson and Seymour M. Farber, eds. New York: McGraw-Hill, 1963.

Jaffe, A. "Reform in American Medical Science: The Inebriety Movement and the Origins of the Psychological Disease Theory of Addiction, 1870–1920." *British Journal of Addiction,* 73 (1978), 139–147.

Johnson, E. Y. "A Few Remarks on Heroin Hydrochloride." *American Practitioner,* 32 (1901), 413–415.

Johnson, Gerald W. *Randolph of Roanoke: A Political Fantastic.* New York: Minton, Balch & Co., 1929.

Jones, Ernest. *The Life and Work of Sigmund Freud,* Lionel Trilling and Steven Marcus, eds. New York: Basic Books, 1961.

Jordan, Phillip D. *Frontier Law and Order: Ten Essays.* Lincoln: University of Nebraska Press, 1970.

Josselyn, Eli E. "An Analysis of Twelve Cases of the Morphia Habit." *Medical Register,* 1 (1887), 195–198.

Joyce, Thomas F. "The Treatment of Drug Addiction." *New York Medical Journal,* 112 (1920), 220–222.

Kahn, E. J., Jr. *The Big Drink: The Story of Coca-Cola.* New York: Random House, 1960.

Kane, Francis Fisher, et al. "Drugs and Crime (Report of Committee 'G' of the Institute)." *Journal of the American Institute of Criminal Law and Criminology,* 8 (1917), 502–517.

Kane, H. H. *Drugs That Enslave: The Opium, Morphine, Chloral and Hashisch Habits.* Philadelphia: Presley Blakiston, 1881.

――――. *Opium-Smoking in America and China: A Study of Its Prevalence, and Effects, Immediate and Remote, on the Individual and the Nation.* New York: G. P. Putnam's Sons, 1882.

――――. "The Rapid Spread of the Morphia Habit (by Subcutaneous Injection) in Germany. A Village of Morphia Takers." *Maryland Medical Journal,* 8 (1881), 337–341.

Kaufman, Martin. *American Medical Education: The Formative Years, 1765–1910.* Westport, Conn.: Greenwood Press, 1976.

Kebler, L. F. "Habit-Forming Agents." United States Department of Agriculture. *Farmers' Bulletin,* no. 393 (1910).

――――. "The Present Status of Drug Addiction in the United States."

Monthly Cyclopaedia and Medical Bulletin, 4 (1911), 13–27.

Keeley, Leslie E. *The Morphine Eater: or, From Bondage to Freedom.* Dwight, Ill.: C. L. Palmer & Co., 1881.

Kempner, I. H. *Recalled Recollections.* Dallas: Egan Co., 1961.

Kennedy, Foster. "The Effects of Narcotic Drug Addiction." *New York Medical Journal,* 100 (1914), 20–22.

Kerr, Norman. *Inebriety or Narcomania: Its Etiology, Pathology, Treatment, and Jurisprudence,* 3rd ed. London: H. K. Lewis, 1894.

Kett, Joseph F. *The Formation of the American Medical Profession: The Role of Institutions, 1780–1860.* New Haven: Yale University Press, 1968.

Keyes, Nelson Beecher. *Ben Franklin: An Affectionate Portrait.* Kingswood, Surrey: World's Work, 1956.

Keys, Thomas E. *The History of Surgical Anesthesia.* New York: Schuman's, 1945.

King, Edgar. "The Use of Habit-Forming Drugs (Cocaine, Opium and Its Derivatives) by Enlisted Men. A Report Based on the Work Done at the United States Disciplinary Barracks." *Military Surgeon,* 39 (1916), 237–281, 380–384.

King, John. *Woman: Her Diseases and Their Treatment,* 4th ed. Cincinnati: John M. Scudder, 1875.

King, Rufus. *The Drug Hang-Up: America's Fifty-Year Folly.* Springfield, Ill.: Charles C Thomas, 1972.

————. "The Narcotics Bureau and the Harrison Act: Jailing the Healers and the Sick." *Yale Law Journal,* 62 (1953), 736–749.

Knerr, Bayard. "Morphinism." *Hahnemannian Monthly,* 40 (1905), 342–350.

Knopf, S. Adolphus. "The One Million Drug Addicts in the United States: A Defense of and Suggestion to the Medical Profession." *Medical Journal and Record,* 119 (1924), 135–139.

Kolb, Lawrence. "Clinical Contribution to Drug Addiction: The Struggle for Cure and the Conscious Reasons for Relapse." *Journal of Nervous and Mental Disease,* 66 (1927), 22–43.

————. *Drug Addiction: A Medical Problem.* Springfield, Ill.: Charles C Thomas, 1962.

————. "Drug Addiction: A Study of Some Medical Cases." *Archives of Neurology and Psychiatry,* 20 (1928), 171–183.

————. "Drug Addiction in Its Relation to Crime." *Mental Hygiene,* 9 (1925), 74–89.

————. "The Opium Addict and His Treatment." *Archives of Neurology and Psychiatry,* 40 (1938), 197–202.

————. "Pleasure and Deterioration from Narcotic Addiction." *Mental Hygiene,* 9 (1925), 699–724.

————. "The Relation of Intelligence to the Etiology of Drug Addiction." *American Journal of Psychiatry,* n.s. 5 (1925), 163–167.

————. "Types and Characteristics of Drug Addicts." *Mental Hygiene,* 9 (1925), 300–313.

Kolb, Lawrence, and DuMez, A. G. "The Prevalence and Trend of Drug Addiction in the United States and Factors Influencing It." *Public Health Reports,* 39 (1924), 1179–1204.

Kolb, Lawrence, and Ossenfort, W. F. "The Treatment of Drug Addicts at the Lexington Hospital." *Southern Medical Journal,* 31 (1938), 914–922.

Kolb, Lawrence C. "Drug Addiction: A Statement Before a Committee of the United States Senate." *Bulletin of the New York Academy of Medicine,* 41 (1965), 306–309.

[Kormann, Ernest.] "Injections of Morphia in the Pains and After-Pains of Labour." *Practitioner,* 1 (1868), 325.

Kramer, John C. "Introduction to the Problem of Heroin Addiction in America." *Journal of Psychedelic Drugs,* 4 (1971), 15–22.

Kremers, Edward, and Urdang, George. *History of Pharmacy,* 4th ed., rev. Glenn Sonnedecker. Philadelphia: J. B. Lippincott, 1976.

Krikorian, Abraham D. "Were the Opium Poppy and Opium Known in the Ancient Near East?" *Journal of the History of Biology,* 8 (1975), 95–114.

Kritkos, P. G., and Papadaki, S. P. "The History of the Poppy and of Opium and Their Expansion in Antiquity in the Eastern Mediterranean Area." *Bulletin on Narcotics,* 19 (1967), 17–38.

Lambert, Alexander. "The Underlying Cause of the Narcotic Habit." *Modern Medicine,* 2 (1920), 5–9.

Lambert, Alexander, et al. "Report of the Mayor's Committee on Drug Addiction to the Hon. Richard C. Patterson, Jr., Commissioner of Correction, New York City." *American Journal of Psychiatry,* 87 (1930), 433–538.

Lang, Charles J. "Heroin." *Medical Times and Register,* 37 (1899), 79–80.

Larner, Jeremy, and Tefferteller, Ralph. *The Addict in the Street.* New York: Grove Press, 1966.

Lathrop, George Parsons. "The Sorcery of Madjoon." *Scribner's Monthly,* 20 (1880), 416–422.

Lazarus, Bernard. "A Contribution to the Therapeutic Action of Heroin." *BMSJ,* 143 (1900), 600–602.

Leahy, Sylvester R. "Some Observations on Heroin Habitués." *Psychiatric Bulletin of the New York State Hospitals,* n.s. 8 (1915), 251–263.

Lee, Harper. *To Kill a Mockingbird.* Philadelphia: J. B. Lippincott Co., 1960.

Lee, Lyndon E., Jr. "Medication in the Control of Pain in Terminal Cancer: With Reference to the Study of Newer Synthetic Analgesics." *JAMA,* 116 (1941), 216–219.

LeForger, George. "Coca in the Opium Habit." *Therapeutic Gazette,* 6 (1882), 458.

"Legal Heroin." *Parade,* May 10, 1981, 6.

Legan, Marshall Scott. "Disease and the Freedmen in Mississippi during Reconstruction." *Journal of the History of Medicine and Allied Sciences,* 28 (1973), 257–267.

Leigh, John. *An Experimental Inquiry into the Properties of Opium and its Effects on Living Subjects: with Observations on its History, Preparations, and Uses. Being the Disputation which gained the Harveian Prize for the Year 1785*. Edinburgh: Charles Elliot, 1786.

Levine, Lawrence W. *Black Culture and Black Consciousness*. New York: Oxford University Press, 1977.

Levinstein, Edward. *Morbid Craving for Morphia (Die Morphiumsucht)*, Charles Harrer, trans. London: Smith, Elder, & Co., 1878.

———. "On Morphinomania." *London Medical Record*, 4 (1876), 55–58.

Lewin, L. *The Incidental Effects of Drugs: A Pharmacological and Clinical Hand-Book*, W. T. Alexander, trans. New York: William Wood and Co., 1882.

———. *Phantastica: Narcotic and Stimulating Drugs: Their Use and Abuse*, P. H. A. Wirth, trans. New York: E. P. Dutton & Co., 1931.

Lichtenstein, Perry M. *A Doctor Studies Crime*. New York: D. Van Nostrand Co., 1934.

———. "Narcotic Addiction: Based on Observation and Treatment of One Thousand Cases." *New York Medical Journal*, 100 (1914), 962–966.

———. "The Truth Concerning Drug Addiction." *Medical Review of Reviews*, 29 (1923), 521–525.

Liggins, John. *Opium: England's Coercive Opium Policy and Its Disastrous Results in China and India; The Spread of Opium-Smoking in America*. New York: Funk & Wagnalls, 1883.

Light, Arthur B., et al. *Opium Addiction*. Chicago: American Medical Association, 1929.

Lindenberger, W. H. "Treatment of the Opium Habit by Codeia." *Medical News*, 47 (1885), 219.

Lindesmith, Alfred R. *The Addict and the Law*. Bloomington: Indiana University Press, 1965.

———. *Addiction and Opiates*. Chicago: Aldine Publishing Company, 1968.

Lindesmith, Alfred R., and Gagnon, John H. "Anomie and Drug Addiction." In *Anomie and Deviant Behavior*, Marshall B. Clinard, ed. New York: Free Press, 1964.

Livingston, Robert B., ed. *Narcotic Drug Addiction Problems: Proceedings of the Symposium on the History of Narcotic Drug Addiction Problems March 27 and 28, 1958, Bethesda, Maryland*. Washington, D.C.: G. P. O., 1963.

Lloyd, B. E. *Lights and Shades of Old San Francisco*. San Francisco: A. L. Bancroft & Co., 1876.

Lomax, Elizabeth. "The Uses and Abuses of Opiates in Nineteenth-Century England." *Bulletin of the History of Medicine*, 47 (1973), 167–176.

Long, Michael T. "The Drug Evil." In *International Association of Chiefs of Police, Proceedings of the Twenty-Second Annual Convention*. Norfolk, Va.: Burke and Gregory, 1915.

Ludlow, Fitz Hugh. "What Shall They Do to Be Saved?" *Harper's Magazine*, 35 (1867), 377–387.

McCoy, Alfred W., et al. *The Politics of Heroin in Southeast Asia.* New York: Harper & Row, 1972.

McFarland, S. F. "Opium Inebriety and the Hypodermic Syringe." *Transactions of the Medical Society of the State of New York* (1877), 289–293.

McGuire, Frank A., and Lichtenstein, Perry M. "The Drug Habit." *Medical Record,* 90 (1916), 185–191.

Macht, David I. "The History of Intravenous and Subcutaneous Administration of Drugs." *JAMA,* 66 (1916), 856–860.

––––––. "The History of Opium and Some of Its Preparations and Alkaloids." *JAMA,* 64 (1915), 477–481.

McIver, Joseph, and Price, George E. "Drug Addiction." *JAMA,* 66 (1916), 476–480.

McKay, Jno. B. "A Clinical History of Three Interesting Cases of Morphinism." *Denver Medical Times,* 27 (1907), 463–468.

Mackin, M. C. "Morphine Addiction." Iowa Board of Control of State Institutions. *Bulletin of State Institutions,* 21 (1919), 171–176.

MacMartin, D. F. *Thirty Years in Hell, or the Confessions of a Drug Fiend.* Topeka: Capper Printing Co., 1921.

McPherson, George E., and Cohen, Joseph. "A Survey of 100 Cases of Drug Addiction Entering Camp Upton, N.Y., Via Draft, 1918." *BMSJ,* 180 (1919), 636–641.

Magid, M. O. "Narcotic Drug Addiction in the Female." *Medical Journal and Record,* 129 (1929), 306–310.

Manges, Morris. "A Second Report on the Therapeutics of Heroin." *New York Medical Journal,* 71 (1900), 51–55, 79–83.

––––––. "The Treatment of Coughs with Heroin." *New York Medical Journal,* 68 (1898), 768–770.

Marsh, F. O. "Morphinism." *Cincinnati Lancet-Clinic,* n.s. 33 (1894), 459–464.

Marsh, J. P. "A Case of the Opium Habit Treated with Erythroxylon Coca." *Therapeutic Gazette,* 7 (1883), 359.

Marshall, Edward. "Uncle Sam Is the Worst Drug Fiend in the World." *New York Times,* March 12, 1911, pt. 5, 12.

Marshall, O. "The Opium Habit in Michigan." Michigan State Board of Health. *Annual Report,* 6 (1878), 63–73.

Martin, W. D. "The Opium-Habit." *Philadelphia Medical Times,* 4 (1874), 231–232.

Mason, Lewis D. "Patent and Proprietary Medicines as the Cause of the Alcohol and Opium Habit or Other Forms of Narcomania—with Some Suggestions as to How the Evil May Be Remedied." *Quarterly Journal of Inebriety,* 25 (1903), 1–13.

Masters, Frederick J. "Opium and Its Votaries." *California Illustrated Magazine,* 1 (1892), 631–645.

––––––. "The Opium Traffic in California." *Chautauquan,* 24 (1896), 54–61.

Mattison, J. B. "Clinical Notes on Opium Habituation." *Medical Record,* 14 (1878), 66–67.

_____. "Cocainism." *Medical Record,* 42 (1892), 474–477; 43 (1893), 34–36.

_____. "The Ethics of Opium Habitués." *Medical and Surgical Reporter,* 59 (1888), 296–298.

_____. "The Genesis of Opium Addiction." *Detroit Lancet,* 7 (1883), 303–305.

_____. "The Impending Danger." *Medical Record,* 11 (1876), 69–71.

_____. "Morphinism in Medical Men." *JAMA,* 23 (1894), 186–188.

_____. "Morphinism in Women." *American Medico-Surgical Bulletin,* 8 (1895), 1399–1400.

_____. "Opium Addiction in Medical Men." *Medical Record,* 23 (1883), 621–623.

_____. "The Prevention of Opium Addiction, with Special Reference to the Value of Electricity in the Treatment of Neuralgic Headache." *Louisville Medical News,* 17 (1884), 113–115.

_____. "The Responsibility of the Profession in the Production of Opium Inebriety." *Medical and Surgical Reporter,* 38 (1878), 101–104.

Maughs, Sydney. "A Concept of Psychopathy and Psychopathic Personality: Its Evolution and Historical Development." *Journal of Criminal Psychopathology,* 2 (1941), 330–356, 465–499.

Maurer, David W., and Vogel, Victor H. *Narcotics and Narcotic Addiction,* 4th ed. Springfield, Ill.: Charles C Thomas, 1973.

Meister, W. B. "Cocainism in the Army." *Military Surgeon,* 34 (1914), 344–351.

"Memorandum on Opium from China." *Report of the International Opium Commission, Shanghai, China, February 1 to February 26, 1909,* 2. Shanghai: North-China Daily News & Herald, 1909.

Merck's 1907 Index, 3rd ed. New York: Merck & Co., 1907.

Meylert, Asa P. *Notes on the Opium or Morphine Habit,* 5th ed. New York: J. J. Little & Co., 1892.

Miller, Stuart Creighton. *The Unwelcome Immigrant: The American Image of the Chinese, 1785–1882.* Berkeley: University of California Press, 1969.

"A Million Drug Fiends." *New York Times,* September 13, 1918, 10.

"Modern Life and Sedatives." *Littell's Living Age,* 238 (1903), 571–574.

Morais, Herbert M. *The History of the Negro in Medicine.* New York: Publishers Co., 1967.

Morel, B. A. *Traité des Dégénérescences Physiques, Intellectuelles et Morales de l'Espèce Humaine et des Causes qui Produissent ces Variétés Maladives.* Paris: J. B. Baillère, 1857.

Morgan, H. Wayne, ed. *Yesterday's Addicts: American Society and Drug Abuse, 1865–1920.* Norman: University of Oklahoma Press, 1974.

"The Morphia Abuse." *Lancet,* 2 (1885), 771.

Morris, F. B. *The Panorama of a Life, and Experience in Associating and Battling with Opium and Alcoholic Stimulants: A Treatise for the Cure of Opium and Alcoholic Inebriety.* Philadelphia: Geo. W. Ward, 1878.

Mortimer, W. Golden. *Peru: History of Coca: "The Divine Plant" of the Incas.* New York: J. H. Vail & Co., 1901.

Mo[tt], F[rederick] W[alker]. "Neuralgia." In *Encyclopaedia Britannica,* 11th ed., vol. 19. Cambridge: Cambridge University Press, 1911.

Murray, John. *A System of Materia Medica and Pharmacy: Including the Translations of the Edinburgh, London, and Dublin Pharmacopoeias.* "From the fourth & last Edinburgh Edition, with notes and additions by John B. Beck." New York: Evert Duyckinck, George Long, Collins & Co., and Collins & Hannay, 1824.

Musto, David F. "The American Antinarcotic Movement: Clinical Research and Public Policy." *Clinical Research,* 19 (1971), 601–605.

————. *The American Disease: Origins of Narcotic Control.* New Haven: Yale University Press, 1973.

————. "Early History of Heroin in the United States." In *Addiction,* P. G. Bourne, ed. New York: Academic Press, 1974.

Musto, David F., and Ramos, Manuel R. "Notes on American Medical History: A Follow-up Study of the New Haven Morphine Maintenance Clinic of 1920." *New England Journal of Medicine,* 304 (1981), 1071–77.

"Narcotics." *North American Review,* 95 (1862), 374–415.

"The Narcotics We Indulge In — Part II." *Blackwood's Edinburgh Magazine,* 74 (1853), 605–628.

Nascher, I. L. *The Wretches of Povertyville: A Sociological Study of the Bowery.* Chicago: Jos. J. Lanzit, 1909.

"Negro Cocaine Fiends." *Medical News,* 81 (1902), 895.

"New York's Junior Gangland." *New York Times Book Review and Magazine,* January 1, 1922, 16.

Nickerson, Harry M. "The Relation of the Physician to the Drug Habit." *Journal of Medicine and Science,* 6 (1900), 49–52.

Nolan, D. W. "The Opium Habit." *Catholic World,* 33 (1881), 827–835.

Nyswander, Marie. *The Drug Addict as Patient.* New York: Grune & Stratton, 1971.

O'Donnell, John A. *Narcotic Addicts in Kentucky.* Public Health Service Publication no. 1881. Washington, D.C.: G. P. O., 1969.

————. "The Rise and Decline of a Subculture." *Social Problems,* 15 (1967), 73–84.

O'Donnell, John A., and Jones, Judith P. "Diffusion of the Intravenous Technique Among Narcotic Addicts." In *Epidemiology of Opiate Addiction in the United States,* John C. Ball and Carl D. Chambers, eds. Springfield, Ill.: Charles C Thomas, 1970.

Olch, Peter D. "William S. Halsted and Local Anesthesia: Contributions and Complications." *Anesthesiology,* 42 (1975), 479–486.

Oleson, Charles W., compiler. *Secret Nostrums and Systems of Medicine: A Book of Formulas,* 10th ed. Chicago: Oleson & Co., 1903.

Oliver, F. E. "The Use and Abuse of Opium." Massachusetts State Board of Health. *Annual Report,* 3 (1872), 162–177.

O'Neill, Eugene. *Long Day's Journey into Night.* New Haven: Yale University Press, 1975.

" 'Opiokapnism' or Opium Smoking." *JAMA,* 18 (1892), 719–720.

"Opium and Its Consumers." *New York Tribune,* July 10, 1877, 2.

"Opium and the Opium Trade." *National Quarterly Review,* 20 (1870), 288–310.

"The Opium Case." *Rocky Mountain News,* October 12, 1880, 8.

"Opium Eating." *BMSJ,* 9 (1833), 66–67.

Opium Eating: An Autobiographical Stretch by an Habituate. Philadelphia: Claxton, Remsen, and Haffelfinger, 1876.

"The Opium Habit." *San Francisco Chronicle,* February 1, 1886. Clipping in CHS scrapbooks.

"Opium Habit in Infant from Kopp's Baby's Friend." *JAMA,* 46 (1906), 1540.

"The Opium Habit in San Francisco." *Medical and Surgical Reporter,* 57 (1887), 784–785.

"The Opium Habit's Power." *New York Times,* December 30, 1877, 8.

"Opium in China. How Many Smokers Does the Drug Supply?" *BMSJ,* 107 (1882), 186.

"Opium in Fevers." *JAMA,* 8 (1887), 265–266.

"Opium 'Joints' in the Black Hills." *Chamber's Journal,* 65 (1888), 654–655.

"Opium Pipes Fed to Flames." *San Francisco Chronicle,* February 7, 1914. Clipping in SCP.

"Opium Smoking." *JAMA,* 34 (1900), 306, 376.

" 'Opium Smoking as a Therapeutic Means.' " *JAMA,* 3 (1884), 100–101.

"Opium Smuggling on Our Northern Border." *JAMA,* 11 (1888), 885.

Osler, William. *The Principles and Practice of Medicine.* New York: D. Appleton and Co., 1892.

Overall, John E. "MMPI Personality Patterns of Alcoholics and Narcotic Addicts." *Quarterly Journal of Studies on Alcohol,* 34 (1973), 104–111.

Owens, W. D. "The Importance of Eliminating the Cocaine Habitué from the Personnel of the United States Navy and Marine Corps." *U.S. Navy Medical Bulletin,* 4 (1910), 204–205.

———. "Signs and Symptoms Presented by Those Addicted to Cocain." *JAMA,* 58 (1912), 329–330.

Paine, William. *An Epitome of the American Eclectic Practice of Medicine: Embracing Pathology, Symptomatology, Diagnosis, Prognosis, and Treatment.* Philadelphia: H. Cowperthwait & Co., 1857.

Papin, T. L. "Morphia and the Morphia Habit." *St. Louis Courier of Medicine,* 9 (1883), 18–23.

Parrish, Edward. *A Treatise on Pharmacy: Designed as a Text-Book for the Student, and as a Guide for the Physician and Pharmacist. Containing the Officinal and Many Unofficinal Formulas and Numerous Examples of Extemporaneous Prescriptions,* 3rd ed. Philadelphia: Blanchard and Lea, 1864.

Parrish, Joseph. "Opium Intoxication." *Medical and Surgical Reporter,* 29 (1873), 343–348, 361–364.

Parssinen, Terry M., and Kerner, Karen. "Development of the Disease Model of Drug Addiction in Britain." *Medical History,* 24 (1980), 275–296.

Patterson, C. E. "Morphine and Other Drug Habits." *Medical Summary,* 22 (1900), 165–167.

Paulson, David. "Morphine and Allied Drug Habits." *Chicago Medical Recorder,* 21 (1901), 415–426.

Pearson, C. B. "Is Morphine 'Happy Dust' to the Addict?" *Medical Council,* 23 (1918), 919–922; 24 (1919), 38–40.

––––––. "Police Powers vs. Science in the Care and Management of the Opium Addict." *American Medicine,* 26 (1920), 35–43.

Penfield, Wilfred. "Halsted of Johns Hopkins: The Man and His Problem as Described in the Secret Records of William Osler." *JAMA,* 210 (1969), 2214–18.

Pepper, William. "The Opium Habit." *Medical and Surgical Reporter,* 38 (1878), 87–88.

Pereira, Jonathan. *The Elements of Materia Medica and Therapeutics,* 3rd American ed., Joseph Carson, editor. Philadelphia: Blanchard and Lea, 1854.

Perkins, Marvin E. "Opiate Addiction and Military Psychiatry to the End of World War II." *Military Medicine,* 139 (1974), 114–116.

Perkins, Roger G., et al. "Report of Committee on Narcotic Drug Addiction." *American Journal of Public Health,* 11 (1921), 1066–73.

Perry, M. S. "Autopsy of an Opium Eater." *BMSJ,* 13 (1835), 319–320.

Pescor, Michael J. "A Statistical Analysis of the Clinical Records of Hospitalized Drug Addicts." *Public Health Reports,* suppl. no. 143 (1938).

Petersen, Howard C., and Stewart, William T., Jr. *A Manual of Conscription Laws and Regulations.* Albany, N.Y.: Matthew Bender & Co., 1940.

Pettey, George E. "The Heroin Habit Another Curse." *Alabama Medical Journal,* 15 (1903), 174–180.

––––––. "The Narcotic Drug Addictions. Etiological Factors; Reasons for Past Failures; Principles Involved in Treatment." *Texas State Journal of Medicine,* 6 (1910), 25–26.

––––––. *The Narcotic Drug Diseases and Allied Ailments: Pathology, Pathogenesis, and Treatment.* Philadelphia: F. A. Davis Co., 1913.

Phenix, N. J. "The Morphine Habit." *Southwestern Medical Record,* 1 (1896), 206–214.

Phillips, Joël L., and Wynne, Ronald D. *Cocaine: The Mystique and the Reality.* New York: Avon Books, 1980.

Phillips, John. "Prevalence of the Heroin Habit: Especially the Use of the Drug by 'Snuffing.' " *JAMA,* 59 (1912), 2146–47.

Pichot, Pierre. "Psychopathic Behavior: A Historical Overview." In

Psychopathic Behaviour: Approaches to Research, R. D. Hare and D. Schalling, eds. Chichester: John Wiley & Sons, 1978.

Pierce, H. B. "Address of H. B. Pierce, M. D., Retiring President, on the Duties of the Hour." *North Carolina Medical Journal,* 14 (1884), 65–78.

Platt, Jerome J., and Labate, Christina. *Heroin Addiction: Theory, Research, and Treatment.* New York: John Wiley & Sons, 1976.

Ploscowe, Morris. "Some Basic Problems in Drug Addiction and Suggestions for Research." In *Drug Addiction: Crime or Disease: Interim and Final Reports of the Committee of the American Bar Association and the American Medical Association on Narcotic Drugs.* Bloomington: Indiana University Press, 1971.

Pohlisch, Kurt. "Psychopathology of Drug Addicts." *Narcotic Education,* 5 (1931), 31.

"Practical Notes on the Morphine Habit." *Asclepiad,* 5 (1888), 301–315.

Prentice, Alfred C. "The Problem of the Narcotic Drug Addict." *JAMA,* 76 (1921), 1551–56.

Pressey, A. J. "Chronic Morphinism." *Kansas City Medical Index–Lancet,* 20 (1889), 613–614.

"The Prevalence of the Morphin and Cocain Habits." *JAMA,* 60 (1913), 1363–64.

Prichard, James Cowles. *A Treatise on Insanity and Other Disorders Affecting the Mind.* Philadelphia: Haswell, Barrington, and Haswell, 1837.

Quinones, Mark A. "Drug Abuse during the Civil War (1861–1865)." *International Journal of the Addictions,* 10 (1975), 1007–20.

R [pseud.]. "On the Use of Opium." *BMSJ,* 6 (1832), 156–157.

Radó, Sándor. "The Psychoanalysis of Pharmacothymia (Drug Addiction)." *Psychoanalytic Quarterly,* 2 (1933), 1–23.

Randerson, J. Howard. *The Cultivation of the Opium Poppy in the United States.* Albany: n.p., n.d. Pamphlet filed with KP.

Reber, Wendell. "The Decadence of Opium Addiction." *Buffalo Medical Journal,* 35 (1895–1896), 392–394.

Richardson, R. B. "Personality, Neurological, and Psychiatric Studies on Drug Addicts." Philadelphia: mimeographed, 1927.

Richmond, Phyllis Allen. "American Attitudes Toward the Germ Theory of Disease (1860–1880)." *Journal of the History of Medicine and Allied Sciences,* 9 (1954), 428–454.

Riis, Jacob. *How the Other Half Lives: Studies Among the Tenements of New York.* New York: Charles Scribner's Sons, 1903.

Risse, Günter B. "The Brownian System of Medicine: Its Theoretical and Practical Implications." *Clio Medica,* 5 (1970), 45–51.

Robb, Hunter. "The Use of Morphia and Other Strong Analgesics in Gynecological Practice." *JAMA,* 18 (1892), 680.

Roberts, J. D. "Opium Habit in the Negro." *North Carolina Medical Journal,* 15 (1885), 206–207.

Robertson, J. W. "The Morphine Habit, Its Causation, Treatment, and the Possibility of Its Cure." *Quarterly Journal of Inebriety,* 19 (1897), 226–235.

Roe, E. P. *Without a Home.* New York: Dodd, Mead & Co., 1885.

Rosenberg, Charles E. "Factors in the Development of Genetics in the United States: Some Suggestions." *Journal of the History of Medicine and Allied Sciences,* 22 (1967), 27–46.

———. "The Place of George M. Beard in Nineteenth-Century Psychiatry." *Bulletin of the History of Medicine,* 36 (1962), 245–258.

Rothstein, William G. *American Physicians in the Nineteenth Century: From Sects to Science.* Baltimore: Johns Hopkins University Press, 1972.

Rountree, W. C. "The Opium Fiend." *Texas State Journal of Medicine,* 8 (1913), 305–308.

Ruppaner, Antoine. *Hypodermic Injections in the Treatment of Neuralgia, Rheumatism, Gout, and Other Diseases.* Boston: T. O. H. P. Burnham, 1865.

———. "Researches Upon the Treatment of Neuralgia by the Injection of Narcotics and Sedatives, with Cases." *BMSJ,* 62 (1860), 193–199, 216–222, 241–247, and 280–289.

Russell, Ira. "Opium Inebriety." *Medico-Legal Journal,* 5 (1887), 144–152.

Russell, James. "Opium: Its Use and Abuse." *British Medical Journal* (1860), 313–315, 334–336.

Sandmeyer, Elmer Clarence. *The Anti-Chinese Movement in California.* Urbana: University of Illinois Press, 1939.

Sandoz, C. Edouard. "Report on Morphinism to the Municipal Court of Boston." *Journal of Criminal Law, Criminology, and Police Science,* 13 (1922), 10–55.

Sanger, William W. *The History of Prostitution: Its Extent, Causes, and Effects Throughout the World.* New York: Harper & Brothers, 1859.

Sapira, Joseph D. "Speculations Concerning Opium Abuse and World History." *Perspectives in Biology and Medicine,* 18 (1975), 379–399.

Savitt, Todd L. *Medicine and Slavery: The Diseases and Health Care of Blacks in Antebellum Virginia.* Urbana: University of Illinois Press, 1978.

"Say Drug Habit Grips the Nation." *New York Times,* December 5, 1913, 8.

Sceleth, Charles E. "A Rational Treatment of the Morphine Habit." *JAMA,* 66 (1916), 862.

Sceleth, Charles E., and Kuh, Sidney. "Drug Addiction." *JAMA,* 82 (1924), 679–682.

Scheffel, Carl. "The Etiology of Fifty Cases of Drug Addictions." *Medical Record,* 94 (1918), 853–854.

Scheppegrell, W. "The Abuse and Dangers of Cocain." *Medical News,* 73 (1898), 417–422.

Schur, Edwin M. *Narcotic Addiction in Britain and America: The Impact of Public Policy.* Bloomington: Indiana University Press, 1963.

Scott, J. M. W. "Drug Addiction." *Medical Clinics of North America,* 2 (1918), 607–615.

Seaman, Valentine. *An Inaugural Dissertation on Opium.* Philadelphia: Johnston and Justice, 1792.

Seeger, C. L. "Opium Eating." *BMSJ,* 9 (1833), 117–120.

Sell, Edward Herman Miller. *The Opium Habit; Its Successful Treatment by the Avena Sativa.* Jersey City, N.J.: Evening Journal, 1883.

Sellew, Paul K. "Heroinism." *Maine Medical Journal,* 4 (1914), 1670–78.

Sewall, J. G. "Opium-Eating and Hypodermic Injection." *Medical Record,* 5 (1870), 137.

Seward, George F. *Chinese Immigration in its Social and Economical Aspects.* New York: Charles Scribner's Sons, 1881.

Shafer, Henry Burnell. *The American Medical Profession, 1783–1850,* reprint ed. New York: AMS Press, 1968.

Sharkey, Seymour J. "Morphinomania." *Nineteenth Century,* 22 (1887), 335–342.

Shipman, E. W. "The Promiscuous Use of Opium in Vermont." *Transactions of the Vermont State Medical Society* (1890), 72–77.

Shoemaker, John V. "The Abuse of Drugs." *JAMA,* 42 (1904), 1405–8.

Shryock, Richard Harrison. *Medicine in America: Historical Essays.* Baltimore: Johns Hopkins Press, 1966.

Sicherman, Barbara. "The Uses of a Diagnosis: Doctors, Patients, and Neurasthenia." In *Sickness and Health in America: Readings in the History of Medicine and Public Health,* Judith Walzer Leavitt and Ronald L. Numbers, eds. Madison: University of Wisconsin Press, 1978.

Sigerist, Henry E. "Laudanum in the Works of Paracelsus." *Bulletin of the History of Medicine,* 9 (1941), 530–544.

Sigma [pseud.]. "Opium-Eating." *Lippincott's Magazine,* 1 (1868), 404–409.

Simmons, Fritz. "The Highbinders, the Girls, and the Pipes are Gone." *San Francisco Chronicle,* November 16, 1947, suppl., 2–3.

Simon, Carleton. "Survey of the Narcotic Problem." *JAMA,* 82 (1924), 675–679.

Simonton, Thomas G. "The Increase of the Use of Cocaine Among the Laity in Pittsburgh." *Philadelphia Medical Journal,* 11 (1903), 556–560.

Simrell, Earle V. "History of Legal and Medical Roles in Narcotic Abuse in the U.S." In *The Epidemiology of Opiate Addiction in the United States,* John C. Ball and Carl D. Chambers, eds. Springfield, Ill.: Charles C Thomas, 1970.

"Slaves to Opium: Increase of the Vice in California." *New York Tribune,* June 19, 1881, 7.

Smith, Edward R. "Seven Years of Pioneering in Preventive Medicine." *Journal of the Florida Medical Association,* 53 (1966), 725–728.

Smith, Phillip T. "Drugs—Use and Sale." In International Association of Chiefs of Police, *Proceedings of the 21st Annual Convention.* Washington, D.C.: Byron S. Adams, 1914.

Smith, William G. *An Inaugural Dissertation on Opium, Embracing Its History, Chemical Analysis, and Use and Abuse as a Medicine.* New York: n.p., 1832.

"Smugglers' Big Profits." *New York Times,* February 17, 1909, 4.

Sollman, Torald. *A Manual of Pharmacology and its Applications to Therapeutics and Toxicology.* Philadelphia: W. B. Saunders Co., 1917.

Somerville, William G. "Who is Responsible for the Drug Addict?" *Southern Medical Journal,* 17 (1924), 108–112.

Sonnedecker, Glenn. "Emergence of the Concept of Opiate Addiction." *Journal Mondial de Pharmacie,* no. 3 (1962), 276–290; no. 1 (1963), 27–34.

Sontag, Susan. *Illness as Metaphor.* New York: Farrar, Straus & Giroux, 1978.

Speer, William. *The Oldest and the Newest Empire: China and the United States.* Hartford, Conn.: S. S. Scranton and Co., 1870.

Spence, Jonathan. "Opium Smoking in Ch'ing China." In *Conflict and Control in Late Imperial China,* Frederic Wakeman, Jr., and Carolyn Grant, eds. Berkeley: University of California Press, 1975.

Spillard, William J. *Needle in a Haystack: the Exciting Adventures of a Federal Narcotic Agent.* "As told to Pence James." New York: McGraw-Hill Book Co., 1945.

Sprague, G. P. "Some Essential Points in the Etiology, Pathology and Treatment of Morphine Addiction." *Cincinnati Lancet-Clinic,* 98 (1907), 585–586.

Stanley, L. L. "Drug Addictions." *Journal of the American Institute of Criminal Law and Criminology,* 10 (1919–1920), 62–70.

———. "Morphinism." *Journal of the American Institute of Criminal Law and Criminology,* 6 (1915–1916), 586–593.

———. "Morphinism and Crime." *Journal of the American Institute of Criminal Law and Criminology,* 8 (1917–1918), 749–756.

Steensen, C. "Misbrug af Opium og Morfin i Amerika." ["Abuse of Opium and Morphine in America."] *Ugeskrift for Laeger,* 7 (1883), 165–167.

Sterne, Albert E. "Have Drug Addictions a Pathological Basis?" *JAMA,* 44 (1905), 609–612.

Stevens, Enos. "Opium." *BMSJ,* 41 (1850), 119–121.

Stewart, W. Blair. "Heroin." *Medical Bulletin,* 23 (1901), 86–88.

Stieren, Edward. "Blindness from Heroin in the Nostrum 'Habitina.' " *JAMA,* 54 (1910), 869–870.

Stimmel, H. F. "Coca in the Opium and Alcohol Habits." *Therapeutic Gazette,* 5 (1881), 252–253.

Stockard, C. C. "Morphinism." *Atlanta Journal-Record of Medicine,* 1 (1900), 865–871.

Stockwell, G. Archie. "Erythroxylon Coca." *BMSJ,* 96 (1877), 399–404.

Stokes, Charles F. "The Military, Industrial and Public Health Features of Narcotic Addiction." *JAMA,* 70 (1918), 766–768.

———. "The Problem of Narcotic Addiction of Today." *Medical Record,* 93 (1918), 755–760.

Street, John Phillips. "The Patent Medicine Situation." *American Journal of Public Health,* 7 (1917), 1037–42.

Street, Leroy, in collaboration with David Loth. *I Was a Drug Addict.* New York: Random House, 1953.

Strode, Hudson. *Jefferson Davis: American Patriot, 1808–1861.* New York: Harcourt, Brace & World, 1955.

Sudduth, W. Xavier. "The Psychology of Narcotism." *JAMA,* 27 (1896), 796–798.

"Survey of Drug Addicts." *JAMA,* 75 (1920), 1655.

Swatos, William H., Jr. "Opiate Addiction in the Late Nineteenth Century: A Study of the Social Problem, Using Medical Journals of the Period." *International Journal of the Addictions,* 7 (1972), 739–753.

Swing, E. V. "The Therapeutics of Opium." *Pennsylvania Medical Journal,* 3 (1900), 505–508.

Swords, M. W. "A Resume of Facts and Deductions Obtained by the Operation of a Narcotic Dispensary." *American Medicine,* 26 (1920), 23–29.

"Symposium on 'The Doctor and the Drug Addict.' " *JAMA,* 75 (1920), 1589–91.

Taylor, Arnold H. *American Diplomacy and the Narcotics Traffic, 1900–1939: A Study in International Humanitarian Reform.* Durham, N.C.: Duke University Press, 1969.

"10 Killed, 35 Hurt in Race Riot Born of a Cocaine 'Jag.' " *New York Herald,* September 29, 1913, 1.

Terry, Charles E. "The Development and Causes of Opium Addiction as a Social Problem." *Journal of Educational Sociology,* 5 (1931), 335–346.

———. "Drug Addictions, A Public Health Problem." *American Journal of Public Health,* 4 (1914), 28–37.

———. "Habit-Forming Drugs." Jacksonville, Florida. *Annual Report of the Board of Health for the Year 1912.* Reports for subsequent years are also cited in the text.

———. "Narcotic Drug Addiction and Rational Administration." *American Medicine,* 26 (1915), 29–35.

———. "Some Recent Experiments in Narcotic Control." *American Journal of Public Health,* 11 (1921), 32–44.

Terry, Charles E., and Cox, J. W. *A Further Study and Report on the Use of Narcotics Under the Provisions of Federal Law in Six Communities in the United States of America for the Period July 1, 1923 to June 30, 1924.* New York: Bureau of Social Hygiene, 1927.

Terry, Charles E., and Pellens, Mildred. *The Opium Problem,* reprint ed. Montclair, N.J.: Patterson Smith, 1970.

Terry, Charles E., Pellens, Mildred, and Cox, J. W. *Report on the Legal Use of Narcotics in Detroit, Michigan, and Environs for the Period July 1, 1925 to June 30, 1926 to the Committee on Drug Addictions.* New York: Bureau of Social Hygiene, 1931.

Terry, Charles E., et al. "Report of Committee on Habit Forming

Drugs." *American Journal of Public Health*, 10 (1920), 83–87.

Thacher, James. *American Medical Bibliography; or Memoirs of Eminent Physicians Who Have Flourished in America*, vol. 1. Boston: Richardson & Lord and Cottons & Barnard, 1828.

"Thomas Davison Crothers, M.D." *Commemorative Biographical Record of Hartford County, Connecticut.* Chicago: J. H. Beers & Co., 1901.

Thrasher, Frederic M. *The Gang: A Study of 1,313 Gangs in Chicago,* 2nd ed. Chicago: University of Chicago Press, 1936.

Towns, Charles B. "The Peril of the Drug Habit and the Need of Restrictive Legislation." *Century,* 84 (1912), 580–587.

Treadway, Walter L. "Drug Addiction and Measures for Its Prevention in the United States." *JAMA,* 99 (1932), 372–379.

———. "Further Observations on the Epidemiology of Narcotic Drug Addiction." *Public Health Reports,* 45 (1930), 541–553.

———. "Some Epidemiological Features of Drug Addiction." *British Journal of Inebriety,* 28 (1930), 50–54.

Tuke, D. Hack, ed. *A Dictionary of Psychological Medicine Giving the Definition, Etymology, and Synonyms of the Terms Used in Medical Psychology with the Symptoms, Treatment, and Pathology of Insanity and the Law of Lunacy in Great Britain and Ireland.* 2 vols. Philadelphia: P. Blakiston, Son & Co., 1892.

Turner, J. Edward. *The History of the First Inebriate Asylum in the World by Its Founder: An Account of His Indictment, Also a Sketch of the Woman's National Hospital by Its Projector.* New York: the author, 1888.

"Two More Arrests in Smuggling Case." *New York Times,* February 16, 1909, 3.

Upham, J. H. J., et al. "Report of the Committee on the Narcotic Drug Situation in the United States." *JAMA,* 74 (1920), 1324–28.

"The Use of Opium." *Supplement to the [Connecticut] Courant,* 6 (October 30, 1741), 56.

"Use of Opium in the United States." *BMSJ,* 72 (1865), 476.

Van Slyke, D. C. *The Wail of a Drug Addict.* Grand Rapids, Mich.: Wm. B. Eerdmans Publishing Co., 1945.

Vice Commission of Chicago. *The Social Evil in Chicago: A Study of Existing Conditions with Recommendations.* Chicago: Gunthorp-Warren Printing Co., 1911.

"Waifs and Strays." *Harper's Weekly,* 26 (1882), 215.

Wain, Harry. *A History of Preventive Medicine.* Springfield, Ill.: Charles C Thomas, 1970.

Waldorf, Dan, et al. *Morphine Maintenance: The Shreveport Clinic, 1919–1923.* Washington, D.C.: Drug Abuse Council, 1974.

Walker, Henry Freeman. "Some Remarks on the Morphine Habit." *Medical Record,* 48 (1895), 692–694.

Waller, Robert A. *Rainey of Illinois: A Political Biography, 1903–34.* Urbana: University of Illinois Press, 1977.

Wallis, Frederic A. "The Menace of the Drug Addict." *Current History,* 21

(1925), 740–743.

Waterhouse, E. R. "Cocaine Debauchery." *Eclectic Medical Journal of Cincinnati,* 56 (1896), 464–465.

Watson, W. S. "On the Evil of Opium Eating." *JAMA,* 14 (1890), 671–674.

Weatherly, J. S. "Increase in the Habit of Opium Eating." *Transactions of the Medical Association of the State of Alabama* (1869), 67–69.

Webster, John C. "The Abuses of Morphine." *Clinical Review,* 20 (1904), 345–348.

Weiss, Emanuel. "Hint as to the Development of Our California-China Trade." *Hunt's Merchants' Magazine,* 47 (1862), 522–526.

"Well Done: The Oriental Opium Eaters Fined Heavily." *Rocky Mountain News,* October 13, 1880, 3.

Werner, [Louis]. "The Illegal Sale of Cocaine." In International Association of Chiefs of Police, *Proceedings of the Sixteenth Annual Session.* Grand Rapids: West Michigan Printing Co., 1909.

Weschcke, Emil. "On Poppy Culture and Production in the United States." *Pacific Medical Journal,* 48 (1905), 457–461.

Whiteside, Henry O. "The Drug Habit in Nineteenth-century Colorado." *Colorado Magazine,* 55 (1978), 47–68.

Whittaker, J. T. "Cocaine in the Treatment of the Opium Habit." *Medical News,* 47 (1885), 144–149.

Whitwell, W. S. *The Opium Habit.* San Francisco: n.p. [?], 1887.

Wholey, C. C. "Psychopathological Phases Observable in Individuals Using Narcotic Drugs in Excess." *Pennsylvania Medical Journal,* 16 (1913), 721–725.

Wilbert, Martin I. "Efforts to Curb the Misuse of Narcotic Drugs: A Comparative Analysis of the Federal and State Laws Designed to Restrict or to Regulate the Distribution and Use of Opium, Coca, and Other Narcotic or Habit-Forming Drugs." *Public Health Reports,* 30 (1915), 893–923.

———. "The Number and Kind of Drug Addicts." *American Journal of Pharmacy,* 87 (1915), 415–420.

———. "Opium in the Pharmacopoeia." *Journal of the American Pharmaceutical Association,* 5 (1916), 688–693.

Wilbert, Martin I., and Motter, Murray Galt. *Digest of Laws and Regulations in Force in the United States Relating to the Possession, Use, Sale, and Manufacture of Poisons and Habit-Forming Drugs.* Public Health Bulletin no. 56. Washington, D.C.: G.P.O., 1912.

Wilbert, Martin I., et al. "Report of the Commission on Proprietary Medicines of the American Pharmaceutical Association for 1915–1916." *Journal of the American Pharmaceutical Association,* 5 (1916), 1374–81.

Wiley, Harvey W., and Pierce, Anne Lewis. "The Cocain Crime." *Good Housekeeping,* 58 (1914), 393–398.

Williams, Allen S. *The Demon of the Orient and His Satellite Fiends of the*

Joints: Our Opium Smokers as they are in Tartar Hells and American Paradises. New York: the author, 1883.

Williams, Edward Huntington. "The Drug-Habit Menace in the South." *Medical Record,* 85 (1914), 247–249.

———. "Negro Cocaine 'Fiends' Are a New Southern Menace." *New York Times,* February 8, 1914, pt. 5, 12.

———. *Opiate Addiction: Its Handling and Treatment.* New York: Mac-Millan Co., 1922.

Williams, Henry Smith. *Drug Addicts are Human Beings: The Story of Our Billion-Dollar Drug Racket: How We Created It and How We Can Wipe It Out.* Washington, D.C.: Shaw Publishing Co., 1938.

Williams, S. Wells. *The Middle Kingdom: A Survey of the Geography, Government, Literature, Social Life, Arts, and History of the Chinese Empire and Its Inhabitants.* 2 vols. New York: Charles Scribner's Sons, 1899.

Wilson, Daniel. *An Inaugural Dissertation on the Morbid Effects of Opium upon the Human Body.* Philadelphia: Solomon W. Conrad, 1803.

Wilson, Edward T. "Notes on the Subcutaneous Injection of Morphia." *Retrospect of Practical Medicine and Surgery,* "Uniform American Edition," 61 (1870), 254–257.

Wilson, Forrest. *Crusader in Crinoline: The Life of Harriet Beecher Stowe.* Philadelphia: J. B. Lippincott Co., 1941.

Wilson, J. C. "The Causes and Prevention of the Opium Habit and Kindred Affections." *JAMA,* 11 (1888), 816–817.

Wilson, Robert Cumming. *Drugs and Pharmacy in the Life of Georgia, 1733–1959.* Atlanta: Foote & Davies, 1959.

Witherspoon, J. A. "A Protest Against Some of the Evils in the Profession of Medicine." *JAMA,* 34 (1900), 1589–92.

Wolff, Pablo Osvaldo. "Narcotic Addiction and Criminality." *Journal of Criminal Psychopathology,* 4 (1942), 35–58.

Wood, Alexander. "New Method of Treating Neuralgia by the direct application of Opiates to the Painful Points." *Edinburgh Medical and Surgical Journal,* 82 (1855), 265–281.

Wood, George B. *A Treatise on Therapeutics, and Pharmacology or Materia Medica,* 1st ed. 2 vols. Philadelphia: J. B. Lippincott, 1856.

Wood, George B., and Bache, Franklin. *The Dispensatory of the United States of America,* 2nd ed. Philadelphia: Grigg and Elliott, 1834.

Wood, Horatio C., Jr. "The Newer Substitutes for Morphine." *Merck's Archives,* 1 (1899), 89–90.

Woods, Arthur. *Dangerous Drugs: The World Fight Against Illicit Traffic in Narcotics.* New Haven: Yale University Press, 1931.

Woodward, Joseph Janvier. *Outlines of the Chief Camp Diseases of the United States Armies as Observed During the Present War.* Philadelphia: J. B. Lippincott & Co., 1863.

Wortman, Roy T. "Denver's Anti-Chinese Riot, 1880." *Colorado Magazine,* 42 (1965), 275–291.

Wright, Arthur Dickson. "The History of Opium." *Medical and Biological*

Illustration, 18 (1968), 62–70.

Wright, Hamilton. "Memoranda on the manufacture of and traffic in morphine and cocaine in the United States and the Philippine Islands, with statement as to opium, in continuation of Senate Document No. 377, Sixty-first Congress, Second Session." *Conference Internationale de l'Opium, Actes et Documents,* vol. 2. The Hague: Imprimerie Nationale, 1912.

————. "Report from the United States of America." *Report of the International Opium Commission, Shanghai, China, February 1 to February 26, 1909,* vol. 2. Shanghai: North-China Daily News & Herald, 1909.

Yore, Clem. *Songs of the Underworld.* Chicago: Charles C. Thompson Co., 1914.

Young, James Harvey. *The Toadstool Millionaires: A Social History of Patent Medicines in America before Federal Regulation.* Princeton: Princeton University Press, 1961.

Young, Oscar C. "On the Use of Opiates, Especially Morphine." *Medical News,* 80 (1902), 154–157.

Zabriskie, Alexander C. *Bishop Brent: Crusader for Christian Unity.* Philadelphia: Westminster Press, 1948.

Zentner, Joseph L. "Cocaine and the Criminal Sanction." *Journal of Drug Issues,* 7 (1977), 93–101.

————. "Prominent Features of Opiate Use in America during the Twentieth Century." *Journal of Drug Issues,* 5 (1975), 99–108.

Index